D0142375

Parties, Policies, and Democracy

Theoretical Lenses on Public Policy

Series Editor, Paul A. Sabatier

Parties, Policies, and Democracy,
Hans-Dieter Klingemann, Richard I. Hofferbert,
and Ian Budge

Policy Change and Learning: An Advocacy Coalition Approach,
edited by Paul A. Sabatier and Hank C. Jenkins-Smith

Institutional Incentives and Sustainable Development: Infrastructure Policies in Perspective,
Elinor Ostrom, Larry Schroeder, and Susan Wynne

FORTHCOMING

Government, Business, and American Politics,
Richard A. Harris and Jay A. Sigler

Parties, Policies, and Democracy

Hans-Dieter Klingemann
Science Center–Berlin and Free University of Berlin

Richard I. Hofferbert
State University of New York–Binghamton and Science Center–Berlin

Ian Budge
University of Essex

WITH

Hans Keman
Free University of Amsterdam

François Pétry
Universite Laval

Torbjorn Bergman
University of Umea

Kaare Strom
University of California–San Diego

Westview Press
BOULDER • SAN FRANCISCO • OXFORD

Theoretical Lenses on Public Policy

Published in 1994 in the United States of America by Westview Press, Inc., 5500 Central Avenue, Boulder, Colorado 80301-2877, and in the United Kingdom by Westview Press, 36 Lonsdale Road, Summertown, Oxford OX2 7EW

Library of Congress Cataloging-in-Publication Data
Klingemann, Hans-Dieter.
Parties, policies, and democracy / Hans-Dieter Klingemann, Richard I. Hofferbert, and Ian Budge with Hans Keman ... [et al.].
p cm. — (Theoretical lenses on public policy)
Includes bibliographical references (p.) and index.
ISBN 0-8133-2068-2 (hardcover). — ISBN 0-8133-2069-0 (paperback).
1. Political parties. 2. Political parties—Platforms.
3. Democracy. I. Hofferbert, Richard I., 1937- . II. Budge, Ian. III. Title. IV. Series.
JF2011.K55 1994
324.2—dc20 94-21322
CIP

Printed and bound in the United States of America

The paper used in this publication meets the requirements of the American National Standard for Permanence of Paper for Printed Library Materials Z39.48-1984.

10 9 8 7 6 5 4 3 2 1

To the memory of Rudolf Wildenmann,
builder, scholar, and friend

Contents

Tables and Figures

Tables

Figures

Preface

To me, party platforms are contracts with the people.

—Harry S Truman

Is there any similarity between what political parties write in their formal programs ("platforms") before an election and the policies enacted after the election? Does it make any difference with respect to policy which party wins the election? Are political parties, and the governments they organize, more accountable in some institutional and cultural contexts than in others? If so, why?

This book addresses these and related questions about the operation of modern democracies. The research is grounded on a massive, newly available body of evidence systematically extracted from election programs of all the major parties in ten democracies, covering the post–World War II period. The data are maintained by the Comparative Manifestoes Project (CMP) of the Research Unit on Institutions and Social Change of the Science Center–Berlin. Most were collected by the Manifestoes Research Group of the European Consortium for Political Research. Data for the first phase of the project, covering 1,018 election programs in twenty countries during the period roughly from 1945 through 1983, are available through the ESRC Data Archive, University of Essex (Colchester, England). The CMP in Berlin is extending the database to all countries that belong to the Organization for Economic Cooperation and Development (OECD) and the new democracies of Eastern Europe. In addition, it is updating the existing country data for each election. These data are part of a number of substantive projects on parties and party systems in democratic regimes. In the near future, the collection will be made available to the academic community by the Zentralarchiv für empirische Sozialforschung, University of Cologne.

The book is organized as follows: The first three chapters present concepts and design; each of the ten succeeding chapters deals with the congruence of party programs and policy priorities over the postwar years in a particular democratic country. Each country study is conducted according to a rigorously equivalent set of procedures. A concluding chapter draws together the most generalizable findings.

The central aim of the research upon which this book is grounded is to advance our understanding of the role of political parties in the democratic policy process. We have taken care throughout the book to adhere to that aim. Thus, we resist the temptation to delve into the peculiarities of any one country's politics or the oddities of a specific policy realm. We do spend some time in the chapter about each country on its institutional and political setting. And we look for cross-country features that may characterize the role of parties in certain types of policy domains. But our interest in specific countries and specific policy areas derives—at the least—from the hunch that the particular features explored might form the basis for a broader, cross-country generalization. Therefore, we test identical statistical models in each country on data that are as close to equivalent as possible.

Because of the commitment to comparative rather than descriptive analysis, the study is able to offer convincing answers to basic questions about the functioning of democratic political systems—questions that have heretofore been addressed with only anecdote and speculation, often leading to skepticism about how *democratic* modern countries can be. By means of rigorous comparative analysis of forty years' experience across ten countries, we find that political parties in contemporary democracies work better than many of their critics have claimed. Especially in their formal election programs, parties present voters with signals that point rather clearly to the kind of policy priorities that are later enacted. Political parties deserve more credit than they often get.

There are good reasons to expect that variations in party accountability are due in significant measure to variations in constitutional structures and institutional practices. Parties should be more accountable in parliamentary systems with clear single-party majorities and strong party discipline than in coalition systems with only loose party control over members of parliament. Parties are expected to be less potent in systems of separated powers than in those where the effective executive is selected by a parliamentary majority. We subject these and other hypotheses about party capacity to careful examination, via measures of the congruence of party election programs and policy priorities. We find wanting many long-standing propositions about the constraint of formal institutions on party accountability. With a few important exceptions, our research offers little basis for blaming institutional barriers for lack of party accountability.

Hans-Dieter Klingemann
Richard I. Hofferbert
Ian Budge

Acknowledgments

This study is one of a series based on the work of the Manifestoes Research Group of the European Consortium for Political Research (ECPR). The ECPR has been a vital force encouraging innovative, comparative political research. It was in the context of the ECPR that the first group of scholars from several countries came together to launch the massive data collection upon which this study and its predecessors rest. Since the inception of the project in 1979, the list of persons who have collected party documents and coded them has grown to considerable length. We thank all of those colleagues and their students who have been engaged in this useful work. Special note must be taken of the documentation and coding efforts of Derek Hearl and Judith Bara. The continuation of the project has been due in large part to the dedicated efforts of Andrea Volkens of the Comparative Manifestoes Project (CMP) in the Research Unit on Institutions and Social Change of the Science Center–Berlin (Wissenschaftszentrum–Berlin).

The Science Center has been crucial for the continuation and progress of the entire project in recent years. In addition to its routine support of the CMP, it supported two conferences of the project working group. Moreover, it provided visiting professorships for Richard I. Hofferbert at various times between 1990 and 1993 and for Ian Budge in 1990.

Several organizations receive our thanks for their financial support of data collection: the Nuffield Foundation (Soc205/125), the Tercentenary Fund of the Bank of Sweden, and the Stiftung Volkswagenwerk (II/38850). The Deutsche Forschungsgemeinschaft (DFG-Be 142/41-1, 1986) provided support for a visiting fellowship for Richard I. Hofferbert to the Free University of Berlin, during which the basic design of this study was put in place. We are also grateful for support for one working conference from the Zentralarchiv für empirische Sozialforschung and its managing director, Ekkehard Mochmann, and for another from the ECPR Joint Research Sessions, organized and convened by Professor Hans Keman of the Free University of Amsterdam.

Projects on individual countries have been supported by the Norwegian and Danish Social Science Research Councils and the British Academy. Our employers, both past and present, have also contributed in various ways: the Free University of Berlin, the Science Center–Berlin, the University of Essex, the European University Institute (Florence), and the State University of New York at Binghamton.

Authorship of this volume is genuinely collaborative, with the major tasks being shared by the three authors. Order of author listing has been alternated throughout the series of publications in the project. Note is taken on the title page of special contributions by Hans Keman, François Pétry, Torbjorn Bergman, and Kaare Strom. Each provided extensive data, and each participated in working conferences during which the design and nuances of the research were refined. These four have also been generous in providing commentary and guidance as the manuscript has evolved. For expenditure data and guidance on their use in the complex case of Belgium, we are grateful to Lievin DeWinter of the University of Louvain de Neuve.

Other colleagues have been generous with their advice and counsel, including in particular Michael D. McDonald of SUNY Binghamton and Thomas Cusack, Dieter Fuchs, Edeltraud Roller, Andrea Volkens, and Bernhard Wessels of the Science Center–Berlin. We are grateful to David R. Cameron for serving as reviewer of the draft manuscript. And for marvelous help in expediting and editing, we admire and appreciate the contributions of Jennifer Knerr, Shena Redmond, and Marian Safran of Westview Press. The final version, complex though it still be, would be far less readable and forthright—not to mention longer—were it not for the excellent critique provided by our series editor, Paul A. Sabatier, to whom we are very grateful.

Errors of fact and interpretation are, alas, almost certain to be contained in this volume. For these and any other shortcomings it may have, we three accept full responsibility.

H.K.
R.I.H.
I.B.

Introduction

Paul A. Sabatier, Series Editor

The field of policy studies—at least for political scientists—is currently in disarray. Much of the problem can be attributed to the absence of a limited set of clearly articulated theoretical lenses through which policy scholars view their field (Sabatier 1991). It is true that those in the subfield in policy evaluation share a framework grounded in welfare economics and benefit-cost analysis. But much of the work in public policy consists of descriptive and prescriptive analyses of a substantive policy area—education, welfare, pollution control—guided by no explicit theory and of little interest to scholars outside that policy area. The best work by policy scholars during the 1970s and early 1980s was done on certain aspects of the policy process, notably implementation and agenda setting. Unfortunately, that work has not been cumulative across policy stages because it is based on a conceptual framework—the stages heuristic of Jones (1970) and Anderson (1974)—that is not really a causal theory at all. It simply divides the policy process into a set of stages (agenda setting, policy formulation, implementation, and evaluation/reformulation) but offers no unifying theory of the factors affecting policy decisions and their societal impacts across stages (Sabatier and Jenkins-Smith 1993, chap. 1).

The Westview Press series Theoretical Lenses on Public Policy seeks to fill this void. It offers volumes that develop one or more explicit theoretical frameworks or that apply such frameworks to specific policy problems, such as health care, education, or water pollution. In all case studies, however, the material must be of sufficient theoretical merit to appeal to students and scholars who have no interest in the specific policy area discussed.

Two volumes have appeared thus far. In *Institutional Incentives and Sustainable Development*, Elinor Ostrom, Larry Schroeder, and Susan Wynne use an institutional rational choice approach that assumes that self-interested, intendedly rational actors operate within decision situations that are strongly framed by institutional rules. They explore the reasons why water and road infrastructures in developing countries are so poorly maintained and suggest how the institutional rules governing those situations should be altered to increase the incentives for effective maintenance. In *Policy Change and Learning*, Hank Jenkins-Smith and I present the advocacy coalition framework (ACF), which assumes that policy change within a specific subsystem or policy domain can best be understood as the result of two major processes: (1) competition among several advocacy coalitions, each composed of actors from a variety of governmental and private institutions who share a given belief system and who seek to manipulate governmental institutions to realize their basic policy objectives; and (2) exogenous shocks from outside the subsystem, such as changes in socioeconomic conditions or major electoral shifts. Six case studies by different authors apply the ACF to a variety of policy domains in United States and Canada, and the ACF is then revised in light of the case results.

It gives me great pleasure to present the third volume in the series, *Parties, Policies, and Democracy*, by Hans-Dieter Klingemann, Richard I. Hofferbert, Ian Budge, and their colleagues. This represents no less than the most comprehensive analysis to date of several critical topics in democratic theory: To what extent are the policy priorities articulated in the platforms/manifestoes of political parties during national elections actually reflected in the subsequent budgetary decisions of national governments? Does the extent of congruence vary by constitutional type, with the strongest congruence in Britain and other Westminster systems and the weakest in multiparty coalition regimes? This is democratic theory with a *policy* focus. The topic of concern is not simply the extent of popular participation but rather whether that participation makes a difference in the policy outputs of governments (in this case, national budgetary priorities).

Unlike the first two volumes of this series, *Parties, Policies, and Democracy* does not primarily seek to make a major theoretical contribution. It is anchored in a long-standing structural-functionalist framework that views political parties as institutions with two critical roles in the functioning of democratic regimes: First, parties select and aggregate a variety of issues and present them to voters in a more or less coherent package, as represented by the party manifesto/platform. Second, the winning parties form the backbone of elected governments, with a general expectation that their campaign promises will be converted into public policies. The major theoretical contribution of this volume is to elaborate and operationalize the "saliency theory" of party competition, originally developed by David Robertson (1976) as an alternative to Anthony Downs's *An Economic View of Democracy.* According to saliency theory, parties are substantially constrained in the positions they can take by past pronouncements and by the need to maintain a cadre of loyal voters. They compete primarily by emphasizing—by manipulating the salience of—different issues rather than by taking different positions on the same set of issues.

The major empirical contribution of this volume is its analysis of great scope and sophistication: the relationship between party manifestoes and subsequent budgetary priorities by national governments in ten countries—Australia, Canada, the United States, Britain, France, Sweden, Germany, Austria, the Netherlands, and Belgium—over a roughly forty-year period from the end of World War II to the mid-1980s. More specifically, the authors and their colleagues first code the manifestoes of all political parties in order to obtain indicators of the relative salience of fifty-four different issues. Then they use regression analysis to examine the influence of three models—agenda, mandate, and long-term ideology—relating those issue priorities to the relative importance of six to ten broad budgetary categories (welfare, health, education, housing, administration of justice, defense, foreign affairs, infrastructure, and agriculture) in the national expenditures of subsequent governments in those ten countries over forty years. With the agenda model, they examine the effects of the saliency of various issues in different parties' election manifestoes on the national budgetary priorities of subsequent governments irrespective of whether that party was a member of the winning coalition. With the mandate model, they look at the additional influence of a party's platform on budgetary allocations if it was a member of the winning coalition. And with the ideology model, they look at the additional influence represented by long-term party loyalties. This is, in sum, a masterful piece of scholarship.

Not surprisingly, the authors come to some very important, and sometimes unexpected, conclusions. First, and most important, political parties in the ten countries have been performing their functions relatively well. On average, the issue priorities in the party manifestoes predict over 50 percent of the variance in national budgetary priorities, ranging from a high of 80 percent in France to a low of 40 percent in Australia. Second, the countries generally fall into two groups. In France, Sweden, and Britain, the agenda model prevails; that is, the primary influence of party manifestoes is in collectively establishing issue priorities, irrespective of which parties happen to form the subsequent government. In the other seven countries, the mandate and ideology models explain more of the total variance than the agenda model. Third, traditional expectations that Westminster regimes—which have single-party governments with a strong cabinet and strong party loyalty—would have the greatest congruence between party manifestoes and budgetary priorities, in large part because of strong mandate effects, are *not* supported by the evidence. Instead, the strongest congruence has been in France, Germany, and Austria; of the three Westminster regimes, the mandate effect has been quite modest in Britain, fairly strong in Canada, and dominant only in Australia. Fourth, contrary to conventional wisdom, in the United States the programmatic differences between Democrats and Republicans are greater than among left-wing and right-wing parties in many European countries; moreover, electoral outcomes (the mandate effect) substantially affect national budgetary priorities. Finally, in one of their most interesting findings, Klingemann, Hofferbert, and Budge conclude that the mandate model is consistently important in countries with political parties that reflect preindustrial cleavages, such as Christian versus secular (Germany, Austria, the Netherlands) or ethnic/linguistic differences (Belgium); this suggests that cleavages founded on personal identity enhance the importance of winning elections, whereas countries dominated by the bread-and-butter issues of the welfare state can accommodate either an agenda or a mandate model.

This study has, of course, its limitations. Many policy scholars will question the use of national budgetary priorities as the sole dependent variable. In most regulatory policy areas, shifts in national policies are likely to be only very poorly reflected by changes in the relative proportion of the national budget accorded regulatory programs. Furthermore, as the implementation literature has surely taught us, with the exception of programs dominated by direct transfer payments, national budgets are only one of many inputs that affect the eventual policy outputs (e.g., quality of educational services or reductions in pollution emissions). However, in a study of this scope—six to ten policy areas in ten countries over forty years—using national budgetary expenditures to examine the effect of party platforms in national elections strikes me as a perfectly sensible decision.

Similarly, many policy scholars—including both Lin Ostrom and myself—have long questioned the utility of the sort of "black box" models used here. In this book the authors simply analyze the relationship between the content of party manifestoes and the subsequent budgetary allocations of national governments via (1) publication of the manifestoes (the agenda effect) or (2) the party's becoming a member of the winning coalition (the mandate effect). Nowhere do they discuss the electoral campaign, the negotiations concerning the formation of the government, the process of putting together a budget, differences among the policy area, or many other relevant topics. Nevertheless, they do manage to explain over 50 percent of the variance in budgetary priorities. More important, they make the excellent point that those who observe the process in detail often get so immersed in the complexities (chaos?) that they fail to see that the systems seem to be working reasonably well; the priorities expressed in party manifestoes somehow get reflected in the budgetary priorities of subsequent governments. Finally, given the scope of this study, the sort of analysis that Lin Ostrom or I would like to do would be utterly impossible. In research of this scope, relatively simple "black box" models are probably all that is possible. Finally, Gary King and Michael Laver have questioned some of the modeling techniques used in this volume, but I am perfectly satisfied with the authors' response (see King et al. 1993).

In the final analysis, however, this is a monumental work of scholarship in the field of comparative public policy. I'm honored to have it appear in the Westview series Theoretical Lenses on Public Policy.

1

A Theory of Democratic Policymaking

This book is concerned with how well the policy priorities of modern democratic governments reflect the issues competing parties put before the voters. Modern democracies are representative democracies. Political parties play a key role in the representation process, and if they fail to play that role, the entire edifice is flawed. Representatives are elected on behalf of the people to act for the people's purposes. The fact that there are representatives, however, means that the political system has a certain autonomy and follows its own logic. It need not respond immediately and to all demands. Rather, the relationship between societal demands and governmental actions is mediated by a competitive party system (Fuchs and Klingemann 1993). This is why the congruence between what parties say and what governments do is important in the theory of representative democracy.

Some critics maintain that competing pressures have destroyed any rationality or orderliness the policy process may ever have had. Diverse interests, media priorities, and various direct citizen initiatives have so pressed on those who would otherwise lead that the political system itself has lost its capacity for autonomous action. Thus the latter half of the twentieth century has brought to maturity a crisis or at least a challenge of grave proportions to representative democracy (Olson 1983). Party systems are no longer functioning as agents selecting and aggregating citizens' demands. However, we shall offer evidence that political parties, integral to representative democracy, perform far better than most critics would lead us to believe.

In this chapter we will first offer a sketch of the role played by political parties in the democratic policy process. Then we will review three critiques of contemporary representative democracy, based respectively on:

- The notion of a hidden power elite
- Comparative policy analysis
- Rational choice theory

We shall argue that parties and, particularly, their formal election programs[1] are far more important in the electoral and governing processes of representative democracy than has previously been believed by expert and lay skeptic alike.

PARTY PROGRAMS AND PUBLIC POLICY: THE BASIC QUESTIONS

To a remarkable extent, the policy priorities of governments in modern democracies reflect the formal programs presented by competing political parties during elections. This congruence between promise and performance is at the heart of what we mean by "democracy." Our book reports on this important connection by examining the experience of ten democracies over the years since World War II. The evidence addresses the claim that political parties have been major actors in organizing the complexities of modern policymaking. The strong congruences that we found between election programs and later policy mean that the policy process is more democratic and probably more orderly than many critics have claimed—and this is so because of the contributions of political parties.

We can make these positive assertions about the congruence between party programs and policy priorities because of the development of a unique body of information: the data produced by the Manifestoes Research Project on postwar party programs in modern democracies. Chapter 3 presents more detail on the nature of the data, but for the reader to understand our endeavor, even at the theoretical level, a brief introduction is required here. We coded every sentence of the published election program of every significant party that participated in the elections of ten modern democracies, for nearly every election between World War II and the mid-1980s, into one, and only one, category from a fifty-four-item classification of possible themes.[2] Thus, a program statement such as: "Our party is committed to the modernization of the country's roads and highways" would be an entry under the coding category *technology and infrastructure.* The statement "Steps must be taken to preserve our natural wonders" would be coded under the category *environmental protection.* This technique was used through the entire document. The percentage of sentences devoted to each category, out of the total number of sentences, was then calculated.

Several statistical procedures, detailed in Chapter 3, were employed to examine the relationship between party program emphases (that is, the percentage of sentences in a program devoted to particular categories out of the fifty-four) and government policy priorities. Such policy priorities were measured by the percentage of central government expenditures devoted to particular activities for each of the years encompassed by the party election programs. These priorities were matched to particular themes in the party programs. Thus, expenditure priorities for the category *highways and public transport* were matched to party program emphases on *technology and infrastructure.*

Motivating our research are questions about the role of political parties in the policy processes of modern democracies: Are postelection policy priorities anticipated by the preelection issue agendas of the parties competing in the system? Do their formal preelection programs anticipate postelection policy priorities? Put differently, do the problems confronted by the parties in the process of competition form an *agenda* that resembles the patterns of government action once the election is over? We shall address this question by examining the match between, on the one hand, changes over time in the total set of concerns stressed in the programs of all the major competing parties and, on the other hand, the relative resources allocated to different policy domains. At this stage we shall not be concerned with which party won but rather with the policy reflection of the programmatic concerns of all the competitors. The goal is to determine if the agenda produced by interparty competition acts as a framework for later legislation. Losers' as well as winners' programs can contribute to such an agenda effect.

Let us suppose that in certain years both the Democrats and the Republicans in the United States increased the emphasis on education in their respective platforms. In other years, they both decreased that emphasis. And let us also suppose that in the years before the subsequent election, the federal government's percentage of outlays for education also went up or down, much in line with the party platforms. This would suggest to us that the platforms of the parties accurately projected the active agenda for federal education-policy priority. We shall be examining those agenda effects and demonstrating their relevance to certain key criticisms of modern democracies.

The second major question we consider is, To what extent is there evidence of a *mandate,* whereby programs of winning parties are more clearly translated into policy than are the programs of the losers? If the process of competition between parties produces and publicizes an agenda that acts as a framework for action, then certain arguments (which we will outline in this chapter) about the openness, structure, and orderliness of the policy process are supported. Furthermore, if there is not only congruence between policy and the general content of competitive discourse (the agenda) but also a better reflection in later policy priorities of the concerns of winners than of losers, we have evidence of a mandate. This would fulfill certain requisites of a democratic process. For evidence of the agenda, we will look to the congruence between policy priorities and the preceding programs of all parties—even those of the losers. For evidence of the mandate, we will see whether the congruences between policy and winners' programs are closer than those between policy and losers' programs.

A naïve observer might well say: "Of course. Parties are supposed to follow the voters' preferences." But ask someone if he or she thinks that political parties have helped make the policy process more structured or more democratic in the United States, for example, and the response is likely to be: "Well, the U.S. is different. We have separation of powers, and so it is just naturally chaotic." Then ask a Dutch observer if the policy process is orderly or democratic in the Netherlands,

Figure 1.1
The Basic Question of
Program to Policy Congruence

Is there any relationship between what parties say and what governments do?

[Operationalization]

Party Program Emphasis on Policy Themes A ... n	=	Central Government Outlays for Policy A ... n

where governments are led by multiparty coalitions that sometimes take several months to be put together after an election or a resignation. The response will be: "Well, of course, the Netherlands is peculiar. We have had these religious differences, you know, in addition to the other conflicts of modern society." Is policymaking in Germany, Sweden, or France more democratic because of the operation of their party systems? Well, maybe in Germany, except that the Free Democrats do seem to have more power than their votes would warrant. But even where things seem to work pretty well, that could be because of peculiar social and historical circumstances. With respect to particular cases, many people would argue that political parties, to the extent that they are important at all, bring disorder to the policy process. As for their contribution to democracy, they are widely seen as contravening popular wishes about policy in the interests of a few power brokers.

This book is concerned with broad patterns, not with national peculiarities. In spite of differences among countries, our research applies a common mode of analysis to ten quite distinct political systems: Australia, Austria, Belgium, Britain, Canada, the Federal Republic of Germany, France, the Netherlands, Sweden, and the United States. All ten are clearly among the world's most democratic countries. All are modern industrial societies. But they differ greatly in their social structure, in their domestic and international history, in their formal political institutions, and in the way they go about confronting collective problems through public policy. Applying a uniform research strategy to such a diverse set is daunting. But we think it can be done. We will present the evidence, and then the reader can judge.

Our basic concern is most simply illustrated in Figure 1.1. The evidence will come later in a series of chapters dealing with the individual countries. Figure 1.1, however, sets out the essential question: Is there any relationship between what parties *say* and what governments *do?* If such a relationship exists, then what politicians do and what observant voters see should be in harmony. We will examine the relationships between the issues emphasized in party election programs and the policy priorities of governments. If the parties, in their published election programs, deal with the same things in pretty much the same priority ranking as do the governments after elections, then the policy process seems to have a good deal of structure and orderliness.

Moreover, if the policies adopted by the winners reflect what they stressed prior to the election—especially if that was different from what was stressed by the losers—it is good evidence, we think, that policymaking is not only orderly but also rather democratic. The voters had a choice, and the choice seems to have made a difference. Such congruence between party election program and government action would reflect the operation of a mandate conferred on the winners by the election process. Before going into the details of the research, however, we shall review the general theory of political parties that underlies our work.

A THEORY OF PARTY FUNCTIONS

Modern politics is party politics. Political parties are the major actors in the system that connects the citizenry and the governmental process. Parties sort through citizens' demands, most of which have been articulated by interest groups and the mass media. The parties turn the demands into political issues by working out policy alternatives in light of the general principles for which the respective parties stand. In this way political parties aggregate demands into loosely coherent policy packages—a process that gives voters a choice in elections. Political parties form governments and act as opposition in legislatures. They may occupy the upper echelons of the bureaucracy. Thus, they are crucial to political decisionmaking and implementation. From this perspective, political parties must choose policies. They have to rule, and they have to take responsibility for their decisions. They are the major actors in representative democratic systems when it comes to solving societal problems.

The Genesis of Political Parties

Historically, parties emerged out of conflicting interests—newly emerging interests versus interests threatened by forces of change. The differences among modern political parties can be traced back to the social cleavages dominant at the time of their founding. These cleavages formed a general pattern across the lands now occupied by modern democracies. Detailed accounts exist of the constellations of cleavages and oppositions that produced mass organizations for electoral action. Building on such evidence, Lipset and Rokkan (1967) developed a theory explaining how major societal conflicts translate into party systems. They conceptualized parties as "alliances in conflicts over policies and value commitments within the larger body politic" (p. 5). They stressed parties' functions as agents of conflict management and as instruments of integration. Most important, they

Table 1.1
Cleavages, Critical Junctures, Issues, and Party Families:
An Amended Version of the Lipset/Rokkan Model

Cleavage	Critical Juncture	Issues	Party family
Center - Periphery	Reformation - Counter-Reformation, 16th-17th centuries	National vs. supra-national religion; national language vs. Latin	Ethnically and linguistically based parties
State - Church	National Revolution, 1789 and after	Secular vs. religious control of mass education	Religious parties
Land - Industry	Industrial Revolution, 19th century	Tariff levels for agricultural products; control vs. freedom for industrial enterprise	Agrarian parties; conservative and liberal parties
Owner - Worker	The Russian Revolution, 1917 - 1991	Integration into national polity vs. commitment to international revolutionary movement	Socialist and Communist parties
Materialists vs. Post-Materialists	The Cultural Revolution, 1968 and after	Environmental quality vs. economic growth	Green/ ecology parties

Source: Adapted from Lipset and Rokkan 1967, p. 47.

convincingly described and systematized the critical lines of cleavage that have historically structured the party systems of Western democracies. Table 1.1 is an adaptation of that theoretical perspective.

In their classic study, Lipset and Rokkan linked the two major cleavages—the Center versus Periphery cleavage and the State versus Church cleavage—to the Reformation and Counter-Reformation (sixteenth and seventeenth centuries) and to the national revolutions (1789 and after). Here the issues of national versus supranational religion and national language versus Latin were dominant. Most of the conflicts taken up by political parties representing ethnically, linguistically, or religiously distinct populations of the peripheries of the newly emerging nation-states of Europe can be traced back to these critical junctures. The same is true of the parties that defended organized religious interests, on the one hand, and of those that attacked the historic privileges of the Church, on the other. The issue was deciding who would control community moral standards.

The nineteenth-century conflict between the landed gentry and newly emerging industrial interests was sparked by the question of tariff levels for agricultural products and the issue of freedom or control for industrial enterprises. Agrarian, liberal, and conservative parties can be traced back to these conflicts.

The owner versus worker cleavage, stimulated by the Russian Revolution, is a fourth major cleavage. This uniquely industrial dimension of conflict was particularly important to the development of working-class parties and their split into revisionist Social Democrats and radical Communists.

In light of more recent developments, Lipset and Rokkan would almost certainly have added the cleavage between postmaterialists and materialists, so aptly described and analyzed by Inglehart (1977, 1990). Its clearest manifestation in the contemporary context is the conflict that pits environmental interests against those favoring economic growth. The Green, or ecology, parties offer the most pointed challenge to established interests in the late twentieth century.

Parties in the Policy Process

In the policy process, parties perform complex, connected tasks. Democracy is not just a description of the way that governments get formed. It also pertains to their functioning. V. O. Key once wrote, "Unless mass views have some place in the shaping of policy, all the talk about democracy is nonsense" (Key 1966; quoted also in Wright, Erickson, and McIver 1988). Our research does not specifically examine the link between public wishes and policy products, but we do look at the connection between what competing parties present to the public and the eventual policy products. Democratic procedures should yield a democratic product. If the procedures fail to produce policies in line with widespread preferences—or with what people have been led by the parties to expect—then the system is not functioning democratically, no matter how universal the formal rules of inclusion.

In the policy process, parties perform numerous functions. They are involved in political recruitment, in the articulation and aggregation of interests, in political communication, in mobilizing and channeling mass political participation. In particular, as Katz (1987, 4) pointed out, political parties have to rule and take responsibility for ruling. Our own view of the role of the parties in policymaking is informed by Fuchs's (1993) model of the formal democratic process. Fuchs distinguished a set of key actors, their environments, functions, and their major action products.

The process of democratic policymaking is summarized in Figure 1.2. The diagram directs attention to the way political goods are produced and to the sets of actors involved in the production process. It is assumed that interests are con-

Figure 1.2
A Model of the Formal Democratic Process

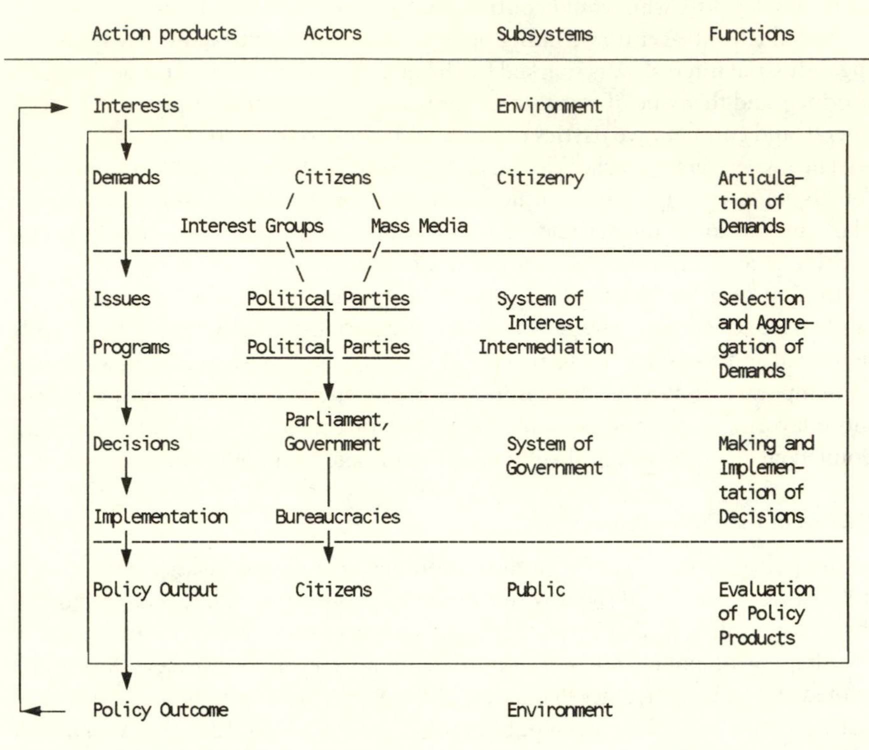

Source: Adapted from Fuchs 1993, Figure 2.

verted into citizens' demands mainly by interest groups and the mass media. This is part of an ongoing policy discourse that takes up murmurs of vague discontent and articulates them, thus giving them the status of demands. Whereas articulation of demands is the dominant function of the actors linked to the citizenry, selection and aggregation of demands are characteristics of the system of interest intermediation. This is the home turf of the political parties. They select demands and turn them into issues. That is, they point out alternative ways to satisfy demands and to address the problems involved. However, parties are typically confronted with not just one but with a multitude of issues that they or their competitors bring to the policy arena. To offer the electorate a choice, they have to package seemingly disparate claims into more or less coherent bundles. In effect, they create predetermined bargains. When multiple parties present the voters with different bundles of issues and solutions, voters have a choice. They can choose from within a more or less crystallized, active policy agenda.

Once that choice is made, parties have to assume their roles as operators of government (and opposition). In this capacity they have to ensure binding decisions and allocations of appropriate resources. Bureaucracies, which are not devoid of partisan influence but which still have to follow narrowly prescribed procedures, are expected to decide in line with enacted policy and to implement the decisions taken. This is what the government system adds to the policy product. Thus, the different steps of policy production consistently reduce options by adding specific qualities to the policy product.

Finally, the citizens are confronted with the policy outcomes that they will evaluate. This evaluation, in turn, affects the configuration of interests, which gives rise to another cycle of the policy process.

Our research does not examine specifically either the link between public demands and issue formation or the citizens' evaluation of policy products. Instead, we look at the congruence between what competing parties present to the public and the eventual policy products. Democratic procedures need to yield a democratic product.

POWER ELITE OR CHAOS?

The amount of structuring and the democratic nature of the policy process have long been a matter of scholarly and popular dispute.[3] Many writers point to the seemingly chaotic nature of contemporary policymaking (Wildavsky 1988; Kingdon 1984). There is a sense that in a bygone age or in a more rational system somewhere else, competing interests, desires, and needs in the public arena were resolved in a tidier manner than seems to be the case in today's democracies. There is a side to democracy that always appears a bit shabby if one chooses to look at it that way. A certain crassness necessarily surfaces when groups of people pursue their self-interest via the mechanisms of compulsion wielded by the state—even when that state derives its "just power from the consent of the governed." It requires some distance from the day-to-day activity for the structural regularity of it all to be visible. The "Iron Chancellor" of nineteenth-century Germany, Otto von Bismarck, is reputed to have remarked: "There are two things one ought not to watch being made—sausage and legislation."

As the reach of the modern state has extended in pursuit of the twin goals of national security and social justice, the stakes of policymaking have broadened and deepened. With that broadening and deepening have come increased complexity and competition between those who seek gain and protection through the channels by which public policy is made.

The Power Elite Thesis

Not all critics of democratic governments, however, have based their disapproval on the seeming disorderliness of the policy process. To some an excess of order, of a rather seamy and less than wholly visible nature, has been the problem. From the time of Karl Marx to the present, critics of democracies have rejected as ultranaïve the simple tenets of popular control of modern government. C. Wright Mills described a structure of control by a "power elite" that is

> in command of the major hierarchies and organizations of modern society. They rule the big corporations. They run the machinery of the state and claim its prerogatives. They direct the military establishment. They occupy the strategic command posts of the social structure, in which are now centered the effective means of the power and wealth and the celebrity which they enjoy. (Mills 1956, 4)

In the 1950s and 1960s a stream of popular and scholarly criticism held that the institutions of democracy were largely a sham to disguise rule by a power elite. Mills, among the most widely read proponents of that thesis, concentrated his fire on the United States, then as now one of the biggest members of the family of democracies. He saw the mainsprings of power being wielded by a "military-industrial complex" of persons with like interests, great wealth, and common backgrounds. Mills and others who pursued comparable lines of inquiry saw the activities of elected officials and their appointees as window dressing, designed to deflect criticism from a real system that was much more closed than that which met the public eye.

Much elitist theory takes its inspiration from the writings of American social scientists who, in turn, were influenced by their own perceptions of their surroundings. Some political scientists of the 1920s and 1930s wrote works of lasting significance on the impact of moneyed interest groups in getting their objectives met through the legislative process (Schattschneider 1935). Sociologists, however, provided the major foundation for an elitist interpretation of formal democracies (Lynd and Lynd 1929, 1937; Warner and Lunt 1941; Hollingshead 1949; Hunter 1953).[4]

American sociologists in the 1920s and 1930s took inspiration from European scholars who had argued that complex organizations, including governments, were almost certain to fall under the control of small, unified groups of self-serving individuals. Marx, for whom the capitalist state was the executive committee of the bourgeoisie, offered the most comprehensive case relating the structure of power to the workings of modern industrial economies. Two European sociologists, Gaetano Mosca and Roberto Michels, seeking to undermine the revolutionary fervor of working-class movements, argued that elite control was inevitable in large organizations, including socialist parties, at any place or time (Mosca 1939; Michels 1915). Michels applied the thesis specifically to these parties, arguing that an "iron law of oligarchy" operated irrevocably in any large organization, leading to specialized leadership, controlled communications, and institutionalized pursuit of elite self-interest.

The Pluralist Counterattack

The major counterattack in defense of the central role of democratic procedures in the policy process was launched in the early 1960s in a series of studies of actual decisions.[5] Issue-oriented research such as that by Robert Dahl or Edward Banfield showed conclusively that democratically elected officials were the central decisionmakers who determined whether particular problems on the agenda would be pursued and, if so, which of the available policy options would be applied to them.

According to the pluralist model guiding the decision studies, multiple actors and groups competed, more or less openly, in the policy contest. For example, Dahl examined sixteen major decisions concerning various policy domains in New Haven. He discovered no elite, in the sense that there was very little overlap of key participants in these different issue areas. The pattern of influence and interaction differed from one issue to another and altered with time. Many individuals moved into and out of the centers of decisionmaking and from one issue area to another. Similar results were obtained by Banfield in his study of major policy decisions in Chicago.

Both Dahl and Banfield found the popularly elected mayor in their respective communities to be the only person occupying a key role in several issue areas. The clear implication was, furthermore, that the stance taken by each mayor was a matter of response to perceived popular preferences and needs rather than one dictated either by inexorable forces or by the preferences of a group of unofficial power wielders.

In the pluralist model—and seemingly verified by the data—citizens' interest in public affairs and a willingness to engage in policymaking activity seem to be more important as determinants of influence than economic resources or status connections. The absence of unified, coordinated, mobilized organizational activity explains the multiple choices available to formal officeholders.

The most telling and enduring criticism of this line of analysis involves the problem of setting the agenda, or what have been called "nondecisions" (Bachrach and Baratz 1962, 1963; Merelman 1968). The pluralists, in their studies of real-world decisions, take the agenda as it is found; the critics argue that decisional inquiry is unable to determine the rules by which particular issues find their way into the process of deliberation. It is reasonable to claim that the most consequential decision is not how to dispose of a particular alternative, once it has been articulated. The appropriate question in the long run concerns the capacity of and means by which the political system discovers and filters the needs and desires that are to be considered in the policy process. The problem is basically this: Once a set of decisions is placed on the agenda for policy deliberation, it is quite easy to discover the relevant actors and to offer some explanation for their actions. But there may well be a "mobilization of bias" in the system that prevents the emergence of particular types of issues and the interests they embody (Schattschneider 1960).

The key doubt about the vitality of the pluralist model of democratic policymaking centers on how items get on the agenda in the first place. If all the issues dealt with by presumably democratic processes were, in a sense, "cleared" by a discrete elite, then the seeming influence exercised by legitimate public officials would be sham (Bachrach and Baratz 1962). If a political system concerns itself only with problems and policy options that are not threatening to some behind-the-scenes power mongers, then the claim that it is democratic is severely weakened. But, of course, if members of the elite work entirely "behind the scenes" and if they skillfully cover their tracks, then there is no evidence of their control. The power elite thesis becomes a matter of faith rather than a demonstrable fact. The pluralist claim that real decisions are being made within the broad framework of democratic procedures is likewise a matter of faith, in that it does not disprove the existence of the "powers behind the scene."

VARIATIONS ON NONRATIONALITY

A system run by a power elite has more apparent structure than an openly democratic one. For all the untidiness of democratic policymaking, however, it does contain implicit structure, at least in theory, as we have suggested in Figure 1.2. Popular perceptions of the policy agenda evolve in response to changing objective circumstances, changing value priorities, and changing views about the purposes of government. Agents of competition, most notably, political parties, aggregate sets of these into bundles of anticipated actions. They steer the electoral process by recruiting and promoting candidates. And they manage to a greater or lesser extent the organization of the formal policy-selection process.

This organization, of course, exists in theory but cannot be assumed to be fact. But it can provide a rich source of interesting questions. Unfortunately for the theory, when some of the interesting questions have been subjected to empirical test, they have come up wanting. Skepticism has been reinforced by comparative policy output research.

Comparative Policy Output Research

Novel quantitative research, beginning in the 1960s, challenged the primacy of political forces as prime movers and shakers of policy. The most lasting message of comparative policy analysis was that "politics does not matter for policy." Newly acquired statistical skills were applied to readily available data, such as expenditures by multiple jurisdictions (for example, U.S. states, Italian cities, or groups of countries) on various policy domains; the findings were that crudely constructed indicators of political differences were unrelated or only weakly related to policy outputs (Dawson and Robinson 1963; Hofferbert 1966; Fried 1971; Cutright 1965). That is, the correlations between the two were low.

Sometimes it was found that socioeconomic data could be manipulated to eliminate any apparent politics-to-policy linkage (Dye 1966; Hofferbert 1966). Urbanization enhances the chances for redistributive welfare policy more than does tight competition between parties. Education expenditures are higher in richer jurisdictions, regardless of which party is in control of government. With variations, this theme was reinforced in the late 1960s in many settings. (See Hofferbert 1972, for a summary and critique of the early work.) Robert Fried found that it matters little for the expenditures of Italian cities which party is in control of government, even when he compared expenditures under Christian Democrats to those under Communists (Fried 1971). Far more important is how far north the city is, with those in the North providing a wider and more costly range of services than those in the South.

Doubt about the policy relevance of democratic government was even more strongly stimulated by Philips Cutright's work (1965). Constructing a multivariate index of democracy and correlating it with a composite index of social security policies across about seventy countries, he found that the social security policies of countries were far more closely related to levels of economic development than to their degree of democracy. There were only minimal policy differences between democratic and patently nondemocratic countries' social security policies, once differences in material resources were taken into account.

These studies found not disorder but only latent patterning of policy and policymaking, with political conditions changing without evident impact on policy. Only "structural" conditions of the society and/or economy seemed relevant to policy, and then not in a theoretically consistent manner.

The early works demonstrating a stronger linkage of policy to socioeconomic conditions than to political circumstances were often challenged by scattered evidence on the importance of party control or competition or other formal institutional features (Lineberry and Fowler 1967; Greenstone and Peterson 1968; Walker 1969; Sharkansky and Hofferbert 1969; Grumm 1971; Flora and Heidenheimer 1980; Castles 1982). Later work has relied on ever-more-elaborate collections of indicators of political and institutional characteristics in the effort to find their possible linkages to, particularly, welfare policy, both across countries and over time.[6]

Alexander Hicks and David Swank opened their 1992 article with the statement: "To date no consensus has been reached on the controversy … over how politics matters for welfare spending in industrialized countries" (Hicks and Swank 1992). The cliché that "politics does not matter" has been largely dispelled. Recent work on the American states by Wright, Erickson, and McIver (1988) even goes so far as to provide impressive evidence of congruence between public opinion, as reported in massive surveys, and broad policy patterns, thereby diluting the force of doubt about democratic influences in the policy process. These various studies, however, while lifting some of the cloud of doubt from democratic theory, do not cohere in any comprehensive, theoretically persuasive manner.

This may be due in part to the fact that party participation in government has necessarily treated interparty differences as static and each party's policy position as intrinsically time-invariant. That is, prior to the availability of the data used here, there was no systematic means by which to track any one party's changes in issue or ideological orientation—in spite of the very obvious fact that few consequential parties have been utterly issue-inflexible. Hicks and Swank (1992) provided a substantively interesting and technically elegant analysis of party and interparty influences on welfare across countries and time, but they could deal with only interparty differences and could not confront intraparty dynamics with respect to issue agendas. Thus there still remains the question how and under what circumstances will what political and institutional features affect what sort of policies.

If party election programs forecast policy, then there is evidence of an important link in the chain of reasoning in democratic theory, providing insight into the fact not only that "politics matters" but also that politics matters in ways that confirm important elements of the theory of what should be found in a democracy. And if we can go further and show the working of a party mandate, we will illuminate yet another set of vital links in the chain of democratic reasoning.

Rational Choice and Voting Cycles: The Inevitability of Chaos

In and around this comparative work, other analysts of the policy process—mostly in the United States—were redesigning the backdrop, in total abstract expressionist form. They produced variations on the theme that the policy process is nonrational and—implicitly, therefore—nondemocratic. "Garbage can" theory claims that policymakers randomly select solutions and then search for problems to which these can be fitted (March and Olson 1984). "Incrementalism" sees policy moving by marginal adjustments without any overall direction (Davis, Dempster, and Wildavsky 1966; Lindblom 1959). Wildavsky's later work views even the order of incrementalism breaking down (Wildavsky 1984). The outer limits of disorder theory were reached by John Kingdon's study (1984), based on close observation of the U.S. Congress in the 1970s and 80s. His ant's eye view led him to conclude that policy is all a product of primeval soup, where elements that go together do so by means of random attractions and evolutionary opportunity—the exact opposite of structured, purposeful, planned action.

All these variations on chaos theory see policy as more or less devoid of purposeful management and as an unguided flow from something that was, to that which is, to that which will be. The very concept of "decision" loses force in such a model, since it lays stress on bounded processes with finite points of transformation that are belied by the seeming seamlessness of the process.

The theory of voting cycles envisions such a chaotic state. If politics is viewed as rational individuals' pursuit of their goals, as economic theories of politics would indicate, one might well feel that there was bound to be a certain order to the policy process—the political equivalent of efficiency in the market (Downs 1957). Not so, according to the predominant rational choice school of political science (Arrow 1951, 1984; Olson 1983). Perfectly rational behavior at the individual level leads to irrational and arbitrary collective outcomes. Thus empirically based policy studies that have found disorder in actual policymaking are reinforced by a critique that says such irrationalities are inevitable in any collective decisions made by rational voters or politicians.

The argument runs as follows: A minimal definition of *rationality* is "transitivity of preferences." That is, a rational individual who prefers policy A to policy B, and policy B to policy C, must logically prefer policy A to policy C. But if there are three or more people and three or more policy options, it is always possible that majority decisions do not produce clear or stable orderings of preference. For example:

- Individual 1 prefers A to B and B to C
- Individual 2 prefers B to C and C to A
- Individual 3 prefers C to A and A to B

In this circumstance, there is a majority for A over B. There is a majority for B over C. And a majority for C over A. Thus rational, transitive preference orders lead to an intransitive collective ordering, otherwise known as a voting cycle, since decisions would go round and round with no clear stopping point.

This critique is devastating for democratic policymaking. It seems to suggest that no matter how hard individuals try to be rational, democratic policy decisions will often fail to reflect majority preferences because no real majority can exist in many cases. This can be seen clearly where resources are being distributed. Enough members of the potential majority, by being promised more for themselves, can always be shifted away from the position that has been taken, thus making every majority unstable.

The rational choice critique of democratic policy processes suggests that groping in the garbage can or fishing in primeval soup is inevitable even for rational decisionmakers. Outcomes can be made to stick only by stopping policymaking at some arbitrary point or by hidden elite manipulation.

Irresolvable issues can come from many sources, not the least of which is the overlap of interests that history has deposited on the contemporary scene. The response to this challenge is to point to the role of parties as organizers of issues. If the process of bundling issues yields fewer than three choices, voting cycles are eliminated. Majorities can rule. Even if there are three or more choices (parties), their various packages of issues (party programs) can be structured in such a manner as to eliminate or minimize the possibility of cycles. This is the process Easton labeled the "aggregation of interests" (Easton 1953; see also Figure 1.2). The result of parties' organizing public-policy deliberation in this way would be clear structure in the "authoritative allocation of values for society."

SUMMARY

We have drawn the outlines of a broad theory of political parties in the policy process. This sets the stage for our comparison of party election programs to subsequent government policy priorities. We see this endeavor as addressing three bodies of writing about the policy process:

- Elite theory, which posits control of policy by forces coming from outside the democratic process, and the pluralist response to it, which argues from observation of policymaking cases that the critical decisions are made openly by legitimate officials
- Comparative policy analysis, which questions the impact of political conditions on policy
- Variations on rational choice theory, which suggest that spontaneously structured, orderly policy processes are probably impossible to find in the real world

Our analysis of the forecasting capacity of political parties' election programs will enable us, if not to "prove" or "falsify" any of these three, at least to provide added weight for or against particular conceptions of the policy process.

The analysis will show that a substantial portion of variation in policy priorities is indeed anticipated by the agendas presented by the parties that have contested elections in the ten countries since World War II. There is an ideological division of labor by which the parties specialize, to some extent, in the issues upon which they focus. Thus it is often in the programs of parties that may be out of office that we find certain agenda items articulated and aggregated for the electorate. That a set of parties competing does cast a broad issue net and that this casting foretells policy priority have several consequences for the critiques we have summarized in this chapter.

Elite theories would identify the preelection period as a stage where issues somehow begin to be suppressed if they pose threats to the interests of ruling elites. Pluralists would insist that the constitutional and other institutional apparatuses of democracy—right to organize, free speech, free press, unfettered party competition—ensure that such gatekeeping is of minimal if any importance. Competing diagnoses become themselves the elements of political discourse. Unlike the decision studies of the pluralist school in the 1960s, our research does not take the policy agenda as found in the formal deliberative processes of sitting governments. As critics have noted, that agenda may itself exclude items threatening to a power elite. The nondecisions may be more important than the decisions, if the hypothesis of elite control is true. We must admit that our research does not definitively dispel the specter of behind-the-scenes manipulation by a nondemocratic elite. But by examining the programmatic antecedents to the formal policy agenda—before even the selection of incumbents—we see our research as possibly diminishing the credibility of the power elite hypothesis. If the policy priorities of governments in several modern democracies over several decades reflect the programmatic options publicly presented in competitive elections, then, we think, the elite gatekeeping hypothesis is hardly credible.

If we can show, furthermore, not only that interparty competition exposes the active policy agenda to public scrutiny but also that it registers voters' choice in a way that favors winners over losers, this is a further point for the pluralist hypothesis. Such a finding likewise casts doubts on the variations on chaos theory discussed above, and it fills in some very important gaps in comparative policy research. It is our contention that the seeming "chaos" is the natural untidiness of democracy viewed close up. The challenge of rational choice theory is the presence of frequently unresolvable dilemmas created by intransitive collective choices. If the party election programs, however, bundle issues in such a way as to reduce the frequency of voting cycles stemming from intransitive choices, then that corner of criticism is less consequential. We will not claim that our research deals with the problem on a highly theoretical level but rather that the apparent importance of party programs minimizes the likely frequency with which such problems are confronted.

Not all who see disorder and randomness in the policy process, however, theorize that things are that way by the very nature of political life. Rather, they see chaos as resulting from particular historical and/or institutional conditions (Wildavsky 1988; Kingdon 1984; March and Olson 1984). If our contention about the structuring revealed through party program-to-policy linkages is true, then the chaos is more apparent than real. It appears as a result of describing and assessing policy processes from too close up.

CONCLUSION

Do the election programs distinguish competing parties from one another? What is the shape of the agenda they have offered to the voters of modern democracies? Do the things about which the parties are concerned seem to structure the contours of policy? How important for getting a program reflected in policy is it for a party to be in government? These are the major questions we ask in this book.

A basic expectation would be that the reflection of party programs in public policy—the accountability of parties—varies according to certain constitutional and institutional features (Powell 1990). Perhaps the more that governmental powers are divided among various actors, the more likely it is that the policy agenda will have been anticipated in the total set of policy concerns considered by the parties prior to government formation. But the mandate, which assumes a distinction between what winning parties do and what was expected from the losers, would perhaps be inhibited by having many parties' participation in the policy process. Majoritarian parliamentary systems along British lines ought to enable governing parties to enact the policies they have signaled in the preceding election. Separation of powers between executive and legislature should inhibit that translation process. Furthermore, multiparty coalitions may be incapable of featuring in the division of policy resources the preelection concerns of any particular party.

The ten countries are presented in a sequence that approximates a scale of institutional coherence. That is, the countries analyzed earliest seem to have constitutional and institutional practices more friendly to the operation of an election mandate. Those analyzed later have more-diffuse policy institutions and practices, suggesting less clarity of linkage between programs and the policies of "winners." First, we present a set of more or less two-party parliamentary systems that have been characterized most of the time by single-party majority governments: Britain, Australia, and Canada. These are followed by two presidential systems with sufficient separation of executive and legislative powers to make possible divided party control: France and the United States. Next comes Sweden, with variations on minority coalitions, followed by two systems characterized by coalitions formed by various pairs from among only three parties: Austria and the Federal Republic of Germany (preunification). And our last two countries are variations on a theme of multiparty coalitions: the Netherlands and Belgium.

Our research does not claim to test all the nuances of party programs as they might or might not get translated into policy. Although we present individual chapters dealing with ten separate countries, our basic interest is not in the individuality of those countries but rather with very broad patterns. Nevertheless, since we are dealing with a relatively novel information base and using a heretofore-untried research design, we do need to build upon a set of real-world cases, explored in some depth.

In each country chapter, we present an overview of the party system and policy processes. Then we seek reasons for the varying performance of our standard models. The goal is to find how far we can fit common models of the party policy agenda and the mandate across democracies with different cultural and institutional features. Where those cultural and institutional features seem to diminish the generality of our research strategy, we nevertheless try to use the seeming peculiarities to build more general statements. We hope this will be justified by the time we get to our concluding chapter.

The plan of this book is fairly straightforward. The present chapter has laid out the concerns that guided our research. In Chapter 2 we will discuss how our research approach, using what we call "saliency theory," fits into the broader processes of party competition and collective choice. This is followed, in Chapter 3, by a detailed explanation of the general methodology, data, and statistical techniques used in the balance of the book. Here we develop a series of statistical models, discuss their rationale, and point out their relevance to the linkage between party programs and policy priorities.

Chapters 4 through 13 are each devoted to the application of the models in a single country. We recognize that some readers will not be equally interested in all ten countries. We suggest that those interested in particular countries read first Chapter 1, then Chapter 3, followed by Chapter 4, chapters on the country or countries of interest, and finish off with Chapter 14. We recommend Chapter 4, dealing with Britain, as part of the core reading because it is a bit more detailed than its successors with respect to the logic of our analysis. It is designed as a guide to the procedures by which we analyze the country data. In Chapter 14, we summarize our argument and try to draw together conclusions based on the ten individual-country studies.

NOTES

1. In the United States, the election programs are called "platforms." Elsewhere, they are sometimes labeled "manifestoes." We use "program" as the generic term. The specific nature of these documents will be discussed in Chapter 2. But the reader should keep in mind that the documents we have analyzed are the formally adopted and published preelection pronouncements of the various competing parties.

2. What constitutes a "significant" party has been defined in accordance with the criteria of governing potential proposed by Sartori 1976.

3. This section draws heavily from Hofferbert 1974, chaps. 2 and 8.

4. For a time, there was a rapid rise in cumulative research within the broad domain of community-power studies, varying the research design and setting. Examples of such studies include Miller (1959), Schultze (1961), Williams and Adrian (1963), Agger, Goldrich, and Swanson (1964). Among the criticisms of the methodology and assumptions guiding it are Bonjean and Olson (1964), Herson (1961), Kaufman and Jones (1954), Polsby (1963), Rossi (1947), Dahl (1958), Clark (1960), Jennings (1963).

5. Robert A. Dahl's *Who Governs* (1961) and Edward Banfield's *Political Influence* (1961) stand out as major decision studies. See also Bloomberg and Sunshine (1963), Martin et al. (1961), and Wildavsky (1964).

6. Throughout the 1970s and into the 1990s, there was a steady accumulation of comparative policy studies from different settings, concerned broadly with the questions raised here. It is not necessary for our purposes, however, to present a full review of that literature, since the relevant overall message remains largely unchanged. Hicks and Swank (1992) presented a reasonably comprehensive listing of the studies examining the party-to-policy relationship up to the time of our research on party programs. Our goal here is not to report everything that is relevant to variations in public policy but rather to assess the specific congruence between party programs and policy priorities, an important difference that is addressed at length in Chapter 3.

2

A Revised View of Party Competition

It is probably a rare voter anywhere who bothers to read the published election programs of competing parties. Why do busy politicians spend their time producing such ephemera? Put differently, if a studious voter had decided to examine, election after election, the contents of the published programs, would that voter thereby have known anything more about the future policies, and particularly policies to be enacted by winners as contrasted to those that would have been enacted by the losers? Would knowledge of the content of contemporary party election programs add anything to the voter's policy-forecasting capacity beyond what could be predicted by impressions of the broad, long-standing differences between the major competitors?

In this book we present some rather impressive evidence that the party election programs really *do* matter in the policy processes of democracies. In data spanning about forty years, for ten established democracies we find support for the seemingly naïve claim that what was written in those documents *before* elections was a good aid to predicting the actions of governments *after* the elections. Furthermore, the particular countries in which the party program-to-policy linkage is found to be most strong are not necessarily those that scholars or journalists have commonly identified as such.

Those scholars who have chosen to study democratic governance have given central place to the form and function of political parties. When the revolutions of the early 1990s took place in Central and Eastern Europe, among the first tasks confronted by the newly active citizenry was to found parties, write formal party programs committing them to certain policies and priorities, and contest elections. As the dust of revolution settled, the most common journalistic and scholarly topic by which the democratic health of those regimes has been assessed was the condition of their fledgling political parties. Our research in ten modern democracies over the postwar period shows that the variation in the universe of policy discourse, as presented in official party programs, does indeed anticipate a large part of the policy actions of governments.

In Chapter 3 we describe in detail the methods by which we analyze party programs and policy priorities. Some additional matters need attention, however, before we get into that much detail. In this chapter we will consider three related topics:

- The character of the election program documents themselves
- "Saliency theory": We reformulate the traditional conception of how party programs are constructed and work in the competitive electoral process
- The way programs may function both to structure the general policy agenda and to be specific mandates for winning parties

THE NATURE OF THE ELECTION PROGRAM

Our data for the parties are based on a content analysis of party election programs, wherein an international team of scholars (the "Manifestoes Research Group") classified each sentence of each document into one of fifty-four unique categories of policy themes. The percentage of sentences devoted to each theme is the fundamental datum we employ in all our analyses. More attention will be given in Chapter 3 to the details of this task. Important here is the nature of the documents themselves.

All democratic parties make some kind of policy pronouncements in the course of the election campaign. The most common way in which these are presented is as a reasonably unified document approved by an authoritative party body. Sometimes this is a large convention, sometimes a small committee especially delegated for the task. In any case, the campaign document is the only statement of policy made with authority on behalf of the whole party.

Appearing as thin pamphlets at the beginning of the postwar period, they have grown steadily in length and can now sometimes resemble paperback books. Their solid appearance and quite dense text often means that they will not be widely read. They are sometimes on sale in bookstores, often acquired by libraries, and commonly distributed throughout the party organizations. However, only in some countries will they be pushed onto individual voters. Extracts from them will appear in other party literature, such as candidates' election addresses, which are distributed individually, but the whole text will not reach the electorate uniformly.

In most democracies the manifesto or platform is launched at a press conference, with great publicity, designed to set the major themes for the whole election. It is through the appearance of programmatic themes—and the contest over them—in the media that the document makes its main impact on electors.

The United States and Britain are the countries where party competition, in the modern sense, originated. These countries have always been associated with published party documents of this kind. As far as possible we have based our analyses in each country on the party pronouncements that most resemble the published election program, but there are many individual variations. Some of these increase the solemn and binding character of the analyses they make. Others bring the document more directly to the people. The variations fall into three groups:

1. The first constitutes a case on its own, as is appropriate for France. Under the Fifth Republic, party leaders have often tended to publish their program, literally, as paperback books, with sales going into millions. Here we have a case where both the authority and circulation of the program are purposefully enhanced.

2. In Australia written manifestoes have been substantially replaced by an hour-long address to an invited audience by prime ministerial candidates, relayed on all television networks and reported in newspapers the next day. This corresponds with Japan, where party secretaries give interviews to specialist reporters from *Asahi Shimbum,* the largest circulation newspaper (about 5 million). In these cases the electoral program is carried by the party into the media, so to speak, and its direct presentation to the electorate enhanced. However, it perhaps lacks the authority of a separately written and legitimized document.

3. In Canada and the countries of northwest Europe, a variety of party documents are issued, often directed to special groups such as farmers or women, and include an *action* program and sometimes an *economic action* program. These are distributed widely, quite often to every elector. Many of these parties also have a *basic* program, which will not be modified except in detail over a twenty- or thirty-year period.

Clearly, the direct impact of the program on electors will be increased by these methods, though the unique standing of any one of them is undermined by the variety of separate documents that are produced and circulated (even if they often repeat one another) and by the status of the basic program as the Bible of the party. We have tended to take the most extensive election-related document as the nearest equivalent to British manifestoes and American platforms.

A SALIENCY THEORY OF PARTY COMPETITION

Selectivity of Issue Emphases

Classical conceptions of party competition assume that all competitors take positions on the same set of issues—tailoring their formulation to calculations of electoral advantage. Voters weigh the individual issues and then assess which party has the right combination to match the individual's preference matrix. Using such an implicit weighting scheme, voters locate themselves in an issue space and then vote for the party whose programmatic commitments are nearest. Parties formulate their sets of positions to seek the maximum number of supporters on the dominant-preference continuum—usually some variation on "left-right." The most widely recognized formal theory of party competition is that of Anthony Downs, set forth in his book *An Economic Theory of Democracy* (1957).

Our mode of analysis rests on certain modifications of this theory of party competition. We adopt David Robertson's terminology and label this modification *saliency theory* (Robertson 1976). The saliency theory of electoral competition reconciles certain inconsistencies within Downs's *spatial model.* Downs assumed that parties that were competing for votes arrayed themselves by means of policy pronouncements on a range of alternatives along a left-right continuum, trying to use their proposals for policy as a means to get as close as possible to major concentrations of voters. Electors signal their preference by voting for the party whose place on the continuum comes closest to their own. In the election, the party closest to the greater number of electors gets the most votes, which then gives it a prominent or, if it got a majority, unique role in the formation of the government. The party thus has a mandate to carry through the policies that had attracted the plurality or majority of votes. Downs's model gives a picture of how mandate theory works in a spatial context. But it is not the only possible means of implementing a mandate.

Downs's model requires that parties have the policy flexibility or mobility to move left or right, as anticipated electoral advantage is perceived. He assumed that the parties can easily place themselves at any point on the continuum. They can do this because leaders are themselves indifferent about policies. They are motivated exclusively by the desire for office and will stand for whatever policies serve that desire. Hence they will alter party policy and their position on the left-right continuum so as to attract the most votes. Of course, this will work only if electors believe parties will do in government what they promise in elections, so the parties also have good, if selfish, motives for carrying through the mandate.

The difficulty in Downs's model comes in specifying how parties move in relation to each other. Specifically, can they leapfrog each other's positions so as to get ever closer to the major concentrations of electors? This might lead to continual movement and confusion as parties jostled each other to get ever closer to the last vote needed to win—that of the *median voter.* Downs (1957), therefore, at one point in his argument, banned leapfrogging by parties. But where there are more than two parties, this prohibition may enable one of the parties to station itself between the major electoral concentration(s) and its rivals, thus invariably winning, as the others would be unable to get any closer to the potential votes (Barry 1970; see also Chapter 11 in this volume).

Besides the logical inconsistency in regard to leapfrogging, Downs's argument also lacks a broader kind of plausibility. If politicians are ideologically indifferent to policy but relentlessly eager to get into office, why do those in losing parties not simply join the winning party—especially given that the Downsian model has a short time perspective, centering on the current election and government? If carried to extremes, this argument would predict new parties at each election, as losers pulled out of their old ones and the governing party(ies) split in the approach to the election, with leaders jockeying for new, favorable, unique electoral positions.

Of course, this does not happen—presumably because leaders, whatever their desire for office, are also attached to their party's enduring ideological stance. Robertson pointed out that this attachment alone would preclude their free movement along a policy continuum, since at a certain point they would feel the strain of ideological compromise.

There is, however, another reason why parties cannot move freely from end to end. If they did so, they would endanger essential and indelible associations with particular issues and policies. As our discussion of party theory in Chapter 1 suggests, parties sustain an identity that is anchored in the cleavages and issues that gave rise to their birth. These issues are packaged by ideology, yielding a history of particular actions in government and enduring association with certain groups of supporters. In other words, even if parties wanted to repudiate their past for short-term advantage, they could not easily do so, and they might not be believed if they tried. Previous actions cast doubt on present promises when the two are not consistent. Parties are historical beings. They stand for something. Each party is expected to stand for something that separates it from the competition.

This is exactly Robertson's point. Past and present promises must be largely consistent to be believed. In spatial terms this means that parties' ability to move along the type of continuum postulated by Downs is severely limited. In particular, parties will not be able or willing to leapfrog: Labour cannot rationally pretend to be Conservatives, nor Communists to be Liberals, nor Republicans to be Democrats. Parties would lose support if they did so and would not be believed anyway. But taken to extremes, this constraint might mean that each party has only one position that can be taken on the spatial continuum and thus must wait for voters to do the moving.

This conclusion of partisan rigidity, however, does not necessarily follow. Parties will be wary of repudiating previous positions outright, to be sure. But there is much less to prevent them from selectively emphasizing or de-emphasizing issues in their policy inventory. We can conceive movement along the spatial continuum as constituted by emphasis or de-emphasis on a party's traditionally favorite issues, along with some adoption of new issues. Contrasted with a process of neat adversarial affirmation versus denunciation of policy positions from a fixed transparty-issue inventory, the process of relative and shifting emphasis and de-emphasis allows parties to push themselves toward the middle from their particular end. But they will usually stick to their own "side" of the center and will rarely leapfrog.

The assertion that parties compete by emphasizing or de-emphasizing characteristic issues, quite apart from the theoretical difficulties that it overcomes within the spatial model, is supported by considerable empirical evidence. Most of the time, party documents such as election programs avoid taking precise positions or making definite statements of what the party will do when in government. References to other parties and candidates as a whole, let alone discussion of their issue positions, take up an average of only 10 percent of the average document (Budge, Robertson, and Hearl 1987). Pledges to take specific actions are made only in peripheral areas of policy (Rallings 1987). The documents generally present the party's views of the history of a certain problem's development and characteristics, while also emphasizing its importance and priority. What specifically is to be done about the problem is implied or minimized.

This amendment of the classical conception of party competition should not itself distort reality unnecessarily. By stressing certain items and excluding others—without overtly denouncing the latter—parties are, to be sure, implicitly taking pro and anti positions. To be for economic planning, for example, implies being against certain forms of the free market. It is not necessary actually to denounce the market in order to take a clear position in opposition to it. If our data set did not specifically include pro-protectionism and antiprotectionism, a stress on the former would imply an opposition to unrestricted free trade. Thus there is direction in the party program data—direction we will acknowledge by constructing a "left-right" scale. However, parties do not usually juxtapose their positions with those of competing parties on the same issues to show the differences between them.

The absence of such sharp conflict, that is, the approach to common symbols from opposite positions, may seem to create some ambiguity. This is more apparent than real, however, partly because what the party will do is in any case already well known. At a minimum, more government action and expenditure can be expected for those issues most emphasized, and withdrawal of resources can be expected from those not emphasized. Parties are, however, wary of more-specific commitments when future circumstances may inhibit implementation and thus make the parties vulnerable to attack for nonfulfillment of promises.

What parties offer electors thus seems to be a choice between selective policy agendas, not between specific alternative policies addressed to items on a universal agenda. Because points of strength for one party are likely to be points of weakness for the others, a program's combination of emphases is likely to be unique to that party. The other parties' issues will probably be ignored or minimized rather than directly repudiated. Overt repudiation focuses attention on the priorities of others and thus risks mobilizing voters for them. Instead of repudiation, the selectivity of each of the competing alternatives constitutes an *implicit* set of priorities, leading to diminution of those items excluded or ranked lower. As Lipset and Rokkan so elegantly phrased it:

> In our Western democracies the voters are only rarely called upon to express their stands on single issues. They are typically faced with choices among historically given "packages" of programs, commitments, outlooks, and, sometimes, *Weltanschauungen*, and their current behavior cannot be understood without some knowl-

> edge of the sequences of events and the combinations of forces that produced these "packages." (Lipset and Rokkan 1967, 2)

These packaging strategies by the parties present electors with the task of deciding which of the competing bundles of issues is most important rather than deciding what specifically to do about any of the contents. This is perhaps an easier choice for them to make and may avoid certain fundamental problems associated with more-specific options. It certainly minimizes the likelihood of voting cycles (see Chapter 1)—sometimes ordering choices in a one-dimensional (for example, left-right) form and sometimes separating out different dimensions and allowing voters to use simple decision rules such as adding up favored priorities in each party package and voting for the one with the highest score (Ordeshook 1986, 250). There is empirical evidence that voters do make choices in these terms (Budge and Farlie 1983; Saarlvik and Crewe 1983; Klingemann 1986).

If social services are stressed, it is generally with the intention of preserving or extending them, in which case the best party to entrust with the job is the one more to the left. Similarly, if defense is a matter of concern, right-wing parties will strengthen it more wholeheartedly. The picture of electoral decision under these circumstances is one in which voters decide which set of issues concerns them. Then, using a simple calculating device similar to the one described above, they judge parties as to whether on balance each will or will not take appropriate action on its own set of issues (Dalton and Wattenberg 1992; Klingemann 1986; Budge and Farlie 1983).

To be sure, there are many channels that can be used by parties and their candidates to convey to the public their relative movement and positioning on policy issues. Candidates make speeches. Advertisements convey at least vague impressions of some policy positions. But it is the formal election program, as issued in the name of the party early in the contest, that, if not consistently touted in detail, is rarely contradicted by other campaign channels. And it is the set of formal programs of the contestants that most clearly constitutes an authoritative statement of the policy concerns of the collective leaders of the parties and that defines and guides the presentation of issues in the media, through which party priorities generally get to the electorate.

If one views competition through the content of party election programs over time, one sees a dynamic system of political information exchange. Emphases wax and wane. Concentrated concern given to national defense at one time will be diminished compared to concern for the economy or the environment at another. If one puts in more issues, they will add to the bundle of policy emphases that differentiates the parties from one another, that sustains the identity of each, but that allows for substantial movement over time in pursuit not only of office but of policy objectives as well.

The Program as a Vehicle for Competition

Whatever their variations in presentation, it is clear that leaders of parties in the countries we have studied feel bound to make policy pronouncements in the course of the campaign, presumably because they think these will help them to win. Why they should think so has been noted above. If enough of "its" issues become prominent in the election, a party will gain a net influx of votes that will put it in a more powerful position in regard to the next government.

Obvious as this may appear, there are theories of voting behavior that downplay the role of policy issues in voters' choices among parties. Those that assert that electors vote in terms of underlying class and other social ties (Berelson, Lazarsfeld, and McPhee 1954; Lipset and Rokkan 1967) or in terms of long-standing party identification (Campbell et al. 1960) contradict the idea that current issues make a great difference, quantitatively, to party votes. According to estimates of "issue voting," only a minority of electors are swayed by issues (Crewe and Saarlvik 1980). Votes seem driven by the standing party loyalties of voters.

As party-identification theorists were the first to point out, however, the distinction between "issue voting" and identification voting is fuzzy. As conceived originally by Campbell et al. (1960) in *The American Voter*, party identification exerted its force by *influencing* reactions to candidates and issues. Candidates and issues, moreover, could have important independent effects in the context of a single campaign. How else to explain the fact that conservative candidates often gain widespread support among working-class voters, whose standing commitment is with parties to the left?

Class, religion, region—the classic social cleavages—also exert their influence not so much through some primordial urge as through the current issues that are brought forth to appeal to such basic electoral orientations (Berelson, Lazarsfeld, and McPhee 1954; Lipset and Rokkan 1967; Budge and Farlie 1977, 1983).

When party leaders assume that what they say will influence the election outcome, they are almost certainly right. They have two problems: how to hold the vote they have, and how simultaneously to attract more votes in order to strengthen their chances of getting into government. Sometimes, of course, as Robertson demonstrated, the leaders' problem is simplified (Robertson 1976; Budge and Farlie 1977, chap. 12). If gaining votes will not put them in a stronger position, they will not bother about attracting new voters but simply seek to strengthen the loyalties of the ones they have by stressing issues traditional to the party.

These different concerns affect the way leaders present the parties in the electoral program. As we have seen, parties cannot dissociate themselves entirely from their past history and ideology—they cannot directly repudiate their founding identity and the issues they espoused in the past. Nor do they necessarily want to. The leaders are, after all, in their own party rather than another one for some particular reasons—and belief in and loyalty to its goals and traditions are very strong ones.

When leaders believe the party is either bound to gain in an election or bound to lose, there is little electoral advantage in departing from traditional issues associated with the party. The task is to please loyalists, not marginal voters. Obviously, the program cannot avoid confronting new problems thrown up by the national or international environment (more on that below). However, the tendency will be to assimilate these new issues to old emphases. Where electoral competition is not a spur, therefore, the party program will in general be resistant to new pressures. However, new problems may still shift net attention among the traditional emphases. The manifest success of market economies, and a proliferation of social problems, for example, may well cause socialist parties to de-emphasize central control in favor of more-general stress on social justice and social services, even when they are resigned to defeat in a particular election. Thus in the case of elections that are already discounted, programs will tend to cast new issues into established frames of reference: For example, the program may treat pollution as a problem of government regulation and control, as coming within Christian teaching of Man's relation to the World, or as a case for making polluters pay in free-market terms—depending on the ideological framework of the party involved.

Opposition parties, in particular, have a strong incentive for innovative framing of alternatives to current policy. Incumbents have a record, but the opposition has only its word. Of course, the impulse toward innovation and novelty must be tempered by the opposition's ideology. One might well maintain that the truly creative politician is the one who can adapt to new issues while maintaining party identity. To the extent that a new issue can be cast in the light of traditional partisan concerns, this challenge is minimized.

Bourgeois parties of the Center and Right have perhaps a wider repertoire of traditional emphases from which to choose. Christian democrats in particular can choose to reemphasize social welfare, perhaps to contrast with coalition partners further to the right. But they can also choose to emphasize the free market or themes of order and morality, especially if they are in coalition with socialists.

"Change in stability" is perhaps the way to describe the reactions of program writers when they are certain of gain or loss in an election. Perhaps this is a generic reaction of parties in multiparty systems, where electoral gains and losses are limited and in any case may have little to do with subsequent government formation (Budge and Keman 1990, Table 6.12).

There is much more pressure for change, however, in a two- or three-party situation where the outcome is seen as uncertain. In this case leaders face the problem of wooing new voters while keeping their old ones. Here a continued emphasis on old party themes may have the effect of putting off the new voters that the party needs. The optimal solution is to pick up new topics not inherently associated with any of the parties. Naturally old themes still have a place. No party can suddenly cease to mention its major concerns. But they can be downgraded relative to newly introduced, free-floating topics.

One of the best examples of this process comes from what is normally taken as a nonideological party system—the United States. Seeking to break the eight-year Republican hold on the presidency, the Kennedy platform for the competitive 1960 election emphasized above all U.S. standing in the world, attempting to seize and promote a new issue and to shift attention from the New Deal–Fair Deal program of social reform. For the clearly discounted 1964 election, President Lyndon Johnson could run on the Great Society programs, hearkening back to solidly Democratic issues, and play down foreign affairs, where the Democratic record could be read as somewhat problematic. At the same time, the Republicans, certain of defeat, could put forth a platform of uncommon right-wing purity, a practice swiftly abandoned when the breezes of potential victory began to blow (see Chapter 8).

The dynamics of electoral competition are therefore one major influence promoting change (or some change) in programs. But politicians are not entirely free to write their own issues. The outside world impinges in the sense that problems that are being discussed, particularly in the media, cannot be entirely ignored by any major party. To try to do so is to risk failing to make an appeal to new voters and to dishearten older supporters by displaying the party's irrelevance to modern developments.

There is thus considerable pressure on party leaders to respond, in their own way and in the manner dictated by electoral circumstances, to problems that consistently attract media attention. Thus parties are forced to choose among different demands (see Figure 1.2). We cannot, obviously, offer a full explanation here of why problems attract media attention in the first place. But one convincing argument why particular topics get consistent attention (as distinct from sensational events that wander on and off the front page) is that they have an actual or potential effect on the well-being of sizable groups in the population.

Ultimately, election programs do seem to be responding, at least indirectly, to issues affecting the total national electorate—and the latter then has an opportunity to increase the governmental influence of whichever of the competing party analyses of the situation most appeals to it. Some support for this assertion comes from other related studies, in particular one that examined the incidence of campaign issues (as reported in the newspapers) in 23 democracies over the postwar period (Budge and Farlie 1983). What emerged very strikingly from this inquiry was the way in which trends in the development of issues mirrored the general evolution of world social and economic conditions: from concern with postwar reconstruction to the problems of the cold war in the 1950s; from concern with the social problems of advancing affluence in the 1960s to coping with the aftereffects of the oil crises in the 1970s and early 1980s.

One last, more focused, question is, To what extent do politicians actually manufacture issues to win elections—issues that have no basis in societal reality, that have no analogue in policy action, and that are thus likely to vitiate the program's utility as a guide to government action? When all the evidence is in, there is remarkably little to suggest that this is a common occurrence. Perhaps the best example is the attention given to the threat of communism in Australia in the 1950s. A country less likely to be taken over by internal subversion or external invasion is hard to imagine. But elsewhere there is very little evidence for issues' being pulled from thin air. Programs do reflect issues that seem to be there in the society, and to that extent electors' endorsement of one party over the other does seem to give a clear indication to government as to which priorities to address.

SALIENCY THEORY AND THE POLICY PROCESS

If electoral programs convey a message to voters about the relative priority of various policy areas, then the mandate that governments acquire by winning is to take some action in those areas. The exact nature of that action is not explicitly spelled out, though often implied by the nature of the emphasis. A stress on social problems is pretty clearly an invitation to governments to spend money on them; the same is true of defense or of law and order. An emphasis on freedom, private initiatives, and government efficiency usually predicts a reduction of government involvement and expenditures over a range of areas. However, this is exceptional. Stressing an area normally implies an intent to increase government involvement and spending. Hence it is quite legitimate to trace out the fulfillment of the mandate in terms of how the budgetary pie is cut.

Democracy depends on losers' continuing to play by the rules. Thinking of policy differences in terms of emphases and priorities rather than direct conflict between opposing alternatives helps resolve the problem of losers' accepting the results, in the sense that disagreement on different priorities may well coexist with recognition of the inherent validity of the lower-ranking objective. That is, a vote for a left-of-center party that stresses social services and environmental protection does not have to imply a disapproval of the right-of-center party's emphasis on, for example, defense. A strong defense force is compatible with other goals. It is just that the elector who votes for the left-leaning party ranks action in the other two areas above defense.

If the rival party wins the election and spends more on defense, the first party's voters will not violently disagree with the policy. They may even regard the expenditure as a direct benefit. Such a situation contrasts to the rare yet dramatic instances in which parties take diametrically opposite positions—as has happened in some countries over the abortion issue—with the result that losers lose and winners win. Those instances are rare in mature democracies.[1] Differential yet not exclusive salience is the norm. In this sense the saliency theory may make more understandable the ready acquiescence of electoral minorities to government policy, even after a hard-fought campaign.

Why should we expect parties to put their programmatic emphases into effect when in government? Perhaps we should answer this question separately for governments composed of a single party and for coalitions. In the former case, only one program is involved—that of the winning party. Obstacles to the fulfillment of the program therefore relate primarily to the party's willingness and ability (in the face of external factors) to carry through its program.

In the case of coalition partners, willingness and ability are not sufficient; the partners, parties that may have vigorously opposed each other in the election, must generate some degree of initial internal agreement on priorities. Clearly, this means, at least at the government level, that none of the priority rankings of any of the parties is likely to be followed in its entirety, but rather some sort of compromise will be found. Although the need to get general agreement may be circumvented in various ways (particularly by giving ministries to the parties that have made the policy area a priority), parties in coalitions can be expected to have more difficulty in following through their programs than do single-party majority governments. We will start with the simpler case.

Single-Party Majority Governments

Parliamentary elections may produce a majority for a single party, which, in turn, forms a government made up exclusively of members who belong to that party. Single-party governments carry a clear responsibility for pushing their priorities through. They are highly visible to the electorate, and they will have to take full responsibility for the government's actions when they face the voters in the next election. These are the kind of arguments used by Downs (1957) in his formal statement of what is essentially a variant of party-mandate theory. From this view, majority parties have no choice but to fulfill election commitments; otherwise they face the prospect of electoral retribution.

Downs's argument, however, assumes perfect information, with electors clearly aware of what government has or has not done, and an absence of disruptive influences (war, economic reverses, domestic discord) that might provide convincing and popularly acceptable reasons for governments to shift direction in midstream. Moreover, governments could exploit ambiguity about what constitutes programmatic implementation, as well as information shortages among the electorate, to make a convincing case for fulfillment even when they had not followed the priorities at all.

It has been plausibly argued that it is the parties' enduring ideological inclinations that should be trusted rather than programmatic pronouncements (Castles 1982; Budge and Farlie 1982). A socialist party is always expected to do more for welfare, for example, than is a conservative party under corresponding conditions. This expectation obtains despite the possibility that economic stringency may force it to do much less than its program had led the electorate to expect.

This point is all the more powerful as it clearly relates to saliency theory, with its emphasis on long-standing party concerns and the impossibility of jettisoning them. Therefore, we do make allowance in each of our ten country analyses for the general influence of long-standing partisan policy attachments. Electors may ground their choice of policy priorities on those long-standing attachments. Part of the mandate given to a party might well be an electoral command to pursue a course consistent with the traditional ideological commitments contained in a party's standing record.

Ideological tendencies, however, are also overtly transmitted through the electoral programs—that is, through the invariant emphases given to topics in the documents, which underlie the strategic and other variations in emphasis made over time. But it is not enough for mandate theory that party leaders act in government on their own and on their electors' ideological predispositions. It is also important that they follow through on the emphases in the specific program with which they obtained office. So we are back with the question: Why should they? Does nonfulfillment matter, especially if our hunch is right that very few people read the published documents?

Part of the answer certainly lies in the potential consequences of nonfulfillment for a governing party in the next election. Whatever the ambiguities of the situation and the pressure of external forces, it is pretty obvious when a party that emphasized housing and social problems in its program has actually cut expenditures on these services. If the voters do not catch the discrepancy on their own, the opposition most assuredly will help them. Besides risking abstentions or countervoting by aggrieved supporters, a party's inability or unwillingness to do what it promised undermines its standing as a firm and effective governing force, threatening consequences for its own internal morale, possible sharp divisions, and a general loss of purpose.

It is probably in this direction that we should look for the second major reason why single-party governments should be expected to follow through their electoral program in office: It is their blueprint for government. No other plan exists that has been so extensively discussed and agreed-upon within the party and so authoritatively enunciated by co-partisans. It would be extremely difficult in democracies for a party to have a secret plan, one not presented to electors, which would go into effect once it took over government. Such a parallel document would inevitably be leaked.

Party leaders really have little choice but to use the electoral program as their basis for coordinating operations and to begin their activities in government from positions that adhere to it. Any initial deviation will be loudly denounced by media and opposition, so there are strong external and internal pressures to stick to it.

Besides pressures for substantive consistency, there is also the push for economy of effort. Party leaders who are taking over a new government or reordering an older one have little time and energy to think up new ideas, let alone to engage in persuasion of others that the fruits of their recent thinking are worthy of collective action. Thus they have no desire to undertake the major and unwelcome task of developing a new political line. Ease, economy, conviction, and rectitude all point in the direction of sticking, broadly, to the stated program. This is what, in most cases, parties do.

These tendencies are reinforced by the nature of the party program document. There are few specific commitments to carry out, since, as we have pointed out, these are deliberately played down. It is the relative priorities indicated by varying emphases that set the central agenda of the government. These priorities are less likely than specific action alternatives to encounter immediate opposition or to arouse internal divisions.

Coalition Governments

Up to now, we have occasionally referred to "winners" and "losers" of elections. In fact, it is often hard to tell them apart, especially given the complexities of proportional representation. In most parliamentary systems it is uncommon for one party to hold a majority of the seats and governments are usually coalitions of parties. Winning may be nothing more than being able to bargain one's way into government or to gain policy concessions. Some of the considerations raised in the previous section—especially the electoral ones—hold also for coalitions. But one should expect most considerations to be altered by the fact that coalitions have no common agreed-upon policy of government to begin with. Indeed, the electoral programs present an initial obstacle rather than an aid to the formation of the government, as some kind of reconciliation among them has to be forged to permit the formation of the coalition and the official policy declaration that usually accompanies it. Such a declaration must necessarily represent a derogation from the electoral program of some of the government members. Very often the easiest way to get agreement may be to omit contentious matters altogether, to stress minor ones where there is agreement, and to emphasize bureaucratic and administrative matters disproportionately. Instead of the formation of a coalition to advance policy, policy emphases are slanted to permit the formation of the coalition (Luebbert 1986). Overall policies of coalitions are unlikely to mirror the exact emphases of members' electoral programs in the same way as do policies of single-party governments. At least, we would not expect this, although we cannot of course make a firm statement until we have weighed the best available evidence on the issue.

It is possible, however, that coalition parties unpack their bundles of issues and search for common ground, as often as not in response to a crisis or mutually attractive opportunity. Thus, parties in disagreement as to the priority of some of their favored issues may come together on a few major policy areas. Again, the answer awaits the analysis. The process of coalition negotiations will, in any case, be eased by the fact that the parties are engaged in reconciling different priorities rather than opposing policies. It is easier to agree to a priority for defense *and* welfare simultaneously than to reconcile one party's overt commitment to cut and the other's to increase defense.

This is a point of convergence, also, between the situation faced by coalitions and that faced by single-party governments: Politicians need an agenda from which to begin, and they find it in the election program. Individual ministers are in the same position. The section of the program dealing with a particular ministry (which the party may hold because of its particular concern with its jurisdiction) gives the minister priorities and ideas for action that otherwise need to be thought out from scratch. Moreover, they are party commitments, and if one wants to advance within the party, one has to show some achievements. The electoral program gives an invaluable basis for coordination with party colleagues within the cabinet—coordination that otherwise might have to be hammered out in time-wasting negotiations.

Presidential Systems and Other Variations

We have so far ignored intermediate types of governments, the presidential systems and minority governments (these last being about a third of all democratic governments). We should expect that presidential systems, which may often have to get measures through a legislature controlled by the opposition, to show some of the characteristics of single-party majority governments and some of the features of coalitions. Given the strength of executive presidencies, one might expect them to tip towards the single-party majority type (Budge and Hofferbert 1990). It is possible, however, in these systems—particularly where one party holds the presidency and the other(s) the majority in the legislature—that all the parties may have some kind of a mandate. Much scholarly criticism of presidential systems, most notably that of the United States, has been concerned with the obscurity of authority and thus the ambiguity if not ineffectiveness of any approximation of an electoral mandate (Burns 1963; Wattenberg 1990). This is a set of circumstances, however, where various arguments could and have been made in the abstract or on the basis of anecdotal evidence. We pay particular attention to these possibilities in our analysis of France and the United States (Chapters 7 and 8).

It is not inevitable that a coalition is formed when there is no parliamentary majority for a single party. Single-party minority governments are frequently found in such cases, based on the expectation of support for legislation in parliament from parties other than the one forming the government, even though those parties do not hold ministries in the cabinet. We would expect minority governments to defer often to the wishes of the other parties in the legislature and hence to be associated with a more diffuse transmission of party emphases into expenditures—one that is spread over a greater number of parties, that is, but less evident for any one party. This is a question we will address on a case-by-case basis, as we encounter those countries where minority governments have occurred.

CONCLUSION

This chapter has been devoted to theoretical reflection. We have offered *saliency theory* as a modification of Downs's traditional theory of party competition. We suggest that parties compete less by taking opposite sides on the same issues and more by selecting their own issue specialties. In addition, we have explored a variety of reasons for parties to be flexible within a rather stable programmatic range during elections but also to be attentive to their promises once in office.

It remains for us to translate these speculations into empirical, statistical form. These technicalities are the subject of Chapter 3.

NOTES

1. But, for a contrast, see Chapter 13 on the consequences of seemingly irreconcilable ethnic conflict over which parties do take clear stands.

3

Measures and Models

We will now explain the manner in which we analyze the evidence from party programs and public-expenditure records. These two bodies of data will be brought together by means of appropriate statistical techniques in order to confront three questions:

- What evidence is there that the variations in the overall agendas of the parties in each of the ten countries have forecast similar variations in policy priorities? The mode of analysis used in this part will be labeled the *agenda model.*
- Do parties that get into government after the election enact policies that conform more to their own election programs than to the programs of parties that do not get into government? The mode of analysis of this question will be labeled the *mandate model.*
- To what extent do parties in power follow more closely a policy reflecting long-standing ideology than one reflecting current programmatic emphases? The mode of analysis for this question will be labeled the *ideology model.*

The chapter is organized around four major topics: procedures by which the party programs were coded; the nature of the policy priority indicators; a set of technical questions on the nature and organization of the data; and a detailed description of the statistical representation of the agenda, mandate, and ideology models. To supplement the material in this chapter, there are two Appendixes, Appendix A, which discusses in considerable detail the procedures and categories used in coding the party program data; and Appendix B, which discusses a variety of statistical alternatives that were considered but rejected for our purposes.

CODING ELECTION PROGRAMS

The information upon which this book is based has opened a new window through which to view the democratic process. No prior research has been able to draw on comparable measures of what party leaders from many countries have agreed will be the issues they present to their respective electorates in the setting of open, competitive elections. Heretofore, party concerns have not been measured in a way that was consistent over time and that could thus be linked to comparably consistent measures of the policy priorities of elected governments. This is the first study that looks across countries, across time, and across policies at the linkage between party program and public policy. We are sensitive to the shortcomings of the information upon which we draw. But we are also mindful of its extraordinary potential.

Coding Categories

The party documents are generally described in Chapter 2. Specific categories, sources, and coding procedures are described in detail in Appendix A. The documents were collected by a multinational team of scholars organized as the Manifestoes Research Group, founded in the late 1970s under the auspices of the European Consortium for Political Research. As a result of several conferences and many communications, the scholars came up with a coding scheme for use across all countries in the project. After considerable experimentation, they agreed on a fifty-four-item classification.[1]

Each sentence, or "quasi-sentence" in the case of clauses in compound sentences or their equivalents in various languages, was assigned exclusively to a single category. Those that absolutely could not be fitted to one of the fifty-four topics were assigned to an "uncoded" category. That category rarely exceeded 20 percent and averaged closer to 10 percent of coded items. International coordination was maintained throughout the coding to ensure as much reliability as possible. The fifty-four categories of our original scheme are described in Appendix A.

Although our expectations based on saliency theory were that contrasting positions on common topics would usually be implicit rather than explicit, there were a few categories created to allow for sharp "pro" and "anti" positions. These included such entries as "pro–" or "anti–European Community," "pro-" or "anti-internationalism," "pro–" or "anti–social services," and a few others (see Appendix A). The "positive" and "negative" codings were in fact included as a check to see whether head-on confrontation between the parties did occur. That is, we wanted to see if there were instances in which Party A declared itself positively for a particular domain and Party B simultaneously declared itself on the opposite side. This seldom happened. References to each topic where positions were distinguishable were overwhelmingly to one position. It is clear that one cannot oppose peace, but what emerged from our earlier work is that parties cannot come down in outright opposition to educational expansion or strong defense either. If they oppose certain policies, they generally do not mention them. The near empty cells under the various "anti" categories provide strong support for saliency theory.

With this established, putting a value on emphases becomes easy. The sentences of each program were simply counted into categories of the coding scheme.

Sentences (or quasi-sentences, where long constructions are divided by conjunctions and/or equivalent punctuation) were used as the basic counting unit because they are the natural grammatical unit in all languages, and they usually convey one unified point. In contrast, paragraphs might contain mutually contradictory elements and do not code easily into a specific category.

The actual figures we use in the analyses below are the percentages of the total number of sentences in the whole election program devoted to each of the fifty-four thematic topics. The programs for different parties and different countries, as we have noted, vary considerably in length. Percentages yield a standardized metric for thematic emphases, irrespective of variations in the length of the different documents.

The original fifty-four-category characterization of election programs has worked very well in all of the contexts in which it has been applied. It clearly distinguished parties in the nineteen countries analyzed in Budge, Robertson, and Hearl (1987). In our own initial analyses of policy priorities we matched up specific codes with functional areas of government action and obtained consistently strong relationships (Budge and Hofferbert, 1990; Hofferbert and Klingemann, 1990; Hofferbert and Budge, 1992).

The Left-Right Scale

Analyses in previous publications of the Manifestoes Research Group have found a strong and cross-nationally consistent tendency for the party programs to array along a left-right dimension (Budge, Robertson, and Hearl, 1987; Laver and Budge, 1993). That is, issues commonly associated with redistribution, such as human services and economic planning, contrast in a patterned fashion to emphases on individual freedom, national defense, free-market economics, and traditional morality.

It seems to us eminently reasonable to test the extent to which such a broad orientation might condition policy-decision making. Thus, in addition to testing the match between more specific categories from the programs and policy priorities (e.g., policy emphases on "law and order" matched to spending shares for law enforcement and administration of justice), we also test for the program-to-policy linkage between a summary left-right program scale and an equally summary indicator of left-right policy orientations over time. The left-right scale of party programs will be discussed here. The equivalent scale of policy priorities will be presented in the context of each country's analyses.

The left-right party program scale we use here is adapted from Laver and Budge's edited book on party programs and coalition patterns (1993). The scale was created in line with a central research finding of the Manifesto Research Group's prior work (Budge, Robertson, and Hearl, 1987) that spatial analyses of party issue positions produces a clearly dominant left-right dimension in most countries.

The scale used here is an aggregation of all the categories that on a priori grounds seemed to belong on such a dimension. Using factor analysis as a check on our reasoning, we found no other, competing, factor across all countries. So the evidence strongly suggests that the best summary representation of the electoral programs is indeed this one dimension.

The index, detailed in Figure 3.1, is constructed by first summing two sets of percentage emphases in the election programs of each party in each country over the postwar period. Thirteen "left" items are summed; thirteen "right" items are summed; and the latter sum is subtracted from the former to yield a net "left minus right" score. The items included are listed in Figure 3.1 in abbreviated form (see Appendix A for more-extended definitions). The result is an interval left-right score for each party in each election in each country. The portion of party programs incorporated by this technique ranges from 35 to 75 percent of total sentences.

In subsequent chapters we make use of the left-right scale to see if it is linked to comparably broad left-right indicators of policy priority. We will go more deeply into our actual analytic procedures later in this chapter, however, after describing the expenditure data that constitute the indicators of policy priorities on the other side of the equation.

POLICY PRIORITY INDICATORS

The Nature of the Expenditure Data

As we have noted, we measure policy priority as the percentage of total central governmental annual outlays devoted to particular functions. Dealing with expenditures might seem more straightforward than coding documents. Indeed, spending indicators are less difficult to acquire, since published public records provide the final raw data. The figures are supplied by government financial offices and are found in national yearbooks or similar statistical sources available in libraries. In fact, as the paucity of long-term cross-national studies using these data indicates, the enterprise has its difficulties. The major one is making sure that the categories of expenditures that we are using are consistent over the years. (Compare, for example, Flora 1986.) This problem will diminish with time as a result of the international standardization of public financial records led by the International Monetary Fund (IMF, annual), the public finance–reporting scheme that incorporates a relatively refined set of codes, attaining as much cross-national uniformity as one can reasonably expect in a diverse world. This system, used by virtually all nation-states, has been in place, however, only since 1972, thus not covering the first generation of data in which we are here interested. We have not used the IMF system, as retrofitting to the pre-1972 years would have been virtually impossible. Rather, we have relied on individual national accounts publications. Among them, those of the Federal Republic of Germany and the

Figure 3.1
Composition of Left-Right Scale

Left Emphases: Sum of %s for		Right Emphases: Sum of %s for
Decolonization		Pro-Military
Anti-Military		Freedom, Human Rights
Peace		Constitutionalism
Internationalism		Effective Authority
Democracy		Free Enterprise
Regulate Capitalism	Minus	Econ. Incentives
Economic Planning		Anti-Protectionism
Pro-Protectionism		Economic Orthodoxy
Controlled Economy		Anti-Social Services
Nationalization		Nat'l Way of Life
Pro-Social Services		Trad. Morality
Pro-Education		Law & Order
Pro-Labor		Social Harmony

United States stand out. These two countries publish a time series that is coded to maintain consistent categories for the period covered in the present analyses.

Elsewhere, our technique has been to start with the latest year of the series, as no category not represented there can be present in all years. We then worked back carefully through the postwar years, checking the consistency of categories both by the labeling in the original language and in terms of the way numbers follow from each other in successive years. Sudden jumps in expenditures or sharp changes in the ratio of one expenditure area to another could, of course, have perfectly good substantive explanations. However, very often in following through on the aberrations, we found indications that the definition of the category had been altered and that the category had to be dropped or aggregated into a larger set. The sources we have compiled both for classification and for the actual figures are given in each of the country chapters.

We generally end up with six to ten broad categories, usually including welfare, health, education, housing, administration of justice (i.e., courts, police, prisons), defense, foreign affairs, transportation, and agriculture. These categories reflect the way that governments keep their books and presumably also conceive of public services, at least as far as expenditures go. As we want to incorporate into our analyses statistical analogues of party and government policy preferences, we have strong grounds for keeping the spending categories as we find them, subject to dropping the ones that are not consistent over the period. Those used cover, on average, 70 to 75 percent of all central government expenditures, which is a figure large enough to serve our theoretical needs.

Four more technical but not unimportant points need to be emphasized with regard to the expenditure figures. First is that, like programmatic emphases, they are in percentages. This is because we are interested in the *relative priorities* in government spending, not in the absolute figures, nor indeed in the total size of the budget. We wish to track relative priorities over time and to observe the extent to which they follow comparable paths in party program emphases. Using percentages controls for total size across time and across countries.

Second, we use actual year-end expended funds rather than budgetary allocations. This is because what is really spent is more important to us than what is simply anticipated to be spent. Many important changes can take place between formal budgeting and actual outlay. We wish to catch those changes.

Third, expenditures are expressed as percentages of total central government expenditures rather than (as is common in much economic research) as percentages of gross domestic product (GDP). The latter figures are much affected by considerations such as the general level of economic activity or the tax yield, which are simply extraneous to our interests. Moreover, as texts on modern budgetary processes make clear, the decision on the total amount of public spending to be budgeted for any fiscal year is customarily separate from the multitude of decisions as to how much is to be the share of that sum appropriated for particular functions.

Fourth, we are concerned with shares of central government expenditures rather than the total of all governments, including semiautonomous entities such as states, localities, or provinces. Subnational outlays are excluded on the grounds that it is to national election programs that we seek to relate the policy priority indicators. The elections in which the parties run and the programs on which they run relate to decisions to be taken by national governments and parliaments. Thus, those are the policy priorities we examine. We are not trying to explain all policies in a country or even the contributions of various levels of government to any one policy domain. Rather, we are concerned with the congruence between national party programs and national policy priorities.

Rationale of Expenditure Data

In statistical terms, the dependent variables of our inquiry are the percentages of central government financial outlays for each of several policy areas. Comparative policy analyses using expenditure indicators are sometimes criticized on the grounds that expenditures are not all there is to policy. But it is not our intent to have indicators of all policy any more than we expect to explore all areas of party programmatic concern. Rather, we accept the premise that spending money is an important element of public policy—of both its content and the debate over alternatives.

Money is not all there is to policy, but there is precious little policy without it. One need watch only a few minutes of the public debate at party conventions or conferences to note that the most frequently invoked indicator of commitment to a particular policy is a promise to spend or reallocate money for it. Over the years, public-policy-output research, examining the factors that have led different governments to cut up the fiscal pie differently, has been productive. That expenditure data are readily available need not be grounds for scientific devaluation, nor is it an argument for the necessity or superiority of data more difficult to acquire.

Policy alternatives may indeed be equally costly or cost may be a trivial consideration. The price of rope is not a determining factor in the preference for hanging instead of life imprisonment. Regulations are important policies for what they do, not for what they cost. They are not as expensive as national defense. Human rights practices are probably at best weakly linked with how much is spent on police, courts, and prisons. Many of the positive accomplishments of environmental legislation have been due to innovative regulations. Spending on regulation is not a valid indicator of its importance relative to that of spending on defense or on social security. But the variation in the share of spending for a regulatory policy over time or across countries provides a good index for comparing differences in the priority of the policy itself. Such indicators are valid not only analytically, but politically as well.

We wish to examine the capacity of party program emphases to anticipate some important policy choices. We have no intention of trying to explain the full array of policy choices themselves. Roughly 30 to 60 percent of gross domestic product is collected and then reallocated by the governments of the countries we study here. That is nontrivial. We see a test of the extent to which those allocations are anticipated by the program of a government's party as also nontrivial.

ADDITIONAL TECHNICAL CONSIDERATIONS

There are several technical points that deserve consideration, mostly having to do with how and why we use or do not use certain statistical procedures. Two important additional matters are (1) creating annual indicators of program emphases, and (2) lagging/leading. (In addition, there are four highly technical aspects of time-series analysis that are addressed in Appendix B. These are [1] endogenous dependent variables, [2] de-trending, [3] autocorrelation, and [4] tests of significance.)

Annualization of Program Data

According to the concept of representative democracy guiding our research, the program of a party elected to govern is the guiding agenda throughout the term of that government. In parliamentary systems, the length of time in office of a government varies. The mandate of a government that remains in office for five years should reasonably be expected to have more cumulative effect than one that is in force less than two years. The unit of time by which most governments arrange their legislative cycle, and by which they keep their books (with some variations), is most often one year.

Furthermore, in order to relate the programmatic emphases to events that are recorded annually—in our case, annual expenditure outlays—it is necessary to take statistical account of the annual recording of expenditure. The party program data are entered for the year of the election if the election is before 1 July, or the year immediately after the election if the election is on or after 1 July. Then the same programmatic percentages are entered for each successive year until a government is replaced or reelected with a new program. Thus, the fifty-four separate thematic percentages indicating the emphases of the election programs presented for the October 1951 British election are entered for each of the three British parties for 1952, 1953, and 1954. A new set of entries is recorded for 1955 for the election held in May of that year, which is then repeated through 1959. This annualization is one technical facet of the arrangement of program emphases.

Leading/Lagging

A further data-organizational concern is leading the policy indicators (or lagging the program data, which yields the same result). We use a two-year lead throughout. Statistical analyses commonly approach the problem of leading/lagging in a more experimental, inductive manner, whereby independent variables are arrayed successively (or as in distributed-lag analyses, cumulatively) at various years prior to the occurrence of the events to be explained until the highest coefficients are discovered. We prefer a more substantively convincing strategy.

The expenditure data are led two years because, under normal circumstances, the budgetary process is on an annual legislative cycle, with a two-year planning lead. Public agencies this year are spending money appropriated last year. Support for next year is being currently debated as formally proposed legislation. And the agencies are preparing estimates and justification of needs for the year after next to be submitted for deliberation next year—a process that might well be neutralized every few years, of course, by the results of an election.

A government that comes into office and brings with it the agenda of its recent election program will have to enter this stream of deliberation, first with at least one year's legislative activity, followed by one year during which the funds are expended. Funds reported spent in 1980 were actually laid out over the whole twelve-month period, from the first to the last day of the 1980 fiscal year, but were appropriated in 1979 on the basis of plans begun no later than 1978. So a report of funds spent—the data we use for measuring policy outputs—indicates funds laid out the year after they were appropriated—for functions anticipated in the election held at least two years before.

To be sure, there are occasional emergencies or other special circumstances in which a government enters office, suspends the commitments of its predecessor, and promptly moves money from one function to another. Those occurrences are rare, however. Even disaster-relief funds are usually appropriated on a contingency basis before the events that they are designed to relieve, in the hope that those events never come about. It is also likely that certain functions require a much longer lead time than others—capital projects versus income transfers, for example. All public obligations, however, have within them mixes of such variations. Capital obligations may be speeded or slowed in stream as a function of a current government's programmatic priorities. What is more, supposedly automatic entitlements can be accelerated or decelerated, likewise according to the current priorities of the party in government.

Although we admit that a computer-assisted search might turn up instances of more statistically powerful lags, we are convinced that two years is most substantively appropriate. It bears repeating that our principal objective is not to explain the maximum amount of variance in particular policy areas or even countries but rather to test the generality of a limited, theoretically compatible set of models. We are interested in broad, comparable patterns, not in the mechanics of particular situations. That is, we are not essentially interested in the myriad reasons why policy priorities vary over time; we care only how well those policy differences are anticipated by the competing parties.

STATISTICAL-MODELING PROCEDURES

We wish, therefore, to relate our annual election program emphases to expenditure data two years ahead. We do so over a time period running in general from the late 1940s through the 1980s.

The Agenda Model

The *agenda model* is based on the hypothesis that policy priorities will reflect the programmatic emphases of one or more of the major parties that competed in the previous election. From the standpoint of policy theory, verification of that hypothesis would suggest that there is considerable structure to the democratic policy process—that it is neither immune to politics nor intrinsically chaotic. The distinction between the agenda model and the *mandate* or *ideology* models (to be discussed) is that the former takes no account of who wins or loses in the race to occupy government posts. Instead, the agenda hypothesis says that the parties together will change their programmatic emphases over time and that these changes will, by focusing the universe of policy discourse, be reflected in similar variations in policy priority.

Whereas in the immediate postwar years, much attention had to be given to building or rebuilding infrastructure, that concern subsided as capital projects were completed. At different times in different countries, fulfillment of the objectives on earlier agendas and also transformation of public values and priorities brought new issues such as the environment and women's rights and a renewed emphasis on policies for culture and the arts, and so on. Not all party programs adapted at the same pace or to the same degree, but all changed their foci. The agenda hypothesis is satisfied if these changes are, in sum, reflected in policy—irrespective of which party or parties are in government.

The function, therefore, is as follows: priority for policy area i = a constant *(a)* plus the program percentage for theme i of Party A P_i^A plus the program percentage for theme i of Party B P_i^B plus the program percentage for theme i for each of all remaining parties P_i^n. This hypothesis takes the form:

Equation 3.1: $E_i = a + bP_i^A + bP_i^B + \dots bP_i^n$

Where: E_i = Percent of expenditures in policy area i, and

P_i^A = Programmatic emphasis of Party A, two years earlier, in domain i from the relevant election;

P_i^B = Programmatic emphasis of Party B, two years earlier; etc., through the number of major parties competing.

The number of parties in the equation ranges from two in the United States to five in Sweden. Three is the most common number of major competitors in the elections of the ten countries in our study.

The other elements in the equation are the common regression terms a (alpha) for the constant and b for the unstandardized regression coefficient, expressing the numeric value of 1.0 percent difference in E_i (expenditure priority) estimated from a 1.0 percent difference in P_i^n (party program emphasis). The sign of the b coefficient is important, as it may confirm or disconfirm our expectations about the relationship that should hold.

The sign of the b coefficient should usually—but not always, as we shall note below—be positive. As the party emphasis on an area goes up, so should the priority for the relevant policy domain. As the party emphasis in the area goes down, so likewise should the expenditure share. Common increases or common decreases yield a positive b. If the sign is negative, this customarily indicates that expenditures tend to vary in a way that is diametrically opposite to our expectations. There are instances, however, in which a negative sign is reasonable, where increased emphasis in the party program should predict reduced spending. For example, a rise in the emphasis on "peace" of a leftist party's programs might reasonably predict a decline in expenditure priority for national defense, thus confirming the agenda effect with a negative coefficient. The emphases in question are of little measurable relevance to policy when b equals 0.

The coefficient of determination (R^2, expressing the percent of common variance between election program emphases and government expenditures) also of course serves as a check on relationships. If the R^2 is small, the expected relationship between emphases and expenditures would not exist at all. Usually, this would suggest lack of support for the party-to-policy hypothesis.

Equation 3.1 will be computed, including all parties of consequence, for numerous policies in each country. This equation says that policy priority will be predicted entirely by the parties' programmatic emphases, regardless of whether the parties have been in government.

It is likely, of course, that certain policies will consistently reflect the emphases of some parties better than they will those of other parties. Some parties are more successful in getting certain facets of their programs across (irrespective of being in government) than are other parties. Some are successful only in specialized policy areas with which they are particularly identified. Thus, for example, welfare policy in Australia is best predicted by the emphases on "social justice" of the Labor party, regardless of whether it is in power (see Chapter 5). This suggests to us that Labor has "hegemonic" influence over welfare policy. That is, it is predominant, irrespective of the programmatic emphases of its opponents, the Liberals, and irrespective of whether Labor is in or out of office. That will be revealed by a larger, statistically significant *b* for Labor in the agenda model equation for welfare policy.

Continuing with the example of Australian Labor, we are not saying that the formal document produced by Labor itself causes welfare policy to vary. But we are saying that the document is a good clue to the role played in the give and take of the policy process by those in the Labor Party who have chosen to express publicly their concern about "social justice" and their capacity (with the acquiescence of the other parties?) to see that concern through to a tangible outcome. Labor's opponents, chiefly the Australian Liberals, have for all intents and purposes yielded to Labor in this domain. By setting the agenda, Labor predicts and determines the policy.

It is rare, however, in the shaping of the universe of policy discourse—in seeking to put concerns on the public agenda—that a party is wholly sealed off from the concerns of its competitors. Saliency theory, as we discussed in Chapter 2, asserts that each party will seek to concentrate on its own favorite themes, leaving other concerns to be discussed by the competition. This by no means suggests that one party is unaware of the concerns of the opposition. The minimizing of emphasis may be a sign of a deliberate effort to draw attention away from a recognized field of advantage for one's opponents. But this most assuredly does not mean that issues absent from the programs of incumbents are stripped of financial support. Thus we have reason to expect instances in which the emphases of multiple parties—even from outside government—may forecast policy. Access to the agenda via party programs may well ensure all serious combatants a chance to get their concerns reflected in policy, at least over a relatively long time span. That is, two or more parties may be able simultaneously to translate programmatic emphases into policy priorities. Such is the case in France: The programs of the Gaullists and the Socialists anticipate equally well the fiscal outlays for foreign affairs.

By analyzing the predictive power of all parties simultaneously, as Equation 3.1 allows us to do, we can assess the several parties' relative long-term strengths in forecasting policy shares. As the techniques of analysis get commensurately more complex, and as the number of variables in the equations increases, the need for caution in interpretation likewise becomes greater. In the case of the agenda model, we are saying that *all* of the parties' programs may forecast variation in spending shares. This is a key to the importance of saliency theory. Competition need not yield mutually exclusive results. All parties can shape and form the agenda, and as that agenda changes over time, policy can likewise change, responsive to the shifts of all parties. Thus, there has been a clear, unanimous but not uniform shift of emphases from traditional policy concerns of each party in most countries to a somewhat common, if differentially accelerated, concern with the environment and quality-of-life issues. No one party's program exclusively captures this shift, but several taken together, moving in fits and starts somewhat independently of each other, show a dramatic change in the agenda.

Let us use the example of education policy. Suppose that all major parties in a country generally recognize in their programs the need for more attention to education. Equation 3.1, the agenda model, will see which of the parties individually predicts best the variation in education-policy priority. But the parties may each predict rather well, and variations in that fit from year to year among the parties may mean that these predictions are somewhat independent of one another. That is, Party A predicts rather well after some elections and Party B after others. But in this case, that variation in predictive capacity is *not* tied to what party is in office (we will cross that bridge later).[2]

The long and the short of the agenda hypothesis is that the parties' programs collectively outline the agenda of action that is effective in the policy process. However, it is an *agenda* and not a *mandate* model because the congruence of program and policy is not predicated on holding office.

All democracies have some variation in separation of powers and checks and balances. Even in the system most unfettered by constitutionally fractured government—Britain—minorities and the losers of elections are not without protections from the tyranny of the majority. Civil liberties and the rights of the opposition are the most basic. But it is rare that a dramatic policy initiative is taken without some nod to the anxieties and expectations of those not formally invested with governmental authority. Governments in the most centralized of democratic systems rarely can get away with acting as though they had a monopoly on wisdom. If nothing else, potential retribution in future elections is a restraint on excess and a stimulus to moderation.

There are occasions when a government does damn the torpedoes. Thus, in the late 1980s, a Conservative British prime minister, Margaret Thatcher, insisted, in the face of wide opposition and consternation, on a nationwide poll tax. Political costs were paid. In the case of that example, Mrs. Thatcher subsequently resigned, for many reasons to be sure, and her successor government (of the same party) pulled the teeth of the offending policy.

We have discussed a case where the coefficients in Equation 3.1 could work out to be negative and still show a positive agenda function, for example, emphasis on *peace* themes in the program and defense-spending priority decreasing congruently. There is a potential for another case of a negative coefficient. Let us suppose there is a rather polarized form of competition between Party X and the others. Party X has a set of concerns that are rejected by the other parties. According to saliency theory, as discussed in Chapter 2, the other parties that do not share these priorities—and even may be opposed to the favorite domain of Party X—will thus ignore these issues favored by Party X. Suppose X is not in the government. X's opponents, in office, enact policies that decrease resources for the domains favored by Party X. That is, the correlation over time between certain of Party X's programmatic emphases, on the one hand, and policy priorities enacted by X's opponents, on the other, is inverse. The other parties, in effect, use X's concerns as a cue to move in the opposite direction, without actually having dealt in their own programs with X's concerns. This would be a *negative agenda* influence.

Thus, for example, the programs of Canada's Progressive Conservatives serve as a good positive predictor of foreign affairs–policy priority (see Chapter 6, Table 6.1) across the whole period, regardless of whether the party wins places in government. That is a good example of an *agenda* effect. But at the same time, the programs of the leftist New Democratic Party (NDP)—which was never in the national government—were *negatively* reflected in foreign affairs spending. Thus when the NDP program had a higher emphasis on foreign policy themes, subsequent spending shares for foreign affairs declined, suggesting a rejection by the more bourgeois parties (that is, either the Progressive Conservatives or the Liberals) in government. There are, indeed, several instances of seemingly cantankerous parties that stay on the electoral scene in spite of writing programs that consistently go against the grain of prevailing policy. We label this a *negative agenda* function.

Cases of negative agenda functions are rarer than are positive agenda effects. Opposition parties and their allies among various collective interests have routes by which they contribute their views to the policy process. Winning rarely means devastation of the dissenters. As we have noted, it is unlikely that democracy could be sustained in such a truly winner-take-all environment. This is the fundamental logic of our "agenda" models.

The Mandate Model

For democracy to mean all that it can mean, however, there must be some policy consequence of elections. A pure mandate theory assumes that winning is everything. Losers' programs are ignored or repudiated. Winners' programs are enacted. James Madison and his fellow authors of the *Federalist Papers* were not the last, however, to see a need for accommodating the views of the greater number in the electorate while still ensuring against majority tyranny. Nor did the 1787 Madisonian formula of separated powers, as inscribed in the U.S. Constitution, exhaust the institutional options for taming winners of the battle for the ballots. The most dramatic alternative, designed for the same purpose, is proportional representation and its common consequence, coalition government. Not a single constitution written for a democracy after World War II has put in place an exclusively single-member-district plurality system, with the result that one-party parliamentary majorities are the exception rather than the rule.

The key to successful tenure in modern democracies has not been a slavish adherence to a single-party program, but rather a dynamic politics of accommodation between and across the parties. Let us assume, as with good reason we do in this book, that the election programs of the competing parties set forth a major part of the agenda to be pursued by governments after the election. Constitutional and practical political considerations structure the situation in such a manner that those (temporarily) invested with authority must take some account of the agendas of "out" parties. What, then, is left as the fruit of victory? Democracy must surely demand not only moderation and protection of losers' rights but also some impact of elections on the products of government. Certainly that is the central tenet of mandate theory.

The *agenda* model (Equation 3.1) assesses the overall congruence of each and all parties to policy priorities. We need, to test for the *mandate*, a model that adds to, and continues to account for, simple agenda effects, that is, influences from the programs of parties not in government as well as those in government. What is needed in addition for the mandate model is a means of assessing that reflection differentially for those parties that get into government, compared to those on the outside. We need an equation that takes account of a party's being in government on the ability of that party's program to forecast policy priorities. But it should, at the same time, allow for reflection of the programs of parties out of the government. In words, it would be: Priority for Policy Area i = a constant plus program percentage for theme i of Party A in opposition relative to program percentage for theme i of Party A in government plus ... [the same for Parties B ... n]. This can be accommodated statistically by incorporating a "multiplicative term" into the equation. Thus, the statistical representation of the mandate model is as follows:

Equation 3.2: $E_i = a + bP_i^A + b(P_i^A \times G) + bP_i^B + b(P_i^B \times G) + \dots bP_i^n + b(P_i^n \times G)$.

All of the terms are identical to those included in Equation 3.1, except for the addition of G in the interactive term $b(P_i^n \times G)$. G is a dummy variable with the value 1 when Party n is in the government and 0 when that party is out of office. Thus, the second term in the equation sees the percentage of the program devoted to theme i entered as its real percentage value when the party is in government. But when the party is out of government, the term has the value of 0. In this equation, in effect, the value of the program is duplicated in those years when the party is in government but stays only as the raw program percentage plus 0 when the party is out.

The result of the full equation is that now (in contrast to Equation 3.1) the term bP_i^A tells us the relative rate at which Party A's platform is reflected in policy because that party was *out* of office—which we can continue to label the *agenda* influence, not unlike Equation 3.1, only in this case clearly distinguished as congruence of policy to the program of the *out*-party while simultaneously controlling for the influence of the *in*-party. The term $b(P_i^A \times G)$ tells us the difference in the translation of program to policy of Party A's program when that party wins, relative to when it loses. We can label this difference the *mandate* influence. Thus the combinations of bP_i^n and $b(P_i^n \times G)$ terms allow us to address the difference winning makes in a party's ability to translate its program into policy, while simultaneously seeing the agenda effect of the out-party program. This program enables us to examine the critique of "pluralist" interpretations of the policy process in that we can assess alternative routes to the effective (that is, policy-relevant) agenda. The increase in variance explained by this model over the agenda model (when the signs are in the right direction) is the difference attributable to governance—the element that is due to the *mandate.*

Both the agenda model and the mandate model accommodate the influence of party programs when the party is out of power. The agenda model makes no distinction as to which party is in power. The more accurate, but too clumsy, label for the mandate model would be *agenda plus mandate.* We trust that the shorter *mandate* label will not be misleading. Thus it accommodates out-party and governing-party programs implicitly. The mandate (that is, agenda plus mandate) model, however, by combining the simple and the multiplicative terms, does so explicitly. We have considered the rationale by which an out-party might nevertheless be able to get its programmatic emphases translated into policy. In that case, the equation's terms bP_i^A and $b(P_i^A \times G)$ would both have positive signs (+). However, as we noted toward the end of the preceding section, there is an interesting wrinkle of the mandate that is nicely accommodated by this model, which might otherwise escape our attention. This is the possibility of the *negative mandate.*

Saliency theory downplays the expectation that competing parties will take programmatic positions that are in head-on opposition to one another—one being strongly pro-welfare and the other equally antiwelfare, for example. However, saliency theory does not require that we dismiss the possibility of specific rejection by incumbents of the programmatic emphases of their opponents who have most recently lost the election. That is, incumbents may have a mandate not only *for* their own particular programmatic emphases but also *against* specific other favorite themes of the losers. If Party A's program stresses welfare and Party B's stresses defense, when Party A wins, its mandate could be read as both a call for *increased* welfare and also for *decreased* defense, on the grounds that the voters' preferences in voting for Party A may have been either positive (pro-welfare) or negative (antidefense). The vote can convey a positive and/or a negative mandate.

Since the statistical embodiment of the mandate model, Equation 3.2, includes indicators of the out-party program and the difference made by being in government, it can accommodate both the positive and the negative mandate. In the case of the positive mandate, the multiplicative terms (1 × the program percent for Party *n*'s emphasis on topic *i* when in government; 0 when out)—$b(P_i^n \times G)$—will have a positive sign (+). In the case of the *negative mandate*, the simple term—bP_i^n—will have a negative sign (–).

Thus, in the United States, there is in the case of the agenda plus mandate model (the *mandate* model) a clear case of the *negative* mandate regarding social security–policy priority (Chapter 8, Table 8.1). The Democrats' programs have little relation to social security–spending shares. But there is a statistically significant positive coefficient (*b*) for the Republicans when they are holding the presidency and a significant negative *b* for the Republicans when the Democrats hold the presidency. This results from the Democrats' having high, but fairly even, emphases on social issues over time, whereas the Republicans vary. If they win, they follow their own program trend. But if the Republicans lose, the Democrats seem to take their cue from the Republicans and do the opposite. We call this evidence of a *negative mandate.*

Equation 3.2 allows us to state how much more is added to what we already know from Equation 3.1 by now knowing whether a party was in government. This comes from a comparison of the (adjusted) R^2s and the signs of the *b*s derived from Equation 3.1 and Equation 3.2. Equation 3.1 says, in effect, if we know the percentage of the prior programmatic emphasis of the parties on a particular policy domain, we can predict how much priority will be given to the expenditure share in the corresponding policy domain. (We use adjusted R^2s throughout our analysis, thus compensating for the total number of independent variables in the equations.) The gain in adjusted R^2 in Equation 3.2 over Equation 3.1 tells us how much better our prediction to policy from the programmatic emphases of the parties will be if we control for their having been in office.

As we shall see in our individual-country analyses, this use of the interactive term for program forecasting while a party is in government proves to be one of the most efficacious tools for opening the window through which we can view parties in the policy process. Commonly, it is the mandate model (or its more expended version, the *ideology* model—see below) that represents best the linkages between the concerns emphasized in the party programs and the policies given priority by the subsequent government. We shall return to discuss this generalization in Chapter 14, but the reader ought to be alerted now to the power of an explanation of policy based on the signaling capacity of parties both in and out of power. To our mind, this mix embodies both the power of majoritarianism and the tendency toward accommodation in modern democracies.

The Ideology Model

In spite of our principal focus, we recognize that the party program is not the only source of a clear electoral mandate. The past record of the enduring historical and ideological orientation of a party can quite conceivably give the voter a strong clue for purposes of projecting from the vote to policy consequences. Conservatives are more conservative than socialists, as a rule, on a *more or less lasting basis.* It is, of course, the "more or less" that is captured by the party election programs, and it would be the "lasting basis" that constitutes the standing differences between parties. The voter in search of useful yet parsimonious information would want to know the weight to attach to such standing differences. If they are clear enough for the voter's purposes, then all that needs to be used to anchor voting decisions is the party label. That logic is the core of the argument that voting doggedly, election after election, according to one's traditional party identification is by no means content-free in terms of policy.

But if party programs are quite variant, then more than a label is perhaps required—namely, a knowledge of not only standing differences but also of current programmatic thrusts. Therefore, just as the *mandate* model added to, but retained the core of, the simpler *agenda* model, so testing for the influence of standing *ideology* involves adding to the *mandate* model—thus allowing simultaneous analysis of all three forms of congruence of party features and policy. Equation 3.3 presents in mathematical form the *ideology* (or agenda plus mandate plus ideology) model, which serves that purpose:

$$\text{Equation 3.3: } E_i = a + bP_A\text{G} + bP_i^A + b(P_i^A \times G) + bP_i^B + b(P_i^B \times G) + \ldots bP_i^n + b(P_i^n \times G).$$

The initial simple measure of ideology, or at least the evidence of ideology provided by the record of a party's standing policies compared to those of its competitors, is a dummy variable $(bP_A\text{G})$, which takes the value of 1 when Party A is in office and 0 when it is not. In most countries we examine here, there is one party that has led postwar governments at least half of the time. Thus, to the extent that long-standing ideological differences can be dichotomized, the initial b in Equation 3.3, when programmatic variations over time are controlled for, assesses the usefulness in specific policy domains (E_i) of simply choosing Party A over its competitors. This is the equivalent of the common independent variable in comparative policy output research that has tried to study the impact of party on policy outputs (e.g., Cameron 1978; Castles 1982; Hicks and Swank 1992).

CONCLUSION

Taken together, Equations 3.1, 3.2, and 3.3 model the different kinds of congruence we would expect from party programs to policy priority. They thus enable a systematic comparison to be made successively between (1) the extent to which the programs forecast policy, irrespective of who is in or out of government; (2) the difference added to (1) by accounting for who is in and who is out of government; and (3) the additional policy-forecasting power gained by controlling for standing interparty policy differences independent of variations in programmatic content. These are, respectively, the *agenda*, the *agenda-plus-mandate*, and the *agenda-plus-mandate-plus-ideology* models.

Most comparative research designed to test the effect of party on policy has used only something akin to the dummy variable in our *ideology* model. But it should be emphasized that the three models are all facets of a single theoretical focus, namely, a central connection in democratic theory whereby parties mediate between disparate interests in the society, on the one hand, and policy production on the other. The essential hypothesis is upheld if significant relationships are found in *any* of the models. The alternative models recognize that we do not know, a priori, which is relevant to a particular country or policy.

We should emphasize, again, that our central objective is broad theory, not country or policy peculiarities. The objective is to assess the signaling capacity of the parties' programs, contrasting those that get into government with those that are left out, and contrasting the impact of variation in party program emphases to standing ideological differences among parties. If our interest were in getting the most "powerful" explanation of policy, as such, we would adapt the models to a variety of conditions specific to particular countries and individual policy domains. We will perhaps pay a price in the overall R^2, but we will avoid the trap of excess specificity. We maximize the comparative potential of the research by rigorously applying the same framework of analysis and the same statistical equations to each included policy in each of ten countries.

For multiparty systems in which more than one party participates in governments—that is, for coalitions—the equations have to be expanded to include more terms, but the basic logic is the same. So rather than going into further complications in the abstract here, we prefer to take these matters up in subsequent chapters, as they apply to specific countries.

Generally we shall proceed in the individual-country chapters by first sketching the overall political context within which the policy process operates. Second, we shall examine for the overall trends in programmatic emphases and in policy priorities throughout the postwar years. This will involve some discussion of graphic displays of time trends. The bulk of our statistical analysis will be concerned with applying the three models to check program-to-policy congruences and with deciding where and how valid these congruences are for which policies in the country concerned.

We will employ two measures of party emphases in the equations: (1) the general left-right program score related to a left-right policy priority score, and (2) the specific programmatic emphases selected to match as well as possible to corresponding categories of policy. This means that the number of regression equations in each chapter equals the number of policy domains (including the general left-right scale) times three. Interpreting the results of around thirty regression equations for each country would clearly be a daunting task for writer and reader alike. Therefore, we shall put the full tables with all regressions in an Appendix. We will select, by criteria to be fully justified, the best-fitting model for each policy. These models will be consolidated into a single table, which will then be the central focus for the discussion of findings for each country.

In Chapter 4, on Britain, we will provide a rather elaborate discussion of the various models. This is to help in illustrating how selections of best-fitting models will be guided in the successive, briefer chapters on the other nine countries.

Our concluding chapter looks back at the ten individual country studies in order to identify general patterns. This will provide a basis for returning to our basic question: Does party democracy work in the policy process?

NOTES

1. The documents described in Budge, Robertson, and Hearl (1987) are generally current through the early 1980s. Those data are available in machine-readable form through the Social Science Data Archive at the University of Essex (England). Responsibility for maintaining currency of the data has been taken by the Research Unit on Institutions and Social Change, Science Center–Berlin (Wissenschaftszentrum–Berlin). The Central Archive for Empirical Social Research (Zentralarchiv für Empirische Sozialforschung) in Cologne (Germany) will be the eventual repository for all original documents and for distributing machine-readable data sets. Other national and international archives will also receive the data for general dissemination. Releases of data for more-recent years will take place as initial analyses are completed by the Manifestoes Research Group. For more detail on coding procedures, see Volkens (1992).

2. But now we encounter a situation where the statistical problem of *multicollinearity* could arise. If Party A and Party B follow similar overall trends, they will be correlated with each other over time—not perfectly, but perhaps closely. It can sometimes happen that each would correlate with a policy indicator positively if analyzed separately, but when analyzed simultaneously, as in Equation 3.1, the (adjusted) R^2 is elevated but the *b*s are misleading. Because of multicollinearity we are unable to discern accurately from the individual *b*s the relative contribution of each. It is even possible that one of the parties that by itself is positively related to policy gets a negative coefficient in the multivariate equation. If we were engaged in truly *causal* analysis, this would be a serious problem, essentially indicating the impossibility of assigning variance accurately to any of the parties in the multiparty equation. However, since our interest is in prediction (i.e., the signaling capacity of the programs), it is less serious for us. The adjusted R^2 in Equation 3.1 tells us how much we gain in knowledge of policy priority by analyzing all parties at once (assuming that the simple correlation for each is positive). And for purposes of testing their combined contribution to the agenda, that is sufficient, assuming we are careful in interpreting the *b*s and signs of the multivariate equations.

4

Britain

INSTITUTIONAL AND POLITICAL CONTEXT

Britain is widely considered the model two-party system, with strong single-party majority governments frequently alternating between Conservative and Labour control. In the years from 1945 through 1987, the voters exchanged either Conservative for Labour or vice versa six times. The absence of a written constitution and the preeminence given to the Parliament in legal theory put great formal power in the government of the day. Internal party discipline among members of Parliament is strict. It is nearly unheard of for the majority-party leadership to lose an important vote in the House of Commons. The presence of another strong party in parliamentary opposition does mean that the ruling party has to be careful about what it does, but this is because of potential trouble at the next general election, not because of any barrier or veto the opposition could impose in Parliament.

The ruling party makes up the government, the core of which is the Cabinet, formed of about twenty senior party figures. These people are led by a prime minister chosen from among them. It is the Cabinet collectively, rather than the prime minister alone, that is the main legal repository of parliamentary sovereignty in Britain. What it decides will be supported by the rest of the government and voted upon favorably by the majority party in the House of Commons.

British constitutional theory is thus very simple: The Cabinet can do anything its party will go along with. Although there are many practical qualifications on the Cabinet's freedom of action, the degree of concentrated power with which it is endowed permits interpretation of the British system of government as a streamlined version of the strict party mandate. If an electoral mandate is going to operate at all in Britain, constitutional theory indicates that it must do so through the governing party. There is nobody else to push a mandate through—no coalition partner, as in many multiparty systems; no opposition-controlled legislative branch, as in systems of separated powers.

Theoretically, opposition parties are irrelevant to policymaking. Their actions are directed at hastening the approach of and winning the next election. In contrast to the separation of powers, or federal, arrangements found in the United

States, or indeed to the internal bargaining of European coalition governments, the politically dominant party in Britain is constitutionally free from having to bargain with anyone or from having to make any policy concessions at all.

This system is often called the *Westminster model* (named for the Palace of Westminster in which Parliament sits, in London's Westminster district). It is not identical to the theory of the *party mandate,* which says a government will keep the promises made in its election program. According to the Westminster model, a government can do anything it wants to—including keeping its election promises. The advantage the British have, formally, however, is that their constitutional and institutional capacity presumably allows the government to be accountable to the voters, should it so choose. It can be argued that in other countries, institutional barriers (such as the separation of powers in the United States) make it impossible for a government to be accountable, even if it is committed to being so.

The fact that a British government has full power is, to be sure, no guarantee that it will carry through its election program. The Cabinet also has the power to lie. Likewise, it has the power to adapt to changing circumstances without being hog-tied by its election commitments. This leaves the way open for leaders of governing parties to change their minds in office or to take over appealing ideas from the opposition. In short, the Westminster model ensures majority-party control rather than accountability.

The Westminster model and the party mandate thus stand or fall to some extent independently of each other. They do overlap, however, in the sense that in the British case the former suggests a simple classical mechanism whereby the mandate can operate, that is, through the ruling party's enacting in government the intentions spelled out in that party's most recent election program. In other countries it comes as no surprise to find some policy decisions that reflect priorities of a different party, for example, the majority party in the U.S. Congress, which is not necessarily that of the president, or of the minor coalition partner, like Germany's Free Democrats, in multiparty governments like Germany's. Given either institutional setup—separation of powers or coalition government—mandates and the claims to hold them are to some extent diffused and shared.

The Westminster version of the party mandate does not, however, surrender to the opposition parties such a claim to a shared mandate. Responsibility for matching programs to official action rests with the government. Therefore, even a government that may choose to exercise its legal prerogative to wander far afield knows that the voters are aware that it *could* have—legally, formally, institutionally—kept its word had it chosen to do so. The clear nature of the accountability is itself a likely check on deviation.

In the Westminster institutional structure, therefore, we have the potential for the mandate in its quintessential form: A single majority party is given an electoral mandate that it implements in government. This simplicity of constitutional theory is reinforced by the actual workings of the British party system. The government effectively needs support in only one chamber of the legislature (the

House of Commons), and the only parties that can secure a majority in it are Labour or the Conservatives. These are the constitutional and institutional features that have caused Britain to be ranked high in terms of formal party ability to carry through a mandate, in contrast to countries with more-diffuse political arrangements, such as coalition governments or separation of powers.

When we come to the real world of society and politics, however, rather than the world of governmental and legal theory, the picture is quite different. Britain has a three-party, not a two-party, system—with additional regional parties, such as the Scottish or Welsh Nationalists. This division has effectively prevented any one party from obtaining a majority of votes in national elections. Thus the strong single-party majority that we see in Parliament is, in fact, based on a popular plurality only, which has less than the vote given to the opposition parties in combination. When the government party faces combined opposition hostility, it does so knowing that its claims on a mandate are less impressive than that of the total of its opponents.

What transmits the diffuse regional, ethnic, and socioeconomic conflicts at the grass roots into a concentrated class-based confrontation between Labour and Conservatives in Parliament is that the members of the House of Commons are elected in single-member districts by simple plurality. That is, each district gets one member of parliament (MP), and whichever candidate gets the most votes, even if not over 50 percent, wins. Contrasted to proportional representation, whereby minor parties win seats in proportion to their nationwide vote, the single-member (or "first past the post") system discourages voters from casting a ballot for an obscure or minor-party candidate, lest their vote be "wasted."

Britain is divided by election law into roughly 630 single-member districts. Because the candidate who gets the most votes in each district wins, in competitions of three or more parties, a party that gets 35 to 40 percent nationally could in theory win all the seats if the losing parties were to split the rest of the vote evenly throughout the country. In practice the system favors parties with regionally concentrated strengths—Conservatives in the Southeast of England and Labour elsewhere. The Liberals, with minority support everywhere, often adding up to a quarter of the national votes, get hardly any parliamentary seats. The regional parties get more seats proportionately than the Liberals, but still a far smaller percentage than they get in votes.

As parliamentary majorities are engineered by institutional means and fit uneasily with social realities, it is difficult to see mandates in Britain following from a straightforward electoral choice between Conservatives and Labour, with governments' being mandated to carry through their winning programs regardless of other considerations. The spirit of the mandate would be more reflected by governments that tried to take over obviously popular ideas from the opposition, particularly of the underrepresented third party, the Liberals, along with their own. This fact gives considerable scope for nongovernment parties in Britain to exercise agenda-setting influence, discussed in Chapters 1 to 3, as an alternative or at least supplement to the strict single winning party mandate.

In Britain, therefore, in spite of the biases of constitutional theory, there are grounds for expecting a significant agenda effect, as in other, less institutionally "advantaged" countries. It may be that in Britain all parties, not just the government one, can get some of their program adopted through moral or intellectual authority or through the ruling party's fears of adverse electoral repercussions. What is even more likely, of course, is that we will find a mandate model operating in some policy areas where the government feels it has clear support, alongside more diffuse agenda-setting influence in other areas where nongovernment parties are surer of their own ground. What will be really interesting—and the ultimate justification for an empirical analysis such as this one—is the extent to which the Westminster version of a mandate model operates in Britain, as compared to other channels of party influence.

PROGRAM AND POLICY TRENDS

In the following section we will discuss party program and policy trends in Britain. First, however, we need to clarify the nature of the data we are going to use.

British Data

We measure policy priorities over time by the percentage of central government expenditures for each of nine areas of policy activity. The selection was guided somewhat by the organization of data by the British Central Statistical Office; we excluded any spending category that was not consistently classified for at least thirty of the thirty-six years covered by our analysis.

Party programs analyzed include those of the Conservative, Labour, and Liberal parties (including the Liberal/Social Democratic Alliance, when they presented a common program) for the elections from 1945 through 1983. The specific categories we use in our analysis add up to about 20 percent of the content of the programs, on the average. They are important categories, but constitute only seven out of the original fifty-four. Specific categories corresponding to policy domains are as follows:

Party Program	*Policy Area*
Foreign Special Relationships +	Defense & Foreign Affairs
Law and Order	Administration of Justice
Agriculture	Agriculture
Social Justice	Social Security
Social Justice	Health
Social Justice	Education
Social Justice	Housing

Technology and Infrastructure	Transportation
Environmental Protection	Environmental Protection

As we have already mentioned, there is one important restriction on the policy data. We employed only those expenditure categories that were recorded in a consistent manner for nearly all the time period. Thus, on average, the expenditure categories account for a bit over 70 percent of outlays per year. The rest are categories that were changed at some point after 1945 and hence cannot be used for time-series analysis. Although we draw on a minority of party program emphases, we utilize over two-thirds of British central government expenditures.

The tables indicate that the years of analysis are from 1948 through 1985. Reliable expenditure figures are available for 1950 through 1985. With the two-year lead, then, the first data point for election programs is the 1948 entry for the 1945 election programs listed adjacent to 1950 expenditures. The last entry is the 1985 expenditures matched to the 1983 election programs. Thus, the election programs run from 1948 through 1983, with adjacent spending data for 1950 through 1985. Although we have program data for more recent elections, there is an unfortunate break in the expenditure data in 1985, owing to a massive reformatting of records published by the Central Statistical Office.

Left-Right Trends

Figure 4.1 shows the positions of the leading British parties' postwar program emphases on the left-right dimension (the construction of which is described in Chapter 3). The percentage of space devoted to "right-wing" emphases (defense, law and order, freedom, and initiative) has been subtracted from the percentage given to "left-wing" themes (social services, peace, and international cooperation, among others). The more right-wing the emphases, the more the party finds itself at the bottom of the graph; the more left-wing the emphases, the higher up it goes.

It is clear that Labour and Conservatives are sharply distinguished. They never "leapfrog" each other. And the changes that do occur are very comprehensible in terms of general interpretations of postwar history. The parties came close to each other in a leftward direction during the era of consensual "Butskellism" in the 1950s (a nickname formed from Rab *But*ler—a moderate Conservative—and Hugh Gait*skill*, a moderate Labourite). They moved rightward in the 1960s as Labour stressed new topics such as technology, and the Conservatives adopted New Right thinking late in that decade. The rightward movement continued, accelerating in the 1980s under Margaret Thatcher's prime ministership. Labour meanwhile experienced a resurgence of the Left, which was modified only by a new, more moderate leadership in 1987. The match between Labour and Conservative shifts and the general political history of the postwar period add credibility to our codings and statistical analysis.

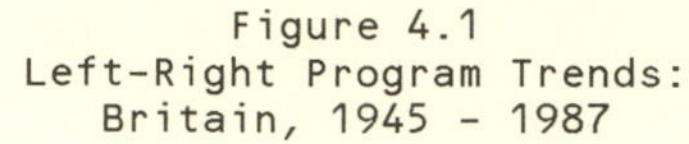

Figure 4.1
Left-Right Program Trends:
Britain, 1945 - 1987

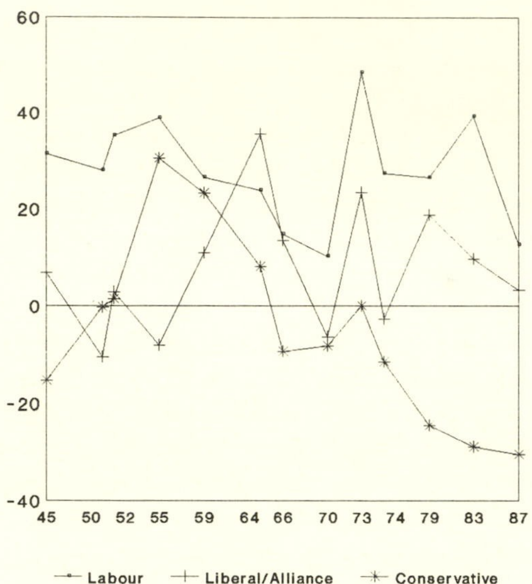

Figure 4.1 is interesting also in terms of our general argument because of something that is not so clearly interpretable—the Liberal positions. The Liberals oscillate wildly between left and right, leapfrogging over the other parties. Only after 1970 do they stay between the other two, but even then they maintain a see-saw motion. The Liberal shifts illustrate the difficulty of third parties in a system that focuses most political debate and discussion on the left-right divide favored by the two larger parties. The most important Liberal topics (copartnership in industry, additional concern for regional interests—especially Scotland and Wales—and electoral reform) do not get in, and the party is forced to locate itself in terms of an ideological space set by its opponents.

So far we have examined party programs in terms of generalized left-right differences. We can start to see how these may correspond to policy by constructing an equivalent scale of left-right policy priorities. The latter scale is built by a factor analysis of British expenditure priorities. This produces as its leading dimension a clear left-right continuum. To eliminate statistical "noise" (from expenditures not very closely related to the left-right dimension) we have built a summary scale taking the expenditures that contribute most highly to left-right distinctions (Figure 4.2). At the "left" these are health, education, and social security; at the "right" they are agriculture and defense/foreign affairs. (See the note to Figure 4.2 for the specific structure of the left-right policy score.)

It is the factor scores from this summary scale that provide the vertical dimension of Figure 4.2. This shows a leftward policy trend, with social services climb-

Figure 4.2
Left–Right Expenditure Priority Factor Scores:
Britain, 1950 - 1985

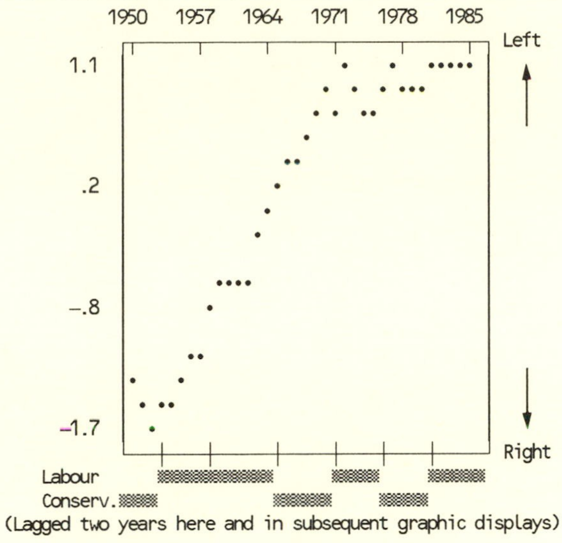

Structure of Policy Priority Factor

Policy Area	Factor Loading
Health	.90
Social Security	.78
Education	.76
Environment	.53
Agriculture	–.97
Defense & Foreign Affairs	–.97

ing steeply at the expense of defense and agriculture, up to 1971, when, after two dips, the trend seems more or less to level out. The trend in Figure 4.2 illustrates the extent to which "leftist" expenditures were favored in the postwar period. What will later also be noted is the way this tendency appears, with only minor variations, in other countries (see the comparable figures in the succeeding chapters).

Figure 4.2 seems to show some tendency for rises in leftist spending to be associated with Labour governments and pauses or dips with Conservative governments. For example, a plateau under Conservative prime ministers in the early 1960s is followed by clear favor being given to leftist policy priorities under Labour. The same happens in the mid-1970s after a change in a rightward direction by the Conservatives. The rises and falls in spending, however, are not consistent,

Figure 4.3
Trends in Expenditure Priorities: Britain, 1950 – 1985

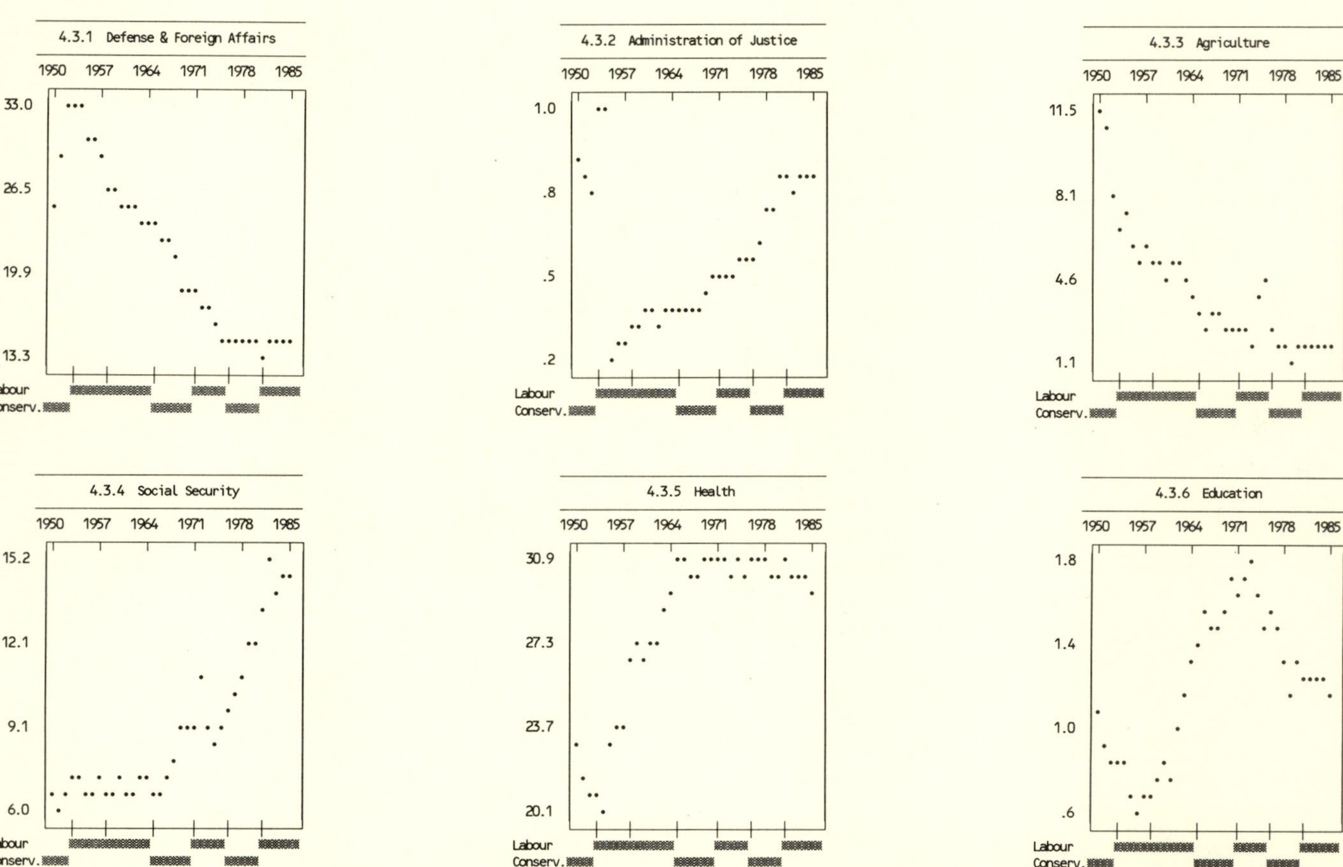

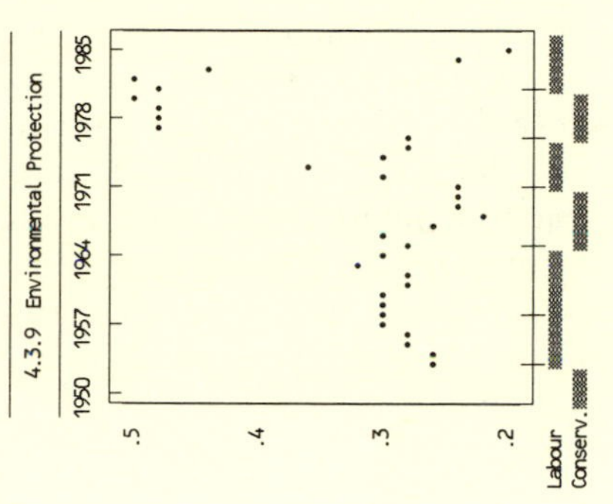
4.3.9 Environmental Protection
1950
1957
1964
1971
1978
1985
.5
.4
.3
.2
Labour
Conserv.

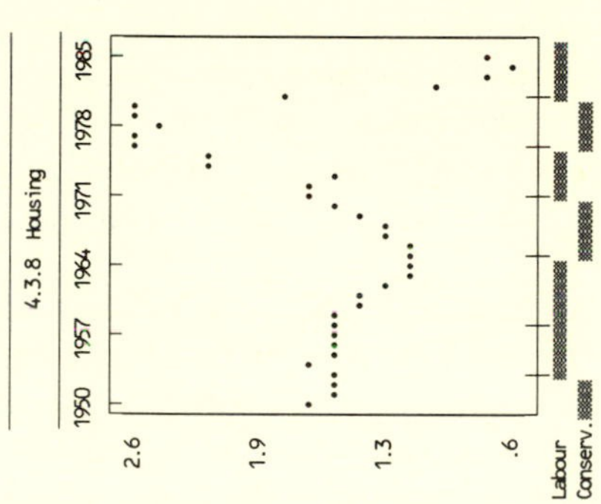
4.3.8 Housing
1950
1957
1964
1971
1978
1985
2.6
1.9
1.3
.6
Labour
Conserv.

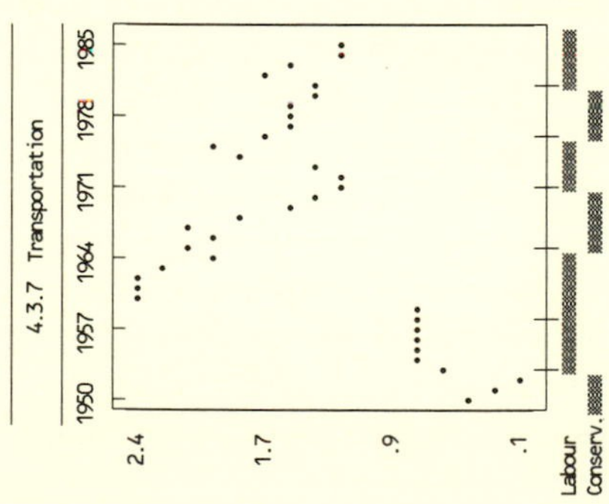
4.3.7 Transportation
1950
1957
1964
1971
1978
1985
2.4
1.7
.9
.1
Labour
Conserv.

since the Labour government of the late 1970s shifted expenditures once more to the right, and the Thatcherite Conservative governments returned just a bit to the left. Moreover, the heating up of the cold war earlier had forced the Labour government to reverse post–World War II military demobilization, followed, ironically, by a shift leftward under the Conservative administrations in the 1950s. Such complexities are not to be divined from simple trend lines, but must be subjected to statistical analysis to expose patterns more clearly. The alternation is sufficiently regular, however, to suggest some influence by party ideology, which may be reflected in the broad left-right trends of policy.

SPECIFIC POLICY TRENDS

The particular trends shown in Figure 4.3 give some indication of how far Labour and Conservative priorities were carried over into government action in a broad range of policy areas. Although some expenditures, such as defense and foreign affairs (4.3.1), have declined under every government and although others, such as administration of justice (4.3.2), have risen inexorably, there are still some apparent party differences. Conservative governments, for example, have been generally associated with increased priority for transportation (4.3.7) and decreases in housing (4.3.8) and environmental protection (4.3.9). Despite a net declining priority for agriculture, the Conservatives have consistently given it a larger share than has Labour (4.3.3).

In some areas where we might expect a clear differentiation between left- and right-wing parties—generally the social-service areas and education—there seem to be left and right movements under both Conservatives and Labour. This may be due either to pressing social needs that override ideology (rising and then falling numbers of children of school age, for example) or fixed entitlements such as unemployment benefits, which often rise under Conservative governments, possibly because of the impact of other economic policies.

There is one clear party-related trend in social-policy priority, however. That is the tendency for the Conservatives to cut housing priorities (Figure 4.3.8), most spectacularly after 1979 under Mrs. Thatcher's Conservative government. A massive program of public housing had been nurtured by Labour, expected by a sizable proportion of the electorate, and protected by the public-housing bureaucracy. It was one of the pillars of the British welfare state—the very ideal-typical case of an entitlement. That is, persons were eligible for housing if their family and economic circumstances met specified criteria—and the public budget had to be adjusted accordingly. Cutting of long-standing entitlements is rare, but this case shows that it can be done. In general, patterns of expenditure priorities in most policy areas show considerable similarities across countries. This exception strongly suggests that elections matter and that those elected can, when sufficiently committed, encroach on even the most cherished preserves of the opposition, guarded by seemingly invincible bureaucracies.

PARTY PROGRAM-TO-POLICY CONGRUENCE

At this point in the other chapters dealing with individual countries we will discuss only the best-fitting of the three models for each policy area, supported by a summary table displaying the statistical results of just those three sets of equations. As we noted earlier, however, we are going into much more depth in the chapter on Britain. We use it to illustrate the full range of our analysis and how we select the "best-fitting" models. Thus, in the text of this chapter, instead of only one table, we have four, containing the results for a particular model over all policy areas, plus a summary table of the best-fitting equations.

Agenda Models

The extent to which the party programs together constitute a delineation of the universe of relevant policy discourse—the public-policy agenda—should be visible in the relationship between each of the party's programmatic emphases and the corresponding policy priorities (see Table 4.1). This involves doing a series of regressions matching appropriate program emphases for all three parties to expenditures for all thirty-six years. The regressions are of the form of Equation 4.1:

4.1 Agenda: $E_i = a + b\text{Con}_i + b\text{Lab}_i + b\text{Lib}_i$
Where: E_i is the percentage of central expenditures for a particular policy area (i);
Con/Lab/Lib_i is the percentage of sentences in Conservative, Labour, or Liberal programs devoted to the substantive area most approximating E_i.

Substantively matched emphases are related to expenditure shares two years later, to take account of the normal budgeting and expenditure cycle. The *b* is the regression coefficient showing the form of the relationship—how much change in the percentage of expenditures (two years later) is associated with a 1.0 percent change in party program emphasis. The regression coefficients should, in most cases, be positive and significant if our ideas about party influence over government action are at all correct. Some, however, may actually be zero or even negative (indicating a contradictory relationship in which the more a party is concerned about an issue area, the smaller the share of expenditures in that issue area). Other coefficients may not be significant at the .05 cut-off point. These are parenthesized in the tables, indicating that the value for *b* we have in the table is unstable and might, if we had data for a longer period of time, turn out to be quite different. The other statistic associated with the regressions is the adjusted R^2, indicating what proportion of the variation over time in policy shares is associated with differences in program emphases (regardless of the direction of the relationship).

Table 4.1
Agenda Models: Britain, 1945 – 1985

Expenditure Area (Program Emphasis)	a	b Con	+ b Lab	+ b Lib	Adj. R^2
Left – Right (Left – Right)	.70	–.02	– .03	+ .02	.33
Defense & For. Affs. (Spec. For. Rel's)	14.3	1.63	+ (.25)	+ 1.95	.49
Admin. of Justice (Law & Order)	.32	.06	– (.02)	– (.02)	.49
Agriculture (Agriculture)	.26	.46	+ .78	+ (.22)	.38
Social Security (Social Justice)	6.10	(.25)	+ (.20)	+ (.21)	.12
Health (Social Justice)	28.5	.71	– (.15)	– (.54)	.15
Education (Social Justice)	1.37	.06	– (.03)	– (.05)	.10
Transportation (Tech. & Infrastr.)	.59	.15	+ .14	– (.06)	.25
Housing (Social Justice)	1.12	.11	+ (.01)	– (.00)	.53
Environ. Protect. (Environ. Protect.)	.24	(.00)	+ .02	+ (.00)	.17

With the exception of the left-right indicators, which will be discussed later, Table 4.1 contains no statistically significant negative *b*s, which we would label "contradictory" relationships. The table does contain some striking findings in which both the *b*s and the R^2s support the same interpretation. Reading down the column under "*b* Con," we see that Conservative emphases through the agenda alone (that is, regardless of the party's being in or out of government) relate positively to policy shares to some degree in every one of the policy areas, except environment. Relative to the other parties, the relationship for the Conservatives is quite strong in three areas: defense and foreign affairs (1.63), administration of justice (.06), and housing (.11). Liberal emphases, in contrast, are the strongest of all three in defense and foreign affairs ($b = 1.95$).

Unexpected is the fact that Labour—which over the postwar period has regularly alternated in and out of government—has statistically significant agenda influence in only three policy areas: agriculture, transportation, and environment (*b*s = .78, .14, and .02). The pattern of *b*s is generally significant and positive for the Conservatives, but nonsignificant for the Liberals and Labour, as is shown by the number of parenthesized *b*s for the latter two parties.

The regressions thus seem to indicate high program-to-policy congruence for the Conservatives' programs, with only patchy policy reflection from either Liberals or (surprisingly) Labour. However, it would be risky to put too much weight on this apparent pattern until we see how the relationships are affected once account is taken of a party's being in or out of government. In fact (to anticipate our findings), only two specific areas (aside from the general left-right anomaly)—housing and transportation—remain as cases of exclusively agenda congruence after the other tests are made.

Mandate Models

The preceding analysis related programs to policy without attention to whether parties were in a position to enforce their priorities directly through control of government. To be sure, parties may hope to influence political thinking in a general way, through the force of their arguments or through special links with bureaucrats and interest groups (the agenda-setting processes). In Britain, of all countries, however, given the bias of constitutional theory toward a party-mandate doctrine, we should expect control of government to be a crucial part of the program-to-policy linkage.

In this section we add to the agenda congruence of programs and policy the element of mandate. This is accomplished, as explained in Chapter 3, by adding to the equation a multiplicative term for each party. These are specified in Equation 4.2:

$$4.2\ \text{Mandate: } E_i = a + b\text{Con}_i + \boldsymbol{b(\text{Con}_i \times \text{PM})} + b\text{Lab}_i + \boldsymbol{b(\text{Lab}_i \times \text{PM})} + b\text{Lib}_i.$$

The items in this equation that are not in Equation 4.1 appear in bold type. There are no multiplicative terms in this equation for the Liberals, since they have never been in a government. E_i refers, as before, to the percentage of expenditures on a particular policy area. $\text{Con}_i/\text{Lab}_i/\text{Lib}_i$ refers to the percent of the program devoted (by the Conservatives or by Labour or by the Liberals) to the corresponding theme. The new term in this equation—$\text{Con}_i/\text{Lab}_i \times \text{PM}$—multiplies the program-thematic percentage by 1 if the party holds the prime minister's office (that is, if it is in government) and by 0 if it is out of office. As each term in a multiple regression equation controls for the influence of the other terms, $b\text{Con}_i$ or $b\text{Lab}_i$ (that is, without the multiplier for PM) in Equation 4.2 is in effect converted to a term for party emphases because of the party's having been sometimes out of office. Moreover, the interactive term $b\text{Con} \times \text{PM}$ or $b\text{Lab} \times \text{PM}$ catches the added prediction from a party's programs because of the party's having been in government.

Table 4.2
Mandate Models: Britain, 1945 – 1985

Expenditure Area (Program Emphasis)	a	b Con	+ b (Con x PM)	+ b Lab	+ b (Lab x PM)	+ b Lib	Adj. R^2
Left – Right (Left – Right)	.78	–(.01)	– (.02)	– (.03)	+ (.00)	+ (.02)	.29
Defense & For. Affs. (Spec. For. Rel's)	12.4	(.35)	+ 2.80	– (.06)	+ 1.35	+ 2.64	.74
Admin. of Justice (Law & Order)	.35	.06	+ (.01)	+ (.19)	– (.21)	– .10	.60
Agriculture (Agriculture)	.53	–(.01)	+ (.55)	+ .57	+ (.78)	+ .20	.37
Social Security (Social Justice)	5.72	(.22)	+ .70	+ (.19)	– (.11)	+ (.29)	.21
Health (Social Justice)	27.8	.56	+ .84	– (.16)	+ (.32)	– (.49)	.18
Education (Social Justice)	1.27	(.03)	+ .10	– (.03)	+ (.07)	– (.05)	.25
Transportation (Tech. & Infrastr.)	.56	.12	+ (.08)	+ .15	– (.01)	– (.05)	.27
Housing (Social Justice)	1.67	.13	– (.04)	+ (.01)	– (.04)	– (.003)	.52
Environ. Protect. (Environ. Protect.)	.23	–(.006)	+ (.004)	+ (.01)	+ .05	+ .01	.33

This equation assesses the relative relationships between Labour and Conservative programs owing to the party's having been sometimes out of office (*b*Con or *b*Lab) and to its having sometimes formed the government (*b*Con × PM or *b*Lab × PM). The former might be labeled the "opposition" effect; the latter could be called the "governing" effect. The equation also includes the Liberals, who, of course, have always been out of government in the postwar years (*b*Lib, applied also to the Liberal Alliance in those years when the Liberal party teamed up with the rather short-lived Social Democratic Party).

The results from this more extended equation are shown in Table 4.2, which should be compared with Table 4.1 to see the difference made by the inclusion of the two governmental terms. At least as judged by the R^2s, there is a clear difference across most areas of policy (with the exceptions of housing, transport, and left-right, to which we will return).

One should bear in mind that the agenda model (Equation 4.1) measures the congruence of the parties' programs and policy priorities irrespective of how many years a party has controlled the government. The mandate model includes that measure but adds to it the impact of the amount of time a party has been in government. Thus, Equation 4.2 measures both agenda and mandate congruence (although for simplicity of discussion we shall label it *mandate*).

To show the differences between Table 4.1 and 4.2, let us use the case of defense and foreign affairs. According to Table 4.1, the emphases of all three party programs on "special foreign relations" predicts 49 percent of the variation in defense- and foreign affairs–spending priorities (which we have summed, given that defense and foreign affairs priorities correlate over time nearly perfectly) over the years 1945 to 1985 in Britain, indicated under "Adj R^2" in the right-hand column. Above a constant (*a*) of 14.3 percent, one could have expected for each percentage of each party program's total sentences devoted to special foreign relations increases in defense and foreign affairs spending, as a percentage of total outlays, as follows: 1.63 percent for a percentage of Conservative program emphases; .25 percent for Labour (but not reliably, given that it lacks statistical significance—indicated by the parentheses); and 1.95 for each percentage of Liberal party emphasis.

Moving to Table 4.2, we see that controlling for years in government by the multiplicative term (that is, program percentage for a certain theme times 1 if the party is in government) has increased the percentage of congruence—or, in customary statistical parlance, the "explained variance"—from 49 to 74 percent, a gain of 25 percentage points. That is the relative gain on the program-to-policy congruence from taking account of a party's being in government.

The interpretation of the row to the right of "Defense & For. Affs." in Table 4.2 is as follows:

- The "constant" (*a*) is 12.4, to which one adds the coefficient for each of five *b*s times that party's program-emphasis percentage to get the predicted policy priority.
- "*b* Con + *b* (Con × PM)" gives two coefficients that together tell us the relative addition to the prediction of defense priority we get from knowing the Conservative program *and* whether that party occupies the prime ministership (which also means controlling the Cabinet). Thus, addition of the mandate to the equation increased the predictive capacity by the difference between .35 + 2.80 over the simple agenda effect of 1.63. But some caution must be exercised in interpreting the .35 (*b* Con), since it is not above the .05 level of significance (indicated by its being parenthesized in Table 4.2).
- "*b* Lab + *b* (Lab × PM)" gives two coefficients, which together tell us the relative addition to the prediction of defense priority we get from knowing the Labour program *and* whether Labour occupies the prime ministership. Thus, addition of the mandate to the equation increased the predictive capacity by the difference between –.06 + 1.35 over the simple agenda effect of .25 (Table 4.1). Labour's program impact is virtually all a result of that

party's winning elections, since both the .25 agenda effect and the –.06 are not statistically significant.

- In Table 4.1, the Liberals, who were never in government, had a *b* of 1.95—larger than either of the major parties. But when we take into account which of the major parties has been in office, plus their program emphases, we have a better prediction than the Liberal program alone provides—although the latter provides very valuable information (*b* = 2.64). Controlling for both major parties and their incumbency still shows the Liberal program making an important contribution to the defense and foreign policy agenda.

The overall conclusions for defense and foreign policy in Britain would be as follows:

- All three parties' programs have anticipated the shifts in the place of defense and foreign policy on the British policy agenda (R^2 = .49). The policy agenda is fairly congruent with the programs presented in the electoral contests.
- The election process has produced policies more congruent with the forecasts of winners than of losers. "Losing" party programs do not provide reliable guides to future action, with one major exception.
- The Liberals, who have never participated in government, seem to be accommodated to a certain extent, perhaps as a sort of conscience, in spite of their status as perpetual outsiders.

In Chapter 3 we discussed in some detail the possibility of the *negative mandate,* that is, when the "opposition" effect is significant and negative. In the tables on Britain there is only one case that fits that category. Priorities for expenditure on administration of justice tend in the opposite direction from that expected based on the Liberals' emphasis on law and order in their programs. Although not significant in the agenda model (Table 4.1), it is significant in the mandate case (–.10, Table 4.2). The Liberals' programs have simply been out of step with administration of justice priorities of both Labour and Conservative governments.

We have no intention of burdening the reader with this much detail for each policy in each of ten countries. But as indicated earlier, we are using the British case and examples within it for the purpose of illustrating our general mode of analysis. In subsequent chapters we will present only a summary table of best-fitting models, from which we will draw conclusions based on general patterns rather than on detailed instances.

Overall, Table 4.2 offers a clear picture of the operation of the party mandate in Britain. Being in government is important. Theoretically consistent increases in R^2s are attained in five policy areas by adding the governing terms to the basic agenda equation. However, the added congruence for the Conservatives is greater than for Labour. What the Conservatives say in their program gives a useful indication, for several policies, of what they will do in government. This is indicated by the relative size of the *b*s under the column "Con"—the measure of program impact owing to the Conservatives' having been out of government—compared to the column under "Con × PM," which measures the gain in relative programmatic congruence with policy gained from incumbency.

On the Labour side, apart from defense and foreign affairs and environment, what they say before winning an election seems to bear little relationship to what actually gets done in government. This is worrisome not only for mandate theory but also for the whole focus of representative government in Britain. Taken in conjunction with Tables 4.1 and 4.2, it implies a pattern of Conservative ability to see their commitments enacted, in or out of office, and of Labour's inability to do so, which raises serious questions about the real nature of party competition in the country. Again, however, it is only an alert, subject to amendment by still-more-detailed analysis.

From the models reviewed up to this point, it appears that the only area where Liberals make a substantial independent contribution is in the domain of defense and foreign affairs. Presumably this is due to a tradition of bipartisanship in external policies that encourages governments of Labour or Conservatives to listen to the Liberals, regardless of the latter's exclusion from government. By the logic followed in the example given here, the mandate model is best-fitting for administration of justice and for education policies.

Ideology Models

A possible explanation for the Conservative/Labour contrasts is, as we noted, that Labour may be a more ideologically dedicated party seeking to change society in accordance with a long-term blueprint, whereas the Conservatives are inherently more pragmatic. To see if voters would do better to vote for Labour on the basis of past record and underlying ideology, and deciding for the Conservatives on their current set of programmatic priorities, we add to Equation 4.2 a new term covering both past record and ideology (*b*ConPM):

4.3 Ideology: $E_i = a + \mathbf{b\text{ConPM}} + b\text{Con}_i + b(\text{Con}_i \times \text{PM}) + b\text{Lab}_i + b(\text{Lab}_i \times \text{PM}) + b\text{Lib}_i.$

The new term, ConPM (in bold type), takes on a value of 1 for Conservative and 0 for Labour governments. This is, in effect, a second constant value (in addition to *a*)—one that accommodates the gross average difference between spending priorities of the Conservative and spending priorities of the Labour governments that have been in office between 1945 and 1985, contrasted—in the two-party case of Britain—to those of Labour. It is thus capable of reflecting long-standing policy differences between the parties that can be attributed to historic ideological commitment rather than the possibly shorter term consider-

Table 4.3
Ideology Models: Britain, 1945 – 1985

Expenditure Area (Program Emphasis)	a	b ConPM (Dummy)+	b Con +	b (Con x PM) +	b Lab +	b (Lab x PM) +	b Lib	Adj. R^2
Left – Right (Left – Right)	.37	(.62) –	(.02) –	(.01) –	.04 +	(.02) +	(.02)	.28
Defense & For. Affs. (Spec. For. Rel's)	16.4	–6.20 –	(.49) +	3.91 +	(.22) –	(.43) +	3.24	.76
Admin. of Justice (Law & Order)	.41	–(.07) +	.05 +	(.03) +	(.20) –	(.24) –	.11	.60
Agriculture (Agriculture)	–2.38	5.28 +	.94	–(6.10) +	(.11) +	1.32 –	(.08)	.52
Social Security (Social Justice)	2.97	(3.51) +	(.21) +	(.47) +	.08 +	(.35) +	.50	.23
Health (Social Justice)	24.9	(3.68) +	.54 +	(.60) –	.28 +	(.80) –	(.26)	.19
Education (Social Justice)	1.42	–(.20) +	(.03) +	.11 –	(.02) +	(.05) –	(.06)	.24
Transportation (Tech. & Infrastr.)	.68	–(.32) +	.10 +	(.12) +	.18 –	(.08) –	(.04)	.26
Housing (Social Justice)	1.56	–(.51) +	.13	–(.006) +	(.03) –	(.10) –	(.03)	.54
Environ. Protect. (Environ. Protect.)	–.15	.40 +	.05 –	.06 +	(.01) +	.18 +	.01	.68

ations written into election programs. It was this long-term commitment that we discussed in Chapter 2 as severely constraining the flexibility necessary for the competitive process to work in the fashion envisioned by Downs (1957). Table 4.3 reports the results of this comparison.

With respect to increasing the overall strength of relationships, as indicated by the adjusted R^2, the new term (ConPM) makes a significant contribution in the domains of defense and foreign policy ($b = -6.20$), agriculture (5.28), and environment (.40)—the latter two being areas in which a Labour government consistently has *reduced* spending priorities, but where its programmatic commitments as a government (Lab × PM) also give a good indication of what it is likely to do. In the cases of agriculture and environment, the introduction of the dummy variable, ConPM (which gets *b*s of –2.38 and .40 respectively), is sufficient to qualify them for the best-fitting models. The .40 for environment indicates that there is an overall four-tenths of a percentage more devoted to environmental affairs under Conservatives than under Labour (controlling for differences in their election programs). In contrast, there is 6.20 percentage less for defense and foreign affairs under the Conservatives than under Labour.

In the latter case, with introduction of the ideological term, it seems that Labour's long-term association with increased defense/foreign affairs expenditures overwhelms any effect of its programmatic emphases. The ConPM term, with a b of –6.20, shows this inversely, that is, it shows a reduction of 6.20 percent for Conservative governments, which is exactly the same as an increase by Labour when it forms the government. The important influences in this area appear according to Table 4.3 to be the ideology term (ConPM), Conservative commitments as a government party (Con × PM, $b = 3.91$) and general Liberal influence (Lib, always out of office, $b = 3.24$).

As we indicated at the outset of this discussion of British parties and policy, it will not be our habit to drown the reader in a sea of regression coefficients in every chapter. We have risked that here as a way of illustrating the process by which "best-fitting" models are selected. In the rest of the country chapters, we use one summary table instead of the three presented here. We now turn to a table providing just such a summary for Britain.

Summary Table: Mechanics

For the rest of the country chapters, we will place the detailed tables equivalent to Tables 4.1, 4.2, and 4.3 in the Appendix. In each country chapter, for clarity of presentation, we will present a single summary table, containing the individual policy areas as they best fit to the agenda, mandate (plus agenda), or ideology (plus agenda and mandate) models. The R^2 is used to select best-fitting models, even if the selection is contradictory to our theoretical concerns, as indeed is the left-right situation in Britain (to be discussed). Coefficients not attaining .05 level of significance are left blank in the summary table, as seen here in Table 4.4. A general version of the equation is also included under the section of the table for each model.

The summary table is read much as were the detailed Tables 4.1, 4.2, and 4.3. However, there are a few additions for the mandate and ideology versions. These are seen in Table 4.4 in the second and third sections. The labels at the top are for the constant (a), indicating the base percentage of expenditure devoted to a particular policy domain before any account is taken of the variables listed to the right. The next columns are labeled:

(+) Agenda or (–) Mandate	Mandate	(+) Agenda or (–) Mandate	Mandate
Conservative (Out)	(x Gov)	Labour (Out)	(x Gov)

Table 4.4
Best-Fitting Models Between Party Program Emphases and Policy Priorities: Britain, 1945–1985*

Agenda Models

Policy Priority (Program)	a	Conservative	Labour	Liberal	Adj R^2
Left–Right (Left–Right)	.70	$\underline{-.20}$	$\underline{-.03}$	.02	.33
Housing (Social Justice)	1.12	.11			.53
Transportation (Tech.&Infrastr.)	.59	.15	.14		.25

[$E_i = a + bP_i^A + \ldots bP_i^n$]

Mandate Models

Policy Priority (Program Emphasis)	Constant a	Conservative (+)(–) Agenda or Mandate (Out)	Conservative Mandate (x Gov)	Labour (+)(–) Agenda or Mandate (Out)	Labour Mandate (x Gov)	Liberal Agenda (Out)	Adj R^2	Added by Mandate
Admin. of Justice (Law & Order)	.35	.06				$-.10^{\underline{n}}$	.60	.11
Education (Social Justice)	1.27		.10				.25	.15

[$E_i = a + bP_i^A + b(P_i^A \times G) + \ldots bP_i^n + b(P_i^n \times G)$]

Ideology Models

Policy Priority (Program Emphasis)	Constant a	Ideology Conservative Gov = 1	Conservative (+)(–) Agenda or Mandate (Out)	Conservative Mandate (x Gov)	Labour (+)(–) Agenda or Mandate (Out)	Labour Mandate (x Gov)	Liberal Agenda (Out)	Adj R^2	Added by Mandate	Added by Ideology
Defense & For.Affs (Spec.For.Rel's)	16.4	−6.20		3.91			3.24	.76	.25	.02
Environ. Protect. (Environ. Prot.)	−.15	.40	.05	$\underline{-.06}$		.18	.01	.68	.16	.35
Agriculture (Agriculture)	−2.38	5.28	.94			1.32		.52	.00	.25

[$E_i = a + bP_A + bP_i^A + b(P_i^A \times G) + \ldots bP_i^n + b(P_i^n \times G)$]

* Indicating only those b's (unstandardized regression coefficients) that attained .05 statistical significance. Coefficients in the opposite direction from theoretical expectation are underlined. Coefficients for negative mandate are indicated by $\underline{n}$.

A coefficient entered under "(Out)," such as the .06 to the right of "Admin. of Justice" in the Conservative column, if it is positive (+), indicates the agenda (or "opposition") effect from a party's program reflection in policy. If that same coefficient is negative, it indicates the reversal of that party's program by the opposite party in government, which we have called the "negative mandate." In this case, the Liberals indeed suffer that experience, with a –.10 for administration of justice. Of course, whenever the Liberals get a negative coefficient, it is by definition a negative mandate, since they have never been in power over the period studied here. Negative mandates are indicated in the summary table of each chapter by the superscript ^{N} (e.g., $-.10^N$). Parties that never get into power have no possibility for a positive mandate.

The coefficients entered under "(× Gov)," under "Mandate," indicate the relative congruence of the party program accounting for the party's having served in government rather than having been in opposition. In the mandate models (as contrasted to those for agenda or ideology), only education shows such a congruence, and then only for the Conservatives (.10).

To the right of the equations for the mandate models is a column labeled "Added by Mandate." These figures (.11 and .15) indicate the added explained variance (addition to R^2) that results from adding the multiplicative terms for programs of parties out of and in government, as contrasted to the simple agenda model. Thus, the R^2 for the agenda model applied to administration of justice, in Table 4.1, is .49. However, in Table 4.2, the mandate model, it is .60. The latter is also the best-fitting model for administration of justice (since there was no gain by adding the ideology term, as seen in Table 4.3). The gain from the agenda to mandate is .11, that is, the difference between .49 and .60. The last column for the mandate models thus gives a quick glimpse of the importance of the mandate's being added to the agenda.

The latter portion of the summary tables presents the cases in which the ideology model offered the best fit. The ideology effect is indicated under:

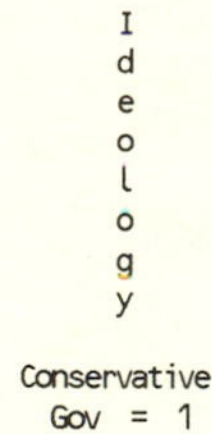

In addition, there is a double column to the right of the adjusted R^2 column, labeled "Added by Mandate/Ideology." This performs for both mandate and ideology terms the function described above for the rightmost column of the mandate models. It shows, respectively, the added prediction of the mandate over simple agenda and the addition of ideology over mandate + agenda. (These figures can be readily reproduced by successive subtractions of R^2s in Table 4.1 from Table 4.2 and Table 4.2 from Table 4.3.)

Aside from the mechanics, we should again stress that the three models represent, not separate theoretical conceptions, but rather cumulative readings on a single theoretical concern. That is, the mandate equation is, in fact, agenda *plus* mandate; ideology is a shorthand phrase, in fact, for agenda *plus* mandate *plus* ideology. They are pieces of a single theoretical whole. They should be assessed, therefore, in terms of how much congruence between election programs and policy priority is found by means of increased levels of complexity and theoretical elegance.

Nonconformists and Contradictions

In line with the scientific caution to give special attention to that which challenges one's theory, we shall examine specifically those findings for each country that do not conform or that actually contradict our theory. The first row of numbers in Table 4.1 is a striking challenge to our theory. It reports the *b*s between the left-right program scores (illustrated in Figure 4.1) and the left-right policy priority scores (illustrated in Figure 4.2). To the right of the constant (*a*, .70) are the three coefficients, first for the Conservatives' program left-right score versus left-right policy ($b = -.02$), then for Labor (–.03), and finally for the Liberals (.02). These are all statistically significant and thus not enclosed in parentheses (as are some other coefficients farther on in the table). The R^2 of .33 at the right of the "left-right" row means that 33 percent of the variance in left-right expenditure variations could have been anticipated by someone knowing the general left-right tilt of the three parties' programs.

But there is a problem. The coefficients for the two major parties—which are presumably the most consequential—are *negative.* The smooth policy move leftward and then more or less horizontally, as seen in Figure 4.2, is not forecast by the left-right programmatic emphases of either major party (Figure 4.1). This is not at all what we expected from our theory.

Figure 4.1 reports only agenda congruence. That is, there is no account taken of whether a party is in government, that is, of the mandate. If we look at the corresponding row of numbers in Table 4.2 and Table 4.3, however, the picture is no better. In Table 4.2 the terms "Con × PM" and "Lab × PM" take account of whether there was a *Con*servative or a *Lab*our prime minister in office. That is, they include the party program scores only in those years when the respective governments are in office. If there was a mandate effect, these terms would be significant (that is, not parenthesized in the tables) and positive, whereas the terms to their left ("Con" and "Lab") would either be insignificant or negative. What actually happens, however, is that none of them are statistically significant. Adding the mandate to the agenda for left-right renders all the coefficients below the acceptable level (.05) of statistical significance.

Table 4.3 does the same thing as Table 4.2, but it goes further and includes the dummy variable for the presence of a Conservative government. The coefficient for that variable has a value of .62, as indicated under "ConPM" in Table 4.3. But it is not statistically significant. We have introduced this term to represent the standing differences in policy-relevant ideology between the parties. Thus, we read the left-right coefficient in Table 4.3, under "ConPM" as saying that adding standing ideological differences along the left-right dimension to mandate and agenda does nothing significant to help our ability to predict the left-right tilt of policy.

Aside from methodological considerations, what are we to make of the substantively uninspiring noncongruence between left-right policy priority and the programmatic emphasis of or shift in governments between Conservatives and Labour? We have no convincing, generalizable explanation for this reversal of expectation. We could discuss it in terms of specific governments, but knowing what is to come in later chapters, we are hesitant to do that. Britain's postwar general left-right policy curve looks nearly identical in broad outline to that of most countries in our set. Thus, the left-right policy curve is more appropriately discussed in the concluding chapter of the book rather than here in terms of apparent oddities in one country.

Many of the larger lessons of this research will become apparent only as similarities across countries unfold. As we will discover later, a strong left-right program-to-policy linkage is rare. Rather, the correspondence between specific programmatic emphases and policy priorities is more fine-tuned—more regularly apparent at the level of particular policies and particular program themes (rather than general aggregated trends).

This is not true, however, for two specific policy domains in Britain, social security and health, which serve, in addition to outright contradiction, as examples of the second kind of deviation from our theoretical expectations, namely, null findings. None of the three models was able to explain 25 percent or more of the variation in priority for either of these policies. As used here, "social security" includes a full range of income-redistribution policies—public pensions, unemployment assistance, and general welfare for various categories of low-income groups. "Health" includes not only a wide array of public health research and services but also the enormous British commitment to the National Health Service, which provides universal medical care at virtually no direct cost to the recipient.

Both of these policy domains have attained the status of "entitlements." Unlike most other public functions, for which a budgeted amount of money is provided to agencies, with the understanding that those spending it must live within the allocation, there are some public services to which persons have a legislatively defined claim, based on their particular characteristics. When persons are unemployed because of specified reasons, they are *entitled* to financial benefits. When one reaches a specified age within the pension system, one is *entitled* to a certain income for life. When one's personal circumstances are such that one's income is below a defined level, one is *entitled* to welfare payments. The general trend embodied in the leftward movement shown in Figure 4.2 is largely composed of expanded entitlement programs. Expenditures in such programs are usually driven by social and economic circumstances rather than by specific allocative decisions of sitting governments. It is harder to change entitlements than it is to change priorities for other functions, where bureaucrats spend what they are appropriated rather than to which their "customers" are entitled.

The absence of robustness of our models regarding health and social security in Britain leaves us tentatively suggesting the hypothesis that party programs, through either the agenda or the mandate, are less relevant to entitlements than to other, more flexible, domains of public policy. We will return to this consideration in Chapter 14, where we reflect on the lessons provided by the ten country studies.

CONCLUSION

In seeking to introduce the reader to the methods of our analysis, via the British example, we have risked burying the actual substantive results for that country. In these concluding remarks, we attempt to rectify that situation.

As noted, the selection of best-fitting British models is summarized in Table 4.4. Only the left-right scales yielded contradictory results, completely counter to all our theoretical expectations. Social security and health policies have failed to attain the minimum R^2 of .25 on any model, leading us to entertain, tentatively, the hypothesis that entitlement programs are insulated from party influence.

Interestingly, for the remaining seven substantive areas of policy, we need all three theoretically relevant models. The crudest, but still useful, means for assessing the value of the increased complexity added by mandate and ideology to agenda is to compare R^2s, although this is compromised by a few statistically insignificant but nonetheless anomalous signs ("–" when a "+" is expected). Omitting the aggregated left-right equation, the agenda models predict an average of 29.8 percent of the variance in policy priority. Taking account of incumbency—that is, the mandate—increases this to 47.5. In other words, winning or losing provides an additional 18 percentage points' accuracy in matching party programs and policy priority. If further analyzed by inclusion of a measure of standing ideological differences between the two major parties, the average prediction is not increased but actually is reduced to a level of 44+ percent. This is possible because we use the "adjusted" R^2, which equalizes for the number of variables in the equation. Thus, on average the ideology term (*b*ConPM) seems to detract more than it adds.

Such a conclusion, however, illustrates the problem with averages. The relative worth of the agenda versus mandate versus ideology models is widely varying across policy domains. The spread across the models is evidence of the usefulness of this rather broad strategy for testing agenda and mandate effects of party programs. But it detracts from the goal of generalization. At best, we can argue that the relative mix of agenda versus mandate versus ideology may be specific to particular policy areas—if we find the same policies in the same categories in other countries. That is yet to be seen.

As we have noted, two areas of British policy, social security (including direct welfare and old-age pensions) and health, seem to have been so heavily circumscribed by entitlements over the years that no amount of influence from party programs or from long-standing differences has been sufficient to control them. They seem essentially insulated from partisan control. However, a lesson might be drawn from the ability of Prime Minister Thatcher's Conservative government after 1979 to shift support away from housing. Prior to the Thatcher government, most experts considered housing in Britain to be a virtually unassailable entitlement. Yet the Conservatives were able to establish control over it, in line with a de-emphasis on housing in their programs. But the very drama of this case made it so exceptional that it was probably a once-in-a-generation phenomenon. We will continue with the hypothesis that neither party alternation nor programmatic salience, through agenda or mandate influences, will be generally controlling in those domains of social services that have taken on entitlement status. Or, at least, such influences will be less with respect to entitled policies.

In spite of institutional arrangements that should allow for a strong mandate in British policymaking, there is considerable evidence of a politics of accommodation. We might expect that accommodation of out-party concerns would show up in policies generally growing in prominence, as incumbent parties attend to their support base at the margins. But there is no British evidence that agenda or mandate models work best on policies that are rising in relevance, compared to those that are declining. Administration of justice has been a gainer, whereas agriculture and defense/foreign affairs have been decliners. Yet all get R^2s between .52 and .74. Transportation and education experienced early gains and later declines in priority. Both hover around the minimum R^2 of 25 percent, whereas environmental protection, which has a similar up and down trend, has 68 percent of its variance explained by a complex model.[1]

Two areas are heavily affected by sheer alternation between the parties: environmental protection and agriculture (*b*ConPM = 40 and 5.28, respectively). That does not provide, as yet, any grounds for speculating about the general impact of constant, long-standing, ideological differences between the parties compared to the impact of contemporary programmatic foci. But these cases, plus the clear evidence of general programmatic distance between the parties, coupled with their mutual flexibility (see the left-right summary trend in Figure 4.1), encourage us in our commitment to continue testing their mutual impact with the ideology mode.

With respect to relative programmatic impact, there is a tilt in favor of one party's being more influential than the other, via any of the mandates. Of the twelve statistically significant program-to-policy *b*s reported for the two major parties in

Table 4.4 (again, aside from left-right), eight are for the Conservatives and four for Labour. Some politics of accommodation is apparent, however, in that the Liberals' programs get significant, positive *b*s in two areas: defense/foreign affairs and environmental protection. There is, however, a negative mandate evident in the case of the Liberals' emphasis on law and order and its congruence with administration of justice policy ($b = -.10$). As we have seen, this means that incumbent governments tend to go in the opposite direction from what would be expected from the Liberal programs. Incumbents seem to have been more dedicated to enacting justice policy *contrary* to the concerns of the Liberals' programs than of enacting policies *consonant* with their own.

Further evidence of positive accommodation is found if we tally the significant *b*s for agendas and mandates, across all three equations. Agenda terms are significant in the best-fitting models nine times, versus eight (including the one anomaly) for any of the terms based on incumbency. That is, a comparison of the out-of-power prediction with the in-government prediction (along with the dummy variable for ideology) shows the agenda ahead nine to eight.

Although mandate theory goes far in explaining party influence on British policy, the processes involved are clearly more complex than can be accommodated within such a strict, relatively pure, theoretical framework. Indeed, as we shall see, both Austria and (surprisingly) the United States conform better to this model than does Britain, its original home. Not only tenure in government but also a free marketplace of ideas without monopolistic tendencies by governing parties are reflected in policy priorities in Britain in ways that will become clearer once we take the experience of other countries into account.

NOTES

1. In the entire summary table, Table 4.4 (aside from left-right), there is only one seemingly contradictory relationship. That is the statistically significant –.06 *b* for the Conservatives in government related to environmental protection priority (Equation 4.3). Given that the simple correlation is not contradictory, we conclude that this is not a case of an actually perverse relationship (unlike the "left-right" situation) but rather an instance of collinearity of Conservative party programs with other terms in Equation 4.3.

5

Australia

INSTITUTIONAL AND POLITICAL CONTEXT

More closely than any other country in our set, Australian governments resemble the single-party majority administrations of Britain. It is true that in Australia there are, officially, three government parties. The right-of-center Liberals were in coalition with the primarily agrarian National Party (formerly the Country Party) throughout the 1950s and 1960s, alternating in recent decades with the left-of-center Australian Labor Party. The National Party is a small party with its main base in Queensland, drawing additional support in rural Victoria and New South Wales. It has been in nearly permanent coalition with the Liberals. The two parties in tandem have competed against Labor in every election since World War II, with the long-term understanding that, if the former gained a majority, they would form a government together. When in government, the Liberals get the prime ministership and the National Party gets a few cabinet posts. A comparison to the relationship between the West German Christian Democratic Union and its Bavarian-based partner, the Christian Social Union, would not be wholly out of place for the Liberals and the National Party in Australia.

Thus, although the two parties have offered separate electoral programs, the National Party can hardly be regarded as a serious contender for power or for coalitions without the Liberals. The National Party's programs emphasize a very narrow set of concerns, with no entries in most of the coding categories. The only comprehensive programs have been issued by the Liberals and by Labor. We will, therefore, concentrate on them in the subsequent discussion.

The Australian Labor Party has no junior partner, but rather competes on its own independent terms. When in the majority, it forms a single-party government. Labor was effectively prevented from doing this in the 1950s and 1960s by the activities of the small Democratic Labor Party (DLP), a predominantly immigrant party. The DLP was encouraged by conservative, anti-Communist Catholic bishops in the 1950s to get voters to divert their second-preference votes away from Labor to the Liberals. Australia has a complicated electoral system whereby voters rank all candidates in a district in order of preference. After Labor reorganized itself under a new leader, Gough Whitlam, in the 1960s, the DLP practically disappeared. Labor was in power from 1972 through 1975 and again in the 1980s.

Australian politics were formed much in the British mold, most by the ideas of descendants of British settlers, supplemented up to the 1930s by fresh waves of immigration from Britain. In spite of a modestly strong federal structure and an upper legislative house (the Senate) with considerably greater powers than the British House of Lords, party organization and activities resemble those in Britain, as does Australian constitutional theory. Legal principles place little restriction on what an Australian government with a majority can do, though there are stronger overt checks from the Senate and from state governments than from any comparable institutions in Britain.

Essentially, however, we have the same expectations of a Westminster model of party government for Australia as we did for Britain—certainly in regard to the opposition in the federal lower house. This means that we would expect programs of the governing party to be most congruent with public policy, with probably some effect from long-standing ideological differences between the parties.

As in Britain, the opposition may be expected to act more with an eye on the next election than out of any hope of affecting current government policies. Thus, even parties in opposition should tend to draw a sharp contrast between their policies and those of the government, rather than adopting a conciliatory tone, which might get some of their own policies adopted. When an opposition party seems to have little chance of winning elections, as happened to Labor in the 1950s and 1960s, we would expect little incentive for the government to respond to it. Thus, as was our natural expectation in Britain, we expect the mandate to be relatively strong.

PROGRAM AND POLICY TRENDS

Australian Data

There are no serious flaws in the Australian data. The program indicators are straightforward. Expenditure data come directly from National Accounts' publications. Unlike most countries, Australia does not publish detailed governmental expenditure data in its statistical yearbook. Furthermore, there have been a few rather substantial changes in the categories used in National Accounts' publications. Consequently, consistent time series for the bulk of the period could be confidently constructed for only eight policy domains. And one of those—agriculture—was available from only the mid-1960s on.

All countries occasionally update and correct data published earlier, usually in later editions of multiyear summaries. Thus, in all our records of expenditure data, we try to use the most recent publication of figures for earlier years. The keepers of Australia's national accounts, however, exceed by far the data-amendment rate of other countries. Data are reported in each year's *National Accounts* for several prior years. But the specific entry for, say 1960, which is published first in the 1962 volume, will then be amended each successive year until it is dropped for the currently reported series. These changes are never of great magnitude—never more than a percentage point or so. But they are sufficient to distort time series somewhat. Thus every effort has been made to use the latest publication of earlier years' data. This leaves us moderately unsure, however, as to the precision of the latest indicators of expenditures in our analysis. None of the amendments, over the years, was such as to make a serious dent in any regression coefficient, but it could create small and misleading blips on a time chart. Caution is advised in interpreting small fits and starts, therefore, in any of the time charts on policy priorities.

The reader should be reminded that in our analysis of specialized program-to-policy relationships we are unable to match the content of party programs to exactly corresponding areas of policy output. The program data have been coded for maximum cross-national reliability into fifty-four comparable categories. Expenditure data, however, usually reported in generic categories, suffer from many nation-specific idiosyncrasies. As in the preceding chapter with Britain and in subsequent chapters, we have here sought to obey a few sensible rules in matching specific thematic concerns of the party programs to policy categories. Some decisions were easy, such as the match between emphases on *agriculture* and expenditure on *agriculture,* or even the correspondence between party program emphases on *law and order* and expenditures for *administration of justice.* In an area like *welfare policy,* however, there are competing program themes, such as emphases on *social justice* or *social services.* The program-coding scheme is also more refined in some areas than in others. Thus there are multiple coding categories dealing with external relations—emphases on *special foreign relations,* on *peace,* or on *internationalism.* But there are many cases where only one category is reasonable, such as agriculture.

Although we have high confidence in the general reliability of the program-coding categories and the measures they yield, we recognize that they should not be thought to have more precision than is reasonable, especially given that a score of languages have had to be accommodated in the larger project of which this volume is a part. Sharp distinctions between such adjacent categories as *social justice* and *social services* or *peace* and *internationalism* are, in all likelihood, unwarranted. In cases where there are multiple candidates within the program coding categories, we experimented to find the theme or combination of themes that seemed to perform best in the analyses. In the Australian case, emphases on social justice performed better than emphases on social services in the various models for explaining welfare-spending shares. In other countries, social services proved to be more useful. Likewise, in modeling spending shares for defense and for foreign affairs, we found that the sum of several categories (foreign special relations, military +, peace, and internationalism +) produced a coherent and effective indicator—one we have labeled *foreign policy.* The matching categories are as follows:

Party Program	*Policy Area*
Foreign Policy*	Defense
Foreign Policy	Foreign Affairs
Law and Order	Administration of Justice
Agriculture	Agriculture
Social Justice	Welfare
Technology and Infrastructure	Housing
Technology and Infrastructure	Transportation
Education +	Education

*Sum of Foreign Special Relations (+), Military (+), Peace and Internationalism (+).

Left-Right Trends

The predominance of the government party in the Australian parliament lends interest to the map of left-right ideological movement. It is constructed for each country out of the same programmatic items by subtracting such typically right-wing emphases as defense, law and order, freedom, and market economics from characteristic leftist emphases on peace and internationalism, social welfare, and government intervention (see Chapter 3). The left-right trends for the Liberals and for Labor are shown in Figure 5.1.

What's in a name? Clearly the Australian "Liberals" are the right-of-center, or "conservative," party, comparable to such parties elsewhere. They do not occupy the middle ground of the left-right spectrum, as we have seen with the British Liberal Party or as we will see with the German "liberals." They are even unlike the Canadian "Liberals," which, although one of the two major parties, nevertheless programmatically look like the smaller "liberals" in other countries.

Figure 5.1 is convincing not only for the way it models party policy emphases but also for the fact that it shows clearly that the two parties have fairly distinct ideological stances. The Australian Liberals and Labor were generally well separated in the 1950s—at the height of the cold war, when they divided sharply on foreign as well as domestic policy. In the prosperous 1960s, the parties actually converged and even "leapfrogged" in one election. But the Liberals then moved to a New Right stance in the face of economic difficulties in the 1970s and 1980s. They were trailed by Labor, which, when it took up power in the 1980s, adopted fairly orthodox fiscal positions.

Australian parliaments have a fixed maximum term of three years, though under exceptional circumstances, they may be dismissed earlier. Because, as noted in Chapter 3, we assume that the programmatic priorities under which an election is

Figure 5.1
Left-Right Program Trends:
Australia, 1946 - 1987

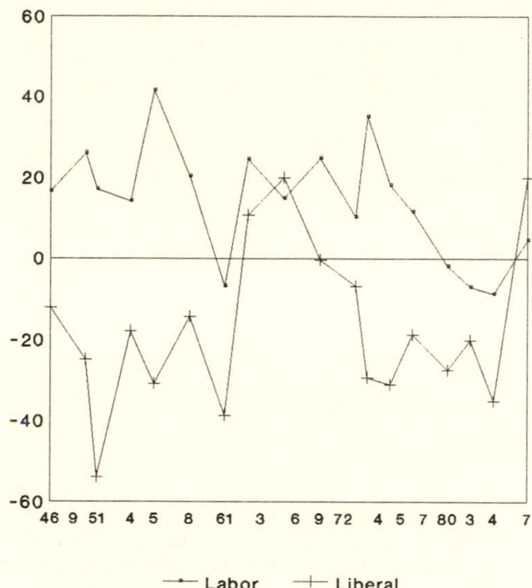

contested are controlling on the winning party until the next election, most of the party positions in Figure 5.1 are in triplicate.

How far ideological positions are reflected in the general tendency of government policy is shown in Figure 5.2. The left-right policy scores are based on a clearly distinguished factor that includes the percentage devoted to education and welfare, as contrasted to the percentage devoted to defense. The loadings on this single factor distinguish tidily between a positive .90 for education and welfare and a negative .97 for defense. Thus, the higher up the vertical scale, the more *leftist* the priorities of outlays by Australian national governments.

The trends are remarkably comparable to those in other countries, the first of which we have already seen in Britain. After the initial cold war shock—driven by Australia's heavy commitment to the Korean conflict—policy priorities moved steadily leftward (upward, in our graphic presentation in Figure 5.2) from the mid-1950s through the mid-1970s, followed by a plateau thereafter. Clearly this reflects the turn away from further expansion of the welfare state common across the Western world in the 1980s. It has been reflected in the movement toward classically orthodox fiscal policies by recent Australian governments of both parties.

There is a general correspondence between the curves for the Liberals' programmatic emphases (Figure 5.1) and the leftward movement of policy (Figure 5.2), at least during the first half of the period covered here—at the very time when the Liberals enjoyed their longest stretch of power in government. And one

Figure 5.2
Left-Right Expenditure Priority Factor Scores:
Australia, 1947 – 1989

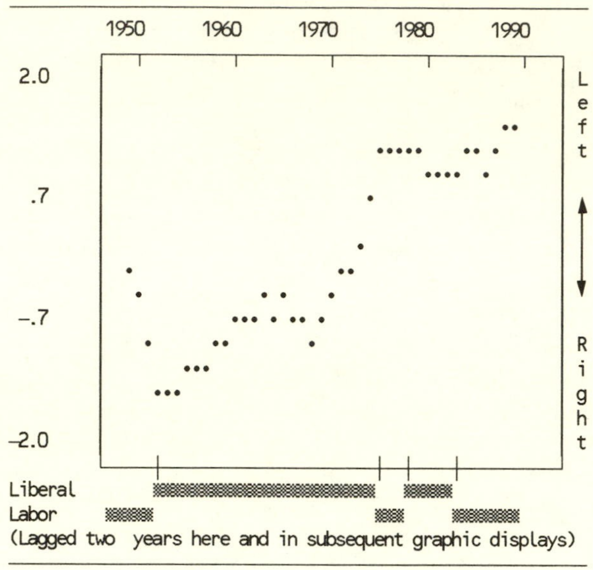

Structure of Policy Priority Factor

Policy Area	Factor Loading
Education	.90
Welfare	.90
Defense	–.97

could claim with some warrant that the post-1960s rightward tilt of programmatic content by both parties (Figure 5.1) was an exaggerated foretaste of the policy plateau reached in the late 1970s (Figure 5.2).

Government policy priorities measured in this manner are by no means fine-tuned to the specific programmatic adaptations of the parties from election to election. Indeed, given the clear divergence in the latter half of the postwar period between the left-right leanings of party programs, on the one hand, and policy priorities, on the other, it appears that if we are to find tight program-to-policy linkages, they will be in the realm of specific policy areas rather than in broad left-right patterns of programs and policies.

Specific Policy Trends

Trends in expenditure priorities for specific policy domains are illustrated in Figure 5.3. Australia responded to the early cold war more vigorously than any other of the ten countries we study, with defense receiving over three-quarters of all federal outlays at the peak of the Korean War (Figure 5.3.1). But as in other countries, that priority declined steeply (with a short, sharp reversal during the Vietnam War) until it bottomed out in the 1970s. Likewise with the much smaller priorities for agriculture (for which, unfortunately, we have only limited data—Figure 5.3.4) and transportation (Figure 5.3.7). Increases in social policy (welfare, housing, education) are broadly similar to those in other countries.[1]

These are the more specific trends that contribute to the summary measures of Figure 5.2. Not only leftist expenditures, however, but also spending on the presumably right-wing domain of administration of justice increased. And there were declines in the share devoted to education and housing in the 1970s, yielding the plateau we noted in general left-right priorities (Figure 5.2).

There are no strikingly obvious cases, in Figure 5.3, where a change of party is clearly and consistently accompanied by a comparable shift in policy priority. There was visibly more change *within* the long rule of the right-of-center Liberals from the 1950s to the 1970s than there appears to have been at the time of alternations in government. We doubt, on the basis of this visual inspection, that simple alternation in power between Liberals and Labor will be of much consequence in explaining broad policy reallocation. In order to say anything more about the policy consequences of party alternation in government, we need the support of careful statistical analysis.

PARTY PROGRAM-TO-POLICY CONGRUENCE

In this section we report on the same set of regression analyses tested in all countries in our study. The theoretical grounds for each model were discussed in the first three chapters. In Chapter 4, we reported the detailed applications for the British case. It is rather tedious, however, to go through each model for each of the ten countries in this book—especially as many of them simply do not fit in every country.

We will be selective in the following discussion. Generally, it can be assumed that where we do not cite specific statistics for a relationship, the particular R^2 will be under .25 and the regression below the .05 level of statistical probability. We will not use our sorting mechanisms, however, to disguise or ignore cases where the sign (+ or –) is in the opposite direction than expected, is statistically significant, and is not reversed in a more theoretically elegant model. That is, we will report cases of nonconforming relationships where they occur. As additional insurance against loading the dice in favor of our theory, we present the full array of statistical results for Australia and the succeeding countries for all of the models tested, across all policy areas, in the tables in the Appendix.

In the summary table of best-fitting models, for purposes of clarity, we leave the cells blank for regression coefficients below the .05 level of significance, not to reject outright, as we are not applying tests of significance in the usual manner,

Figure 5.3
Trends in Expenditure Priorities: Australia, 1946 – 1988

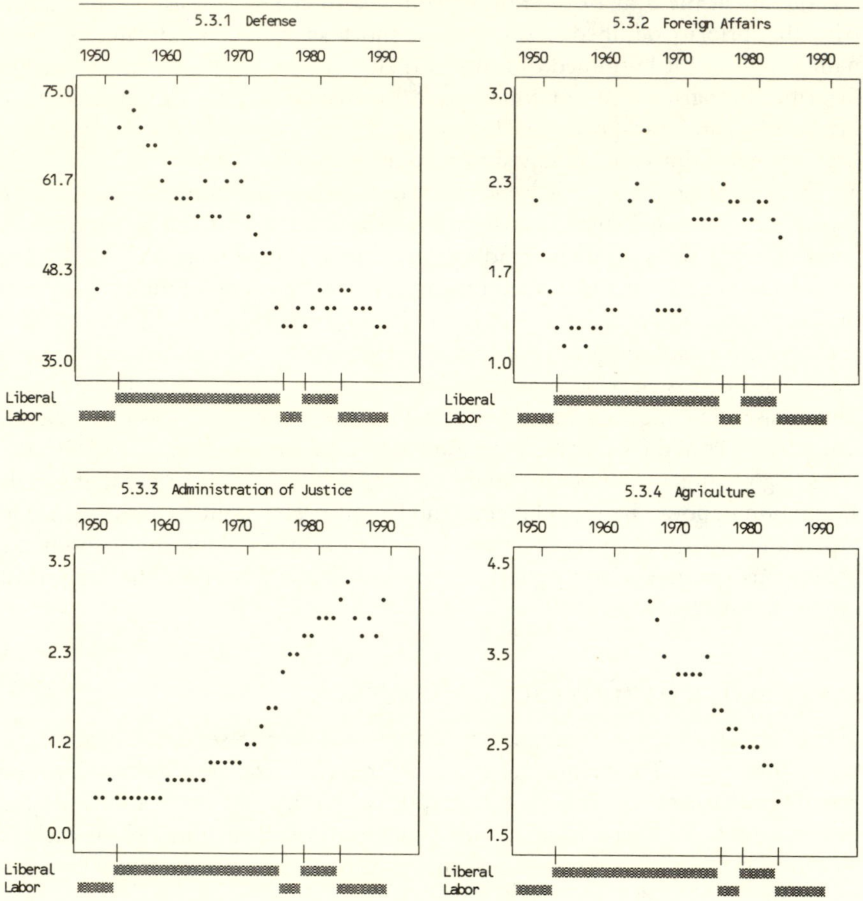
5.3.1 Defense
1950
1960
1970
1980
1990
75.0
61.7
48.3
35.0
Liberal
Labor
5.3.2 Foreign Affairs
3.0
2.3
1.7
1.0
5.3.3 Administration of Justice
3.5
2.3
1.2
0.0
5.3.4 Agriculture
4.5
3.5
2.5
1.5

but to indicate that the estimate is unstable and might be radically changed by the addition of new observations. This procedure is also consistent with our goal of identifying patterns that are most comparable cross-nationally, as contrasted to exploring the nuances of the party-to-policy process peculiar to any one of the ten countries.

Best-Fitting Models

There is considerable programmatic structuring of policy in Australia, but it works itself out in specific policy contexts rather than as a general left-right pattern. The program-to-policy connections are not as strong, measured by R^2, as in most other countries, but they are sufficiently interesting to support a claim to the relevance in Australia of the general ideas guiding our research strategy.

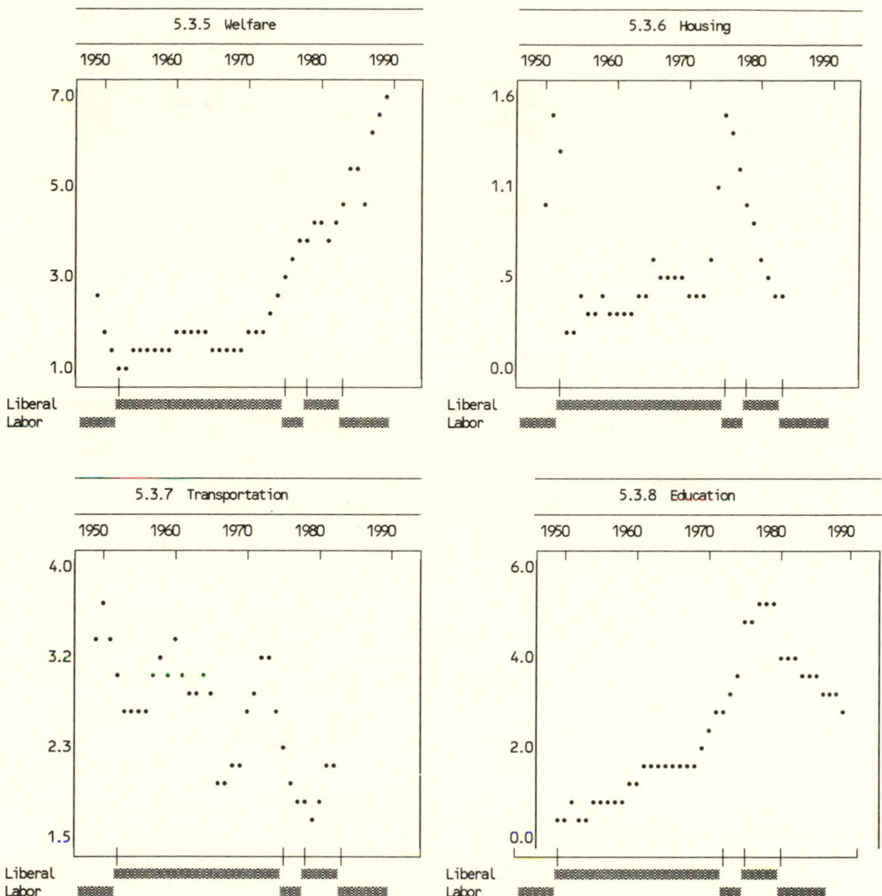

In each of the seven substantive policy domains, either the mandate model (agenda plus mandate) or the ideology model (agenda plus mandate plus ideology) provided a superior explanation to the simple agenda version. That is, in all cases, taking account of governing effects and/or standing differences between Liberals and Labor yielded a superior explanation to that provided by the party programs alone, regardless of incumbency.

Each party's emphases are linked to each area of policy, first through a test for the agenda model, and then through the more complex models described in Chapter 3 and illustrated by the British case in Chapter 4. Again, the entire array of computations is presented in the Appendix. Table 5.1 gives a summary, presenting the best-fitting model for each policy area where the corresponding programmatic emphases forecast at least 25 percent of the variance.

Table 5.1
Best-Fitting Models Between Party Program Emphases and Policy Priorities: Australia, 1950 – 1988*

Mandate Models

Policy Priority (Program Emphasis)	Constant a	Liberal (Out) (+)(–) Agenda or Mandate	Liberal (x Gov) Mandate	Labor (Out) (+)(–) Agenda or Mandate	Labor (x Gov) Mandate	Adj R^2	Added by Mandate
Defense (Foreign Policy)	45.7	–1.14$^{\underline{n}}$	1.65			.49	.18
Foreign Affairs (Foreign Policy)	1.96			–.07$^{\underline{n}}$		.37	.17
Admin. of Justice (Law & Order)	1.34	.02	1.01	–1.45$^{\underline{n}}$	1.89	.32	.20
Agriculture (Agriculture)	3.37			–.03$^{\underline{n}}$		.29	.06

[$E_i = a + bP_i^A + b(P_i^A \times G) + \ldots bP_i^n + b(P_i^n \times G)$]

Ideology Models

Policy Priority (Program Emphasis)	Constant a	Ideology Liberal Gov = 1	Liberal (Out) (+)(–) Agenda or Mandate	Liberal (x Gov) Mandate	Labor (Out) (+)(–) Agenda or Mandate	Labor (x Gov) Mandate	Adj R^2	Added by Mandate	Added by Ideology
Welfare (Social Justice)	4.95	–3.05	–1.02$^{\underline{n}}$		.40		.52	.03	.15
Housing (Tech. & Infrast.)	1.12	.68					.52	.41	.11
Education (Education)	.82					.42	.32	.21	.02

[$E_i = a + bP_A + bP_i^A + b(P_i^A \times G) + \ldots bP_i^n + b(P_i^n \times G)$]

* Indicating only those b's (unstandardized regression coefficients) that attained .05 statistical significance. Coefficients in the opposite diection from theoretical expectation are <u>underlined</u>. Negative mandates are indicated by $\underline{n}$. There were no cases in Australia where the agenda model was best-fitting.

As mandate theory would lead us to expect, models that do best in Australia are those that measure the congruence of policy to the individual and collective agendas of the major parties and add the impact of the specific party's having been in or out of government. The Australian findings also highlight the role of the *negative mandate,* that is, the extent to which policy priorities are formed in seeming reaction to the programs of the opposition. There seems to be a vigor to partisan competition in Australia that gives focus to the differences in emphases between the parties, not only in terms of what will be done, but also in terms of what will not be done. Liberal governments' policy priorities go in the direction opposite to that predicted by the losing Labor program in foreign affairs (–.07), administration of justice (–1.45), and agriculture (–.03). A comparable reaction to Liberal programmatic emphases under Labor governments shows up in welfare (–1.02) and defense (–1.14). Saliency theory says that the parties are more likely to select their own peculiar areas of emphasis, to the exclusion of those of their opponents, rather than to line up on opposite sides of the same inventory of issues. But saliency theory, when carried through to the policy process, does not exclude the possibility, very evident in Australia, of incumbents in effect punishing the losers by de-emphasizing those policy domains emphasized in the latter's programs. The structure of Westminster-style systems would seem to encourage such sharpness of policy competition. Although the negative mandate is not a prominent feature of the British situation, it is very much in evidence in Australia.

Interestingly, instances of negative mandate are more common than instances of the *positive mandate,* wherein the program of the winners is the best predictor. These cases occur under the Liberals in defense (1.65) and administration of justice (1.01) and under Labor in administration of justice (l.89) and education (.42).

Ideology, as measured by the simple difference in policy that results from alternation between Liberals and Labor, in no policy area completely dominates the influence of the agenda or the mandate alone. In three policy domains, welfare, housing, and education, the addition of the "ideology" term does produce a superior R^2, but only in welfare and housing is that term itself statistically significant, with the liberals de-emphasizing welfare (–3.05) and favoring housing (.68). These two instances are, in our minds, insufficient to suggest that standing differences between the Liberal Party and the Labor Party in Australia are of such magnitude as to render inconsequential the shifts and maneuvers reflected in contemporary party election programs.

The notable effect of the mandate and the somewhat less but still consequential fit of policy to standing interparty differences are not sufficient to suggest that agenda congruences are absent in Australia. Table 5.1 does not include the simple agenda model, not because it was unimportant, but because in all cases something was added by mandate and/or ideology considerations. Most of the variation in policy priorities in postwar Australia reflects strong agreement across the two major parties. A crude index of this is the fact that in three of the seven policies presented in Table 5.1 (welfare, defense, and agriculture) the mandate and/or ideology terms did not add to the R^2 as much as was already explained by the agenda alone. Furthermore, there is a positive agenda (opposition) congruence at a statistically significant level in two policy areas (welfare, Labor = .40; administration of justice, Liberals = .02). Australia's policy process is not cleft by fundamental, pervasive interparty conflict.

Broad agenda influence, however, does not mask one instance of virtual single-party dominance—welfare. In addition to the clear effect of alternation in office (–3.05, indicating a positive effect from Labor), noted above, the Labor *program* is also congruent with policy, but in an interesting manner. When the Liberals are in power, they nonetheless respond with welfare shares congruent with Labor's most recent emphases on social justice (.40). Yet when Labor is in, it goes in the direction opposite to that predicted by the most recent Liberal program (–1.02). This is an especially sharply defined instance of the type of competition discussed above, which here suggests that Labor is largely the driving force for welfare expansion, as could be expected by the party of the Left in a highly competitive situation.

Labor is the only party whose programs count in regard to education policy. But unlike the linkage with welfare, this one is not exclusively due to agenda or negative mandate congruence but is a clear case of a positive mandate (b = .42). That this impact is nearly hegemonic is suggested by the absence of a statistically significant coefficient for the Liberals in the education realm.

Nonconformists and Contradictions

The theoretical expectations for Australia are similar to those we put forth for Britain prior to the analysis. Tight, two-party competition with strong discipline within parliament should set the stage for operation of a party mandate. Parties have at least the formal capacity to be accountable for what they have said they will do. The duality of party competition, furthermore, has created the conditions for recognizable, long-standing differences in the stances of the parties—differences confirmed by the left-right trends shown in Figure 5.1.

When it comes to policy impact, however, this general ideological distinction between parties is not so clear. Left-right program trends do not forecast left-right policy in any discernible fashion. The R^2s for left-right in all three models remain stubbornly low. When we enter the dummy variable for party alternation (Equation 4.3, *ideology*), an R^2 of .31 is produced. But the extent of multicollinearity is so extreme as to yield totally unstable results (see Appendix Table A5.3).

Were we interested in explaining this country's policy rather than in testing the comparative fit of a set of standardized, theory-driven models, we could probably dissect Australia's data further and find the locus and extent of impact from party alternation on the left-right policy trends shown in Figure 5.2. But such is not our purpose.

There is one additional case, out of the eight domains of specific policy, that does not conform to any of our models. Transportation policy priorities are not accounted for by our strategy. The reader may recall that two policies lay outside the fold in Britain—social security and health. We speculated there (Chapter 4) that it is their status as "entitlements" that immunizes them from partisan impact. But transportation—the Australian misfit—is not in the set usually viewed as entitlements. That hypothesis, therefore, must remain on hold. And we offer here no special speculation on the causes for the Australian deviation regarding transportation. Transportation, as in other countries, enjoyed a strong postwar boost as capital investments flowed to infrastructure modernization and then declined relatively as those programs reached a level of infrastructural maturity (see Figure 5.3.7). In the case of transportation in such a sparsely populated, sprawling country as Australia, either there was such widespread consensus as not to require partisan notice, or, alternatively, policy has been driven by forces beyond the ken of the parties.

Aside from these two cases of nonconformity—left-right and transportation—there are no instances in Australia where the best-fitting version of the model contains statistically contradictory coefficients, that is, significant coefficients that have a sign (+ or –) opposite to theoretical expectation. In Chapter 14 we will review the country findings, paying attention to the cases of nonconformity, in order to identify patterns. At the moment, however, we shall draw the conclusions that seem warranted in the particular instance of Australia.

CONCLUSION

Compared to most other countries, as we shall see in later chapters, the party program-to-policy linkage in Australia is weak. Left-right and one of eight specific policy areas fell beneath the .25 R^2 threshold. But Australian parties and their programs are by no means unimportant policy predictors. Seven of eight policy areas are above the threshold in one of the three versions of the model, with the average R^2 for those six at nearly 40 percent. That is hardly to be ignored.

Furthermore, our analysis generally shows that the relationship between party programs and federal policy in Australia is even more consistently mandatory than in Britain (although at somewhat lower statistical levels). In that sense, Australia is comparable to the other countries we shall examine later in the book. That is to say, when parties emphasize particular areas of policy in their election programs, subsequent government spending in most instances tends to go up, or down if the reverse is the case.

The Australian case is fairly consistent with mandate theory. The agenda effect is important, but it is a common foundation for congruence with a mandate. For

Australian parties to implement their program emphases or to defeat those of their opponents, they really need to win office. The politics of accommodation, whereby incumbent governments defer selectively to opposition policy priorities, are not much in evidence in Australia.

NOTES

1. There is an interesting contrast between the defense (5.3.1) and the foreign affairs (5.3.2) time lines. The trend in defense is nearly universally downward from the Korean War peak into the 1970s. Foreign affairs spending, which is heavily laced with assistance to developing countries, rises over time, correlating with defense at –.76, indicating that foreign affairs expenditures are driven by forces opposite to those that facilitate funding for the military. In many countries, foreign affairs priority is positively correlated with defense, suggesting that foreign affairs spending is driven by much the same concepts of national security as is spending on the military. We will comment further on these differences as they are encountered.

6

Canada

INSTITUTIONAL AND POLITICAL CONTEXT

The Canadian political system is burdened with some issues not high on the agenda of most long-established democracies. Canada must regularly face two challenges to its fundamental political identity, one internal and one external. Internally, there is a varying, but always visible, threat of ethno-linguistic separatism, particularly from the French-speaking majority in the province of Quebec. Externally, there is simply the big neighbor to the south—the United States. These issues cloud whatever may elsewhere be "business as usual." The capacity of Canadian governments to respond to these challenges, and those of routine policymaking as well, is further distorted by the frequency of minority governments, that is, cabinets that are composed of a single party that lacks a majority of seats in the parliament. These forces keep the policy agenda atilt in a manner not encountered in most of the other democracies examined in this book (with the clear exception of Belgium—see Chapter 13).

Canada finds itself next door to the United States, the major Western constitutional alternative to the British—with thoroughgoing federalism and the separation of powers. Canadian political institutions are, in spirit and in theory, however, purely British. In legal theory, the provinces can do only that which is explicitly devolved to them. There is not even a constitutional fiction, like the one that exists in the United States, that powers not delegated to the central government are reserved to the provinces. Instead, in all matters not explicitly assigned to the provinces, the parliament in Ottawa is sovereign. Indeed, the majority party has the same freedom of action and exclusive responsibility for fulfilling its mandate that is allowed under the British and Australian systems.

In practice, however, Canada is politically a very different country from Britain, Australia, or the United States. Things do not work out quite the same way in Canada. But the way they differ is much more easily recognizable from a European than from an American perspective. That is, although Canada may differ in many respects from Britain, its politics look more continental than they do American.

For a start, Canada has not, for most of the postwar period, had a parliamentary two-party system like those of the United States and Britain, or even (effectively) Australia. Rather, Canada has had a "two and one-half party" system, if not a "two and two halves" system. That is, two smaller parties have had fairly consistent representation along with the two large ones in the House of Commons. Often, particularly in the second half of the postwar period, single-party governments formed by the Liberals or the Progressive Conservatives depended on the tolerance of either the more or less socialist New Democratic Party (NDP) or the rather populist Social Credit Party. The latter disappeared from the national scene in the course of the 1970s. However, one of the forces behind it in its later stages simply took another form: overt French Canadian nationalism, which is a constant preoccupation of the national government and a severe constraint on its freedom of action.[1]

Canada does resemble its southern neighbor in one respect. Neither of its two leading parties is blatantly socialist. Further, like the U.S. parties of former generations, Canada's major parties have regionally distinct bases of support. The Liberals (Canada's approximation of a left-of-center party) and the Progressive Conservatives (generally to the right) owe their origins to political cleavages dating back to around the turn of the century. The Liberals have tended to base themselves on an alliance between French Canadians and poorer English-speaking groups in the East of the country. The Progressive Conservatives have found their core support in the better-off sections, above all, in Ontario. Increasingly, they also speak for the newly rich western provinces, whose inhabitants resent the cultural and financial dominance of both Quebec and Ontario. Prairie populism was also voiced by the Social Credit Party and by the New Democratic Party (the only socialist alternative), which now derives its support equally from the central, wheat-growing provinces and from the economically depressed sections of the eastern seaboard beyond Quebec.

In this lineup, the Liberals can be seen as an old-style progressive alliance, not unlike the New Deal Democrats in the United States. This comparison can be overdrawn, however. Like the Democrats, the Liberals have had populist and radical phases but have contained many conservative elements, notably small-town French Canadian Catholics. And the Liberals have consistently backed established eastern interests against populism and radicalism from the West. These eastern interests have been, however, an important force within the Progressive Conservatives, who, beginning in the 1980s, made a bid to detach French Canadian support from the Liberals by recognizing the autonomy of Quebec.

In many ways, therefore, it is difficult to trace consistent ideological divisions between Progressive Conservatives and Liberals, a point that will come up later when we look directly at their programs. Even from the most cursory reading, it is clear, nevertheless, that major and consistent divisions open up between both major parties and the New Democratic Party. The latter is generally recognized as a socialist party in the European mold, which the Social Credit Party, with its sporadic populism, was not (being once a vehicle for deeply conservative western oil interests and, at other times and in other places, embittered French Canadian small businesses).

Underlying the party system have been the profound social cleavages in Canadian society, which are not primarily matters of class but rather of religion and ethnicity, with a territorial base. Because of that territoriality, more traditional social divisions have not dissolved with time, as they have to some extent in the United States. Politics is increasingly centered on the division between French-speaking Canadians, based in Quebec in the East and constituting 25 percent of the Canadian population, and English-speaking Canadians, on the eastern seaboard, in Ontario (the largest province, just west of Quebec), and in the Middle and Far West. The migration of French Canadians from country to city in the 1960s heightened their perception of disparities in social conditions and political treatment and reinforced their demands for redistributive policies. The western provinces in particular reacted against these pressures, which the Westerners saw as exploiting their oil and mineral wealth to subsidize the East.

Further undercurrents of conflict were introduced by the policy of official bilingualism: Recently arrived immigrants, for example, viewed English as the language of opportunity and thought that the policy forced them to be, in effect, trilingual—and was designed merely to pacify the native French speakers.

Besides internal territorial and ethnic divisions, which have threatened—but never actually brought about—the breakup of the federation, all Canadian governments have had to concern themselves with relations with the United States, relations that the former premier Pierre Elliot Trudeau once compared to sleeping with an elephant. The United States is so overwhelmingly dominant in the Canadian economy and exerts so much cultural penetration that all governments are faced with the question of whether, where, and when to follow the U.S. lead—which has been done with regard to membership in the North Atlantic Treaty Organization (NATO), cold war diplomacy, and more recently with trade policy—or whether to disassociate from it, which was done with regard to the war in Vietnam and the Third World, particularly Latin America. Canada has been able to reconcile political independence with its strong practical dependence on the U.S. market economy by acting internationally as a strong supporter of the United Nations and of development assistance programs generally. Internally, from time to time, this external independence has also helped to secure New Democratic support for minority governments of the major parties.

Given the occasional failure of national elections to return parties with parliamentary majorities, several Canadian governments in the postwar years have been based on a minority of parliamentary seats. Over the whole postwar period, up to 1988, there were twelve years of minority government as opposed to thirty-two years of clear majorities. Minority governments are, however, formed the same way as majority ones. That is, the party with the plurality of seats forms the government, with the tacit support of the smaller parties or party—often the New

Democrats. In practice this takes the form of the cooperative small party's abstaining on votes that would otherwise bring down the government.

Such a situation is clearly restrictive, since a minority government always has to consider the other parties' reactions to what it must do. In practice, however, Canadian minority governments do not seem to act very differently from majority ones. This is partly due to the lack of striking ideological differences between the leading parties, which renders many policies bipartisan, a condition we shall examine in the next section. It is also due to the ideologically charged matters being frequently forced off the government agenda by pressing immediate problems (very often, separatist threats and/or relations with the United States). Accommodation to achieve multiparty support on fundamental constitutional or national questions may result in less guidance from the party program to policymakers than is common in other democracies (Clarke et al. 1984).

Generally speaking, however, one has the impression that a government, either majority or minority, when it has a reasonably clear mandate for some policy, will be allowed (sometimes reluctantly) by the other parties to pursue it. Often the government can count on active support from one of them. Therefore, effectively, the operation of the mandate in Canada may not be so different from its operation in Britain or Australia. We would expect relationships to be attenuated, however, because of the substantial agreement between Liberals and Progressive Conservatives and the minority position of many governments. That minority status may increase the influence of out-parties over what government does and, thus, enhance relationships between the programs of out-parties and policy.

PROGRAM AND POLICY TRENDS

Canadian Data

The expenditure categories and figures for Canada are reasonably well documented by Statistics Canada, the central governmental records office. The party program data, however, present problems, owing basically to an increasing tendency of Canadian parties to disperse and diversify their policy statements and in the case of the major parties, to replace much of the text with captions and pictures. The upshot is that apart from the material from the New Democrats, who issue electoral programs like those of parties in most other countries, we have had to rely on a somewhat varied collection of documents for Liberals and Progressive Conservatives (see Irvine 1987 for a detailed description of these). It is remarkable and reassuring that even given this diversity, we can establish the kind of relationships we do. However, these may be attenuated, not only by the substantive policy agreements and minority status of governments already mentioned above, but also by the limitations of the programmatic data themselves. This must be borne in mind in evaluating our analyses.

Eleven categories of expenditure data could be consistently tracked throughout the period of our analysis. Together, they average just over half of all federal spending in Canada and include the major categories analyzed in the other countries. They have been paired with programmatic emphases as follows:

Party Program	*Policy Area*
Foreign Special Relations (+)	Defense
Foreign Special Relations (+)	Foreign Affairs
Law and Order	Administration of Justice
Agriculture	Agriculture
Social Services (+)	Welfare
Social Services (+)	Health
Social Services (+)	Social Security
Social Services (+)	Education
Technology and Infrastructure	Transportation
Technology and Infrastructure	Housing
Art, Sport, Leisure	Culture and the Arts

Left-Right Trends

In our analyses, we include the three major Canadian parties: the Progressive Conservatives, the Liberals, and the New Democrats. Left and right trends in the Canadian programs are measured in the same standard manner used in other countries (see Chapter 3), subtracting the percentage of references to typically *rightist* themes (defense, law and order, freedom, and so on) from the percentage of references to typically left issue areas (peace and internationalism, social services, and so on). Figure 6.1 plots the trends in left-right programmatic emphases for the three Canadian parties.

The two major parties, the Progressive Conservatives and the Liberals, follow a pattern that is quite different from that of the two major parties in Britain, Australia, or—as we shall see—any other country in our set of ten. For the first twenty-five years of the period, one would have difficulty defining which was left and which was right. The Liberals have situated themselves on the middle of the left-right divide. They are clearly major—indeed, generally predominant—contenders for power, and hence, we might expect them to be more inclined to compromise on ideological positions, given the general complexity of the universe of policy discourse in Canada. This, along with a number of these preliminary expectations for Canada, will be seriously challenged by the evidence.

Although the New Democrats have averaged only about 13 percent of the popular vote, they have virtually monopolized the programmatic left. While moving about considerably, they have nonetheless kept a wide berth away from either of the major parties. This suggests that the New Democrats are doggedly committed to a socialist ideology and, moreover, perceive no national electoral advantage to

Figure 6.1
Left-Right Program Trends:
Canada, 1949 - 1988

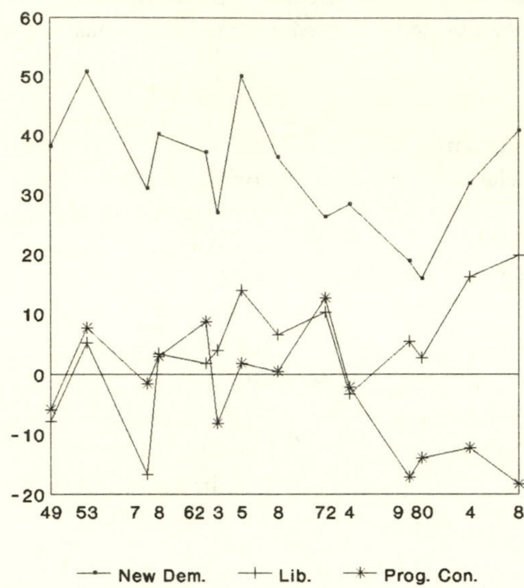

be gained from moving into the space occupied by the centrist parties. However, successes in the 1980s at the provincial level, including winning the right to form the government in Ontario, may have whetted the New Democratic appetite sufficiently for the party to move, haltingly to be sure, to the right ($r = -.56$) over time. But the final two national elections in the 1980s saw a return to the traditional left for the NDP.

It should be kept in mind that our scoring procedure makes possible reasonably reliable cross-national comparison. The Canadian Liberals' average score is well to the right of those of British Labour, the continental social democratic parties, and the U.S. Democrats. The Progressive Conservatives, in terms of left-right averages, are right in the middle of the bourgeois parties of the other countries. If there is a political identity problem in Canada, it is with the Liberals.

An interesting question for us is the following: Does the NDP monopoly over the left represent a sort of utopian resignation, which essentially excludes NDP programs from effective place on the policy agenda? Or do the indistinction and identity problems of the Liberals, if not the Progressive Conservatives, create a set of circumstances where the NDP programs are accommodated in policy, even though the party never gets into a federal cabinet? Using rather different measurements, François Pétry put forth precisely that argument, describing the Canadian system as one characterized by "contagion from the left" (Pétry 1988).

The Liberal/Conservative seesaw may in fact be a sort of Downsian policy adjustment on the part of the major parties, seeking votes directly from the oppos-

Figure 6.2
Left-Right Expenditure Priority Factor Scores:
Canada, 1950 – 1989

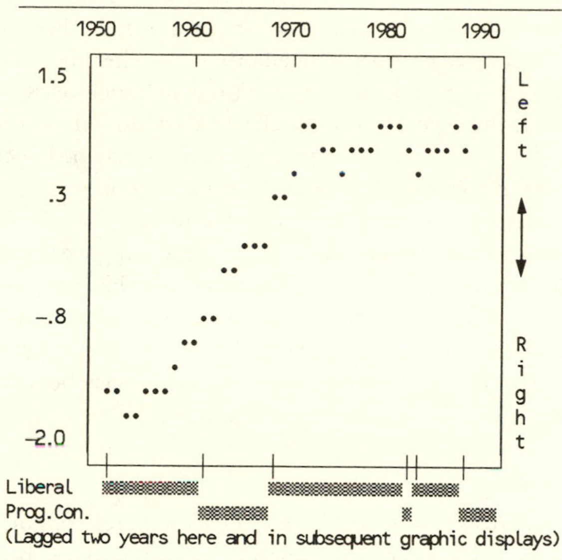

Structure of Policy Priority Factor

Policy Area	Factor Loading
Social Security	.95
Health	.91
Welfare	.90
Education	.89
Defense	–.98

ing bloc by taking policy positions congenial to the median voter. This could be seen in contrast to the relative stubbornness on the part of the only truly ideological party in the system, the NDP.

Further insight into the party program-to-policy linkage can be gained, still with respect to the highly aggregated domain of general left-right leanings, from looking at the left-right policy trend. Following the practice begun in the British and Australian analyses, we have constructed a factor score to measure left-right policy priorities (see Figure 6.2). It includes five of the eleven policy domains, with very clear differentiation between defense, at the right end (factor loading = –.98) and social security, health, welfare, and education on the left (.95, .91, .90, .89, respectively—see Figure 6.2). The trend based on factor scores from that scale is displayed in Figure 6.2.

As in the other countries, Canada's general policy trend shows a steady movement leftward after the initial defense buildup in the early cold war, with a flattening and oscillation from the early 1970s on. The break in the leftward movement came a few years earlier for Canada than for most of the other countries in the study. Perhaps it occurred earlier in Canada than elsewhere because of the severe and quick impact of the economic reverses of the oil-shock years.

Again, however, any expectations of a clear association of leftward policy with a comparable move in the content of party programs may be largely thwarted in Canada, as can be seen even by the simple comparison of Figures 6.1 and 6.2. As in many other countries, the shift from defense to social services actually coincided with a period of right-wing party incumbency in government, during the 1950s and 1960s, whereas left-wing parties elected later had the misfortune to enter office during a time of economic strain and of some heightening of tension between NATO and the Soviet bloc, during the 1970s. The doubt stimulated by comparing left-right programs with policies, however, may be somewhat allayed by examining the trends for specific policy areas.

Specific Policy Trends

The plots in Figure 6.3 show the trends for the eleven areas of policy included in our analysis. Defense follows the same pattern seen elsewhere, being the virtual mirror (and largest single component) of the left-right trend. Although more erratic than defense, foreign affairs follows a similar curve, suggesting that external policy in general, although not so tightly interwoven as in Britain, is still conceived as a common package. The simple correlation between defense and foreign affairs priorities in Britain is .72, and in Canada it is .58. But recall that in Australia, it was strongly negative, –.76.

Only social security, which mainly includes state pensions for the elderly, enjoyed a virtually unabated rise in Canada (Figure 6.3.6). Except for agriculture, most other domestic policies, including administration of justice, welfare, health, education, transportation (and communication), housing, and the modest domain of culture and the arts, rose sharply and then fell, at least a bit. It is the dip in the human services areas that contributes to the leveling of the left-right summary index. None of the curves, however, is entirely smooth. We have the following questions: Were these shifts in policy priority clearly forecast by any or all of the parties? By the governing parties only? Or by none?

The continuing fact of a general income disparity between English- and French-speaking Canadians may serve to elevate human services to the status of a bipartisan policy, on the grounds that income transfers through these programs are a principal means for "buying" loyalty among otherwise restive ethnic sectors. If that tactic is adopted across parties then, of course, it may mute any impact not only of long-standing interparty differences but perhaps also of current programmatic variations.

The trend line for agriculture requires some special attention. Canada is an agrarian nation. Agriculture is big business in Canada—a business that makes Canada a major actor on the stage of international trade. And it is clear from Figure 6.3.11 that governmental assistance to agriculture has varied dramatically over the postwar years. Canada shows a less consistent drop in policy priority for agriculture than any of the other nine countries in this volume. The variation in the pattern over time would suggest that agriculture policy should be quite responsive to party programmatic emphases, relative to other policy areas.

Our argument in the opening discussion of this chapter should create an expectation of low relevance of party programs to policy in Canada. The rationale for our argument is that the challenges to basic political identity simply overwhelm ordinary politics, consistently distracting the parties from the affairs to which they would otherwise attend. However, it is also reasonable to make an argument somewhat at an angle to this null hypothesis. That would be in favor of the *agenda-setting* role of parties. Precisely because of the fundamental tensions in Canada, especially the centrifugal tendencies of ethnic separatism, it may behoove governing parties to be especially accommodating to the programs of those out of office. This then constitutes an argument for the agenda models, but not for the mandate.

The plots in Figure 6.3 are insufficiently precise to suggest even a hint of an answer. As we have seen in previous analyses, it is only through careful statistical dissection of the program-to-policy relationships that we can come close to satisfactory answers to the questions we have posed above.

PARTY PROGRAM-TO-POLICY CONGRUENCE

It is important to keep in mind the tactics we have used in assigning to each of the policy domains a corresponding thematic category from the party programs. Clearly the Canadian record keepers have not classified expenditures with our specific needs in mind. Nor were the party program data coded to correspond precisely to the Canadian expenditure records. The data must be taken as found. It would be possible to recode each country's data using categories that seemed to be closer to that country's policy records. However, that would impose a high cost against the potential for cross-national comparison. If each country had its own, unique, coding system, then it would be impossible, for example, to compare trends in the way we have with the left-right scale.

Using the data exactly as they are seems to us to provide ample insights for our purposes—for testing a set of common models over a set of diverse political and cultural settings. Furthermore, such a use constitutes necessarily a more stringent, more conservative test. Thus, any findings that seem to be consistent with the models should be even more convincing, precisely because of the stringency of the test. That is, not only must our theory work, but it must also work the same way everywhere.

Figure 6.3
Trends in Expenditure Priorities: Canada, 1951 – 1989

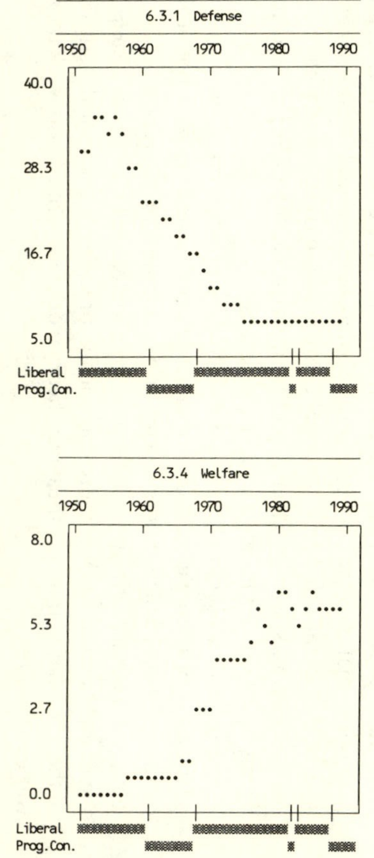

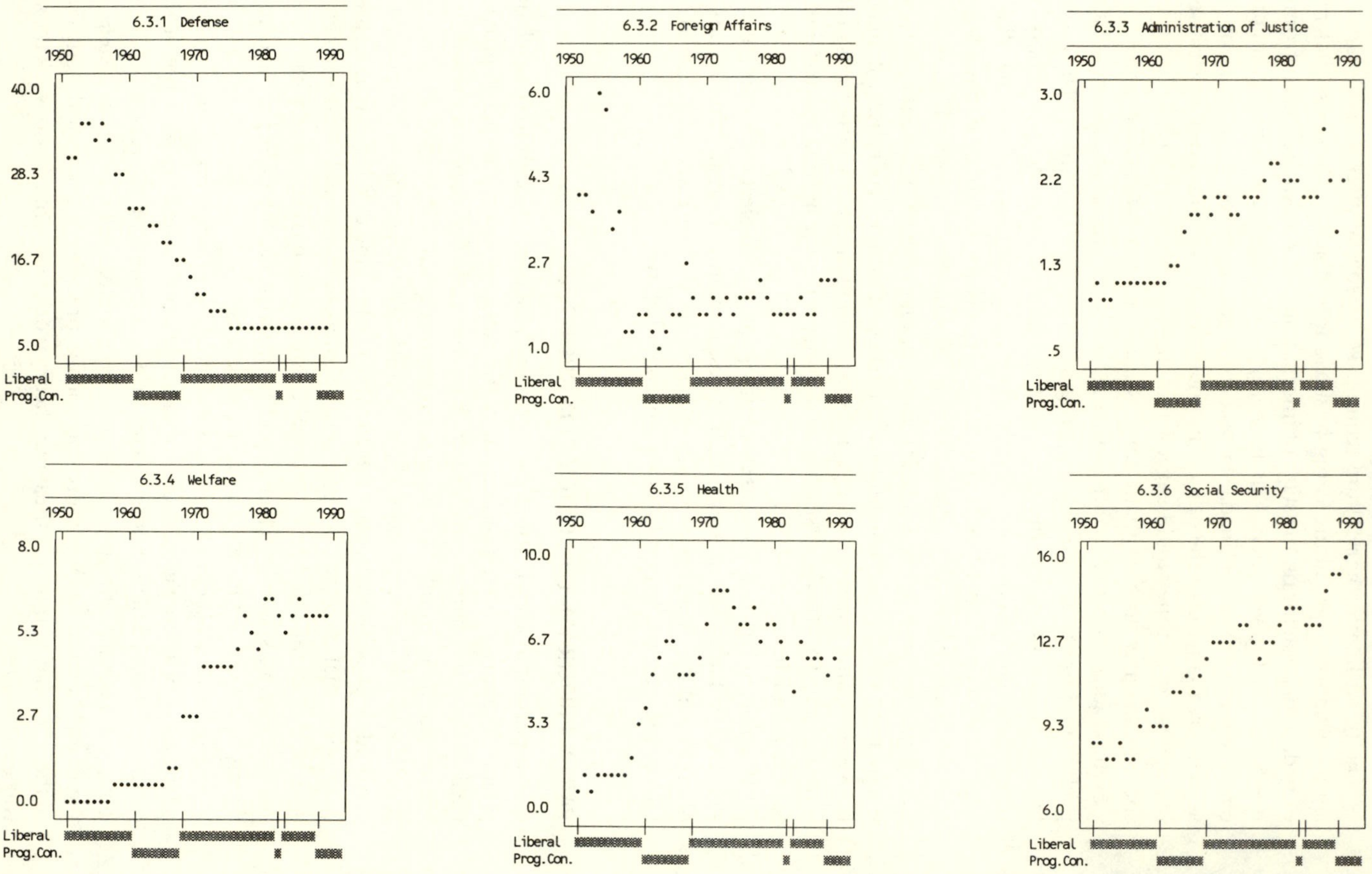

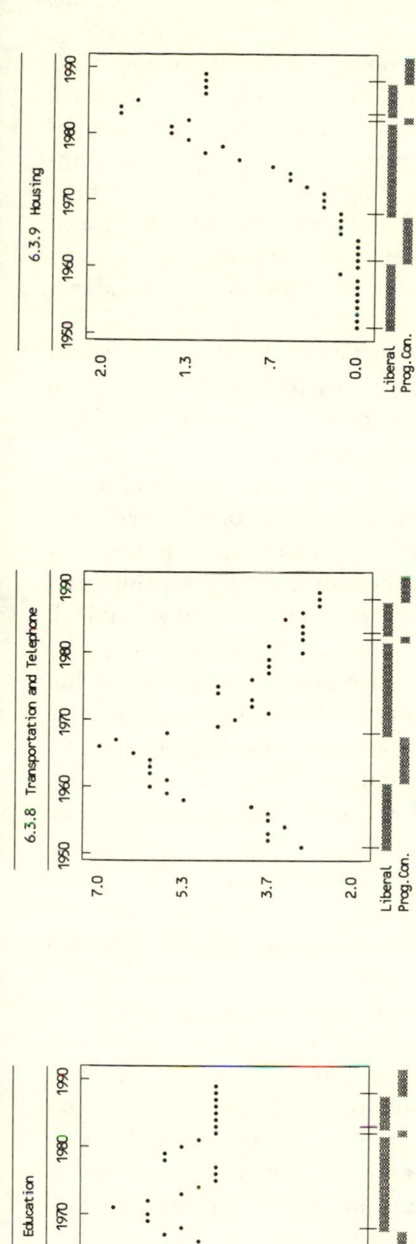
6.3.7 Education
1950
1960
1970
1980
1990
6.0
4.0
2.0
0.0
Liberal
Prog.Con.
6.3.8 Transportation and Telephone
1950
1960
1970
1980
1990
7.0
5.3
3.7
2.0
Liberal
Prog.Con.
6.3.9 Housing
1950
1960
1970
1980
1990
2.0
1.3
.7
0.0
Liberal
Prog.Con.

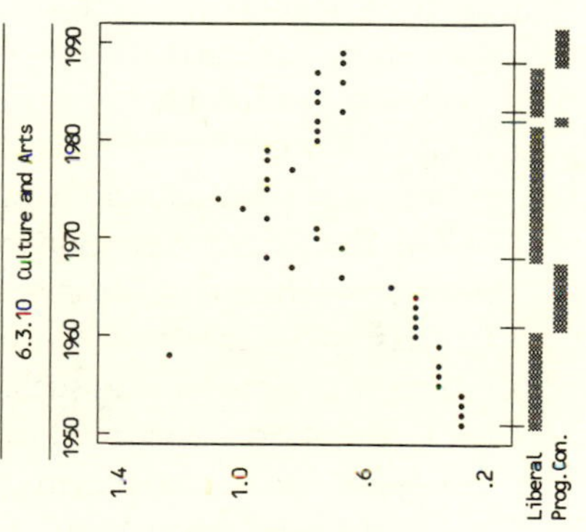
6.3.10 Culture and Arts
1950
1960
1970
1980
1990
1.4
1.0
.6
.2
Liberal
Prog.Con.

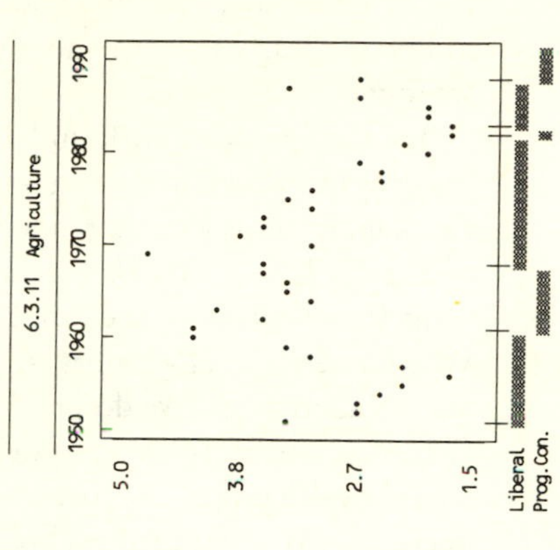
6.3.11 Agriculture
1950
1960
1970
1980
1990
5.0
3.8
2.7
1.5
Liberal
Prog.Con.

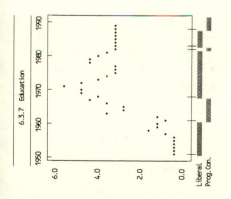

Given that the coding of party data was often done by different persons in different countries and that the categories of expenditure all have modest national idiosyncrasies, we do not adhere slavishly to a fixed set of pairings between specific program categories and corresponding spending indicators across all countries. We might have come closer to uniformity by aggregating categories on both sides of the equation, much as we have with left-right. However, as is confirmed by the relatively poor showing of the left-right pairing, our initial trial analyses indicated clearly that the more we aggregated, the more loss of correspondence we found.

For these reasons, we found the most effective tactic to be to select corresponding program and policy categories by a two-step process: first, selections based on face validity and, second, refinement of those selections by means of a bit of trial and error. Thus we try both *social services* and *social justice* categories as explanations for variation in the range of human services—welfare, health, and so on. Which one we finally report is determined then by which performs better in the statistical analyses. We do not apply a category like *technology and infrastructure* (which we do match to transportation policy) to human services to explain variation in health policy, no matter how high the correlations. Occasionally, a difficult decision had to be made. Thus, it is reasonable to assume that housing policy would be responsive to a party's commitment to *social justice* or *social services.* But it is also reasonable to include housing under a range of policies stimulated by a commitment to modernization of infrastructure, in which case the program category *technology and infrastructure* would be appropriate. This was the most divergent of options considered for any policy, and again, the decision was made on the basis of goodness of fit to the models. In the Canadian case, housing related very strongly to party emphases on *technology and infrastructure.*

On rare occasions, we go against the initial logic of face validity. There are some categories that, on their face, should relate directly to a comparably labeled policy, such as agriculture to agricultural policy or *education* (+) to education policy. The former correspondence is used in every country, but on a couple of occasions—including Canada—we find that *social justice* or, as here, *social services* (+) has far better fit to education policy than do apparent emphases in the party programs on education as such. There is a reason for this. In some political contexts, education is conceived as quite apart from other welfare-state policies. In fact, some have argued that in the United States it has served as a counter-welfare policy, exchanging equalizing of condition for equalizing of opportunity. In other settings, at least at the level of national government, however, education is conceived as part of the redistributive package of welfare-state measures knitting together the social safety net. Taking this potential difference into account reduces our concern about substituting *social services* (+) programmatic emphases for education as a way of forecasting education-policy priority in Canada.

Best-Fitting Models

As explained in Chapter 3 and illustrated at length in the British case (Chapter 4), we have a set of three statistical models corresponding to the variety of ways in which, theoretically, one might expect party emphases to link up with government action. A party's programmatic emphases may influence policy only when the party is in government, as expected from mandate theory, or they may find their way into policy by that party's influence on the overall agenda. Long-standing ideological commitments may be equally as important as specific, current election emphases. All these possibilities are taken into account by the set of equations in Chapters 3 and 4.

In each country chapter, except the illustrative one on Britain, we report only those findings likely to reveal enduring patterns (that is, the statistically significant regression coefficients), while noting clearly the contradictions and nonconforming cases. Here and in the balance of the chapter, our major point of reference will be Table 6.1, which reports the best-fitting models for Canada.

As in Britain, there are policy areas best-fitted to each of the three, increasingly complex, versions of the theory—the agenda, the mandate, and the ideology variations. Of the twelve possibilities (left-right plus eleven specific policy areas), nine are improved by including the dummy variable for party alternation in office—the ideology term. One—culture and arts—is not addressed by any of the equations. One—agriculture—seems best to fit the mandate (i.e., agenda plus governing effects), but as we shall discuss, it is fraught with contradictory elements.

Of the nine instances where the ideology version (agenda plus mandate plus ideology) yields the highest adjusted R^2, it is nonetheless the case that the mandate and ideology elements are built on a strong basis of cross-party consensus. The agenda element is more than half of the measured congruence in six of the nine instances.[2]

The general pattern is one of strong, theoretically consistent relationships. Even after taking into consideration the few nonconforming cases, to be discussed later, we can say that the party programs, in one combination or another, do have noteworthy power to forecast policy.

Foreign affairs is the only policy area examined in which no addition of either mandate or ideology elements improves the prediction of the basic agenda model. And here it is clearly the Progressive Conservative programs (b = .68) that are most consequential; there is a significant negative mandate regarding the New Democrats' priorities (–.42). That is, the best prediction of foreign affairs' share of outlays has been the Progressive Conservative programs, whether or not they are in office, supplemented by a negative prediction from the New Democrats. As we shall see, however, this rejection of the New Democrats' emphases in the area of foreign affairs does not form a pattern. The party does rather well, in spite of its

Table 6.1
Best-Fitting Models Between Party Program Emphases and Policy Priorities: Canada, 1950 – 1988*

Agenda Models

Policy Priority (Program)	a	Prog. Cons.	Liberal	New Dem.	Adj R^2
Foreign Affairs (Spec. For. Rel's)	1.76	.68		–.42	.32

[$E_i = a + bP_i^A + \ldots bP_i^n$]

Mandate Models

Policy Priority (Program Emphasis)	Constant a	Prog. Cons. (+)(–) Agenda or Mandate (Out)	Prog. Cons. Mandate (x Gov)	Liberal (+)(–) Agenda or Mandate (Out)	Liberal Mandate (x Gov)	New Dem. Agenda (Out)	Adj R^2	Added By Mandate
Agriculture (Agriculture)	2.05	.20	–.21	.27	–.26	.03	.57	.41

[$E_i = a + bP_i^A + b(P^A_i \times G) + \ldots bP_i^n + b(P_i^n \times G)$]

Continued ⟶

permanent outsider role, in several policy domains, pointing to the presence of contagion from the left.

Beyond the foreign affairs instance, all the other policy domains reaching R^2 .25 were fitted best by the most complex model, including the dummy variable for party alternation (ideology). The only exception is agriculture, which had contradictory coefficients, as discussed below. That is, eight policies have significantly different priorities, depending on whether the Progressive Conservatives or the Liberals control the government (and thus occupy the premiership). As we noted in Chapter 3, this term—the dummy variable that equals 1 for a Progressive Conservative government and 0 for a Liberal one—is the functional equivalent of the focus of most comparative policy research, concentrating on alternation in government over time. What our model adds is the congruence of party programs, as enhanced by accounting for their opposition versus government status.

Among the equations under "ideology models" in Table 6.1, *left-right* commands our attention. The Liberals have a bit of an agenda effect (.12). That is, the

Ideology Models

Policy Priority (Program Emphasis)	Constant a	Ideology Prog. Gov Cons. = 1	(+)(–) Agenda or Mandate Prog. (Out)	Mandate Cons. (x Gov)	(+)(–) Agenda or Mandate Liberal (Out)	Mandate Liberal (x Gov)	Agenda New Dem. (Out)	Adj R^2	Added By Mandate	Added By Ideology
Left–Right (Left–Right)	2.75	–.60			.12		–.08$^{\underline{n}}$	.68		.06
Health (Social Services)	7.40	–8.19	–.98$^{\underline{n}}$	.98			.26	.79	.12	.08
Housing (Tech.& Infrastr.)	–.56	2.70	–.03$^{\underline{n}}$	–.13	–.19$^{\underline{n}}$	.24	.07	.79	.04	.08
Defense (Spec. For. Rel's)	6.67	7.21	6.88	–14.34			2.63	.72	.05	.03
Education (Social Services)	3.39	–6.87	–.50$^{\underline{n}}$	.63	.32	$\underline{-.34}$	.18	.64	.09	.15
Admin. of Justice (Law & Order)	1.99	–.48			.26		**	.59	.11	.15
Transportation (Tech.& Infrastr.)	5.12	–2.20	–.59$^{\underline{n}}$	.36	–.15$^{\underline{n}}$	$\underline{-.20}$	–.89$^{\underline{n}}$	.46	.19	.05
Social Security (Social Services)	13.4	–10.4	–.62$^{\underline{n}}$	.98			.15	.40	.09	.15
Welfare (Social Services)	5.83	–12.7	–.60$^{\underline{n}}$	1.15				.35	.06	.19

$$[\quad E_i = a + bP_A + bP_i^A + b(P_i^A \times G) + \ldots bP_i^n + b(P_i^n \times G) \quad]$$

* Indicating only those b's (unstandardized regression coefficients) that attained .05 statistical significance. Coefficients in the opposite direction from theoretical expectation are underlined. Cases of negative mandate are indicated by $\underline{n}$.

** The New Democratic Party programs contained no references coded as law and order.

general left-right movement of overall policy priority is rather well tracked by the general left-right tilt of the Liberal programs, whether or not that party is in office. The somewhat far-out NDP is the victim of a negative mandate on left-right. But the most congruent element with the overall left-right shifts of policy has been the simple alternation of power between the Progressive Conservatives and the Liberals. Bearing in mind that the left-right policy indicator is a standardized score (that is, the mean = 0 and the standard deviation = 1), a *b* of .60 for the ideology term is pretty impressive. Canada is one of only three countries out of the ten studied here (along with Germany and the Netherlands) where the ideology term adds significantly to the prediction of general left-right variations in policy priority.

The ideology term is the most potent part of the equation in each of the eight specific policy areas listed under "Ideology Models" in Table 6.1. Two areas—housing and defense—experience significantly higher priorities under the Progressive Conservatives (2.70 and 7.21, respectively). Six are favored by the Liberals (health, education, administration of justice, transportation, social security, and welfare). This magnitude of interparty difference certainly does not comport with the image of party and government impotence conveyed by our introduction to the Canadian institutional and political context.

Examination of the policy congruence of party programs themselves, in addition to that of alternation in office, further erodes that pessimistic assessment. The two parties' columns under "agenda or mandate" portray a vigorously competitive set of circumstances in Canada, with the negative mandate being the dominant condition in eight of the eleven significant coefficients (left-right aside). Positive out-party agenda congruence seems evident in only defense (6.88) for the Progressive Conservatives as well as education and administration of justice for the Liberals (.32 and .26, respectively). The Liberals, especially, seem to reject the out-party's emphases in a systematic manner, as seen by the large number of negative coefficients under "Prog Cons (Out)" (the third column from the left in Table 6.1, under "Ideology Models"). The Progressive Conservatives' concerns for health, housing, education, transportation, social security, and welfare all suffer that common fate—a fate somewhat repaired in most instances when the Progressive Conservatives are able to enact policies positively congruent with their own emphases when in office (the fourth column from the left). Progressive Conservative governments are likewise eager to reject Liberal emphases in at least housing and transportation (–.19 and –.15, respectively), while accommodating them in education and administration of justice (.32 and .26 under "Liberal—Out").

The case of defense calls for some special attention. The agenda model alone, as seen in the Appendix Table A6.1, is quite congruent with defense priorities (R^2 .64), with the NDP gaining the highest coefficient—8.12, as compared to 4.52 for the Progressive Conservatives and 1.44 for the Liberals. Although the ideology model raises the R^2 by only an additional 8 percent (bringing it up to .72, Tables

6.1 and A6.3), entering the dummy variable for ideology noticeably redistributes the variance attributable to the party programs, with the NDP still being significantly congruent, but no longer the most so. What is intriguing is the seemingly contradictory nature of the defense congruence in the ideology model for the Progressive Conservative programs' opposition effect compared to the difference made by their being in government. Controlling for the standing differences attributable to alternation in office (7.21), the out-of-office coefficient is a positive 6.88, whereas the program times governance term is a negative 14.34. That means that the more the Progressive Conservative program emphasized special foreign relations when they were in opposition, the larger the percentage of outlays for defense. The relative "gain" from office is in fact an apparent "loss."

If this were an isolated instance, we would simply chalk it up as a one-country qualification on the theory. However, as we will see, a similar situation will be encountered in other countries—where the relevant programmatic emphasis of a party with respect to defense priority seems to be inverse, with positive signs out of government and negative signs for the relative congruence in office. There may be a substantive reason for this seeming anomaly that could render it theoretically consistent. For certain parties, it may be that reduction in defense expenditures is their conception of an increased concern for the quality of the international atmosphere. Thus, concern for international affairs may mean for some parties—as it seems to mean for the Canadian Progressive Conservatives—a reduction in defense's share of outlays. Recall that increased emphases on special foreign relations is positively congruent with increased priority for foreign affairs outlays. That this need not be a universal phenomenon, however, will be apparent in other countries (such as the United States) where foreign affairs and defense priorities themselves are positively correlated and where there is evidence of a policy of "peace through strength," manifested in positive coefficients for the congruence of programmatic emphases and defense expenditures. More on that later, as the instances demand.

These complexities aside, the strength of the basic agenda model (Table A6.1) and the inverse correlation between defense and foreign affairs suggest that external policy is not a single party's preserve. All three parties independently contribute to what has been a somewhat nonpartisan, but well-forecast, defense policy—the largest consumer of federal funds over the years. Recently, however, it has been well below several other priorities. The NDP does well in seeing its program translated into defense priorities (in any of the three models). It is quite conceivable that national defense lies rather outside the fields of constitutional controversy so widespread in Canada, leaving the one truly alternative party free to contribute to the policy tone. That tone has been to reduce defense relatively much more rapidly from a rather lower cold war base than is the case in some other countries, such as Australia and the United States. Clearly, Canada has carried its NATO burden, but it is also clear that it has not hesitated to reduce that burden. It has done so in a manner forecast rather well by the NDP programs in the give and take of three-party discourse.

Turning our attention specifically to the agenda role of the New Democrats, we find some support for Pétry's (1988) thesis of "contagion from the left." Since the NDP has never been in a national government, it lacks the potential for a positive mandate and can have only an agenda effect or a negative mandate—in the latter case seeing policy priorities consistently going the direction opposite from the NDP's programmatic emphases. The NDP never mentions *law and order* in its programs, so we do not test it for administration-of-justice policy. Of the remaining domains, only with left-right, transportation, and foreign affairs is there evidence of a negative mandate exercised to the disadvantage of the New Democrats. We should keep in mind that the NDP, as noted earlier, is the true "left" party in Canada, with the Liberals and the Progressive Conservatives being uncommonly close to each other—uncommon, that is, for major parties that alternate in office (see Figure 6.1). In fact, this seemingly outlier position for the NDP has not been without its rewards, allowing for its programs to be significantly reflected in over half of the specific policy areas. The NDP programs, in competition with those of the major parties in and out of government, get significant positive *b*s in agriculture, health, housing, defense, education, and social security.

Keeping agriculture aside, in defense (with the sign reversal discussed earlier), health, housing, education, transportation, social security, and welfare, at least one of the parties receives a significant *negative* coefficient for having been out of power, contrasted to a significant *positive* one for having been in. When this juxtaposition is coupled with the consequentiality of the alternation in power between major parties, Canadian politics can be seen as a high-stakes game. The winners win rather impressively, and the losers lose equally impressively. The party in government accommodates policy as much to what the voters voted against as to what the voters voted for. This reward and punishment syndrome most negatively affects the Progressive Conservatives, with the pairing of negative out-party and positive in-party coefficients occurring for that party much more than for the Liberals. The Liberals more often than the Progressive Conservatives fail to exploit their place in government to bring to fruition the forecasts of their own programs. But the Liberals are very much committed to systematically foiling the forecasts of the losing Conservatives.

Standing ideological differences show up clearly in the mainstays of the modern welfare state: health, education, social security (pensions), and welfare (income maintenance). In each case, Conservative governments reduce and Liberal governments increase priority for these policies by 8.2, 6.9, 10.4, and 12.7 percent, respectively. In sheer magnitude, these far surpass the independent predictive capacity of programmatic emphases in these three domains.[3]

The absence of theoretically consistent best-fitting entries under the mandate model is not, as we might have at first assumed, due entirely to the Canadian parties' being mutually accommodative through agenda effects. What would have otherwise shown up as mandates have appeared under the ideology model, not because of positive relationships to out-party programs, but because of significant negative mandates between policy priority and programs of the out-parties. That is the clear message of the minus signs before the *b*s under "out" of government terms in Table 6.1.

Nonconformists and Contradictions

The overall message of Table 6.1 is that the linkages of party programs to policy in Canada are generally pretty tight—certainly tighter than expected, given Canada's special problems and parliamentary complexities. Using the best-fitting models as the base for calculation, Britain's average R^2 was .50, Australia's was under .40, whereas Canada's is .57—rather higher than the other two, somewhat more pure, Westminster-style parliamentary systems. So if Canada is burdened and distracted by identity neuroses, that is not initially evident from our view of the policy system. Closer inspection, however, reveals a few conditions that, although not essentially changing that overall assessment, must be considered as qualifications.

In each country study, we inspect the detailed tables (Appendix Tables) for contradictory relationships, that is, policies for which the party program emphases actually correlate in a direction opposite to our theoretical expectations. Normally, we expect a positive correlation, as, for example, between program emphases on arts, sport, and media on the one hand and policy priorities for culture and the arts on the other. If the data showed that the more a governing party emphasized the former, the lower the percentage of outlays for the latter, that would clearly contradict our theory. It would also mean that something important but not accounted for by our theory is going on in that particular country and/or policy. We shall be attentive to these cases in Chapter 14 precisely to see if there is a pattern, suggesting that our theory has a systematic cross-country rather than a random country-specific weakness.

Likewise, if a policy finds none of the models fits at an acceptable level, which we have arbitrarily set at R^2 .25, then, while not contradictory, it is no feather in our theoretical cap either. That, in fact, is the case with cultural and arts policy in Canada. It is a small but visible and modestly rising domain of policy, averaging around two-thirds of one percentage of federal outlays. As the arts community would probably prefer it, cultural policy lies outside the realm of partisan discourse, as far as we can tell from our analyses.

On the basis of the left-right score and its trends, we could characterize the Liberals as having an identity problem (Figure 6.1). There is only an agenda effect (.12) and no evidence of a significant mandate for the Liberals. In Downsian terms, it is no doubt a problem with which the party has been able to live comfortably, given that the Liberals formed the government for nearly two-thirds of the time between World War II and the late 1980s. But the Liberals may have traded policy, here and there, for power. There are three policy domains where the Liberals' performance as a result of being in government is the reverse of expectations based on their own election programs: agriculture, education, and transportation. In the cases of education and transportation, however, with the exception of the "Liberal × Government" anomaly, the equations are strong and theoretically consistent.

Agriculture, however, remains a puzzle. Note that the best-fitting model (Table 6.1) includes, in addition to a modest positive agenda contribution from all three parties, contradictory *b*s for the Conservatives and for the Liberals in government. For both major parties, their out coefficients show an agenda effect, which can be statistically independent of the fact that the coefficients for being in government are reversed. Fifty-seven percent of the variance in agriculture priority is explained by the party programs' emphasis on agriculture—a tidy correspondence, on its face. The relative distinction of having been in and out of government is important—but in the *opposite* direction from the trend in the governing parties' programs!

Agriculture matters in Canada. It is more than a romantic relic, reminiscent of sentimental films about the tragic loss of the family farm. It is more than a chauvinist symbol for an outmoded conception of national self-sufficiency, such as found in Europe. Agriculture in Canada is real—the largest source of export earnings. Nevertheless, although the year-to-year pattern of policy is uncommonly irregular (Figure 6.3.11), the overall trend has been, as in other countries, a reduction in priority for agricultural policy. But the parties have not dealt with it candidly. All three parties have a long-term, irregular trend downward in the space they devote to agriculture in their programs. Likewise, as is clear from Figure 6.3.11, agriculture's policy priority has declined, also irregularly. But these irregularities of trend in programs and in policy have not coincided. They have, in fact, diverged.

Our suspicion is that the restive nature of the western provinces has caused the parties to bow to agriculture symbolically in their programs, but to decouple that from actual policy commitment. The course of modern agriculture toward ever-increasing efficiency is inexorable, as is the decline in heavy governmental support. Food will get cheaper, in spite of short-term government efforts to the contrary. Support from government has declined relative to other policy domains in all countries. But since agriculture is as crucial as it is in Canada, where it is concentrated in far-off western provinces where voters are angered about obeisance to the French in Quebec, there is a likelihood that lip service will be paid to agriculture by the national parties.

The few instances of misfits and nonconformity are interesting. They should not, however, detract from the overall message, the message conveyed by the bulk of our findings, which is quite supportive of our theory's predictions.

CONCLUSION

The general picture of Canadian politics that we sketched earlier, taking account of the essentially unstable constitutional and cultural conditions, suggested alternative results: Either (1) program-to-policy relationships would be essentially absent, because of the distractions from problems of political identity, both internally and externally; or (2) problems of internal and external identity would lead to a politics of accommodation, whereby party programs would serve more as contributions to a common agenda and less as contentious poles around which combative partisans might rally.

In fact, neither description of the program-to-policy relationships in Canada is accurate. To be sure, as in all the countries we study, there is a strong base of interparty agreement in the directions taken by the policy agenda. Canada is also notably attuned to the mandate. The Progressive Conservatives can generally be relied upon in government to follow the forecast of their program. The Liberals, although not adhering especially closely to predictions based on their programs, can be relied upon to enact policies that disappoint the Conservatives. Canadian voters should pay attention to the Conservative programs. If they signal what the voters want, then the voters should vote Conservative. If they signal what the voters do not want, then the voters should vote Liberal. In either case, the Conservative program is the best guide. The Liberals' long-standing ideological positions are a better guide to policy than are their current programmatic concerns.

Despite their similarity along the broad left-right dimension (Figure 6.1), the Conservatives and the Liberals fight a political battle in Canada that is well forecast by the differences in their programs and by standing ideological differences. Progressive Conservative programs win when that party is in office. With the exception of the few cases of an agenda effect, either alone or in combination with the mandate and the nonevent of culture policy, the out-party that most often sees a positive reflection of its program foci in the policy priorities of governments is the NDP. It is the main beneficiary of a pure agenda influence. The New Democrats do indeed infect some policies of the welfare state with a "contagion from the left." Clearly, the NDP is the conscience of Canada's welfare state.

NOTES

1. French Canadian nationalism is associated with the Bloc Quebecois; western conservatism has reemerged in the Reform Party. Third parties have been fairly successful in forming governments at the provincial level, but they have remained unaligned with the national establishment parties.

2. There is no simple way to display all of the relevant statistical information contained in our analyses. The adjusted R^2 is a convenient summary term, but it is burdened with occasional contradictory signs. As these are uncommon and we give them special attention in

the text, one can nevertheless, with appropriate care, use the R^2 as a crude metric of congruence. Further. it can be used—likewise with care—to set forth the best-fitting models.

But the reader is reminded that the progression from agenda to mandate to ideology is additive. Thus, although the R^2 for a policy domain may be higher under the ideology or mandate heading, it is still often the case that the agenda element would yield quite impressive results alone—ignoring the effect of governance, either in the programs or as a function of simple alternation in office. Thus, in the case of Canadian housing policy priorities, Table 6.1 shows an R^2 of .79 for the ideology model. But the agenda element alone yields a .61, with only .04 and .08 being added by mandate and ideology respectively. That the ideology element, as indicated by alternation between the Liberals and the Progressive Conservatives, is important, however, is indicated by the *b* of 2.70 for that dummy variable—far and away the largest element in the equation. Thus, if we ignore simple alternation in power, we could argue that the party programs do a fair job of anticipating housing policy. However, if we keep in mind that voters can give an electoral mandate by acting on a combination of both the known traditional policy tilt of a party and its contemporary programmatic emphases, then it is important to sort out those influences, as the more complex model does.

3. The seeming contradictory coefficient for the Liberals in education, Equation 4.3 is a bit misleading, due to multicollinearity with the dummy variable for party alternation. Without that term for party ideology, both Liberal terms are significant and in the predicted direction (Appendix Table A6.2).

7

France

INSTITUTIONAL AND POLITICAL CONTEXT

The institutional and political circumstances in France and the United States stand apart from those of the three countries we have examined so far in this book. Despite Canada's particular political and cultural circumstances, its system is clearly recognizable as parliamentary, with only slight variations on the classic Westminster model. It has alternating single-party governments based on legislative majorities or, at least, pluralities. As we have pointed out, the theory underlying such a system is that it should provide very favorable institutional conditions for the enactment of party mandates. There are no political barriers to the government of the day implementing its policy priorities, unless, as often happens in Canada, it is in a minority position.

France and the United States, however, separate some constitutional powers between the executive and the legislature. This may raise obstacles to the execution of a programmatic mandate. Certainly such a possibility is a foundation stone for the most commonly voiced criticisms of the U.S. system. The separation of powers was deliberately designed to obstruct swift, decisive policymaking, lest such action, in the words of the *Federalist,* lead to a "tyranny of the majority."

The French Fifth Republic, however, is designed not so much to induce caution as to minimize the historically obstructive role of the parliament. The constitution seeks to enable the president to lead policy, above the fray, as it were. Charles de Gaulle's 1958 constitution was crafted to accord with his concept of presidential government, with but a modest bow to party involvement.

Neither the French nor the American constitution, in any event, was crafted with an eye toward parties' serving as central instruments of interest mediation and governmental accountability through an integrated policy process. For a start, there may be some confusion if, as is commonly the case in the United States, the party that controls the presidency is different from the one that controls the parliament ("Congress" in the United States; "National Assembly" in France). One could argue that the executive and the legislature receive, in effect, separate mandates, with no guarantee of mutual compatibility. One may be able to block the other politically in such a way that policy enactment becomes much more difficult than in seemingly more coherent parliamentary systems.

For these reasons we have placed presidential systems—and the chapters discussing them—between Westminster-style polities and the continental European coalition systems. Presidential systems endow the chief executive with sufficient autonomy that the tenure of the incumbent is not jeopardized by the partisan composition of the legislature. This distinguishes the president from his or her counterparts in coalition systems, where the effective executive (ignoring the symbolic role of monarchs and figurehead presidents) is always subject to loss of office through abandonment by a coalition partner.

The problems of accountability seem to be more severe in the United States than in France. Rather than a true separation of powers, the French have sought *concentration* of policymaking power in the hands of the president. The president of France in fact could reasonably claim to be the most powerful elected politician in the world. As (de facto) in the United States, he is directly elected by the people. He nominates his own "cabinet of ministers" and the prime minister. The president has considerable reserve powers in foreign policy and security matters. He is elected for a fixed term of seven years, with no limit on running again (the National Assembly is elected for only five years). The president can dissolve parliament and call for legislative elections. He can also initiate popular referenda on matters where he wants to go over the heads of the legislators. In theory, there are some constitutional restrictions on the president's power, but in practice these have been manipulated so as to make the president preeminent.

Parliament may be dominated by a partisan majority opposed to the president. This happened between 1986 and 1988, when parliamentary elections returned a Gaullist-Center majority during the first term of Socialist President François Mitterrand, leading to the first period of "cohabitation." In this period, the president used his powers of initiative to undermine the cabinet, appointed by the antipresidential majority in the National Assembly, in favor of his own Socialist Party.

The president's close connection with a particular party—first the Gaullists up to 1974, then the Center-Right under President Valéry Giscard d'Estaing, from 1974 to 1981, then the Socialists under Mitterrand—has served to consolidate the authority of the presidency. During the period under study, with the exception of 1986–1988, the parliamentary majority or plurality was the same as the one holding the presidency and very much disposed to accept initiatives from the sitting president.

The constitutional effort to concentrate power in the presidency has its roots in French history. French society was riven by social and political divisions that have been reflected in fragmented, unstable multiparty coalitions during the Third and Fourth Republics (1870–1940, and 1946–1958, respectively). The Fourth Republic ultimately foundered on the twin problems of cold war politics and overseas decolonization. Severing ties from the colonies, first in Indochina and then in Algeria, proved militarily and politically humiliating.

General Charles de Gaulle, national hero and chief executive for a brief period immediately after World War II, took over with emergency powers in 1958. His supporters produced a constitution that represented a thoroughgoing change in institutional authority. The weak but sovereign parliament of the Fourth Republic was replaced by a strong presidency. The office gained prestige with de Gaulle's successful pullout from Algeria, the development of a strong, nationalistic foreign policy, which emphasized independence from the United States, and the belated industrialization of the late 1950s and 1960s, which gave the country unprecedented prosperity.

The Gaullist party, founded to support President de Gaulle in the National Assembly, survived his death in 1969. The mechanics of the electoral system under the Fifth Republic and the emergence of the presidency as the great political prize put a premium on parties' consolidating themselves into cohesive electoral blocs. As a result, many of the smaller parties, whose existence had contributed to the instability of governments under the preceding parliamentary regime, disappeared.

The politics of the Fifth Republic for many years was dominated by the Gaullist party, a strongly nationalist party of the Right whose characteristic policy stance is for an independent French position in foreign affairs and defense. Associated with it is the more liberal Union for French Democracy (UDF), with an orthodox economic and fiscal policy.

Opposed to the two allied parties of the Right is the Socialist Party, which from 1965 through 1985 grew in strength to displace the Communists as the largest party of the Left. The French Communist Party has been one of the two (along with its Italian counterpart) largest and strongest Communist parties in Western Europe. With the easing of East-West tension, however, the French Communist Party dropped electorally from 20 to 10 percent over the 1980s (Banks 1992, 232).

In some ways it is more appropriate in the French political setting to talk of "Right" and "Left" than of individual parties. This is because the parties themselves are growing and changing entities, with relatively short histories in their present incarnation. The Gaullists, in fact, have formed different groupings, under different names, to contest different elections, though they were rather more stable, both in composition and name (Rally for the Republic—RPR—since 1976), over the 1980s. The UDF came together out of several smaller cooperating groups in 1978. Even the Socialist Party, whose name goes back to the nineteenth century, was reconstituted under Mitterrand in 1971. The Communists have been by far the most stable grouping organizationally and ideologically, but they have suffered severe erosion since the 1970s.

French politics also have a record of *flash* parties representing petit bourgeois and working-class groups that often feel threatened by the pace and form of socioeconomic change. An example from the late 1980s and early 1990s is the anti-immigrant, hypernationalist National Front, led by Jean-Marie Le Pen. It has collected over 10 percent of the votes in several elections, both local and national.

One reason for party instability in France is the process of consolidation that has gone on under the Fifth Republic. This has been more or less imposed by the logic of the presidential election system. It is a two-ballot system, which also operates for parliamentary elections. In the first ballot, any party can field a candidate. A candidate is elected if an absolute majority is obtained (provided that the absolute majority represents the support of more than 25 percent of registered voters). Otherwise, there is a second ballot two weeks later (one week later for parliamentary elections) in which a majority of those voting is sufficient. In the runoff, which is normally between the two leading candidates from the first round, there is a clear premium on creating "coalitions" of parties of similar ideological *tendances* (tendencies). This brings together Gaullists and UDF, on the one hand, and Socialists and Communists on the other—the Right against the Left. Although relative party strengths decide which candidates represent an ideological tendency, in the second presidential ballot, it is loyalty to the overall *tendance* that determines the final result.

This electoral system has been in effect for all presidential and most of the parliamentary elections of the Fifth Republic. In 1985, the Socialist-led government introduced a system of proportional representation, which was valid for the March 1986 legislative election. However, later in 1986, the incoming government of the Right reintroduced the majority system. And the latter was again the rule for the 1988 election.

France thus experiences a direct confrontation between ideologically based Right and Left, making France unique among the democracies we analyze in this book. But it does so in a setting that may bode ill for the capacity of parties to serve as agents of democratic accountability, both for identifying and packaging issues and for seeing those issues through to legislation. In the tradition of the Fifth Republic's founding father, the president is endowed with sufficient autonomy to be *above politics.* This could mean that the president is also above the programs of his party. And the electoral system encourages organizational and programmatic fluidity among and within the parties. This could mean that the message gets blurred. It remains to be seen if these factors weaken the party program-to-policy linkages or not.

PROGRAM AND POLICY TRENDS

French Data

Problems with the French data are caused by problems of French history. Our analysis is confined to the Fifth Republic, which means that compared to the other nine countries, for France we have an average of about ten years less experience from which to draw. Furthermore, the pattern of government change has been such as to introduce potential distortions in the analysis. At the time of this research, no French party had been voted out of the presidency and then back in. The Gaullists occupied the office, first under de Gaulle and then under Georges Pompidou, from 1958 through 1974. The UDF (which we shall also refer to as the "Center") presidency of Giscard d'Estaing lasted from 1974 until Giscard was replaced by Socialist President Mitterrand in 1981. And most of our analyses run two years into the second Mitterrand term, conditioned upon the recency of expenditure data, which have to be led two years. Thus 1989 policy indicators are related to the 1987 entries in the program data.

The distribution of party control of the presidency—Gaullist, Center, and then Socialist, with no alternation—means that there is a severe skew in all our measures of government control. Yet, for the reasons spelled out in detail in Chapter 3, we still choose not to de-trend the data. That would make no difference in our ability to analyze the program-to-policy congruence over time. Rather, we shall, where relevant, alert the reader to the potential problem and to the implications it may have for the results of our analysis.

One consequence of the skewed distribution of party control of the presidency over time, however, can be anticipated. In the various models, we will be unable to include simultaneously the term for standing ideology (here a dummy variable where 1 = Gaullist president, 0 = non-Gaullist) from the interactive term (party in presidency multiplied by program emphases, that is, measuring the difference between *agenda* and *agenda* plus *mandate*). Given the far greater precision of the latter, we have used it. Therefore, we report no instances of standing party differences (the ideology model).

The programs used to establish party positions are those issued for parliamentary rather than presidential election campaigns. This might seem odd, given our emphasis on the power of the president as opposed to that of the National Assembly and the fact that our subsequent analyses credit a party with being in office if its candidate is president, regardless of the party composition of the National Assembly or the cabinet. It is, however, in the context of elections to the National Assembly that parties issue their collectively agreed-upon document and often the most politically important document (the Common Program of the Left in 1973 is the most clear example). Given the personal nature of campaigns for the presidency, with candidates often seeking to distance themselves somewhat from their party, especially for the second ballot, it is difficult to pick out a party program as such. Particularly in the 1970s, presidential candidates wrote books rather than issued programs (Pétry 1987, 331).

Hence, in these analyses we use the party programs issued in National Assembly elections and clearly endorsed by the party organs collectively. This means that the scores for each program tend to come in groups of five, five years being the usual life of an assembly unless some special event intervenes. However, presidential elections are usually followed by assembly elections (so that the president can get a comfortable majority or plurality in the assembly); thus in some cases assemblies are shorter and programmatic emphases are recorded for only one to three years.

The distribution of emphases within the party programs was such in France that it made sense in two cases to build special indices. In the foreign policy and defense domain, the programs had a distribution of entries that was quite unusual. In most countries, there is a concentration of entries in one or two of the categories, special foreign relations (+) or peace or internationalism (+). In this subject area, the original coding frame included several negative possibilities, for example, special foreign relations (–), internationalism (–), as may be seen in Appendix A. It is unusual for any of these negative cells to have any entries. In France, however, the spread across the whole set of foreign policy possibilities was quite broad, but different between the parties and over time. Thus we have created a factor score that distinguishes between an internationalist orientation toward external cooperation and involvement and a more nationalist, isolationist stance.[1] We labeled the score for this measure of program emphases "Internationalism/Nationalism." This score was used as the indicator of programmatic emphases, which we then paired with expenditure priorities for defense and for foreign affairs.

One additional program merger seems to have been effective in the French case. In the coding scheme, there are two (conceptually and organizationally) adjacent categories for concern about public order—law and order and national effort/social harmony. The coding instruction are, respectively:

- Law and Order: Enforcement of all laws; actions against organized crime; putting down urban violence; support and resources for police; and tougher attitudes in courts.
- National Effort/Social Harmony: Appeal for national effort and solidarity; need for nation to see itself as united; appeal for public spiritedness; decrying antisocial attitudes in a time of crisis; support for public interest; national interest; and bipartisanship.

To construct an index of public order, which can be paired with administration of justice policy, we simply summed the entries for the two categories. This seemed to eliminate some gaps and apparent minor idiosyncrasies in the coding of each category, with results that proved to be relatively interesting (Table 7.1, later in chapter).

Policy indicators are relatively straightforward. In the French yearbook, *Annuaire Statistique de la France,* expenditures by major categories are reported in sufficiently uniform fashion that we could confidently construct time series for nine policy domains, summing to an average of over 90 percent of central governmental outlays. One should also bear in mind that France is one of the most centralized systems among modern democracies. Thus with these policy data, unlike those from federal systems such as Australia or Canada—or even Britain, where there are major functions, such as education, that are devolved to local authorities—in the French case, we have a grip on the bulk of public activity. The paired categories used in the analysis are as follows:

Party Program	*Policy Area*
Internationalism/Nationalism	Defense
Internationalism/Nationalism	Foreign Affairs
Public Order*	Administration of Justice
Agriculture	Agriculture
Social Justice	Welfare
Social Justice	Education
Technology and Infrastructure	Housing
Technology and Infrastructure	Transportation & Communications
Art, Sport, Leisure	Culture

* Additive score of "Law and Social Order" + "National Effort/Harmony."

Left-Right Trends

Left-right positions are measured as in other countries by subtracting party emphases on such traditional right-wing topics as defense, law and order, freedom and initiative, from traditional left-wing emphases on welfare, peace, government intervention, and so forth. Figure 7.1 shows French party scores on this measure from the beginning of the Fifth Republic.

The actual pattern of left-right movement in Figure 7.1 is what we would expect. The Communists generally define the left (upper) edge of the spectrum and the Gaullists define the right. The Communists are not, however, so distinct as one might expect, overlapping with the Socialists on several occasions, and issuing the Common Program in 1973. On the right, the Gaullists and Center (UDF) maintain more distinction through the 1970s. But they come completely together in the Common Program of 1981. (No program data are available for the Center after the 1981 program, which we treat as in force through 1985.)

The uncommon issuance of the Common Program by the Communists and Socialists in 1973 was due in part to the need for the left parties in opposition to present a unified front and to bolster their credibility as a political alternative to the incumbent Center-Gaullist collaboration. That 1973 Common Program was a major turning point for the French Left, which is reflected in the relative coincidence of their programs for the next few elections. Many observers maintain that the Common Program was critical in paving the way for the ultimate Socialist victory in 1981.

The Gaullists and UDF adopted their Common Program in 1981 to combat the increased threat from the Left. However, taking the time period as a whole, one sees more ideological similarity between the two leftist parties than between

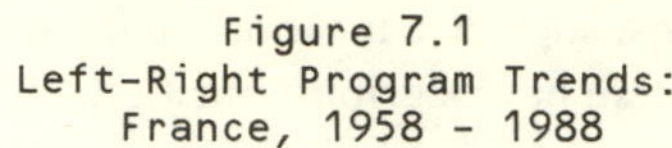
Figure 7.1
Left-Right Program Trends:
France, 1958 - 1988

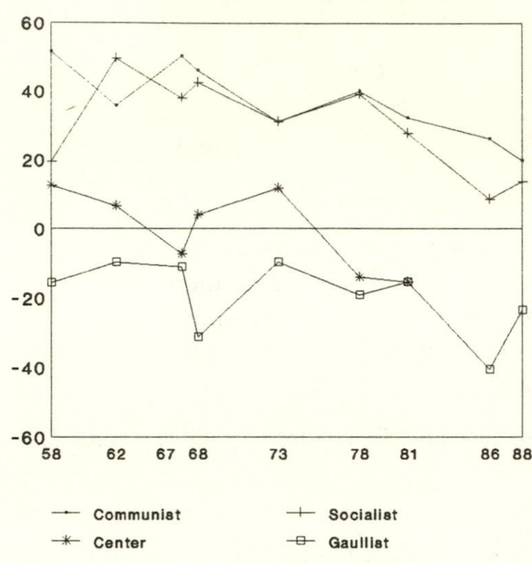

Joint Programs:
Communists-Socialists, 1973
Gaullists-Center, 1981

the center-right ones, even outside the common programs. It is noticeable also that the Socialists and the Center UDF never leapfrog or overlap each other. Left and right *tendances* are clearly distinguished in terms of ideological trends.

These trends are overlaid, however, by a general rightward shift of all the parties over time, which is visible in Figure 7.1. This broad shift coexists with many short-term changes of position, particularly but not exclusively in the case of Gaullists and Socialists. The Communists, ideologically as well as organizationally, remain the most consistent of the parties.

How do these programmatic emphases compare with general patterns of policy over these years? If parties do affect government policy either by enacting a mandate or by affecting the political agenda, we might expect there to be a visible correspondence. Moreover, we should anticipate policy priorities in France to be clearly structured along a left-right dimension, given the very focused confrontation between these two *tendances* in the second ballot of the presidential elections.

As we have done elsewhere, we can identify and contrast left-wing areas of policy (welfare, education, and social services generally) to right-wing favorites (such as agriculture and defense). To give more precision to this distinction, we followed our customary practice of factor analyzing expenditure items from each end of the policy spectrum. The loadings from which the factor scores were computed are indicated, along with the factor score trend, in Figure 7.2. The unusu-

Figure 7.2
Left–Right Expenditure Priority Factor Scores:
France, 1958 – 1987

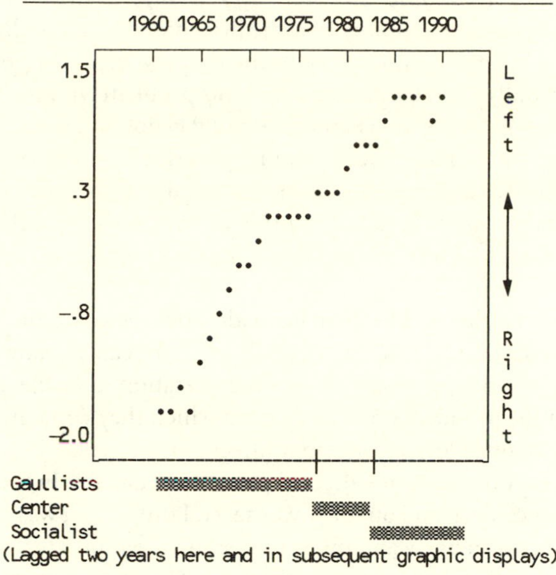

Structure of Policy Priority Factor

Policy Area	Factor Loading
Welfare	.97
Culture	.90
Education	.59
Agriculture	–.46
Defense	–.86

ally strong French priority for culture and the arts (averaging 3.3 percent of central governmental outlays) loads at .90, along with welfare at .97 and education at .59. These contrast clearly with agriculture (–.46) and defense (–.86).

Although the time period is shorter than in other countries, the same general trend is evident, but without the flattening or rightward tilt in the mid-1970s found elsewhere. The leveling that does take place can be attributed clearly to the brakes applied on expanding social services early in Mitterrand's first term. Overall, the importance of social services—education, welfare, and so on—increases steadily relative to that of defense and agriculture, up to 1983. Afterward there is no decline, but there is a clear cessation of leftward growth. On the basis of the pattern in other countries, one should expect this trend to endure for some years.

At first view, Figures 7.1 and 7.2 seem to say that party priorities have little to do with government actions, at least at this level of general aggregation. That is certainly true for the undifferentiated party positions shown in Figure 7.1, though it leaves open the possibility that the priorities of the Gaullists in the early years may have sustained policies more to the right, whereas the Socialists veered leftward more rapidly later. Earlier we noted this problem with the time distribution of party control. On the one hand, one could claim on the basis of Figure 7.2 that policies were to the right under Gaullist presidents, in the middle under the Center, and to the left under the Socialists. Unfortunately for such a simple interpretation, we have seen the results from other countries with different distributions of partisan control, and we thus know that the French curve is far from peculiar.

Some headway on this problem will be made when we go beyond graphic presentation and undertake the statistical analyses. One can already see, however, from the raising of this possibility of misinterpretation, that the alternations in party control of the presidency and the way in which they come in sequence and thus coincide with one block of time may affect our inferences in the French case in a way the alternations have not affected preceding analyses. In the Anglo-Saxon countries, parties came in and out of power several times, so it was possible to distinguish better between party and other unmeasured temporal effects.

The French situation, however, is real-world. This is the way it happened, so we have to cope with it. We should be aware in making inferences that some such effects may complicate the analyses. As we shall later see, however, most of the problems remain potential rather than real. The apparent smoothness of the line in Figure 7.2, in fact, conceals quite a lot of variation, not only from time to time, but in specific areas of policy as well.

Specific Policy Trends

The apparent absence of correspondence between broad left-right party emphases and general left-right policy trends leaves open the possibility that there is congruence between specific policy areas. Accordingly, we will, as in other countries, concentrate our analyses on those fine-tuned correspondences. As a prelude to those analyses, we will profit from an examination of specific policy trends, as shown in the plots of Figure 7.3. Defense and foreign affairs are quite closely linked, as seen in 7.3.1 and 7.3.2. ($r = .81$)—not enough to justify merging the indicators as we did in Britain, but clearly different from the negative relationship between comparable policies in Australia. As elsewhere, defense's share of outlays has dropped, but a bit more erratically in France than in most other countries. In France, unlike the other countries, it did not level out in the 1970s and then bounce back a bit later. Rather, the decline was reversed in the mid-1960s and then began again in the 1970s. Foreign policy (heavily influenced by other overseas development assistance programs), although correlating highly with defense, is a bit more idiosyncratic in the way it varies over time.

Administration of justice—principally police, courts, and prisons—follows the general upward pattern found elsewhere, as does welfare (which here includes pensions and other income maintenance policies), education, and culture. The latter includes such activities as promotion of the French language and France's achievements in literature and the arts generally, overseas as well as at home. This has been a central concern of all French governments of whatever political complexion.

Spending shares for transportation and infrastructure peak later in France than elsewhere (7.3.9) but show the now familiar growth and decline pattern as a one-time capital investment was made to cope with modern communications needs. Housing steadily declines in priority under the Fifth Republic (7.3.6). It is clearly decoupled from other welfare-state programs in ways for which we have no obvious explanation. This is a pattern found also in some of the other countries, perhaps reflecting early concentration on capital construction, followed by less-expensive management and maintenance.

Education priorities (7.3.7) also follow the pattern we have seen elsewhere and will meet again in other countries—first steeply upward and eventually downward. Our concern here is not the social origins either of programmatic commitments of the parties or of the priorities of governments—but rather the congruence between them. In the case of education, as we have mentioned in other chapters, the driving force is, no doubt, the relative size of the school-age population. But different parties in different countries respond differentially to whatever it is that stimulates them to emphasize a particular domain, such as education. Thus the implicit socioeconomic roots in the process of agenda specification may remain highly interesting, without in any way diminishing the relevance to democratic theory of the party program-to-policy priority linkage examined here (Appendix B).

PARTY PROGRAM-TO-POLICY CONGRUENCE

To get beyond the general trends and to make the link with party, we follow the same conventions used in the preceding three chapters. Thus we record for each year the party program's emphases presented in the preceding National Assembly election. We regard these as continuing to guide policymaking over the whole of the period to the next parliamentary election campaign. We relate these to policy two years later in order to allow for the budgetary process and the actual outlay of funds. And as usual, we have to experiment somewhat in relating the programmatic emphases to expenditure areas, as in the cases of the nationalism-internationalism index and the summed score for public order.

Figure 7.3
Trends in Expenditure Priorities: France, 1958 – 1987

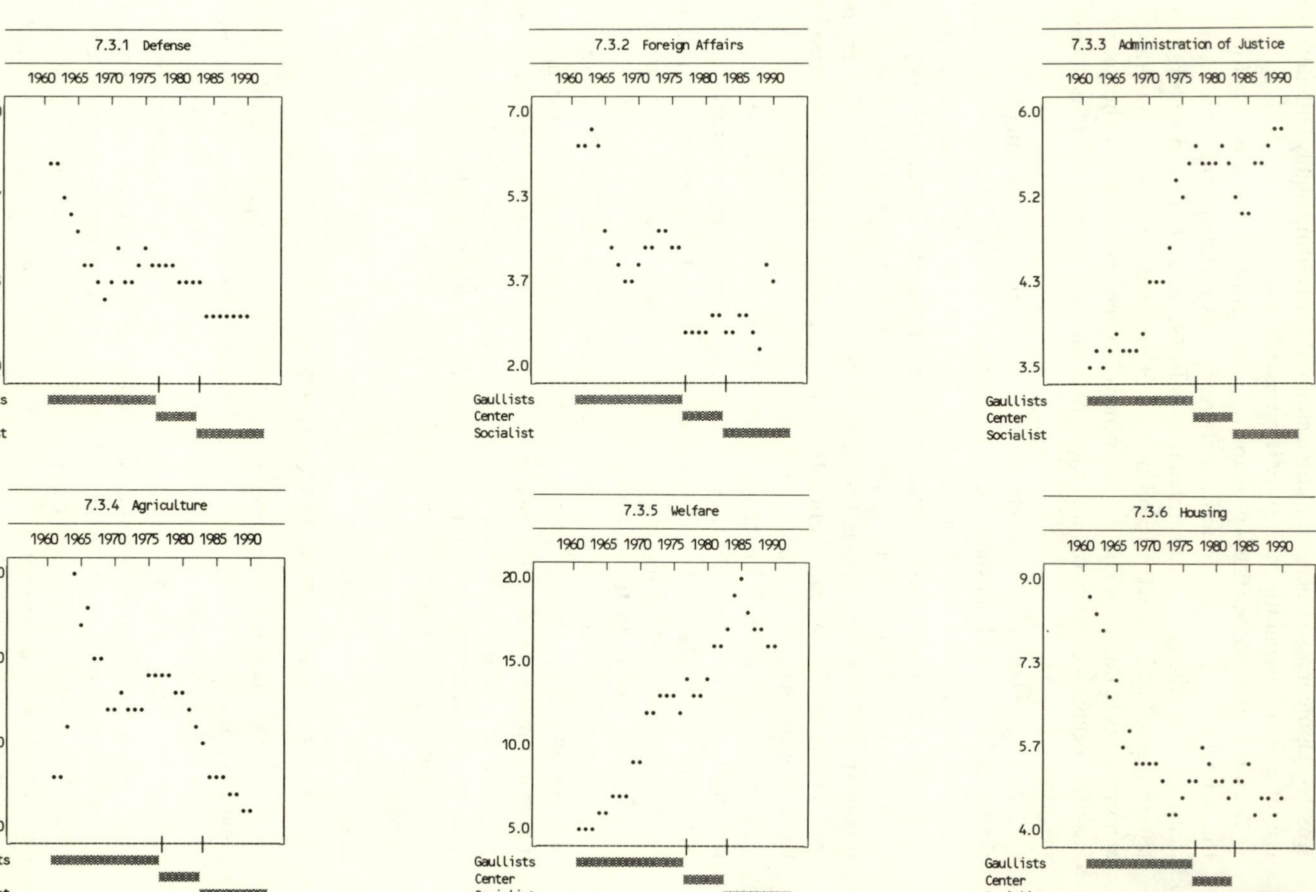

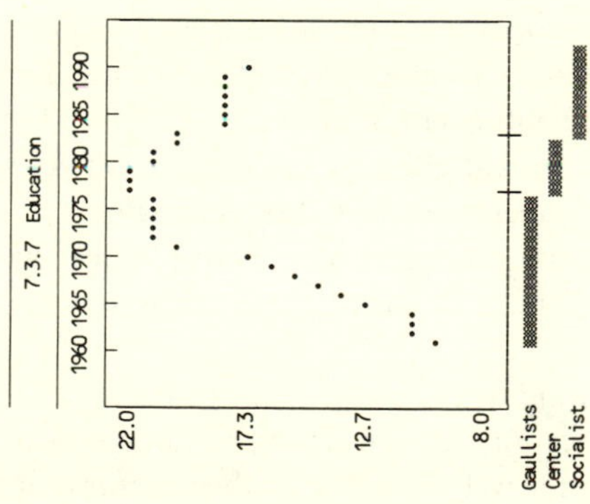
7.3.7 Education
1960 1965 1970 1975 1980 1985 1990
22.0
17.3
12.7
8.0
Gaullists
Center
Socialist

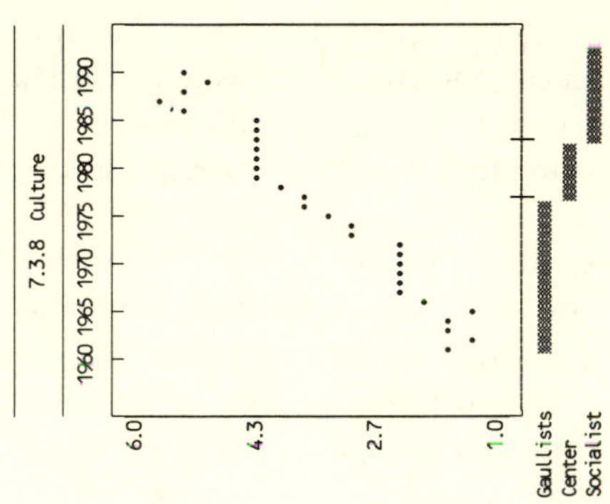
7.3.8 Culture
1960 1965 1970 1975 1980 1985 1990
6.0
4.3
2.7
1.0
Gaullists
Center
Socialist

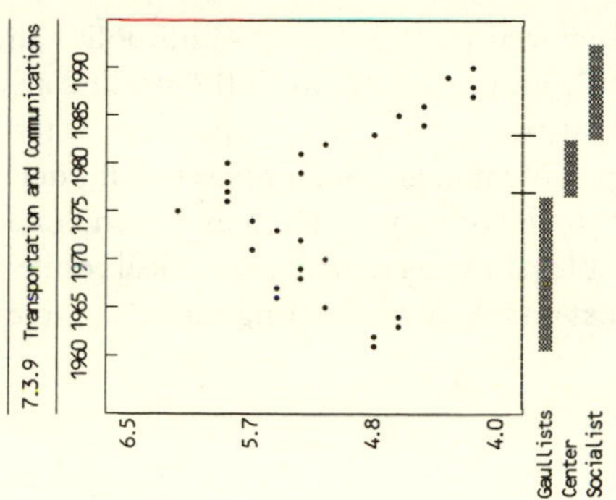
7.3.9 Transportation and Communications
1960 1965 1970 1975 1980 1985 1990
6.5
5.7
4.8
4.0
Gaullists
Center
Socialist

The measurement of correspondence between party programs and policy in France involves applying two models (agenda and mandate) to all the specific areas and to the general summary of left-right policy trends. To some extent, the process of fitting models to the data is experimental, although the set of models shares a quite focused theoretical base. As in all country chapters except the one on Britain, however, we put the full set of tables showing detailed statistical results in the Appendix, while presenting in the text a table of best-fitting models (Table 7.1).

Best-Fitting Models

A reminder is in order that because of the multicollinearity introduced by the odd sequence of party alternation in France, we were unable to run the ideology model, including the party alternation measure. Obviously, if we look only at the R^2s reported in Table 7.1, we need not view the French results as somehow ambiguous or theoretically disappointing. The mean R^2 is 80, well ahead of any other country in our study. Furthermore, a quick glance at Table 7.1 confirms that only one policy area—welfare—is so fraught with contradictory signs as to be clearly beyond the pale of our theory. As is our practice throughout the individual-country chapters, we will shortly give careful attention to that and the other, less severe, contradictions.

The dominant message of the table of best-fitting models is the pervasiveness of agenda influence, reflecting a deep and broad process of policy accommodation by the government of each partisan composition to the programmatic concerns of all the other major parties. The agenda model alone fits best in four cases (education, foreign affairs, administration of justice, and agriculture). Agenda influences are strong even when the mandate adds to the amount of congruence between programmatic emphases and policy priorities. Of the six domains where that occurs (left-right plus five specific areas), the average addition from the mandate is 22 percent, on top of the 63 percent accounted for by the simple agenda effect. Put differently, if we omitted the case of welfare and then analyzed only the agenda models and ignored which party occupied the presidency, the average congruence of party programs and policy priority would have been over 67 percent! As we shall note later, however, there are enough contradictions to qualify seriously the extent that our theoretical expectations fit in France.

We do see, however, a substantially wider agenda effect, suggesting a good deal of cross-party accommodation rather than preeminence of clear mandates. The very mixed case of welfare (to be discussed at more length), for example, is heavily affected by opposition agenda congruence (12.3, Gaullists; .63, Socialists; 1.88, Center; and .17, Communists).

The mandate (i.e., $b(P_i^n \times G)$) adds nothing to the congruence of party program and policy priority in four areas—education, foreign affairs, administration of justice, and agriculture. All four are generally well predicted by the programs of

Table 7.1
Best-Fitting Models Between Party Program Emphases and Policy Priorities: France, 1958 – 1988*

Agenda Models

Policy Priority (Program)	a	Gaullist	Socialist	Center	Communist	Adj R^2
Education (Social Justice)	–26.4	4.60	<u>–.62</u>	2.80	.15	.88
Foreign Affairs (International)	3.48	1.44	1.42	<u>–.57</u>	.38	.84
Admin. of Justice (Public Order)	4.70	<u>–.21</u>	.21	.36		.68
Agriculture (Agriculture)	3.08	<u>–.35</u>	.26		.33	.47

[$E_i = a + bP_i^A + \ldots bP_i^n$]

Mandate Models

Policy Priority (Program Emphasis)	Constant a	Gaullist (+)(–) Agenda or Mandate (Out)	Gaullist Mandate (x Prs)	Socialist (+)(–) Agenda or Mandate (Out)	Socialist Mandate (x Prs)	Center (+)(–) Agenda or Mandate (Out)	Center Mandate (x Prs)	Comm. Agenda (Out)	Adj R^2	Added by Mandate
Left-Right (Left-Right)	3.6	.06		.03^n	<u>–.04</u>	–.09^n	.66	–.09^n	.92	.07
Culture, Art, etc. (Art, Sport, etc.)	–4.4			.56			1.12	1.70	.91	.08
Welfare (Social Justice)	–19.6	12.3	<u>–9.13</u>	.63	<u>–9.63</u>	1.88	<u>–5.50</u>	.17	.91	.26
Defense (International)	20.9	4.46			5.93	–2.85^n		1.72	.82	.25
Trans.& Communic's (Tech. & Infrastr.)	11.2			–1.51^n	<u>–2.44</u>	.39		–1.6^n	.81	.59
Housing (Tech. & Infrastr.)	9.5	.49		3.62	3.24	–.86^n		3.82	.79	.12

[$E_i = a + bP_i^A + b(P_i^A \times G) + \ldots bP_i^n + b(P_i^n \times G)$]

* Indicating only those b's (unstandardized regression coefficients) that attained .05 statistical significance. Coefficients in the opposite direction from theoretical expectation are <u>underlined</u>. Coefficients for negative mandates are indicated by ^{n}. In France, with the Gaullist presidency as the control variable, there were no cases where the ideology model was best-fitting.

the parties, irrespective of governance. To be sure, there are four out of fourteen coefficients in the agenda (only) models that are contradictory, besmirching the theoretical tidiness of those equations.

The thesis of accommodation applies particularly to the congruence between policies and the Communists' programmatic emphases. Although there are two instances of negative mandate, where the incumbent party's policies veered away from the Communist program (left-right, –.09; transportation and communications, –1.56), the Communists obtained positive, statistically significant coefficients in eight policy areas. We would maintain that for a party whose reputation is one of antisystem opposition, a party that is suspected of control from abroad, that is a striking record of accommodation of the policy agenda.

Second to the Communists in the number of policy areas where a party was accommodated while accounting for time out of the presidency were the Gaullists. The out-of-office congruence of their programs-to-policy priorities was significant in the general left-right direction of policy (.03), as well as in the areas of welfare (12.3), defense (4.46), and housing (.49). Their record under the pure agenda models was more mixed, with positive predictions in education (4.60) and foreign affairs (1.44), but it was sullied by the negative reflections in administration of justice and agriculture, (–.21 and –.35, respectively).

Compared to either the Communists or the Gaullists, the Socialists and the Center have had a less consistent history of opposition agenda, that is, in seeing a significant out-of-office policy reflection of their programmatic emphases. Socialists' out-party agenda congruence is seen in culture (.56), welfare (.63), and housing (3.62). The Center has a comparable effect in welfare (1.88) and transportation/communications (.39).

Most indicative of a governing effect is the incidence of the negative mandate. There are only four instances of a statistically significant positive mandate congruence: Socialists in defense (5.93) and housing (3.24), and the Center in left-right (.66) and in culture and art (1.12). Negative mandate effects, where the incumbents enact policies opposite to those of the out-parties, are found, however, in six cases, again to the disadvantage of the Socialists (transportation, –1.51) and the Center (left-right, –.09; defense, –2.85; and housing, –.86), as well as instances of left-right and transportation/communications already noted for the Communists.

Nonconformists and Contradictions

There are no clear cases of nonconformity, since all of the nine policy domains were well above the R^2 minimum of .25, the smallest being .47 (agriculture). Second, mention should be made of an expected nonconformity that did not happen—left-right. Quite the contrary, with only one contradictory coefficient out of seven possibilities, left-right yields the highest R^2 we have yet obtained, .92.

The Socialists receive four contradictory coefficients: one for their agenda influence in education (–.62) and, under the *mandate* heading, for left-right(–.04), welfare (–9.63), and transportation/communications (–2.44). This is a rather worse record of accountability than could be attributed to any of the other parties, including the Communists—who never were in government but who experienced only two areas of negative mandate (left-right, –.09, and transportation/communications, –1.56). Those familiar with French politics in the early 1980s will recall the dramatic reversal of leftward policy taken by Socialist President Mitterrand only one and one-half years into his first term. Our analysis seems to document that reversal.

Neither the Gaullists nor the center party (UDF) fared consistently better, however. The presumably dominant Gaullists had two cases under simple agenda congruence with negative signs—administration of justice (–.21) and agriculture (–.35). And when given the opportunity to fulfill a mandate via winning the presidency, the Gaullists had one negative coefficient (welfare, –9.13) and no significantly positive ones. The Center, likewise, had one negative agenda coefficient (foreign affairs, –.57) and one where they "should" have had a positive mandate (welfare, –5.50).

Contrary to the superlatives expressed earlier, this frequency of contradiction suggests a rather spotty record for party reliability in France. The "best-fitting" welfare equation is fraught with contradictions. Welfare, however, is the only policy area (even including left-right) that is virtually dominated by coefficients contrary to theoretical expectation. None of the other domains has more than one contradictory coefficient, and those are generally smaller than the ones that are theoretically consistent. Likewise, were it not for the poor programmatic fulfillment of the Socialists, the national pattern would not be so uneven. Even with such possibilities for redeeming theory, however, one must conclude, at least tentatively, that France is not a model for the mandate. But neither is it a case to the contrary.

CONCLUSION

The analyses demonstrate that the mandate works moderately well in certain areas of French policy, and the most notable exceptions compared to the other countries are the general left-right indicators of policy and programmatic emphases. However, the most interesting and to some extent surprising aspect of these findings, given the concentration of power in the president, is the extent to which influencing the agenda, rather than implementing the mandate, seems to operate as a significant mode of party congruence with policy priorities. If our analyses of left-right are not severely disturbed by the time distribution problem, then that measure of overall party and policy orientation is particularly interesting as providing a substantive interpretation of French policymaking under the Fifth Republic.

Elsewhere, however, policy is influenced more by a general debate, which we have called the *universe of policy discourse,* within which even the Communists, as the anchors of the left *tendance,* have been the beneficiaries of sympathetic programmatic accommodation. During the Fourth Republic (1945–1958), the Communists commonly held more seats than any other party in the National Assembly. The electoral system of the Fifth Republic severely disadvantaged them, but they continued as a force with which to be reckoned, at least through the resounding success of the Socialists in 1981. The Communists occupied only a few cabinet seats for a brief time during the early 1980s, but they certainly have had weight in the policy process.

Both left- and right-wing parties seem to have had effective input into policy debate regardless of who held the presidency. The ones who have effective input most consistently, from our examination of Table 7.1, seem to be the Gaullists rather than the Socialists.

From an overview of French practices, one might expect that parties would play a modest or weak role in the policy process. The French president is much more independent, constitutionally, than a prime minister in a true parliamentary system. Furthermore, parties in the Fifth Republic have been much more organizationally unstable and fluid than their counterparts in most other democracies. Even though the Fifth Republic constitution certainly corrected for the party fractionalization of its Fourth Republic predecessor, it did so more by giving power to a president *above politics* than by ensuring accountable parties. It is more appropriate to speak of left and right *tendances* rather than of parties as such in France. A president above politics and parties that are not really parties do not make for a salutary environment within which parties may define the effective policy agenda, let alone serve as a vehicle for a mandate from the voters carrying through to passage of legislation consistent with a clear party-defined policy line.

Just as the Westminster systems do not conform exactly as one might expect, so the French situation does not deviate exactly as expected. Detailed interpretations of our findings should not be allowed to detract from the fact that the Fifth Republic seems quite comparable in its modes of operation to the "Westminster" systems previously examined. The same kinds of models fit overall, even with greater apparent statistical power. Agenda setting is relatively more important than the mandate, compared to the Anglo-Saxon countries. Perhaps most important of all for the French political process, the evidence suggests that the political parties often perform their dual role as issue mediators and instruments of accountability, though the former role is more evident than the latter. The president, endowed with formal powers that might run afoul of democratic tenets by being entirely too far "above parties," in fact, seems often to use the constitutional instruments and political opportunities in aid of the essential partisan elements of democracy.

It now remains to be seen whether this broad pattern of accommodation is an attribute of presidential systems or whether it is peculiar to France. We make some progress on those concerns by examining another presidential system—the United States.

NOTES

1. Initially, we experimented with a number of additive scales, but they seemed to attenuate the variance. As we will see later, that would have concealed some very important linkages between program emphases and policy priorities. More sensible was a pooled factor, that is, we merged all parties, extracted a single factor, and then computed the scores for each party in each year. The policy domains and factor loadings were as follows:

[Internationalism]	
Military (–)	.88
Peace	.70
Decolonization	.63
Internationalism (+)	.57
EEC (+)	.24
For. Special Rel's (+)	.03
EEC (–)	–.15
Internationalism (–)	–.42
Military (+)	–.56
[Nationalism]	

8

United States

INSTITUTIONAL AND POLITICAL CONTEXT

There is a compelling argument that the United States has the best-defined and longest-established two-party system in the world. The Democrats can document their continuous existence back to the early nineteenth century. The Republicans trace their origins at least as far back as the 1860s. Since the turn of the twentieth century, Democrats have dominated the Left and Republicans the Right, competing throughout the country for national and state office, only rarely challenged by additional parties. Seldom have the votes received by the two major parties together in national elections dropped below 96 to 98 percent. True to a model of strong interparty competition, the Democrats and Republicans have alternated in the most conspicuous public office, the presidency. Following the record-setting multiple tenure of Franklin Roosevelt, the Democrat Harry Truman served as president until replaced by the Republican Dwight Eisenhower, beginning a process of eight-year rotation that lasted until Jimmy Carter served only one four-year term after the Richard Nixon/Gerald Ford presidencies. Ronald Reagan again brought about a party rotation. With the George Bush victory after eight years of Reagan, the Republicans in 1988 had won the White House for three successive terms—a feat that had not been accomplished since 1908.

The American Constitution was designed as much to limit as to empower the national government. During the forty years between 1952 and 1992, Republicans occupied the White House for twenty-eight, but they had a majority in both houses of Congress for only four years. The electoral strength of otherwise impressive two-party competitiveness is counterbalanced by a constitution that makes the separation of powers a central principle in the organization of government. Each of the main political institutions—the elective presidency, the Congress, the Supreme Court, the separate states—not only has autonomous spheres of action and entrenched rights in regard to the others but also usually exercises some kind of veto over what the others can do.

The political parties, which in other countries coordinate and control the other elements in the system, in the United States have adapted themselves to fragmented institutional structures. They are decentralized into state parties and congressional parties, and within them, individual politicians have substantial autonomy. There is no visible structure for party discipline of legislators comparable to that found in most parliamentary systems. The president has general influence over a loose party confederation, but for detailed policymaking he relies mainly upon his own campaign and executive organization, built up within the party but quite separate and distinct from its other structures.

If we add to the institutional fragmentation of parties the heavy dependence on pressure groups and special interests for campaign finance, there seems considerable justification for the controversial critique made for the American Political Science Association under the title *Toward a More Responsible Two-Party System* (APSA 1950). This report of the U.S. political science discipline's premier professional association attributed much of the apparent looseness, confusion, and waste in U.S. policymaking processes to the amorphous political parties and the absence of clear-cut ideological differences between them. The report urged their restructuring, with associated changes in the presidency and Congress, to nudge practice gently but firmly in the British direction. This would enable parties to offer sharper policy choices to the electorate and to provide real support for implementation of the winning program (the party "platform") in government. Parties would shape the agenda and see to its enactment. Voters would be provided a choice and clear evidence of partisan accountability.

In spite of the critical reception given to the APSA report, its spirit lives on in many modern discussions of American politics. In a comparison of the capacity of national institutions to carry through policy mandates, the United States was ranked lowest—below such multiparty systems as Italy and Israel—precisely because of its institutional fragmentation and absence of clear-cut party differentiation and policy influence (Powell 1990).

It is this assessment of the weaknesses of the U.S. parties as policy coordinators and programmatic implementers that has prompted us to locate the American analyses at this point in the book. We have dealt mainly with parliamentary systems, characterized by alternating governments of a clearly defined ideological complexion and hence a fairly concentrated capacity for enacting the winning party mandate. The one other presidential system—France—has enough legal concentration of power to distinguish it sharply from the United States. We will go on to consider European coalition systems, where no party has the formal autonomy to push through its program fully, but where all may hope to carry some points in coalition or legislative bargaining. Consequently, such systems may be expected to operate with a much more diffuse conception of the mandate.

On the face of it, bargaining between the president and the two houses of Congress might impose similar constraints on American parties, in spite of their winning electoral majorities. But is this true in practice? There is conflicting evidence (Budge and Hofferbert 1990): We hope to resolve the issue to some extent in the following analyses.

In any case, it is interesting that the critiques of American parties focus heavily on one of their aspects of particular relevance to us—the uses of the party mandate in coordinating and directing policymaking. We could not concur more on the centrality of the parties in this respect, but we dissent from the general tone of self-criticism adopted by most American policy analysts in writing about their own system. The analyses presented here suggest not only that the Democrats and Republicans are reasonably cohesive internally, when compared with political parties in other systems, but also that their platforms are quite clearly differentiated from each other in an ideologically consistent fashion. They are thus as capable of giving a choice of policy alternatives to electors as are socialist and bourgeois parties in European democracies, and they are equally able to bring into effect their programs in government, despite institutional fragmentation—owing above all to the central position and pivotal forces of the presidency within the federal system.

In Chapter 1 we discussed several critiques that find American policymaking to be more or less chaotic. The chaos view is that policymaking serves *no one's* interests. Elite theory, although seeing policymaking as more orderly, says that it serves the exclusive interests of a privileged few. The evidence we present supports our dissent from both brands of pessimism.

PROGRAM AND POLICY TRENDS

U.S. Data

The coding procedures used on the U.S. party platforms were completely consistent with those used for the rest of the countries included in the Manifestoes Research Group's efforts. In fact, it was with the United States and Britain that the project originated (Robertson 1976). For the present analysis, the data have been updated through the 1988 election.

The U.S. Office of Management and Budget (OMB) maintains policy data in a form that should serve as a model for other central statistical agencies. OMB publishes several series of annual reports on budgetary and expenditure statistics (OMB, annual), including the *Historical Tables* on the U.S. budget. These volumes contain, along with other entries, full, consistent, and rather finely classified expenditure data (as well as multiyear projections from budget estimates). The data are organized in such a way that categories no longer in use are carefully fitted to contemporary functions, with full documentation of what has been classified where. It is this documentation that provided the general guidelines that we followed in our own effort to retrofit expenditures from other countries. Only in Germany were we able to benefit from a comparable document for a full, consistent financial retrospective. The U.S. data are presented for the entire postwar period. Because of the consistency of these indicators, we were able to analyze thirteen policy domains, plus the left-right summary measure. The thirteen policy areas include an average of 88 percent of expenditures by the federal government.

In our analyses here, the latest expenditure data were for fiscal year 1990, which were paired with party program data for 1988. Thus, the first year in the series is 1949, which pairs the appropriate 1948 party platform entries with 1951 expenditure shares. The platform was for the November 1948 election, but the government took office in January 1949. The last entry analyzed is 1990 expenditures against 1988 party platform entries. Those platform entries, in turn, actually represent the last year of the 1984 platform, since the 1988 election was for a government that took office in 1989, for which 1991 expenditures would have been required. Those expenditures were not yet available at the time of our analyses.

We needed to make only one combined policy measure. Health expenditures in the United States are recorded separately from Medicare. Medicare, which provides (through the social security system) health insurance for the elderly, was introduced into the data stream in 1965. It was a wholly new service and did not represent a reclassification of a former category. In order to get a reasonably full picture of health-policy indicators, which would maximize comparability to other countries, therefore, we summed "health" and "Medicare" expenditures. Except for left-right, which we discuss below, no other special indices or summary categories were constructed from either the program or the expenditure data. The categories we relate are as follows:

Party Program	*Policy Area*
Special Foreign Relations (+)	Defense
Special Foreign Relations (+)	Foreign Affairs
Law and Order	Administration of Justice
Agriculture	Agriculture
Social Justice	Social Security
Social Justice	Health and Medicare
Education	Education
Technology and Infrastructure	Transportation
Technology and Infrastructure	Energy
Technology and Infrastructure	Commerce and Housing
Technology and Infrastructure	Community and Regional Development
Environmental Protection	Environmental Protection

Left-Right Trends

The U.S. parties, contrary to the "Tweedledum and Tweedledee" thesis, have maintained enduring ideological differences. This conclusion is justified by historical evidence of party activities in the modern period and from detailed re-

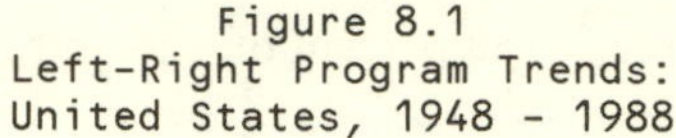

Figure 8.1
Left-Right Program Trends:
United States, 1948 - 1988

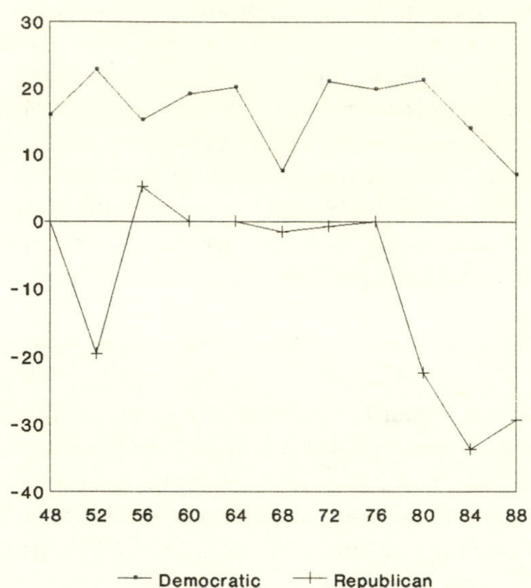

search on their role in the policy process (Pomper 1968; Ginsberg 1976). Figure 8.1 shows graphically how Democrats and Republicans have related to each other in terms of the generalized left-right scale that we have also used to trace the movements of parties in other countries.

A first obvious conclusion from Figure 8.1 is that, at least at the programmatic level, American parties are just as distinctive as those of other political systems. Democrats tend to put welfare and education at the top of their list of priorities, to support peace initiatives and international organizations, and the other issues that make up the measure of *leftism.* Republicans, as would be expected of a conservative party anywhere, put more stress on national strength at the world level and on law and order, individual freedom, and a market economy. The actual distance between the parties is up to the norm shown in our previous chapters for countries with presumably "more responsible" parties.

The pattern of general difference between the parties is likewise interesting, not for its peculiarity—as might be expected from the critiques that have been leveled at the U.S. parties relative to their European counterparts—but for its *lack* of peculiarity. There is no "leapfrogging," that is, the Republicans stay to the right of the Democrats. A comparison of Figure 8.1 with the British ideal of the critics (Figure 4.1) or with the presumably more sharply delineated German parties (Chapter 9) shows no less difference or distinctiveness in the United States than elsewhere. In fact, the U.S. Democrats appear to have been more ideologically consistent, if not downright stubborn, than the leftist parties in most other countries. As do rightist parties generally, the Republicans show more flexibility in the central focus of their platforms over time than do the Democrats.

It could be argued, of course, that the platforms for the presidential race are little more than a papering over of cracks—that they are produced strictly for electoral consumption and are not to be taken as serious statements of party intent or even of party ideology. This public fakery may be necessary, given the internal divisions and fragmentation of the parties (where, for example, a Minnesota Republican might be far to the left of an Alabama Democrat). Political parties in all countries, however, encompass a considerable ideological range, with a welfare-oriented European Christian democrat being much more "leftist" than a European moderate socialist, for example. The role of the platform in this context can be seen as a major effort to pull the contesting wings of the party together around a set of immediate priorities that they can support. In this sense, the platform is central to what the party does, and its shifting priorities (most visible in Figure 8.1 for the Republicans) are good indications of its general thinking. It also of course represents the priorities specifically endorsed by the party voters, in the sense that the platform has a unique standing as a document of party principle.

The trends in Figure 8.1 certainly conform to what we know historically about party stances. The New Deal–Fair Deal era of Franklin Roosevelt and Harry Truman (1932–1952), with its emphasis on establishing the American brand of the welfare state, dominated Democratic policy positions over most of the post-war period, reinforced by the Great Society programs of the 1960s and of the New Left of the 1970s. In the 1980s, Democratic platforms tentatively explore centrist emphases, but they remain relatively closely tied to their ideological heritage.

Republican programs swing more between center and right, as can be seen in the contrast between the platforms of 1956 and 1964, one written to accommodate the centrism of the incumbent Eisenhower, and the other by the same Republican National Convention that nominated the conservative Barry Goldwater as the Republican presidential candidate. In 1968 and 1972 Nixon adopted an almost-leftist position. But after Nixon there was a steady trend to the right under the influence of Reagan and Bush—often commented upon in general terms by political analysts and historians, but more precisely measured, of course, by this evidence from the platforms themselves.

The conclusion that parties make a difference in the United States is also supported by previous analyses of a somewhat shorter time series, where substantial congruence between party programmatic emphases and government expenditures was found by Budge and Hofferbert (1990). In several policy domains, they also report a specific effect from changes in party control of the presidency (which we have related to underlying party ideology) in line with those observed in many other democracies (Castles 1982).

A hint of this can be seen by a left-right policy indicator, constructed by means of factor analysis in the same manner as for the other countries discussed so far. The factor loadings, displayed beneath the graph in Figure 8.2, contrast core wel-

Figure 8.2
Left–Right Expenditure Priority Factor Scores:
United States, 1946 – 1988

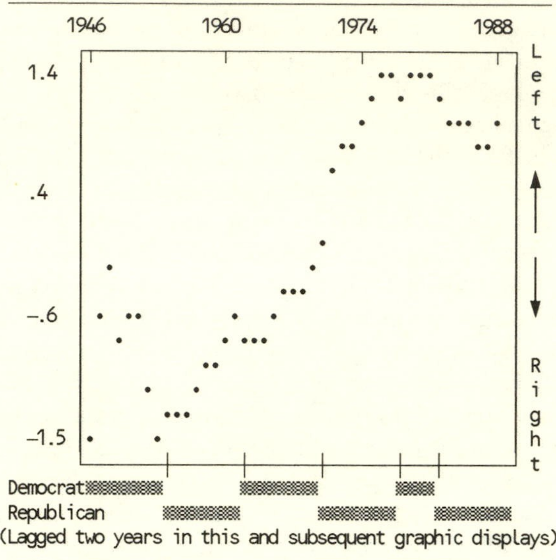

Structure of Policy Priority Factor

Policy Area	Factor Loading
Health & Medicare	.94
Welfare	.92
Education	.88
Agriculture	–.40
Defense	–.91

fare-state policies (health and Medicare = .94; welfare = .92; education = .88) with clearly conservative favorites (agriculture = –.40; defense = –.91). And even more interesting from a comparative standpoint is the striking similarity to the trends in the other countries in the left-right factor scores. That is, the rightward lurch at the beginning of the cold war veers steadily leftward into the 1970s, then flattens and moves rightward again in later years. Again, the United States proves to be less different from the other countries in our analysis than some of its social and institutional peculiarities might lead one to expect.

The initial cold war move to the right trapped the Democrat Truman. Furthermore, much to the disappointment of many conservatives, his successor, the Republican Eisenhower, did not repeal the elements of the welfare state put in place under twenty years of Democratic rule. This is a not uncommon response for right-wing parties following a period of left-wing policy innovation. But it clouds the consistency of any association of general left-right policy development with corresponding left or right governments. Eisenhower indeed paused a bit in the later 1950s, but Lyndon Johnson's reassertion of a leftward shift in the mid-1960s did little more than restore the curve to where it would have been forecast to be by the line from the middle Eisenhower years. And the flattening to the right was not a Reagan innovation but rather took place solidly within the Carter administration in the latter half of the 1970s.

In sum, as in virtually all other Western democracies, the United States reversed its postwar demobilization by taking up arms in the aftermath of the Berlin Blockade and in the face of the Korean War. Without ever abandoning the commitment to contain Soviet communism, this rearmament was followed, however, by a long-term trend to the left, reaching what appears to have been a near-universal leveling in the 1970s, with only modest adjustments from then on. It is not clear whether this trend will remain relatively flat or, in the face of the revolutionary developments in the world's political situation in the 1990s, whether there will be a reassertion of a leftward shift. Moreover, it is not clear that the outcome could be predicted from knowing which party is in the White House. Although we still need to investigate the left-right program-to-policy connection, statistically the expectation is that it will be a weak linkage at most.

Specific Policy Trends

The ebb and flow of policy priorities can be better seen in the trends for specific domains than in the broad left-right index. The time plots for the thirteen specific policy areas are displayed in Figure 8.3. The manner in which the individual components made up the left-right scale is very clear from these plots. Defense and foreign affairs follow similar curves (8.3.1 and 8.3.2) sharply downward from the 1950s and then flatten in the 1970s. These contrast most sharply with the mainstays of the welfare state—social security (i.e., pensions, 8.3.5), welfare (8.3.6), health and Medicare (8.3.7).

The upward trend in federal priority for administration of justice (8.3.3) is not quite as steep or as seemingly inexorable as in some other countries, with an uncommonly sharp drop after the mid-1970s. Other policies rising and then dipping are the same ones we have seen following such a curve elsewhere: education (8.3.8), transportation (8.3.9), and community and regional development (mostly various urban renewal programs: 8.3.12).

Agriculture (8.3.4), which everywhere tends downward, in the United States follows a somewhat more erratic path (as it does in Canada—see Figure 6.3). Also lacking a clear, overall secular trend are energy, which enjoyed a flurry of activity in the immediate years after the Organization of Petroleum Exporting Countries (OPEC) embargo (8.3.10), housing (8.3.11), and natural resources and environment (8.3.13).

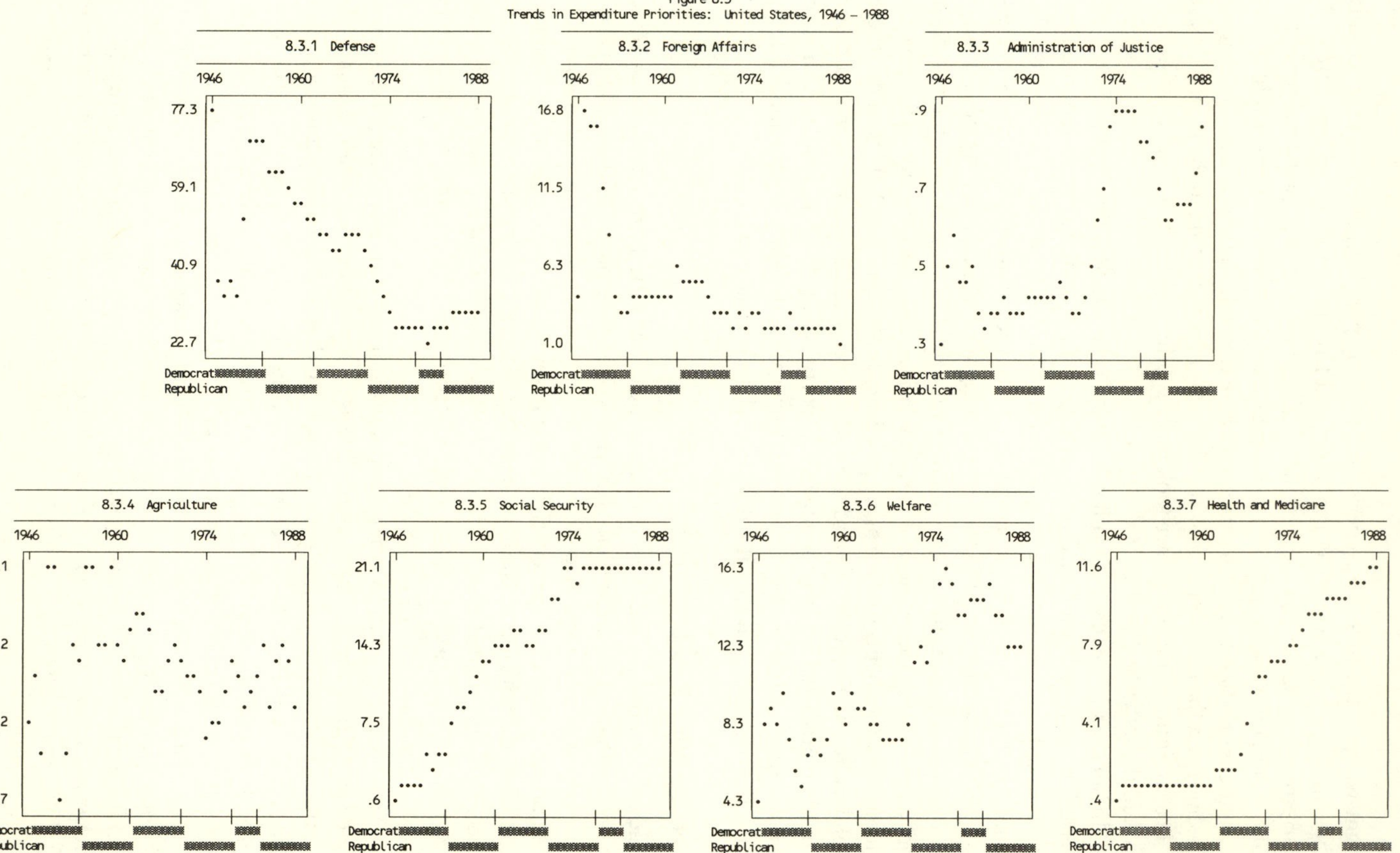

Figure 8.3
Trends in Expenditure Priorities: United States, 1946 - 1988

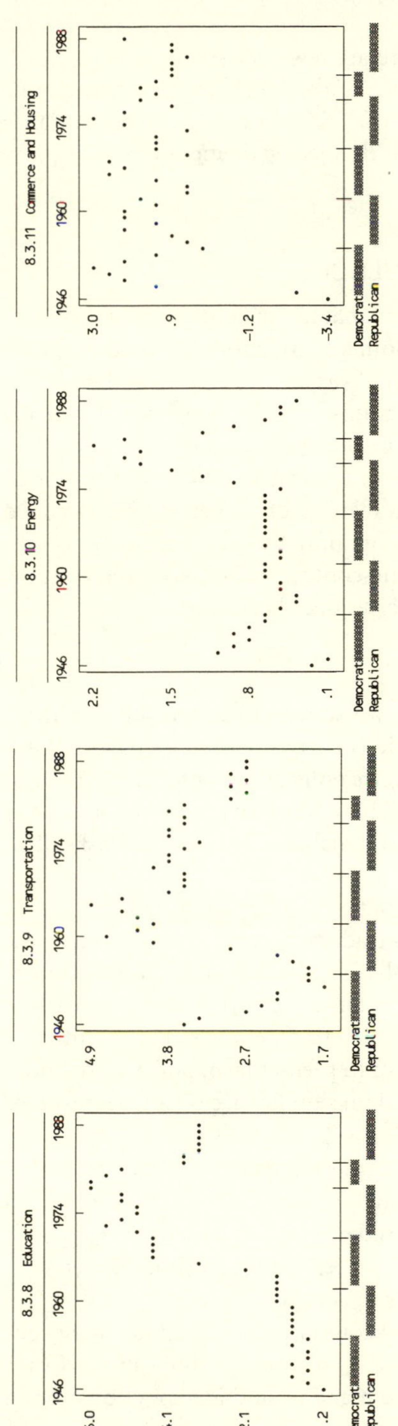

8.3.8 Education
6.0
4.1
2.1
.2
1946
1960
1974
1988
Democrat
Republican
8.3.9 Transportation
4.9
3.8
2.7
1.7
1946
1960
1974
1988
Democrat
Republican
8.3.10 Energy
2.2
1.5
.8
.1
1946
1960
1974
1988
Democrat
Republican
8.3.11 Commerce and Housing
3.0
.9
-1.2
-3.4
1946
1960
1974
1988
Democrat
Republican

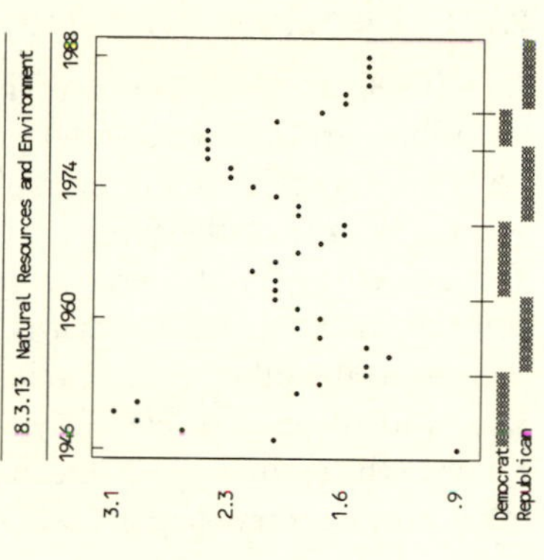

8.3.13 Natural Resources and Environment
3.1
2.3
1.6
.9
1946
1960
1974
1988
Democrat
Republican

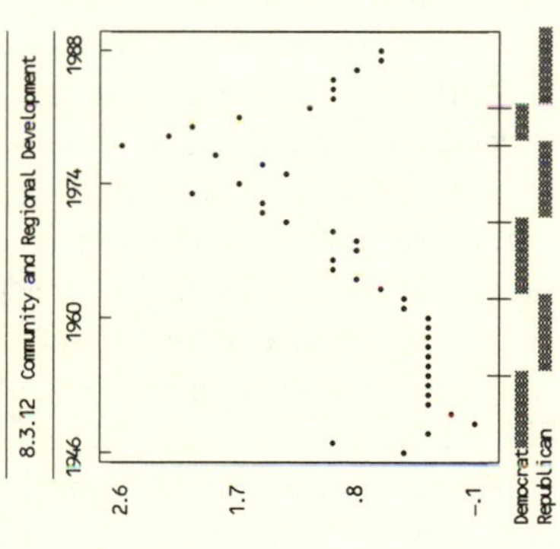

8.3.12 Community and Regional Development
2.6
1.7
.8
-.1
1946
1960
1974
1988
Democrat
Republican

Across the different policy domains, there are few very smooth curves. Each has ample short-term as well as long-term variance, which argues against some sort of automated, incremental explanation of U.S. policy. In fact, that variance invites the study of its congruence with relatively specific themes in the U.S. party platforms.

PARTY PROGRAM-TO-POLICY CONGRUENCE

As Table 8.1 makes abundantly clear, the United States is hardly the land of irresponsible parties. Twelve of thirteen policy domains attain or exceed our customary minimum R^2 of .25. A mean of 52 percent of variance over time in those is explained by one of the three models of program-to-policy congruence. Agenda elements alone are of consequence in only one policy domain (agriculture). And controls for governance—that is, the platform mandate—add an average of 16 percent to the other eleven policies, with an average of 12 percent being added also by ideology in seven policy areas. There are only three contradictory coefficients in the entire table. Nonconformities and contradictions, however, as in the other nine country chapters, will shortly receive special attention.

Best-Fitting Models

Before examining the exceptions, however, we should focus on the dominant message in Table 8.1. It has two parts. America's party system does its job. But it does so in a complex fashion. Seven of the twelve policies presented in the table fit into the most elaborate of the three models. This complexity, however, in no way supports the criticisms that the U.S. parties are unable to perform the tasks of issue mediation or of enhancing accountability.

Agriculture policy priority in the United States, although not in a statistically spectacular manner, is not dominated by contradictory coefficients, as is the case in some other countries. The Republican platforms, which over time have devoted less and less attention to concerns of farmers, have best described the downward trend of policy—irrespective of which party controls the executive (b = .11). The failure of the Democratic platform to predict farm policy or of either interactive term (Program × Presidency) to attain significance is sufficient to suggest a certain Republican "hegemony" over farm-related policy.

Perhaps ironically, two welfare-state centerpieces, social security (pensions) and welfare (income maintenance), are heavily influenced by the Republican platforms—negatively under Democratic presidents (social security = –6.35; welfare = –2.64), with the Republicans following their own platforms rather well, 4.12 and 1.61 for social security and welfare respectively.

The Democrats generally, like their Liberal counterparts in Canada, use occupancy of the presidency as a means to work *against* the Republican platforms more often than to work *for* their own. In the mandate and ideology equations a positive sign under the "out" party column, without the interactive term (" × Gov") indicates accommodation of that out-party's programmatic emphases by the other party in the presidency. A negative sign under the same columns indicates policies pursued by the other party in office that go against the out-party platforms. The latter (–) is consistent with the mandate; the former (+) with the agenda-setting model. In the eleven equations including such a term, the Democrats yielded to the out-of-office Republicans only three times, including the very ambiguous case of energy ($b = .21$) as well as in transportation (.09) and regional development (.17). The opposite, a negative mandate effect, was implemented by the Democrats in six instances: social security (–6.35), welfare (–2.64), defense (–8.70), education (–.09), foreign affairs (–68), and health and Medicare (–4.32).

The Republicans were only a bit kinder to the Democrats, using their occupancy of the White House to go significantly against the Democratic platform trends in three cases: transportation (–.14), regional development (–.17), and environmental protection (–.06). At the same time, the mandate and ideology models show the Republicans accommodating the Democrats in only two cases, education (.99) and energy (.08). (And this took place while the Democrats were in solid control of the House of Representatives for the entire time and of the Senate for all but six years.)

The interparty contrast is shaped by the Republican's simultaneous positive policy response to their own programmatic emphases in the mandate and ideology models. The interactive term for Republican program congruence as a result of occupying the presidency is positive in eight instances (administration of justice, .09; social security, 4.12; defense, 6.54; welfare, 1.61; education, .49; foreign affairs, .47; environmental protection, .19; and health, 2.95). This compares to only three areas in which the Democrats use their occupancy of the White House to pursue the signals sent up by their own platform: defense, 8.0; transportation, .60; and regional development, .22.

Looking back to Figure 8.1, we see that the Republicans have been generally much more flexible in the central tendencies of their programmatic concerns than have the Democrats. The diversity of interests loosely woven together by the Democrats has kept them rhetorically close to their rather leftist ideological domain, without necessarily guiding their actions in office. The oppositional role they have cultivated through congressional dominance may have carried over into the tactics pursued in the White House as well.

The fact that seven of the twelve policy domains are best anticipated by the equation including a dummy variable for party alternation (ideology) is a very insightful finding. That term (1 for a Republican president, 0 for Democrat), if we control for current platform emphasis, says that election of a Republican rather than a Democrat has increased the percentage for transportation (2.60) and regional development (.79). Election of a Democratic president has increased spending shares for education (2.18), energy (.52), and environmental protection (.46). And in two additional areas (foreign affairs and health), although the spe-

Table 8.1
Best-Fitting Models Between Party Program Emphases and Policy Priorities:
United States, 1948 – 1990*

Agenda Models

Policy Priority (Program)	a	Republican	Democrat	Adj R^2
Agriculture (Agriculture)	1.27	.11		.28

[$E_i = a + bP_i^A + \ldots bP_i^n$]

Mandate Models

Policy Priority (Program Emphasis)	Constant a	Republican (+)(–) Agenda or Mandate (Out)	Republican Mandate (x Gov)	Democrat (+)(–) Agenda or Mandate (Out)	Democrat Mandate (x Gov)	Adj R^2	Added by Mandate
Admin. of Justice (Law & Order)	.40		.09		.08	.84	.04
Social Security (Social Justice)	19.9	$-6.35^{\underline{n}}$	4.12			.55	.11
Defense (Spec. For. Rel's)	46.9	$-8.70^{\underline{n}}$	6.54		8.00	.48	.08
Welfare (Social Justice)	13.1	$-2.64^{\underline{n}}$	1.61		$\underline{-1.52}$	.29	.15

[$E_i = a + bP_i^A + b(P_i^A \times G) + \ldots bP_i^n + b(P_i^n \times G)$]

Continued ⟶

Ideology Models

Policy Priority (Program Emphasis)	Constant a	Ideology: Republican Pres. = 1	Republican (Out): (+)(–) Agenda or Mandate	Republican (x Prs): Mandate	Democrat (Out): (+)(–) Agenda or Mandate	Democrat (x Prs): Mandate	Adj R^2	Added by Mandate	Added by Ideology
Education (Education)	.51	–2.18	–.09^{n}	.49	.99		.92	.35	.05
Transportation (Tech. & Infrastr.)	.55	2.60	.09		–.14^{n}	.60	.64	.22	.32
Commun.& Reg.Dev't) (Tech. & Infrastr.)	.09	.79	.17		–.17^{n}	.22	.58	.45	.12
Energy (Tech. & Infrastr.)	1.22	–.52	.21	–.10	.08		.58	.16	.03
Foreign Affairs (Spec. For. Rel's)	4.06		–.68^{n}	.47			.43	.02	.22
Env. Protection (Env. Protection)	1.85	–.46		.19	–.06^{n}		.40	.08	.06
Health & Medicare (Social Justice)	11.5		–4.32^{n}	2.95		–3.27	.27	.09	.03

$$[\quad E_i = a + bP_i^A + bP_i^A + b(P_i^A \times G) + \ldots bP_i^n + b(P_i^n \times G) \quad]$$

* Indicating only those b's (unstandardized regression coefficients that attained .05 statistical significance. Coefficients in the opposite direction from theoretical expectation are underlined. Negative mandate coefficients are indicated by ^{n}.

cific variable does not itself attain statistical significance, it does restructure the equation. In those instances, the party alternation term, although not significant at .05, was the largest coefficient in the foreign affairs equation (–3.14) and second largest in health (–4.11; see Table A8.3).

The one policy that is perhaps the oddity of our entire study is administration of justice. Spending for police, courts, and prisons by central governments has risen in priority in every country we examine. Most people would consider this a policy, on its face, favored by the right. Most "right-wing" policies have, as our trend analyses make very clear, suffered relative to those on the left, at least into the 1970s. The share of national outlays for administration of justice, however, has risen in nearly every country, making it look like a "left-wing" policy. The ability of party programs, as built into our models, to account for this seeming deviation from the long-term leftward policy trend of all countries is quite varied. Interestingly, in the United States it is a case where the mandate model performs very well, with an R^2 of .84. Both parties increased their emphases on law and order (correlation with time, Republican = .42, Democrat = .62), and each party is highly correlated with the other (.87). Either one has provided a reliable guide to successive policy, irrespective of holding office. Nevertheless, by a slight edge, the best prediction would be to use the program of whatever party wins in order to predict what it would do in office with respect to administration of justice. In the retrospective and summary discussion in Chapter 14, we will reconsider whether it is reasonable to interpret this area of policy as "right-wing" or whether, in fact, it may have taken on a decidedly "leftward" tilt.

Nonconformists and Contradictions

Two policy indicators fell below the .25 R^2 cutoff: housing and the left-right scale, leaving the twelve for which significant coefficients of the best-fitting models are given in Table 8.1. We will not speculate here about the peculiarities of partisan treatment of housing policy, along with some commercial development assistance, in the United States. The lack of left-right linkage to party control seemed apparent from the trends in Figures 8.1 and 8.2. This is confirmed by the statistical analysis, in which no model was able to produce an R^2 greater than 13. The absence of left-right platform/policy statistical linkages suggests that U.S. policy processes are not being overtly driven by broad ideological orientations. That is the general pattern, with few exceptions (e.g., France) elsewhere, with left-right program-to-policy equations being either inconsequential or heavily laden with contradictions. In most other settings, as in the United States, the realization of democratic theory takes place in the specific program-to-policy relationships.

Aside from the complete nonconformity of housing policy, there are only three statistically significant contradictory coefficients in Table 8.1. Two are for the Democrats: welfare, under Mandate models, at –1.52, and health and Medicare, under Ideology Models, at –3.27. These instances of welfare-state entitlement being poorly forecast by the party most overtly identified with them hearkens back to the discussion in the British case. There we suggested that human services entitlements may simply not be congruent with party programs, given the more or less automatic manner in which policy must match objective socioeconomic conditions and changes in them. That a similar pattern was not seen in Canada, Australia, and France naturally stimulates skepticism, but the hypothesis should be at least put on hold until the retrospective in Chapter 14.

The Republicans have only one statistically significant contradiction: the –.10 for energy policy, matched to platform emphases on technology and infrastructure. The time distribution of priority in this field is uncommonly skewed, as is evident in Figure 8.3.10. The Republicans enjoyed some agenda effect, with their programmatic emphases relating positively when out of office to energy policy (b = .21). We suspect that this policy has been entirely too volatile, in response more to short-term external conditions such as the OPEC embargo, to be brought under control in response to clear partisan concerns. We would not want to use the .58 R^2, therefore, as strong evidence in support of our theoretical concerns.

As we have done in previous chapters, however, we are here risking that the acknowledgment of these few deviations will detract from the general power of the agenda/mandate models to forecast policy priorities in the United States. That forecasting power is really quite high and generally theoretically consistent.

CONCLUSION

In 1964, Barry Goldwater took the Republican Party well to the right, running on the claim that he was offering the voters a "choice, not an echo." Senator Goldwater articulated the common claim that America's two major parties usually offer little choice to the electorate. To that claim can be added the weight of scholarly argument that the American system is confounded by insurmountable barriers to the presentation and enactment of a voter-endowed mandate.

Our conclusions show, on the contrary, that the historical Republican-Democratic duopoly over national elections may be due to conditions that enhance the parties' potential to act as formulators and implementers of clear policy mandates. This monopoly is encouraged by legal conditions—first-past-the-post elections in single-member constituencies (even for the presidency in what is, in effect, a single national district). Yet the parties' policy potential is widely regarded as being diluted by the constitutional and institutional peculiarities of the American system—separation of powers, checks and balances, federalism, decentralized party organization. These factors lead some scholars to expect minimal policy differentiation and maximum fluidity in substantive issue choices offered the electorate. They further expect the party-to-policy linkage will be different and weaker in the United States than in parliamentary systems, and particularly weaker than in majoritarian parliamentary systems, exemplified by Britain.

These expectations are not confirmed by our analysis of American party platforms, in terms either of the choices they have offered the voters or of the capacity they have had to anticipate postelection policy priorities. Giovanni Sartori, basing his argument on Downs, predicted that a party system with only two significant combatants would take indistinct policy positions, close to the center, with no daring leaps toward the edges of any major dimension of competition, such as the left-right continuum (Sartori 1976). Our cross-national, cross-temporal, cross-party standardized measures of left-right, however, show that the American parties are distinct from each other in a highly predictable manner. The Republicans are consistently to the right of the Democrats. Moreover, the Republicans have frequently veered well away from center, matching the adventurousness of their European and Anglo-Saxon counterparts. American voters who have sought to base their decisions on differences in the broad leanings of the two major parties have not, in the post–World War II period, lacked a choice equivalent to that of electors in other democracies.

The record of the general left-right tilt of party programs as forecasts of commensurate general policy leanings has not been stunning. By the early 1950s, most Western democracies, in some respects paced by the United States, had engaged in the cold war via their budgets, only to spend the next thirty years shifting from defense-related policies to a basket of human services and income transfers. The leftward policy shift then generally leveled in the 1970s. This movement is sometimes well and sometimes badly tracked by the general left-right orientations of party programs. Relationships can be blurred by the fact that this macropolicy shift represents a basic, evolutionary transformation of the policy consensus of Western societies. In spite of the continued distinctiveness of the two American parties from each other, there is no evidence that the degree of left-right programmatic orientation significantly signals a comparable orientation of policy.

The election mandate, however, as we have argued in Chapter 1, can take many forms, broad or narrow. It can be as simple as the voter's resting a decision on the established record of one party, contrasted to the other. Such a mandate, in effect, tells the winner to stay the course. The mandate can be narrowed somewhat—but still be quite broad and based on general historical orientations—if the party wins on the basis of its aggregate left-right leaning in a particular election. Or the mandate can be much more specific, attached to the particular bundle of programmatic emphases which a party has presented to the voters in a specific election.

The American party mandate is not about broad historical orientations or even about more temporally bounded left-right leanings. Rather, it is a choice between alternative bundles of rather specific policy concerns. It is in this domain that the American parties come into their own, demonstrating a set of specific party program-to-policy priority linkages that is as strong as that usually found elsewhere—in spite of the institutional and constitutional disadvantages with which a process of mandate implementation would seem to be burdened in the United States.

The average R^2 for the U.S. best-fitting models is .54—a bit above the mean for all ten countries in our study. It is in a tie with Canada, well ahead of Australia, and even modestly ahead of the very home of the Westminster model, Britain. This is, of course, a summary, including both agenda and mandate influences. For a mandate theory of the parties' mediating role to be fully upheld, however, it is essential that the electorate's decision make a discernible, systematic, and predictable difference on policy. Saliency theory argues that the mandate does not require pro versus con choices on each policy issue. It is sufficient that the parties stake claims to concrete priorities, specifying their particular and distinct domains of concern. Head-to-head issue conflict is not essential for the mandate. But winning helps a great deal. Mandate theory calls for the programmatic emphases of winners to be favored and those of losers to be relatively diminished in ensuing policy decisions.

Unfortunately for the tidiness of theory, it is often difficult to establish precisely who has *won.* Two major families of exceptions exist in modern democracies: (1) multiparty coalition governments (of which we can consider actual minority governments a subset) and (2) the specific peculiarity of separated powers in the presidential systems. Who had the mandate when Republican presidents faced a Democratic Congress? It is necessary to test for both parties simultaneously to address that question. Of course, if the party program of neither party predicts policy priorities, then finer distinctions are irrelevant. But if both predict, then there may indeed be a split mandate working its way through the peculiar American institutional labyrinth. In fact, as in the other countries, there is the possibility that one or both of the party programs simply reflects a dominant agenda of policy discourse, divorced from the election or the capture of office.

By and large, misgivings grounded on the peculiarity of American institutions are unwarranted. The particular best-fitting combination of party platform emphases and party office-holding varies from policy to policy, as is clearly demonstrated in the summary of findings in Table 8.1. But there is an unquestionable push from the evidence toward a conclusion that mandate enactment is the major form in which party accountability occurs in the United States.

The standing choice between Republicans and Democrats over the postwar years has made a major difference in many policy areas. Beyond that distinction, winning the presidential race has distinctly enhanced the congruence of party platforms and subsequent policy priority. The efficient voter would be better off reading the Republican platform than reading that of the Democrats. If what the Republicans stress is to that voter's liking, he or she should vote Republican; if not, he or she should vote Democratic. The Democrats are generally more sharply focused on veering from the Republicans than they are in serving the specifics of their own, rather standardized, offerings. But that the American voter has a clear choice in a current election—or grounds for attributing accountability for the last one—is solidly supported by our data.

Our conclusion, therefore, is that the United States need not seek "a more responsible two-party system." It already has one.

9

Sweden

INSTITUTIONAL AND POLITICAL CONTEXT

Sweden is the first country of the six encountered so far in our analysis where coalition governments are a normal political arrangement. There is a twist to the Swedish situation in that, in addition to coalitions, minority governments are common, usually led by the largest single party, the Social Democratic Party (SDP). The Social Democrats have often won just under half of the seats in parliament. Sweden has a Communist Party that has gained, on average, about 5 percent of the seats in parliament. That statistic, in itself, would not be worthy of much attention were it not that the Communists, although never gaining portfolios in the cabinet, provided a cushion for SDP-led minority governments—a circumstance that could well have given them a role in policy larger than seemingly warranted by the mere number of votes.

Majority coalitions, however, are also quite frequent in Sweden. In the mid-1950s the red-green coalition of Social Democrats and Agrarian Party (now called the Center Party) provided an alternative to minority governments. In more recent years, three parties have combined on occasion to exclude the SDP from government: the Center Party, the Liberals (People's Party), and the Conservatives. Their combination and alternation since the mid-1970s have been quite complex. In the graphic material discussed in the next section, we attempt to simplify this alternation of governments in Sweden.

We expect coalitions, and to some extent minority governments, to be less accountable to their electorate than either majority governments under the Westminster model or systems headed by a popularly elected chief executive, as in France and the United States. This is because the parties forming the coalition must make initial compromises with each other in order to get a cabinet together. These compromises may water down the separate party programs in some areas in order that a viable government can be formed at all out of parties that may just have completed a vigorous campaign against each other. It would seem, therefore, that they cannot help but abandon many of their electoral commitments. Anglo-American political scientists often criticize coalitions for being ineffective, weak, and internally divided—all of which must surely limit any ability to implement their mandate or even to influence the agenda. We would expect that, if parties are accountable at all under coalition governments, agenda influence of several parties, rather than a mandate enacted exclusively by parties in government, would be the main mechanism of accountability.

In line with these ideas, we began with the three Westminster countries, moved to the two presidential systems, followed by Sweden with frequent minority or coalition governments, Austria with grand coalitions over much of the period, Germany with almost permanent coalitions between the Free Democrats and one or the other of two large parties. Finally, we present two countries with multiparty coalitions: the Netherlands and Belgium. If ideas about diminishing party accountability under coalition systems are correct, we ought to have increasing difficulty fitting our models as we move through this sequence of systems.

Already, however, we have found several reversals of the expectations of varying accountability based on the presumed consequences of different institutional arrangements. The party mandate is weaker in Britain relative to the United States than was previously expected. Larger than expected program-to-policy linkages are present in Canada and France. We need not be unduly surprised if the relevance of institutional arrangements does not work out as expected in Sweden.

There are, moreover, ways in which we might, a priori, expect coalition parties to accommodate themselves to each other without weakening accountability on core issues. It has been shown, for example, that agreements on the distribution of ministries involve sharing these out so that each party gains control of its own areas of central concern, where through administrative and other measures it can bring policy around to its own preferences (Budge and Keman 1990). Thus it is not a foregone conclusion that parties are less accountable under coalition systems than under single-party governments.

There is one hypothesis that we would fully endorse at this stage: Coalitions invest several parties with some degree of governmental authority. This reduces the differentiation between in- and out-parties. Under short-term coalitions, what is an opposition party one day will be in government or supporting a minority cabinet the next. Therefore, we do expect that under coalition systems, general influence over the agenda is likely to be more widespread than strict implementation of a party mandate. But this question, like all relationships discussed here, can finally be settled only by statistical investigation of what actually takes place under coalitions.

The question of how far programmatic emphases are reflected in policy priorities is of particular relevance to Sweden, which has at times had proportionately the largest public sector of any Western democracy. By the 1980s, public expenditures consumed approximately two-thirds of the gross national product (GNP), as compared to somewhat over one-third in Britain and the United States. Public consumption alone accounted for almost 30 percent of total economic output in Sweden. In 1983 over 400,000 persons out of a population of 8.25 million worked for the national government. How much has this proportionately massive state been guided by sheer inertia? How much has it been in congruence with the articulation of societal needs and alternatives by the political parties?

Swedish institutional forms should facilitate the translation of party concerns into public policy by neutralizing some of the weaknesses of minority and coalition governments. Party discipline in Sweden is sufficient to ensure cabinet policy initiative. Moreover, the traditional instruments of leadership available were further strengthened by a set of constitutional reforms in 1970 whereby all political authority was lodged in the one-chamber parliament. The king no longer has a power of initiative, even in the process of government formation. And although the courts can challenge the constitutionality of government actions, in practice they never do so. Local governments are formally subordinate to the national authorities. Although earlier postwar arrangements differed in detail from present ones, they actually worked very similarly. Power was all the more concentrated because the dominant Social Democrats monopolized the cabinet for all of this earlier period.

Inside the policymaking institutions a rather hierarchical organization renders the imposition of central directives quite easy. The cabinet—the central decision-making body—is supported by disciplined parties in parliament. In the 1980s the cabinet consisted of the prime minister and his deputy, twelve ministers who were also heads of departments, and six ministers without departmental responsibilities. All members of the cabinet formally share responsibility for all policy decisions, including those affecting only a particular area. The ministries and other agencies of the executive branch have considerable authority in implementing cabinet decisions. Given that the cabinet is usually dominated by a single party (the SDP), it can be seen that the potential for political direction is really rather great.

There are also social factors making for clarity of policy leadership in Sweden. The society is unusually homogeneous by Western European standards, and perhaps even more so by the standards of larger countries around the world. There are none of the regional, religious, or ethnic differences that characterize even neighboring Norway. The only ethnic minorities in Sweden are the native Lapps and Finns in the northern provinces, who are numerically insignificant. There has also been very limited immigration in recent times, compared to most other countries.

All these factors make for a centralized, somewhat hierarchical, structure that one can assume to be capable of quick and effective response to political directives. However, two other tendencies render it likely that such directives will be broadly defined by all parties rather than emanating simply from the dominant one.

First of all, Sweden is a small country. There are no divisions between different religious groups; most people are Protestant. There are no remnants of former conquerors who have left behind the rudiments of ethnic conflict.

National homogeneity in a small country makes possible widespread discussion, consultation, and consensus building. In such a consultative setting, decisions generally have not had to be undertaken urgently; therefore, time and effort are devoted to hammering out widely acceptable policy strategies. Parliamentary commissions, with strong representation of all political parties, play central roles in setting the policy agenda and in identifying acceptable alternatives. Evidence is taken and discussion held with all concerned groups. Quite detailed proposals for eventual action by parliament emanate from the commissions. It is unusual for a government to go against such commission recommendations.

Second, Social Democratic dominance has alternated with periods of coalition: Social Democrats with the Center (Agrarian) Party for much of the 1950s; and bourgeois coalitions of Center, Liberals, and Conservatives after 1976. Since 1970, in fact, there has been a standing possibility of alternating SDP and bourgeois governments, though the latter have often been hampered by divisions between member parties. These divisions have given the Social Democrats considerable opportunity for influence from the outside. And as we pointed out earlier, SDP minority governments have often relied on support from the small Communist Party. In contrast, the Center, Liberal, and Conservative parties have gained around 15 percent of the vote each, with considerable fluctuations and transfers between them.

PROGRAM AND POLICY TRENDS

Swedish Data

The Swedish party program data are not unusual. Our analyses include the election programs of all four parties that have served in government, plus the Communists. The reason for including the Communists is to check the extent to which their occasionally influential position as, more or less, "silent partner" has given them a wedge into the active agenda. The categories include a bit under 30 percent of the entries in the election programs.

There is a problem with the time series that is similar to, but not as serious as, the one encountered in France. This concerns the skew in distribution of party control of government over time. Our time series for the policy analysis begins in 1948. The SDP headed every government from then through 1976. This was followed by alternation between governments headed by the Center and by Liberals, then by a return of the SDP for the last period we include, ending in 1985. The return of the SDP reduces the skew, compared to France, where each of three parties held the presidency successively, with no repetition. The French case meant that any extraneous trending would be statistically indistinguishable from the party in government. The return of the Swedish SDP helps minimize that somewhat. However, all statistical terms that include an indicator for governing party—either the interactive term for each of the four parties (which multiplies by 1 their party program percentage when in government and enters 0 when not) or the dummy variable (1/0) for SDP prime ministers—have to be viewed with some caution, given the imbalance of partisan composition of governments over time. The amount of necessary caution is minimized, however, since we find that the indicators for control of government tend, in Sweden, to be of less consequence than elsewhere, without in any way producing especially low or ambiguous R^2s.

The expenditure data are, unfortunately, less than fully comparable with those used in most of the other countries. The Swedish data are not for functional categories of policy, as such, but rather are the expenditures of particular ministries. The data have been checked carefully for continuity, since ministries change, merge, and disappear—although not dramatically. A few functions performed at one time by one ministry have been, for political or administrative reasons, shifted to another. We use only seven ministries, as they are the most consistent. They also represent the major functions examined in the other countries.

Most ministries' fields of competence have remained fairly constant across the various Swedish governments. Of course, since ministries are usually organized along functional lines, we can take their spending record as being roughly equivalent to spending in equivalent functional areas. Thus expenditures by the Ministry of Education and Culture, for example, can be considered more or less equivalent to the record for education spending, as a function, elsewhere. Dealing with the education and culture ministry as a whole does mean, however, that we cannot separate educational from cultural expenditures. But other ministries are more specifically dedicated to one area—defense or agriculture, for example. Thus, employing ministerial rather than more substantively consistent categories should not make too much difference to our results.

The election program categories and corresponding ministries are as follows:

Program Category	*Ministry*
Peace	Defense
Peace	Foreign Affairs
Agriculture	Agriculture
Law & Order	Justice
Technology & Infrastructure	Transport and Communications
Social Services (+)	Health & Social Affairs
Education	Educ. & Cultural Affairs

Again, a reminder: The expenditure indicators are the percentage of central government outlays spent by each ministry, with a lead of two years. This means that the first entry in our analysis is 1948, for which we pair the last entry for the 1944 election programs against the 1950 expenditure priority. The last entry in

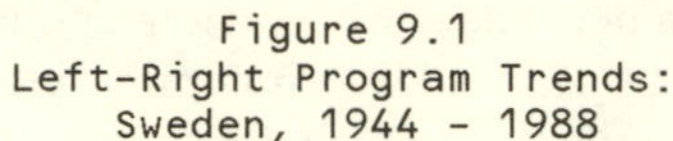

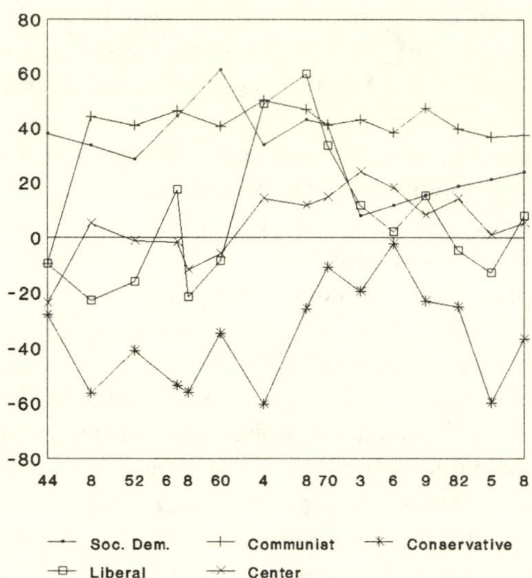

our data set is for 1985, which pairs the 1982 election program data (entered for 1983, 1984, and 1985) against the 1987 policy indicators.

Left-Right Trends

We will soon see that the ideological structure of Swedish parties and policies is tighter than that in any other country we study. The summary left-right program-to-policy linkages are very strong, even though the visual representation does not convey a more obvious message than its counterparts elsewhere.

Figure 9.1 presents the trends for left-right orientations of the party programs. As one might expect, Social Democrats and Conservatives set the ideological boundaries, by and large, within which the other parties move. This results from the Social Democrats' emphasis on social services, welfare, government intervention, and peace, as compared to the Conservative focus on such themes as law and order, freedom, lower taxation, and national defense.

There are two peculiarities of the Swedish left-right trends that distinguish them from party configurations elsewhere. First, there is substantial overlap between the Social Democrats and the Communists. This overlap results from both the occasional radicalism of the Social Democrats, especially prior to the 1970s, and the relative stability of the Communists' program emphases. However, the Social Democratic party is the only one in Sweden that has moved fairly steadily to the right, coming, in recent years, well within the range of such parties as the German SPD, British Labour, and even the American Democrats.

Figure 9.2
Left-Right Expenditure Priority Factor Scores:
Sweden, 1950 – 1987

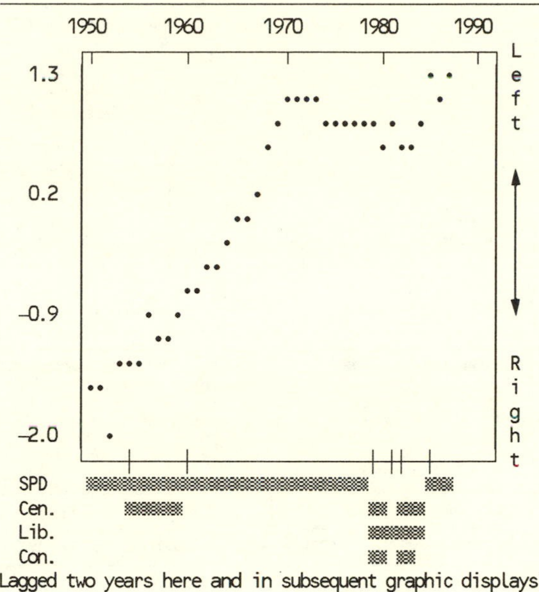

(Lagged two years here and in subsequent graphic displays)

Structure of Policy Priority Factor

Policy Area	Factor Loading
Foreign Affairs	.91
Education & Cultural Affairs	.76
Social Security & Services	.37
Agriculture	–.66
Transportation & Communication	–.91
Defense	–.94

Second, it is noticeable that the Liberals and the Center Party are closer to the Socialist position (even to the extent of sometimes crossing over it in the 1960s and 1970s) than they are to the Conservatives. This helps account for the internal divisions of bourgeois coalitions and for the fact that a minority Liberal government could survive with support from all parties in the late 1970s. The bridging role of the two centrist parties explains why consensus with a tilt toward Social Democratic policies is a notable feature of Swedish party politics.

How far this carries over into policy priorities is shown by Figure 9.2. Again, a factor score arraying leftward against rightward expenditure domains yields a measure that has strong face validity. Note that in Sweden, as in Australia, foreign

Figure 9.3
Trends in Expenditure Priorities: Sweden, 1950 – 1987

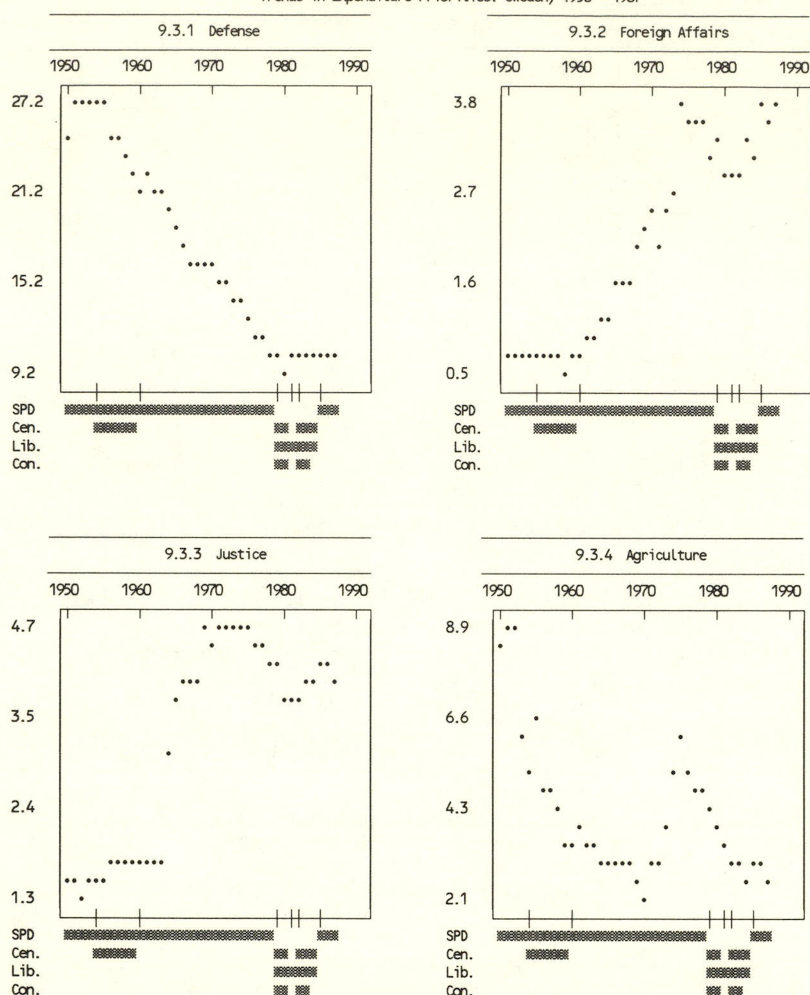

policy (loading at .91), heavily affected by development assistance to the Third World, is polarized with national defense (–.94). That is, when defense shares have been high in Sweden, foreign affairs spending has been proportionately lower, and vice versa. And along with foreign affairs spending have gone the favorites of the welfare state—education (.76) and human services (.37). Contrasted to these, and going along with defense (.94), are the basic infrastructural (–.91) and agriculture policies (–.66).

The left-right policy trend in Sweden is strikingly similar to that found in most other countries in our study. In the 1940s and 1950s, heavy investment in infrastructure accompanied a strong commitment to national defense. In spite of for-

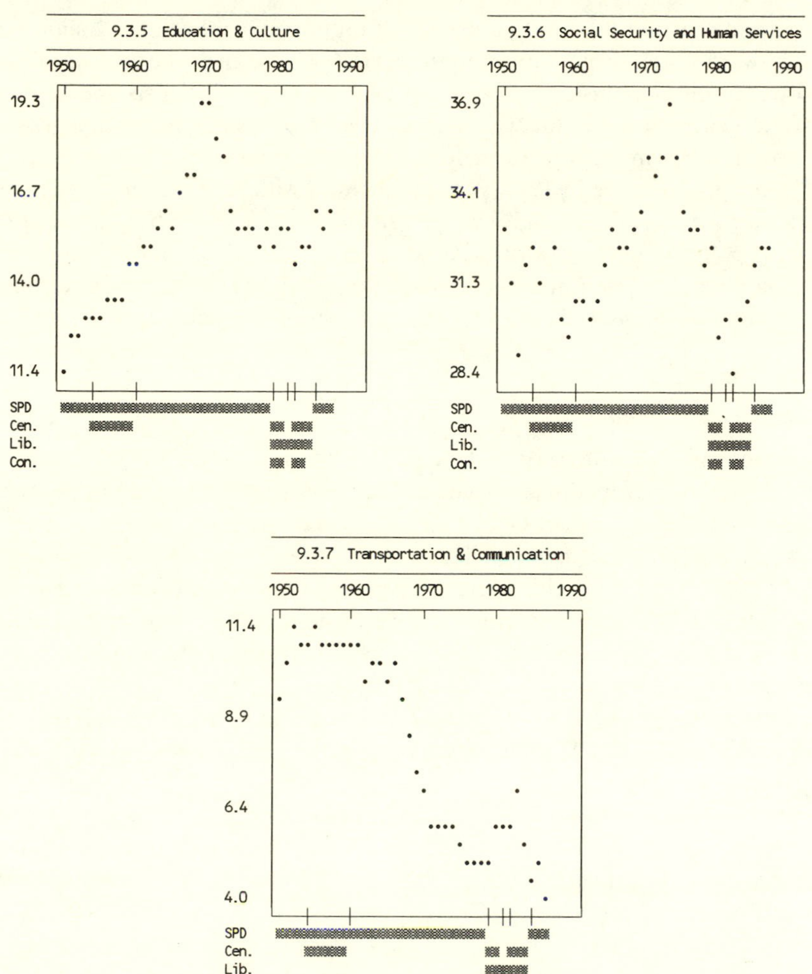

mal neutrality, Sweden did not escape the cold war. This was followed by a sharp leftward trend that moderated in the 1970s and 1980s. Comparing Figure 9.2 with Figure 9.1—policy priorities and ideological orientation of parties—one sees that the peak of leftward policy movement occurred at about the same time as three out of five parties interrupted their programmatic trends to the left. The policy trend tilted rightward under the bourgeois coalitions but reversed again after 1983 under the new Socialist government.

There is essentially little here to distinguish Swedish developments from those of other countries—except for the appearance of left-right policy shifts associated with particular changes in government. With regard to the similarity of programmatic and expenditure trends, a juxtaposition of Figures 9.1 and 9.2 shows that the leftward drift of expenditures to the early 1970s parallels the general leftward movement of the bourgeois parties, but not that of the Socialists and Communists. In general, programmatic emphases (Figure 9.1) show many changes from election to election that are not reflected clearly in policy priority trends (Figure 9.2). The great change in 1976, when a coalition without Socialist participation took over for the first time in forty years, also seems to have been a temporary turning point for policy priorities. We may expect then that some reflection both of programmatic commitments and of the long-standing ideology of government parties may be found in the manner that Swedish governments have cut the fiscal pie.

Specific Policy Trends

The trends in expenditures broadly confirms our assumption of the ministries' equivalence to the functional categories used elsewhere. Inspection of the trends in specific spending domains (Figure 9.3) serves to put detail in the picture conveyed by the summary measure (Figure 9.2). Defense starts high and dips until the 1970s (Figure 9.3.1), with foreign affairs spending being nearly the mirror opposite (9.3.2); likewise (with some variation) with agriculture and transportation (9.3.4 and 9.3.7), although with a bit less regularity. As in other countries, Sweden's priorities for education seem to reflect the baby boomers' passage through the system (9.3.5). The share of national outlays for administration of justice rises in Sweden (9.3.3), just as it does elsewhere, although, as in the United States, it dips in the later years.

Only the category of social security and human services—the heart of the welfare state—seems to follow a peculiarly Swedish pattern. That is, rather than rising monotonically, it varies widely. This probably reflects the fact that Sweden's neutrality during World War II allowed it to emerge from that period with its welfare state largely intact, at quite a high level of priority, compared to those countries whose national outlays had been devoted to the Allied war effort. Sweden's postwar welfare-state policies, therefore, were more adjustment than major redirection—that is, until the redirection rightward in the 1970s.

The expenditure shares displayed in Figure 9.3 constitute an average of over 85 percent of central government outlays. As is usual, the need to match programmatic categories with predetermined expenditure areas requires some experimentation to get the best fit, within limits of a priori plausibility. As it happens, the pairings in Sweden are by and large fairly obvious, for example, justice with law and order, agriculture with agriculture, social and human services with positive references to social services, education and culture with education, transport and communications with technology and infrastructure.

The less obvious case is where emphases on peace were matched with both defense and foreign affairs spending priorities. Expenditure on foreign affairs is largely for aid, development, and support of international organizations. Positive relationships are to be expected with party program emphases on peace. In the case of defense, however, party program references to peace may indicate either a negative or a positive tilt toward defense spending—with the rightist parties positive (peace through strength) and leftist parties negative (peace through disarmament and collaboration). We will return to this point as we report on the analyses.

PARTY PROGRAM-TO-POLICY CONGRUENCE

The best-fitting model linking party program emphases to each policy priority in Sweden is presented in Table 9.1. As in previous chapters, we present the full analyses of all models and expenditure domains in the Appendix. Consistent with our objective of mapping the broad sweep of patterns in policy agenda formation and implementation of mandates, we concentrate here on the most generalizable findings.

Left-right and all seven specific areas are predicted at or above the .25 R^2 threshold. It is interesting for the Swedish context, as we shall discuss at greater length below, that the agenda model is the most common, and agenda effects are very much in order even for those policies gaining congruence from the addition of the mandate terms. In no instance did the ideological differences measured by a dummy variable for Social Democratic governments add power to the models.

Best-Fitting Models

Essentially, we are performing three tasks in these analyses. The first is to see whether there is any relationship at all between party emphases and policy priorities in Sweden. The second is to specify the areas in which there is such a relationship. It is quite plausible that the parties would be more important in some areas than in others, and that we may, eventually, note some cross-national patterning to those differences. Our third task is to identify which kind of relationship holds between party program and policy in various areas. Broadly speaking, can it be described as the parties—even those in opposition—that are setting an agenda, or are governing parties carrying out a mandate?

In a multiparty system, with frequent coalition governments, the parties may effectively stake out territorial claims on particular policy domains. This would be evident in patterns of what could be labeled *policy hegemony.* Are there any instances of party policy hegemony in Sweden? None that are very striking. The one policy for which the best prediction of policy shares is provided by a single party's program, irrespective of government or opposition status, is also the weakest (R^2 = .25, b = .61) in our set of analyses. This is the case of transportation and communications policy, which seems best predicted by the Center Party program's emphases on technology and infrastructure. This seems a reasonable domain for dominance by an agrarian party concerned with the marketing conditions of its

Table 9.1
Best-Fitting Models Between Party Program Emphases and Policy Priorities:
Sweden, 1948 – 1987*

Agenda Models

Policy Priority (Program)	a	Soc. Dem.	Liberal	Center	Conservative	Communist	Adj R^2
Left-Right (Left-Right)	.14		.02		.03		.71
Admin. of Justice (Law & Order)	.68		<u>–.21</u>	.60	.16		.68
Defense (Peace)	17.3	–1.34	<u>.75</u>			$.33^{\underline{n}}$	.58
Foreign Affairs (Peace)	1.60	.19				.07	.54
Trans.& Communic.) (Tech.& Infrastr.)	6.25			.61			.25

$$[\quad E_i = a + bP_i^A + \ldots bP_i^n \quad]$$

Mandate Models

Policy Priority (Program Emphasis)	Constant a	Soc. Dem. (+) Agenda or (–) Mandate (Out)	Soc. Dem. Mandate (x Gov)	Liberal (+) Agenda or (–) Mandate (Out)	Liberal Mandate (x Gov)	Center (+) Agenda or (–) Mandate (Out)	Center Mandate (x Gov)	Conservative (+) Agenda or (–) Mandate (Out)	Conservative Mandate (x Gov)	Comm. Agenda (Out)	Adj R^2	Added By Mandate
Agriculture (Agriculture)	3.90			$–.23^{\underline{n}}$	.97	.57		.18			.69	.12
Soc.Sec.& Servs. (Pro-Soc.Services)	31.7	$–.45^{\underline{n}}$	.38	.07	.29	.18				$–.15^{\underline{n}}$	.59	.21
Education (Education)	16.2		<u>–.90</u>			.22	<u>–.47</u>	$–.37^{\underline{n}}$			.56	.47

$$[\quad E_i = a + bP_i^A + b(P_i^A \times G) + \ldots bP_i^n + b(P_i^n \times G) \quad]$$

* Indicating only those b's (unstandardized regression coefficients) that attained .05 statistical significance. Coefficients in the opposite direction from theoretical expectation are <u>underlined</u>. Cases of negative mandate are indicated by $\underline{n}$. In Sweden, there were no cases where the ideology model was best-fitting.

main clientele. In general, there is little evidence that a monopoly over specialized policy areas is given to competitors in exchange for coalition participation in Sweden. The evidence, rather, leans much more toward broadly accommodating or consensual policies, whereby the parties share influence on the agenda and the mandate matters little.

The most general indicators of program emphases and of policy priorities are the left-right measures. To what extent was the movement of policy leftward in the 1950s and 1960s, followed by a plateau and slightly rightward tilt (Figure 9.2), anticipated by the general orientation of the party programs? At the level of simple correlations, all three bourgeois parties—Liberals, Center, and Conservatives—anticipated these trends in their election programs. When entered together in the agenda model, only the Center, because of high correlation with the other two, drops below statistical significance. The left-right tilt of the dominant Social Democrats, in spite of their being far and away the biggest player in Swedish politics, offered no programmatic guidance to the voters that would have enabled them to anticipate general policy allocations accurately. These relationships were earlier noted in the discussion of the trend lines portrayed in Table 9.1.

When submitted to the alternative models, the broad left-right program-to-policy linkages do, however, yield very interesting results. The strongest theoretically consistent congruence found in any country we have so far studied is yielded by the agenda model, which includes no term for governing but merely examines the collective predictive power of the agendas provided by the competing parties. Taken together, the joint party program left-right emphases predict 71 percent of the left-right trend in Swedish policy priorities. And the two statistically significant contributors to this relationship, the largest found in any country in our study, are the Liberals and the Conservatives. Even though these parties have gained only between 25 to 35 percent of the seats in parliament, they have provided Swedish voters with the best overall guide as to what broad policy directions to expect after elections.

This same joint, consensual pattern of multiple party programs, irrespective of whether parties are in government or opposition, provides the best explanation for four of the seven domains of policy (which, we should again note, are over 85 percent of all government expenditures in Sweden). Between 57 and 68 percent of the variance in these domains is explained by the combination of party programs. There are differences within this overall pattern, however, that deserve attention.

First, the cases of defense and foreign affairs together present the pattern seen previously only in Australia. Our earlier examination of the Swedish time trends focused on the inverse relationship between these two obviously related policy domains. As defense has declined, expenditures for foreign affairs—principally in the form of development assistance—have risen. The more the Social Democrats emphasize peace in their programs, the lower the percentage of expenditures for defense and the higher for foreign affairs. The *b* of −1.34 for defense and +.19 for foreign affairs affirms the predominant role of the Social Democrats' policy of détente, that is, stressing peace in the party program and implementing it by reducing the priority given to defense expenditures.

For the Liberals, however, pursuit of peace is either contradicted by policy priority or is a case of "peace through strength," that is, an increased investment in the military ($b = .75$) as a means to attain the peace discussed in the election program. As can be confirmed by consulting the Appendix, the same holds true, although not at a statistically significant level, for the other bourgeois parties. In the preceding section, we viewed this coefficient for the Liberals as a likely contradiction, and we have indicated it as such in Table 9.1. But we would not argue vigorously against the "peace through strength" explanation without more detailed exploration than is really warranted, given our goal of identifying general patterns.

The other two policy areas best explained by the joint impact of multiple party programs, irrespective of participation in government, are administration of justice and transportation. And here there is no significant impact from the seemingly dominant Social Democrats. The Center Party's and the Conservatives' emphases on law and order have together provided the best forecasts of the rising priority accorded to justice policy ($b = .60$ and .16, respectively). The Liberals, like their counterparts in other countries, have refused to join the law-and-order bandwagon, resulting in one of the few statistically significant *contradictory* relationships in the Swedish findings.

In contrast, however, the declining emphasis of the Center on technology and infrastructure has strongly forecast the course of reduced priority for transport and communication. We earlier commented on the likely concern for transport and communication by this historically agrarian party in Sweden. Seen here is the joint dynamic of change in that linkage. The trend in the Center Party's emphasis on technology and infrastructure is –.47 (r with year); moreover, the trend in transport and communication's share of outlays is an even steeper –.91; whereas the simple correlation between the two is .52. This is the statistical essence of the hegemony already noted.

According to the mandate model, we should expect the second term under each party ("× Gov") to be positive and significant (except in the special instance of peace vs. defense policy). The "Program × Government" term brings into play on program congruence with policy priorities the added effect of the party's having served in the government. Yet for both the Socialists and the Center Party the expectation provided by program emphases on education is the reverse of what comes out of the policy process (–.90 and –.47, respectively). The positive .22 b for the Center party out of government effect is not opposite to expectations but rather indicates agenda influence, outside the confines of the electoral mandate. The –.37 under the Conservative "out" column is consistent with the theory, as an indicator of negative mandate.

Mandate theory is redeemed somewhat further by the pattern of relationships in social security policy, especially with respect to the Social Democrats. The simple correlation between Social Democratic emphases and social policy priority is near zero. But in the mandate model, if the programs of the other parties and especially their participation in government are taken into account, the Socialist's situation becomes more clear, with a negative mandate of –.45 for having been out of government and a +.38 for governing. This sustains the reputation of the Social Democrats as the archetypical proponents of the modern welfare state.

Social policy is not reflective solely of the SDP programs in government, however. It is also affected by those of the Liberals, especially as a consequence of the Liberals' having been in government (.29) and, to a lesser extent, by some impact on the agenda from the Liberals (.07) and the Center (.18).

We should note again that there is no instance where a superior model is produced by including the dummy variable for Social Democratic occupancy of the premier's office. Long-standing interparty policy differences outside those accommodated by variation in the formal, written election-program content do not seem to be of consequence for policy in Sweden.

Nonconformists and Contradictions

There were no cases of nonconformity. Transportation received the lowest R^2, at exactly .25. Of the significant coefficients in Table 9.1, only two policy areas contain clear contradictions:

- Justice: *b* for the Liberals = –.21
- Education and culture: *b*s for the Socialists and the Center = –.90 and –.47, respectively.

With one contradiction but two consistent coefficients, we might conclude that the administration of justice is moderately well covered by our theory. But education is a clear case of contradiction. The chronicling of deviations is offered only as a possible base for later generalization, once we have completed our cross-national tour. Thus we do not speculate at any length about the contradictory *b* (–.21) between Liberal emphases on law and order and the expenditure priority for the Ministry of Justice, accounting for the Liberals being in government. Do Liberal parties, generally, tend to dissemble in such an area? It is usual for them to tilt relatively more than their competitors in the direction of individual liberty on any order versus liberty scale. Does that color their ability to signal their governing behavior through their party program? We would not use this single deviation to reject the whole equation for justice policy, although it does weaken the otherwise strong impression of an R^2 of .68. Among other reasons for retaining a positive view toward the robustness of the equation is that the Liberal contradiction is based on only six years in government over the entire period of thirty-eight years.

The contradictions in education and culture, in contrast, ought to be taken much more seriously, first because there are two contradictions and only one statistically significant supporting coefficient in the best-fitting equation, and second because the contradictions involve two major parties, one or both of which have participated in government nearly the entire time since the war—the Social Democrats and the Center. The most appropriate conclusion is that we can have little confidence in the linkage between program signals and education-policy priorities in Sweden. In sum, we are inclined to claim success for six of seven policy areas, plus left-right.

The policy success of the Communists is rather mixed. They show a modestly strong agenda contribution in foreign affairs (.07), where Communist emphases on peace are independently associated with increased policy priority. However, we hypothesized a negative coefficient as confirming effectiveness in defense when related to party emphases on peace. That indeed is the case with the Social Democrats (–1.34). However, the more the Liberals (.75) and the Communists (.33) stress peace, the higher the priority for the military. The usual proximity of both these parties to the Social Democrats would lead us to expect comparable program-to-policy congruence, yet that is not the case. We must accept the likely message of the coefficients to be that the Liberal and Communist cases in defense are indeed contradictory. The same, we would hold, is true for the Communist coefficient in social security and human services (–.15). These negative findings for the Communists are not contrary to our basic theory but rather are examples of the negative mandate for out-parties. But we had expected the Swedish Communists, small though they are, to be exempt from that form of "punishment," given their ideological proximity and general history of assistance to the Social Democrats. Such a reward, however, has apparently not been tendered.

The clear and possible contradictions reviewed here for the Swedish case, while deserving of note, are not nearly so impressive as is the overall pattern of cross-party accommodation, with occasional implementation of the mandate.

CONCLUSION

The conclusion is precisely the one that we suggested in our introductory remarks on the Swedish political environment: Sweden's is a broadly consensual policy process, with institutionalized mechanisms of accommodation. The absence of policy shifts associated with long-standing ideological differences is additional evidence of consensual politics. But consensus does not mean impotence, as is seen in the dramatic reflection in policy of left-right movements by the bourgeois parties. Overall, the Swedish mixture of a Social Democratic Party mandate on welfare, with general agenda-setting roles in the other areas incorporating the habitual opposition parties, seems to ensure a voice for nearly everyone. The nearly 50 percent left-wing voters (Social Democratic plus Communist) generally see a translation of the programs they have voted for into government priorities, and supporters of the minority parties also influence this translation process through debate and discussion. The different representational roles of the parties are broadly appropriate to their numerical strengths. And the fact that the Center has somewhat more say than the Right seems fair, given the overall distribution of preferences, as reflected in the popular vote. The formal absence of a dual mandate seems counterbalanced in Sweden by effective informal processes of minority representation.

In sum, the homogeneity of Swedish society has helped bridge potentially serious policy differences. Party pronouncements effectively guide the policy agenda. But the fact of being in or out of government, with some important exceptions, is not crucial to party program implementation, forcing us to doubt that any pure form of mandate theory applies in Sweden. Risking a speculation on the basis of one case, we might conclude that mandate theory makes sense only under social and economic conditions that produce at least moderately serious policy divisions.

10

Austria

INSTITUTIONAL AND POLITICAL CONTEXT

The singular peculiarity of Austrian politics in the postwar period has been the tendency of the two large parties to form coalitions, even when one of them had enough support to form a government on its own. One of the few well-attested generalizations in political science is the tendency of proportional representation (PR) at the electoral level to be associated with government by coalitions (Riker 1962). In systems of cabinet government, where the formation and survival of the executive depends on parliamentary support, PR tends to produce a multiparty system without clear parliamentary majorities. Heightening the paradox of coalitions in the Austrian case is that, almost uniquely, an electoral system of strict proportional representation has produced two large, potentially majority parties, the Austrian Socialist Party (Sozialistische Partei Österreichs—SPÖ) and the Austrian People's Party (Österreichische Volkspartei—ÖVP). Yet for half the postwar period those parties chose not to form governments on their own, even when they could have done so. From 1945 to 1966 the two major parties were in a grand coalition together, excluding the small Austrian Freedom Party (Freiheitliche Partei Österreichs—FPÖ), which had almost 10 percent of the vote. In 1966 the ÖVP formed a single-party majority government that lasted until 1970, when the SPÖ won the first of several general elections, governing on its own until 1983. At that point, a reduction in the SPÖ's vote forced it into a coalition with the Freedom Party. In 1986 this coalition broke down as a result of quarrels between the two parties, with the SPÖ reconstituting the grand coalition with the ÖVP—the last government included in our analysis.

Surplus majority is a term applied to coalition cabinets that could have included a different combination of parties closer to, but still above, 50 percent of the seats in parliament. Such coalitions cannot be explained in terms of narrow party competition aimed at exclusive power holding. In Austria, they are partly understandable in terms of the country's unusual history and international position after World War II. In the interwar years, the Socialists and the precursor of the People's Party (the Christian-Social Conservatives) had actually used armed force against each other, in a near civil war, which brought about the downfall of the First Republic and its absorption into Nazi Germany (1938–1945). After the war, Austrian governments coexisted with Western and Soviet occupying forces until their withdrawal in accord with the State Treaty in 1957. The treaty itself was achieved in part through the maintenance of a united front by the Austrians, so there was a considerable premium on the two major parties' forming the grand coalition.

The real peculiarity of the Austrian situation, however, is that the major parties continued in government together long after coalition ceased to be a necessary response to external pressures. They even returned to such a surplus majority in 1986. Clearly their earlier experience of working together provided a precedent for this kind of arrangement. The SPÖ and the ÖVP have well-established procedures for hammering out a detailed coalition agreement, which covers the distribution of ministerial portfolios between the parties and the general policies they will pursue in government. The document is detailed enough to provide strict reference lines for government action, and it can be appealed to in the case of disputes.

The existence of a precedent for cooperation cannot be a full explanation, however, for the proclivity to grand coalitions in Austria. If the past had been totally determining, there should not, after all, have been single-party majority governments between 1970 and 1983. The extreme contrast that might open up between these situations—one in which constant consultation with a powerful partner is necessary and one in which the majority party need not, constitutionally, consult anyone—offers a controlled situation in which to compare the operation of the election mandate and to examine the effects of diffuse party influence over the broad agenda. But it also requires systematic explanation.

PROGRAM AND POLICY TRENDS

Austrian Data

The Austrian program data have one striking oddity. The April 1970 election produced a short-lived government—the first of a string of SPÖ governments under the leadership of Chancellor Bruno Kreisky. That particular government, however, was destined to be brief and returned to the voters for renewal in November 1971. The programs for the 1970 election were uncommon for all parties—focusing on a very narrow range of issues. The consequence was a wild swing leftward. However, the data we employ show that this is due to a concentration of emphases in only a few categories. Therefore we exclude the 1970 data from our examples.

Austrian expenditure data are included for 1953 through 1988. They are reported in the general yearbook *(Statistische Handbuch für die Republic Österreich)* in quite fine detail. Unfortunately for our purposes, the categories are frequently changed. Some clear aggregation could be done with confidence of consistency throughout the period. But enough was changed to prevent incorporation of more than an average of 45 percent of the total. We are reasonably confident of the consistency of the nine categories that make up that total. The categories are generally comparable to their counterparts in the other countries. The largest set of omissions are several subsidies that varied considerably in definition over time.

After the usual preliminary experimentation, the following pairings were used in the Austrian analyses:

Program Category	*Policy Area*
Internationalism (+)	Defense
Peace and Internationalism*	Foreign Affairs
Law & Order	Administration of Justice**
Agriculture	Agriculture
Social Justice	Social Security (Pensions & Welfare)
Social Justice	Family Assistance (Children's Allowance)
Education	Education
Technology & Infrastructure	Public Utilities & Communication
Art, Sport, Leisure	Culture and the Arts

*Sum of "Peace" plus "Internationalism (+)."
**Sum of spending for police, courts, prisons, etc.

As a result of our leading the expenditure data and the elimination of two years, the actual times series is a bit complicated. Spending data could be assembled consistently for the years 1953 through 1988. The analysis employs program data for the years 1951 through 1986. They begin with the second year of the November 1949 election programs (which were entered in the party program files for 1950, 1951, and 1952). This entry, for 1951, is paired to the 1953 spending data. The last entry in the data file is for 1986, which pairs the programs for the June 1986 election against 1988 expenditures. This should yield thirty-six years—1951 through 1986. However, the elimination of 1970 and 1971, because of irregularities in the party data, leaves a total of thirty-four years.

An additional variation in the Austrian analyses is required because of the length of time the Socialists have participated in government. The SPÖ was the junior partner (that is, it did not occupy the chancellorship) during the long period of grand coalition, from 1945 through early 1966, or for the first fifteen years of the period included in our data set (1951 through 1965). Then, after four years of ÖVP majority government, the SPÖ headed the government, in coalition beginning in 1983. The two years excluded from our statistical analyses (1970 and 1971) were years of Socialist government. Nevertheless, during thirty of the thirty-four years included, the SPÖ was in government.

If we were to follow our standard procedure for the interactive term, used to separate in- from out-parties, we would multiply the SPÖ's program percentages by 1 for the years in government and by 0 for the years out. This would yield a separate variable that actually included identical values for the out-party variable for all but four years. The same, of course, occurs in reverse for the liberal FPÖ, but we consider it less severe, given that the FPÖ is by far the least consequential of the three parties. We have chosen, therefore, to use as the Socialist interactive term a 1 for the years when there was a Socialist *chancellor* and a 0 for the years when there was none. This gives a near-even break and contrasts to the skew that would have resulted from using the dummy variable to indicate Socialist participation *in government,* as is our custom in the other countries.

This choice does incur two other risks, however. First, it treats the SPÖ programs during the years of the grand coalition as though the party was "out of government." That we can deal with by using appropriate caution in interpreting differences between out-party and government terms for the Socialists.

The second risk, however, brings us once more against the problem of skew in party control. The use of an indicator of whether the Socialists were in or out of the chancellorship as the interactive multiplier concentrates the "in" indicators in the second half of the time period and the "out" indicators in the first half. That also will call for qualifiers, much as we have had to invoke in the French case and, to a lesser extent, in the Swedish.

The irony of all of this seeming exceptionalism for Austria is that it is all done in the interest of bringing the data closer to uniformity with those from the other countries. Unfortunately, we have one more exception in the interest of consistency. This concerns the left-right policy score.

Unlike the other countries, where we were able to use a few expenditure priority measures to construct a tidy left-right policy factor, minor instances of missing data plus the peculiarities of the Austrian experience prevent the construction of such a clearly differentiated measure. As will be clearer (or more murky, depending on one's view) in the graphic illustrations, Austria's policy pattern is the most deviant of all in the set. This deviance is principally driven by the uncommon history of national defense policy, which is, in turn, tied to the peculiarity of Austrian neutrality.

Austria was, in effect, an occupied country until 1955, at which time all four Allied forces were withdrawn in return for a firm pledge of neutrality by the Austrian government. A consequence of the occupation was a defense budget of virtually nil prior to 1955. Austria remained outside both NATO and the Warsaw Pact. But being directly between them made a Costa Rican solution—no military as such—highly risky. As a consequence, the defense buildup, which elsewhere took place in the late 1940s and early 1950s, did not occur in Austria until ten years later, peaking in 1966. But it peaked at only 6.1 percent of total spending, well below the peak of 24 percent for the next lowest defense spender in our set of countries—the Netherlands. Austrians did not feel secure without some defense, but they likewise did not wish to create a fuss with their superpower neighbors, shouting over them, as it were.

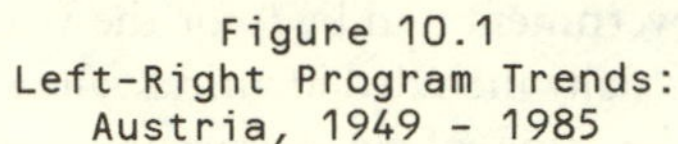

Figure 10.1
Left-Right Program Trends:
Austria, 1949 - 1985

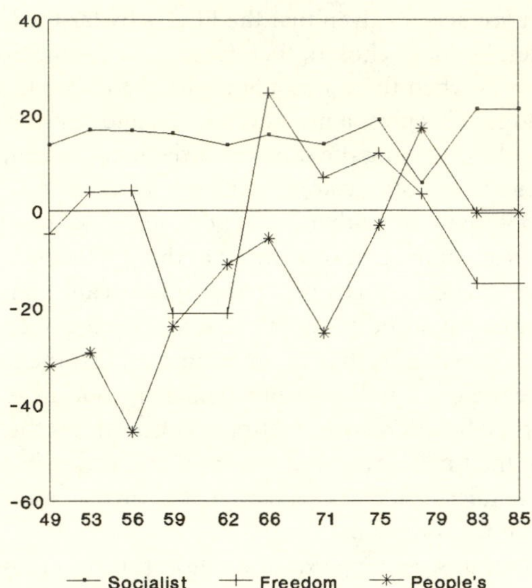

This absence of a defense pole anchoring the scale, in effect, has left the Austrian policy profile less structured than elsewhere. The profile was further complicated by some gaps in the time series, such as the absence of consistent data on health or transportation expenditures. Factor analysis did not help sort out the problem. Therefore, we opted for a strategy that would produce an index with maximum face validity compared to the other countries. In each of the other countries, the left-right factor score anchors defense and agriculture on the *right* and a variety of human services on the *left.* For Austria, we constructed an additive/subtractive index of left-right composed of the following: [Education + family assistance + social security] minus [defense + agriculture].

Again, the motive behind these irregularities is, counterintuitively perhaps, to attain as much regularity in the measures as possible. We want very much to ensure that Austria, peculiar though it may appear on the surface, is analyzed in such a way as to yield maximum comparability of indicators, thus enabling us to view the results as valid readings rather than as strange numbers describing a peculiar country.

Left-Right Trends

No peculiarities are involved in the measurement of left-right programmatic trends in Austria. Figure 10.1 shows a set of trend lines much like those found elsewhere—which, in itself, challenges at least one long-standing assumption about Austria's parties. Commentators have often suggested that the two major Austrian parties are closer in many ways to each other than either is to the Freedom Party, thus explaining the preferences of the former for grand coalitions instead of minimum-winning coalitions between the small FPÖ and either the SPÖ or the ÖVP. The FPÖ, heir to a legacy of prewar pan-German nationalism as well as economic liberalism, was widely regarded as a home for Nazi survivors and sympathizers after the war, and it has been distinguished by certain strident nationalist stands since.

Even apart from these historical considerations, the major parties could be averse on broad political grounds from giving the FPÖ the kind of blackmail potential exerted by the German Free Democrats (see Chapter 11). However, the strong Christian-social element in the ÖVP is sympathetic to many of the interventionist, welfare-oriented stances taken by the SPÖ. This resonance is reflected in policy practices that stress consensus between business and labor, commonly labeled *neocorporatism* (Lehmbruch and Schmitter 1982, 16). Strong corporatist tendencies are at work throughout Austrian society—indeed Lehmbruch and Schmitter identified Austria as one of the purest examples of postwar neocorporatism. The tendency to seek national economic policies based on agreements between business and unions also facilitates cooperation between their political representatives, the People's Party and the Socialists, respectively.

There are, however, countertendencies at work in Austria, the most striking of which are the cumulative sociopolitical cleavages that produced the two-party-dominated system (in spite of PR) in the first place. In Austria the major class, religious, and territorial divisions do not cut across each other, as they do in many West European countries, where they produce the typically fragmented party system, magnified by proportional representation. Instead, the cleavages in Austria are cumulative and mutually reinforcing, dividing the basically working-class, industrialized, secularized East—centered in Vienna—from the bourgeois, small-town, Catholic West. Such a sharp and unmediated opposition of political and social forces must have some effects on the ideology and relationships of the two major parties. It certainly suggests that, on occasion, they might find it congenial to push their policies through from an untrammeled majority position, rather than suffer the constraints and compromises of coalition.

We can settle some of these points by looking at the left and right movements of the three parties, as we have done for all the countries analyzed so far in this book. The picture revealed in Figure 10.1 is very like the ones that emerge elsewhere. The Socialist Party's and the People's Party's stances rarely overlap (only once, in the late 1970s). It is interesting that they diverged most in the 1950s, the period of repeated grand coalitions, and since then have generally come closer together, although they may be sharply differentiated at a particular election. However, these left and right movements bear little relationship to the parties' going into coalition together. Indeed, there is something of an inverse relationship, with the ÖVP at any rate going the furthest to the right during coalitions with the SPÖ—perhaps because the former feels it must differentiate itself at that point.

The FPÖ, despite its general reputation for being ideologically far out, seems in Figure 10.1 to follow a path mapped out by many other liberal third parties (e.g., the British Liberals, the German Free Democrats) of moving indecisively between its two major rivals—going, for example, from the extreme of overlapping with the ÖVP in 1959 to passing the SPÖ on the left in 1966. There is nothing here to indicate why the FPÖ should not have been preferred as a coalition partner by either of the two major groups. If anything, it seems more ideologically centrist than the German FDP, which has performed such a role as minor coalition partner throughout most of the postwar period.

It may, of course, be that the left-right scale is not the most appropriate dimension along which to measure variations in the ideological orientation of the FPÖ, or of other liberal parties, for that matter. That is, it may have distinguishing marks that are not captured by Figure 10.1. As far as that representation goes, however, it does not seem exceptional in any respect from other national counterparts.

Policy trends, however, as we have noted in the previous section, are rather unlike those of other democracies. Figure 10.2 displays the left-right policy score for Austria. Clearly, this is an idiosyncratic distribution, and it is so in spite of, not because of, the modest adjustments in measurement. In all the other countries in this study there was a steady postwar movement leftward until (usually) the early or mid-1970s, after which the policy score either remained stable or moved slightly rightward. In Austria, no such pattern is evident. In some small part this may reflect the rather different basis of construction of the scale. But it also reflects undeniable tendencies of individual policy areas, such as the rise rather than the decline in defense expenditures and the relatively static nature of social and educational spending priorities. These ratios are very much affected by the postwar history of occupation followed by neutrality, outlined earlier in the chapter. The result is that Austria does not display the inexorable leftward push of spending priorities evident, for example, in the United States (Figure 8.2). Taking Figure 10.2 as a whole, we can point to a weak secular decline in *left* as opposed to *right* expenditures, a decline that is unique among our ten countries.

Figure 10.2 does not show much surface relationship to Figure 10.1, on the right and left movements of parties, though it does display a rightward shift under the ÖVP single-party government of 1966–1970. We check out congruence with the statistical models below. The absence of any very evident reflection of ideological shifts in policy priorities makes it clear, however, that congruence between emphases and government priorities have also to be sought primarily in specific areas of policy, as with other countries, rather than along the broad left-right spectrum.

Figure 10.2
Left-Right Expenditure Priority Scores:
Austria, 1953 – 1988*

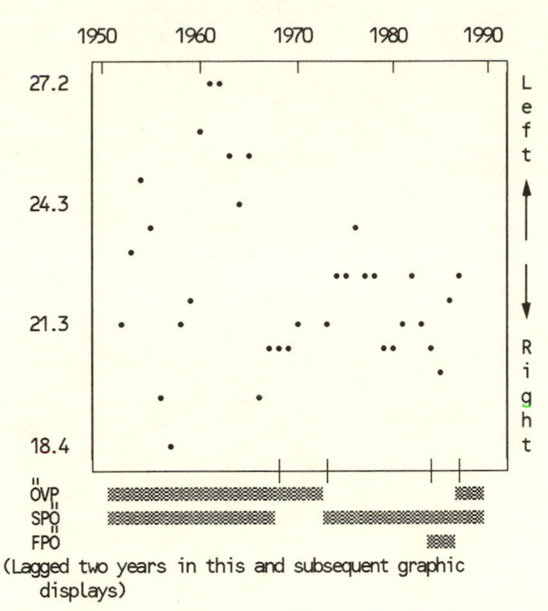

* Additive score composed of percentage of central government expenditures for education, social security, and family assistance minus percentage for defense and agriculture.

Specific Policy Trends

As a prelude to more-detailed analysis, we shall examine expenditure trends within specific areas. One peculiarity of the Austrian data should be noted: Shifts in budgetary categories over the postwar period meant that we could construct time-consistent series for only about 45 percent of total central governmental outlays. Thus, even though each area is measured by the percentage of total expenditures, all or most of them can go down simultaneously without implausibility. The separate elements of Figure 10.3 show that this in fact happens with the indicators we have.

A first concern, however, is how policy priorities vary with the different types of postwar government. In particular, does the era of single-party Socialist government (1970–1983) show markedly different patterns from those of the grand coalitions?

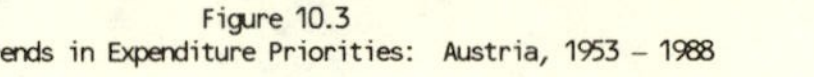
Figure 10.3
Trends in Expenditure Priorities: Austria, 1953 – 1988

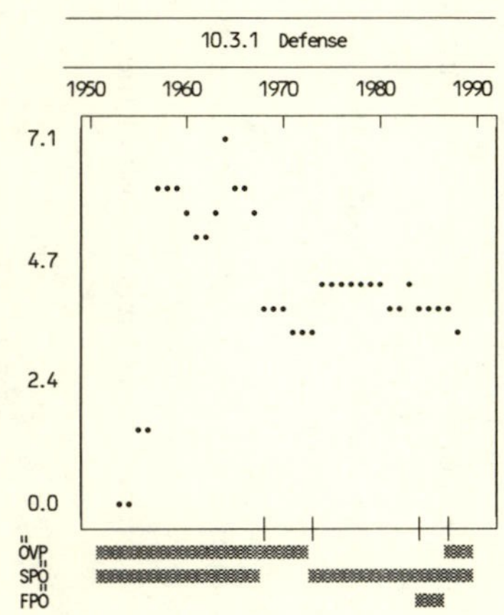

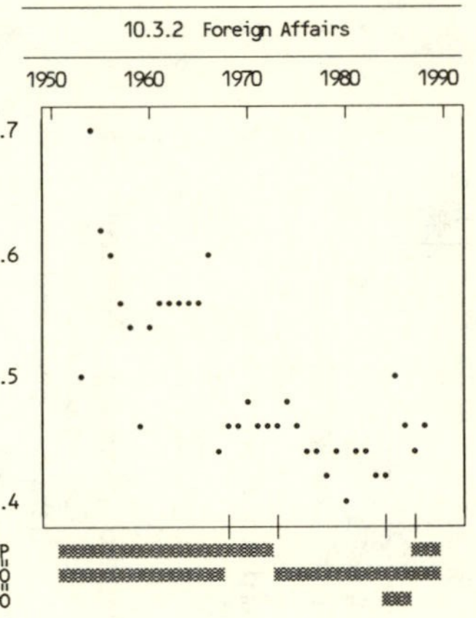

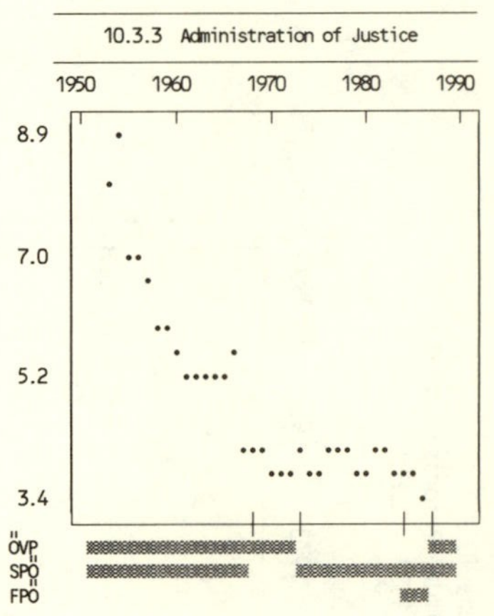

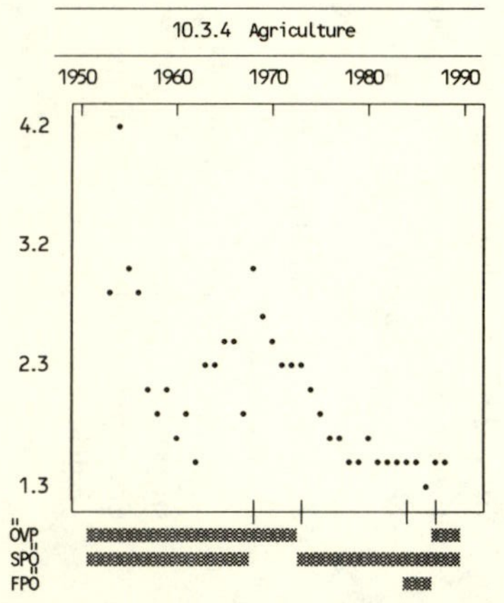

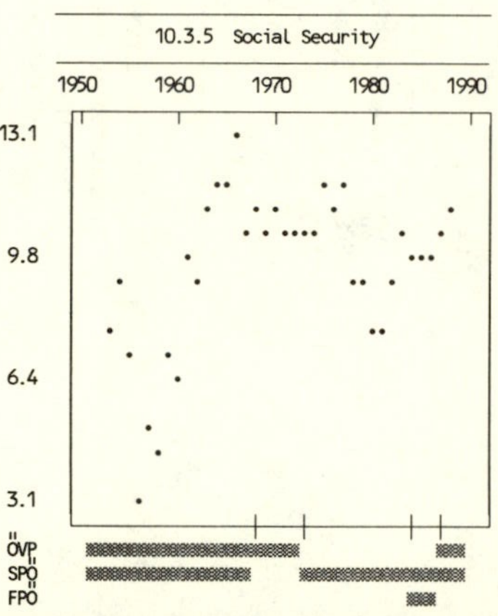

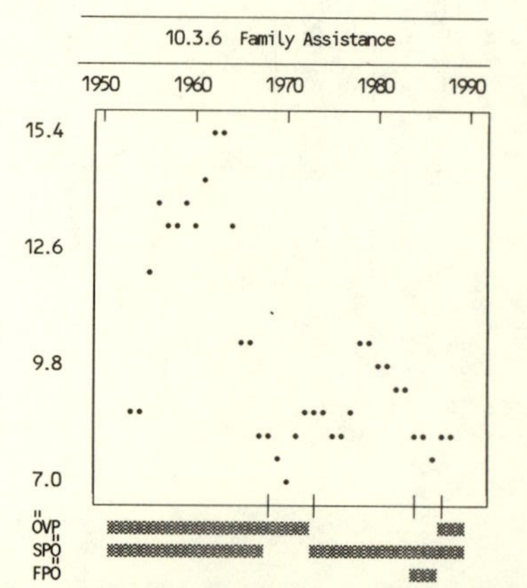

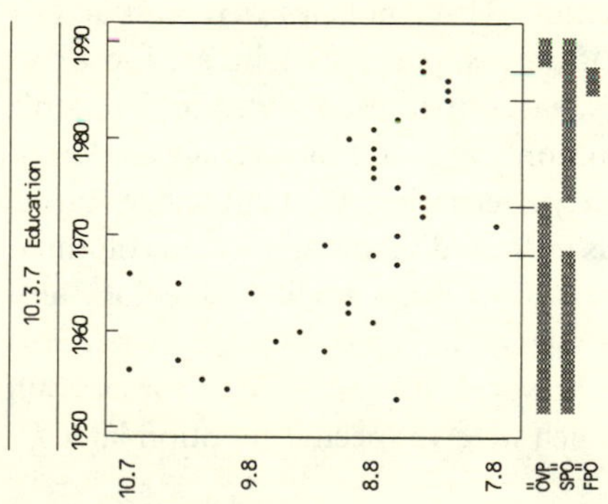
10.3.7 Education
1950
1960
1970
1980
1990
10.7
9.8
8.8
7.8
ÖVP
SPÖ
FPÖ

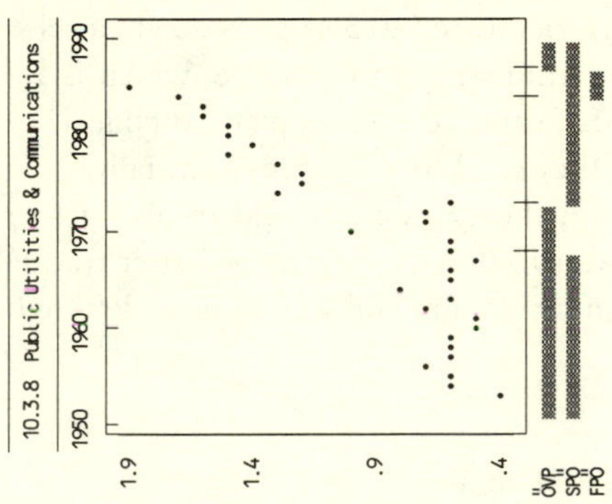
10.3.8 Public Utilities & Communications
1950
1960
1970
1980
1990
1.9
1.4
.9
.4
ÖVP
SPÖ
FPÖ

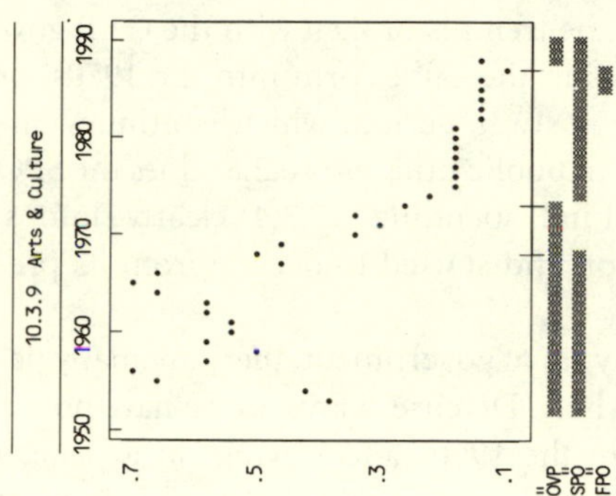
10.3.9 Arts & Culture
1950
1960
1970
1980
1990
.7
.5
.3
.1
ÖVP
SPÖ
FPÖ

The answer on the whole is no. Either the trend is broken with the ÖVP government beginning in 1966 and continues in the same form into the 1970s, or there is a clear tendency over the whole postwar period, which continues unchanged into the Socialist decade. Only with public utilities (10.2.8) does the SPÖ have a possibly distinctive profile. Agricultural spending (10.3.4) clearly slumps, but had done so under the grand coalition and started to decline from its previous high point under the ÖVP in 1966.

Despite the lack of difference between types of government, there are many peculiarities of Austrian policy trends as a whole. Defense shares, as we have noted, contrast with other countries, peaking in the 1960s and staying on a plateau thereafter instead of declining from a peak in the early 1950s (10.3.1), as in most other countries. Clearly this has to do with the late gain of political independence. Spending abroad (foreign affairs, 10.3.2) varies inversely with defense (as in Australia and Sweden, but not as in Britain, the United States, Canada, or France), most strikingly in the earlier years (Figures 10.3.1 and 10.3.2). But unlike the case in the other countries, it is the defense policy priority in Austria that goes up and foreign affairs policy shares that decline. Agriculture (10.3.4) goes down, as elsewhere, but so also does funding for the administration of justice, which is less usual. Family assistance and education (10.3.6 and 10.3.7) drop and then level off in the postwar period, whereas elsewhere they tend to rise, at least initially.

As we have noted, such deviations from the comparative norm also get reflected in left-right policy priorities (Figure 10.2). But they may be better tracked by program changes in specific areas than by the general measures of left-right programs and left-right policy.

PARTY PROGRAM-TO-POLICY CONGRUENCE

The long periods of grand coalition led us to expect a general pattern of accommodation, much like the one found (for different reasons) in Sweden. However, the opposite is the case in Austria, as is clear from Table 10.1. In no instance did the relatively simple agenda model, taking no account of a party's being in or out of government, yield the best-fitting equation. Three policies were best accommodated by the mandate model. Six specific areas, plus left-right, are most congruent with the ideology model. The statistical contribution added to the agenda model by the mandate term is also uncommonly high. Of the average 65 percent of variance explained by programs and party alternation, the mandate term contributes an average 38 percentage points, as indicated in the right-hand column of Table 10.1. In those seven equations where it contributes at all, the ideology term adds an average 12 percent to that of the agenda and the mandate. A relatively high number of apparent contradictions, however, suggests a need for care and caution in interpreting average R^2s—to which we give specific attention later.

Table 10.1
Best-Fitting Models Between Party Program Emphases and Policy Priorities: Austria, 1951–1988*

Mandate Models

Policy Priority (Program Emphasis)	Constant a	People's (+)(−) Agenda or Mandate (Out)	People's Mandate (x Chan)	Socialist (+)(−) Agenda or Mandate (Out)	Socialist Mandate (x Chan)	Freedom (+)(−) Agenda or Mandate (Out)	Freedom Mandate (x Gov)	Adj R^2	Added by Mandate
Public Utilities (Tech.& Infrastr.)	.47	$-.02^{\underline{n}}$			.05		.39	.96	.70
Foreign Affairs (Peace & Int'natl)	.41			.02	$\underline{-.02}$			.60	.48
Education (Education)	9.61			$-.17^{\underline{n}}$	$\underline{-.25}$			.59	.38

[$E_i = a + bP_i^A + b(P_i^A \times G) + \ldots bP_i^n + b(P_i^n \times G)$]

Ideology Models

Policy Priority (Program Emphasis)	Constant a	Ideology People's Chan = 1	People's (+)(−) Agenda or Mandate (Out)	People's Mandate (x Chan)	Socialist (+)(−) Agenda or Mandate (Out)	Socialist Mandate (x Chan)	Freedom (+)(−) Agenda or Mandate (Out)	Freedom Mandate (x Gov)	Adj R^2	Added by Mandate	Added by Ideology
Left-Right (Left-Right)	21.2	−11.7		.07	.92	$\underline{-.82}$	$-.13^{\underline{n}}$	.28	.42	.15	.07
Culture & Arts (Arts, etc.)	.08	.30			$-.02^{\underline{n}}$		.02		.89	.75	.07
Admin. of Justice (Law & Order)	2.06	4.28	1.53		$-.36^{\underline{n}}$	.84	$-.35^{\underline{n}}$	$\underline{-.27}$	.88	.38	.12
Family Assistance (Social Justice)	3.06	11.2		$\underline{-1.12}$			.33		.81	.41	.09
Agriculture (Agriculture)	.95	1.85				.25			.51	.32	.19
Social Security (Social Justice)	21.6	−11.8				$\underline{-.65}$	$-.77^{\underline{n}}$		.46	.09	.10
Defense (Internationalism)	4.72	3.62			$-.98^{\underline{n}}$	.95			.38	.07	.21

[$E_i = a + bP_A + bP_i^A + b(P_i^A \times G) + \ldots bP_i^n + b(P_i^n \times G)$]

* Indicating only those b's (unstandardized regression coefficients) that attained $\underline{.05}$ statistical significance. Coefficients in the opposite direction from theoretical expectation are $\underline{\text{underlined}}$. Coefficients for negative mandates are indicated by $\underline{n}$. There were no cases in Austria in which the Agenda model alone provided the best fit.

Best-Fitting Models

The dummy variable for People's Party (ÖVP) chancellor appears to be by far the most informative partisan indicator for predicting policy priority, as indicated in the second part of Table 10.1, under "Ideology Models." In other words, the most valuable information an Austrian voter can have in projecting the division of the fiscal pie is the choice between parties. Nine of ten coefficients for the party alternation term are statistically significant. It is, in effect, a time demarcation for the years under ÖVP versus SPÖ chancellors. And it serves as a great divide in Austria policy priorities.

The mandate conferred on party programs, however, is not to be ignored, even after account has been taken of differences apparently owing to party alternation in power. Moreover, given our expectation of a politics of accommodation in the heavily corporatist Austrian setting, it is surprising that programmatic congruence is most often through the *negative* mandate—that is, through negation of the emphases of a program owing to a party's having been out of the chancellor's office rather than in a positive congruence owing to incumbency. Only one of these is to the detriment of the People's Party (ÖVP): public utilities, –.02. Four, however, are against the programs of the Socialists: education, –.17; culture and the arts, –.02; administration of justice, –.36; and defense, –.98 (if we accept the premise that an emphasis on internationalism should yield increased priority for the military). And the Freedom Party receives nearly as much rejection by the incumbents as do the Socialists. Negative mandates affect the FPÖ in regard to left-right (–.13) as well as administration of justice (–.35) and social security (–.77).

Positive mandates are a bit less frequent than negative ones, occurring in only seven instances: one for the ÖVP (left-right, .07), four times for the SPÖ (public utilities, .05; justice, .84; agriculture, .25; and defense, .95), and twice for the ÖVP (public utilities, .39; and left-right, .28).

Agenda congruence, that is, positive predictions from out-party programs, is conspicuous by its infrequency in Austria, suggested earlier to be the ideal setting for a politics of accommodation. We find such out-party forecasts to be statistically significant, relative to the other forces in the equations, in only five instances: administration of justice for the ÖVP (1.53); foreign affairs (.02) and left-right (.92) for the SPÖ; and culture (.02) and family assistance (.33) for the FPÖ.

In spite of the fact that the FPÖ's ideological trends do not support the longstanding reputation it holds as a rightist maverick (Figure 10.1), when it comes to specific programmatic emphases, the FPÖ does not enjoy the favor of the major parties. Its most frequent apparent input is through the negative mandate. This would seem more natural if it were not for the fact that on the ideological spectrum and in the electoral balance, they take a position not unlike that of the German Free Democrats, who, as we shall see in Chapter 11, often occupy a potential for policy blackmail.

One policy domain—the only one that showed dramatic rise in priority (Figure 10.3.8)—public utilities and communications, deserves special attention. This policy, receiving an average of just under 1.0 percent of central government expenditures, enjoyed a checkered history under the grand coalition, rising steadily in the years of Socialist leadership. The mandate model explains an astounding 92 percent of the variance in public utilities priority, with the in-government terms for the SPÖ and the FPÖ (*b* = .05 and .39, respectively). The large coefficient for the FPÖ-in-government term, in spite of that party's brief cabinet tenure, is visible in the singular jump displayed at the right-hand side of Figure 10.3.8, which reflected a heavy emphasis by the FPÖ on technology and infrastructure in its 1983 program.

These agenda and program mandate elements are minor, however, compared to the apparent impact of party alternation. Under ÖVP chancellors, policy was strikingly more rightist than under the Socialists (–11.7), as also was social security priority (–11.8). Five policy areas, in contrast, saw the switch from ÖVP to SPÖ as a loss: culture and arts (.30), administration of justice (4.28), family assistance (11.2), agriculture (1.85), and defense (3.62).

The apparent importance of party alternation over Austrian policy priorities should not be accepted uncritically, in spite of the weight of evidence presented. The simple dummy variable divides not only parties but also time periods. In Chapter 2 we give what we feel are sound reasons for not incorporating into our analyses a range of statistical controls that would purge temporal effects from the findings. The fact is that the world is as we find it. And in Austria, the ÖVP headed the governments in the first half of the postwar period and the SPÖ headed them during the second half. This means that we could be confusing something else that coincided with that break in time with the alternation of parties. But we cannot somehow scramble Austrian history to suit our statistical convenience. We have a theory of party influence. The test of theory is made a bit tenuous by the oddities of the facts. But the facts, however odd, do say that the policy priorities before the switch in parties were very different from what they were afterward. In the absence of better theory accompanied by valid and reliable indicators, we are willing to let that observation stand.

Nonconformists and Contradictions

The most systematic apparent contradiction is under the Socialists' mandate column, with four of the eight coefficients negative where they are expected to be positive. This suggests that the Socialist programs, when one accounts for occupancy of the chancellorship (as was the case for half the period covered), are as often misleading about up-coming policy priorities. They mislead in terms of general left-right directions of policy as well as in foreign affairs, education, and social security. This poor fit of the model is not a function of particular policies, but rather a particular problem of the Socialists. The other terms in the equation, even when not reaching statistical significance, are usually in the predicted direction (see Appendix Table A10.3).

The only other contradictions are one each for the FPÖ (administration of justice, –.27) and the ÖVP (family assistance, –1.12). Given that the FPÖ has been in government only four years out of the thirty-four included in the analysis, their one contradiction should be taken with a grain of salt. Their mandate term is included more for symmetry of presentation across countries than for well-warranted substantive reasons.

The ÖVP situation in family assistance, however, is more serious. It must, however, be viewed in the context of the 11.2 ideology effect. That is, there is a dramatic difference between family assistance priorities under ÖVP chancellors and those under Socialist chancellors. Once that very predictable element is controlled, the conservative ÖVP programs are not reliable indicators of future priorities in this area.

As to patterning of contradictions, however, only one general statement is warranted: The Socialist programs do not provide reliable bases for forecasts across policy domains in Austria. It is possible, however, that even these deviations for the SPÖ are a consequence of the time skew in the years when the SPÖ was in the chancellery, much like the situation in France. The ÖVP headed all the governments under the long grand coalition; then there were a few years when it was the sole occupant of a majority government. Thus all the years with an SPÖ chancellor are concentrated in the latter part of the time period, except for the latest return of the ÖVP, which is recorded for only one year in our analysis. However, this lack of fit for Socialist or Social Democratic party programs is apparent in several countries, a circumstance to which we shall return in the discussion of cross-country patterns in Chapter 14.

On the basis of the graphs in Figure 10.3 as well as the statistical analysis, we are inclined to accept at face value the message that there are striking differences between policies enacted under governments headed by the conservatives and those enacted under governments headed by Socialists. Accepting that logic, however, means that we must also accept the evidence of unreliable SPÖ programmatic congruence.

CONCLUSION

Austria's policy-relevant partisanship stands in striking contrast to the agenda-driven politics of Sweden, or even those of France, countries where all parties, whatever their place in or out of government, seem to contribute substantially to the definition of policy priorities. Clearly, the Austrian findings, which illustrate the conferral of a mandate on the basis of standing ideological differences, is of major substantive importance.

One must remember that standing differences between the parties are a perfectly valid basis for conferral of a mandate. As long as it can be demonstrated that such a choice is indeed consequential for policy—a claim long disputed by scholars of comparative policy analysis—it is as valid a basis for a mandate as is the current party program. And from that viewpoint, the mandate in Austria is stronger even than the mandate in Britain, home of the Westminster model.

Besides characterizing Austria as having a rather power-driven, mandate-based policy process, these findings may also indicate why a predominant party is not unwilling to go into a grand coalition with its main rival. If the party controls the chancellorship, government policy goes its way regardless.

It is, of course, more puzzling why the junior partner in the grand coalition sticks with it. Possibly, however, the party feels there is an electoral payoff to be seen as capable of governing. And the party does differentiate itself clearly in ideological terms (Figure 10.1), perhaps hoping to be seen as an alternative to the current government, even though it forms part of it.

We have expressed our concern about the time series. But even if more changes had taken place around 1970, it would be difficult to dismiss them as pure artifacts without relevance to party politics. There were, after all, good substantive reasons for the SPÖ's becoming the plurality party at that time and for its displacing, and continuing to displace, the ÖVP. One of these was the greater attractiveness of its overall policy stance. Changes around 1970, whatever their other causes, can therefore also be credited substantively to differences in ideology between the parties. The contrast over time is inextricably mingled with the contrast between the parties because they overlap in the real world.

On the basis of our graphic and statistical assessments, it is difficult to resist the conclusion that Austria, in spite of grand coalitions and corporatist sub- or extra-governmental arrangements, tends strongly toward a mandate rather than an agenda-setting model of party representation. There is little evidence for consistent party influence out of government—except through the negative mandate. In marked contrast to the programs of British and German liberals, those of the Austrian FPÖ show little positive relevance to policy priorities, and certainly no domains where the party approaches hegemony. It must be said, in spite of more mixed evidence, that the same is generally the case, with several noteworthy exceptions, for the SPÖ's and the ÖVP's programmatic priorities. In deciding how to cast their votes, therefore, Austrian electors would be well advised to consider primarily differences in general approach and past record between the parties rather than current programmatic emphases.

The case of the SPÖ raises the question of the conditions under which being in coalition leads parties to compromise, if not to abandon altogether, short-term goals. We shall have a clearer idea on this after we analyze a closely related coalition system, that of Germany—to which we turn in the next chapter.

11

Federal Republic of Germany

INSTITUTIONAL AND POLITICAL CONTEXT

From the founding of the Federal Republic of Germany (West Germany) in 1949 until the first election of the newly reunited country in 1990, three parties have occupied the center of the German political stage. The Christian Democrats (Christlich Demokratische Union/Christlich Soziale Union—CDU/CSU) averaged a little over 45 percent of the popular vote across the twelve national elections. This exceeded that of the second-place Social Democrats (Sozialdemokratische Partei Deutschlands—SPD) in all but one election (1972), with the SPD averaging just over 37 percent. This split, with neither the right-of-center CDU/CSU nor the left-of-center SPD ever receiving either a majority of the popular vote or, with the exception of one four-year period, a majority of seats in the Bundestag, has created a superb opportunity for the centrist liberals, the Free Democrats (Freie Demokratische Partei—FDP). The FDP, with an average vote under 10 percent, has played a continuing role as kingmaker. The FDP has been included in all cabinets of the Federal Republic except for the time of the CDU/CSU majority, 1957–1961, and the Christian Democratic/Social Democratic grand coalition from 1966 through 1969.

The CDU is, in fact, a federation of two parties: the CDU, which is nearly nationwide in its organizational base, minus Bavaria, and the CSU, which is an independent but exclusively Bavarian party. At the national level, the two parties have always combined, formed a party in parliament, and presented a common electoral program. Furthermore, the CDU does not compete on the Bavarian turf of the CSU. Thus, although they maintain separate organizational hierarchies and membership lists, they may be considered a single party for most analytical purposes. The CDU/CSU partnership (which we shall subsequently designate merely "CDU") has been the dominant governing party in modern Germany. It held the chancellor's office for all but twelve years of the period under study, most of that time governing in coalition with the FDP.

The FDP, in contrast, has never occupied the chancellery but has been the cabinet partner not only with the CDU but also with the SPD—during the Willy Brandt (1969–1974) and Helmut Schmidt (1974–1982) governments. Thus, the

FDP has served in cabinets for more years than either of the two major parties. Furthermore, the kingmaker role of the FDP has not been an idle threat, as shown with the withdrawal of FDP support from the social-liberal coalition in 1982, ushering in the long reign of Helmut Kohl as (CDU) chancellor.

Although it shares the leftist roots of the other socialist parties across Europe, the SPD long ago gave up any pretensions to revolutionary ideology or a program of widespread nationalization and massive redistribution. It overtly denounced its already tattered radical tradition in a famous declaration issued in 1959 at a party conference in Bad Godesberg. That declaration clearly indicated the intent of the SPD to accept the rules of the mixed-economy game. The game was well on the way to being won under CDU Chancellor Konrad Adenauer, and his economic czar, Ludwig Erhard, in the form of the German postwar economic miracle, or *Wirtschaftswunder.*

The CDU has a social Catholic, conservative ideology very similar to that of the Austrian People's Party (ÖVP), but distinguishable from more conventionally conservative European parties in its acceptance of a benevolent (some might even say "paternalistic") role for the state in the regulation of economic and social affairs.

The smaller German liberals—the FDP—also, from one angle, look much like their Austrian counterpart, the FPÖ. The German liberals even carry some of the stain of not having been wholly pure during the early years of National Socialism. But the stain is neither so broad nor so deep as is that of the Austrian liberals, which may lessen the barrier to the FDP's playing a key role in German governments. This is most visible, perhaps, in the Foreign Ministry, which was headed by liberals for a very long time, including the longest-serving foreign minister in a Western democracy, the FDP's Hans-Dietrich Genscher.

The interesting question, given the peculiarity of German coalitions, is the following: How do party programs get reflected and refracted into policy through such a multifaceted lens? In Austria, the FPÖ—rarely in government—saw very little policy reflection of its election programs, even though it obtained voter support roughly equivalent to that of its German counterpart. But in spite of the general similarity of political landscape, government politics are actually quite different in Germany and Austria. To get a majority, the FDP and whichever of the major parties was its partner at the time often campaigned in electoral alliance for a continuation of the existing coalition, while still presenting distinct election programs. Thus the governments may be said to have had a direct popular endorsement, unlike most coalition systems, where alliances are made by interparty bargaining after the election. Equally, the election programs of both coalition parties can be seen as having a popular mandate. Despite major disparities of size, both parties—one of the major parties and the FDP—are crucial to government formation. Thus have comparable political authority.

The Free Democrats' ability to break the coalition in the interelection period (as it did in 1982) and let in its partner's rival gives it potent leverage. This can be seen both in the disproportionate number of ministries it takes, relative to the number of parliamentary seats it controls, and in the substantive importance of these ministries.

With the FDP's firm hold on selected ministries, which are important in framing and implementing specific policy measures, it is natural to assume that governmental priorities as a whole are also heavily influenced by the FDP, even though it is supported usually by less than 10 percent of the electorate. In fact, previous research on the congruence of party emphases and policy priorities in Germany found many areas with stronger and more consistent links for the FDP than for the major parties. This was attributed to its "blackmail potential" as the arbiter between a CDU and an SPD coalition (Hofferbert and Klingemann 1990).

PROGRAM AND POLICY TRENDS

German Data

Matching programmatic emphases to expenditure categories raises the same problems in Germany as elsewhere. First there is the difficulty of establishing consistent expenditure categories over the whole postwar period. Actually, this is less troublesome for Germany than for any other country except the United States, as consistency has been a concern of the Federal Statistical Office itself, and a specific document addresses the problem directly (Statistisches Bundesamt, annual). The standardized, cross-time consistent records are a great aid to research.

The party program categories selected cover, on average, about 30 percent of the total content. The policy indicators included, in contrast, cover an average of two-thirds of total central governmental expenditures.[1]

In the German case we find that a modest degree of aggregation of coding categories works well, statistically, in regard to defense and foreign policy as well as health and welfare policy. In the first case, we add up the references to all foreign policy categories in each of the party programs. This imparts to the program measure a decidedly pro-peace and cooperative internationalism tinge, given the balance of references. We label this aggregated measure *foreign policy.*

In the analysis of linkages of programs to welfare and to health-spending shares, it turns out that the sum of all references to social justice and to social services (+) matches welfare and health expenditures better than either welfare or health spending on its own and better than any other programmatic candidate. The rest of the pairings for Germany are of specific program categories to obviously related expenditure areas, where no comparable problems of interpretation arise. The complete set of pairings is as follows:

Party Program	*Policy Area*
Foreign Policy*	Defense
Foreign Policy*	Foreign Affairs

Law and Order	Administration of Justice
Agriculture	Agriculture
Social Justice/Social Services	Welfare
Social Justice/Social Services	Health
Education	Education
Technology and Infrastructure	Transportation
Technology and Infrastructure	Energy, Water, etc.
Technology and Infrastructure	Housing and Community Dev't
Art, Sport, Leisure	Culture & Arts

*Sum of categories in foreign policy emphases.

The indicator of left-right policy orientation is very similar to that used in the other countries (except Austria). The factor analysis weights four indicators in such a way as to produce a neatly differentiated score. The factor loadings for the various areas of policy priority are education, .93; health and medical care, .88; agriculture, –.80; defense, –.87.

Left-Right Trends

There is a strong ideological structure in German politics that we should expect to see reflected later in the statistical analysis. The pivotal position of the FDP arises largely because of the reluctance of the two large parties—unlike their Austrian counterparts—to enter into a semipermanent grand coalition. The potential for a grand coalition would undermine the leverage of the third party. This reluctance of the CDU and SPD to combine may be due to a lesser degree of ideological overlap than was shown by their respective counterparts in Austria (compare Figures 10.1 and 11.1).

In the 1980s, a possible alternative to the FDP as a partner, at least for the Social Democrats, did emerge—the Greens. But the latter never mustered enough parliamentary strength to provide an alternative governmental basis to an FDP alliance. (In the 1990 all-German election, the West German Greens failed to obtain the minimum 5 percent of votes required for representation in the Bundestag.)

The FDP also gains of course by wandering about ideologically in the center ground between the two major parties on the left-right dimension, which so strongly structures German politics (Figure 11.1). The FDP's flexibility, sometimes overlapping the positions of the main parties, sometimes oscillating in the middle, is really no different from that of the other liberal parties (e.g., in Britain or in Austria), constrained to take up positions in a left-right space that they are trying in part to transcend. The important point is, however, that this makes them a congenial partner for Socialists or Christian Democrats alike, when the only alternative is a grand coalition.

We summarize overall policy priority trends with the scoring procedure that contrasts left-wing and right-wing expenditure shares, much as we contrast left-

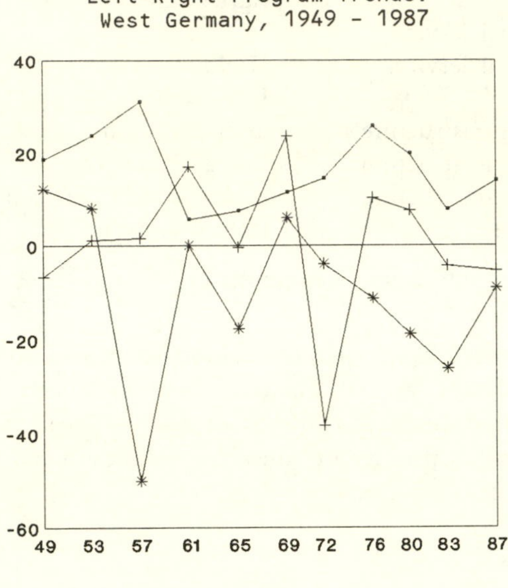

Figure 11.1
Left-Right Program Trends:
West Germany, 1949 - 1987

right programmatic scores in Figure 11.1. Figure 11.2 presents the overall left-right trends in German policy.

As in most of the other countries, there is in Germany a leftward policy trend that reaches a plateau in the 1970s. However, in Germany the leftward lurch comes later, is steeper, and then flattens more markedly. Indeed, these changes are sharper and seemingly more closely associated with changes in government than in the other countries. The two great turning points are 1969 and 1983, both associated with transfers in the chancellorship between the major parties.

A comparison of the left-right program and policy trends (Figures 11.1 and 11.2) reveals no obvious linkage between the two. In fact, the general rightward trend in program emphases, at least roughly since the mid-1960s, is juxtaposed to the leftward slope of policy.

But the changes in government in 1969 (from the Kurt Georg Kiesinger chancellorship in the CDU/SPD grand coalition to the SPD/FDP coalition headed by Brandt) and the 1982 switch from SPD/FDP to CDU/FDP are clearly reflected in the general left-right trends in policy (Figure 11.2). The great leap leftward accompanied Brandt into the chancellery. It was stepped down a bit with the return of the CDU under Kohl.

Specific Policy Trends

The specific content of these shifts is seen in the individual policy trends, illustrated by the graphs in Figure 11.3. Although these curves conform broadly to

Figure 11.2
Left–Right Expenditure Priority Factor Scores:
West Germany, 1950 – 1988

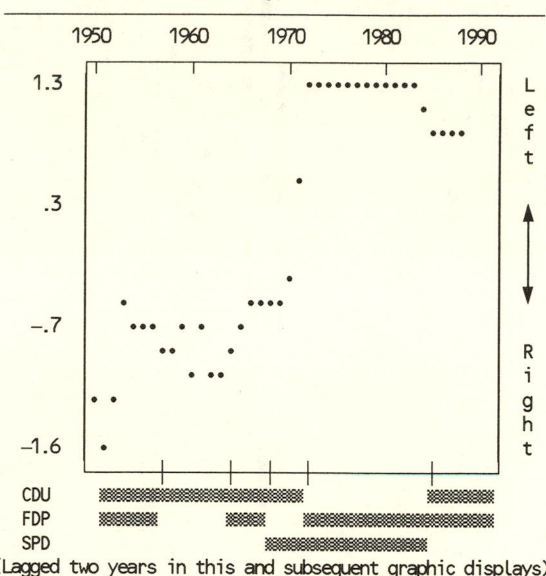

(Lagged two years in this and subsequent graphic displays)

Structure of Policy Priority Factor

Policy Area	Factor Loading
Education	.93
Health & Medical Care	.88
Agriculture	–.87
Defense	–.80

patterns found elsewhere (e.g., defense and agriculture declining; health and administration of justice rising), there are certain German peculiarities, owing to the unique intensity of the wartime destruction and the subsequent reconstruction through the mid-1950s. For example, housing expenditure (11.3.10) is at its peak in the 1950s and tails off sharply thereafter. The education bulge seen in the other countries is delayed in Germany owing to the decimation of the wartime generation and consequent relative delay of the baby boom (11.3.7). Spending on "luxuries" such as public utilities, transport, better health provisions peaks after the economic boom of the 1960s, contrasted to the preceding period of relative austerity.

The great political watershed of German postwar history occurred in 1969 when a CDU chancellor gave way to an SPD nominee and a CDU-dominated government yielded to a social-liberal coalition. The policy adjustments associated with that kind of shift have, as seen in all countries examined so far, a certain

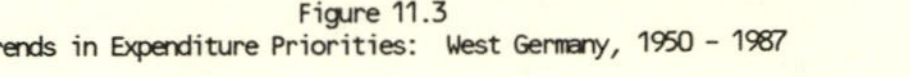

Figure 11.3
Trends in Expenditure Priorities: West Germany, 1950 - 1987

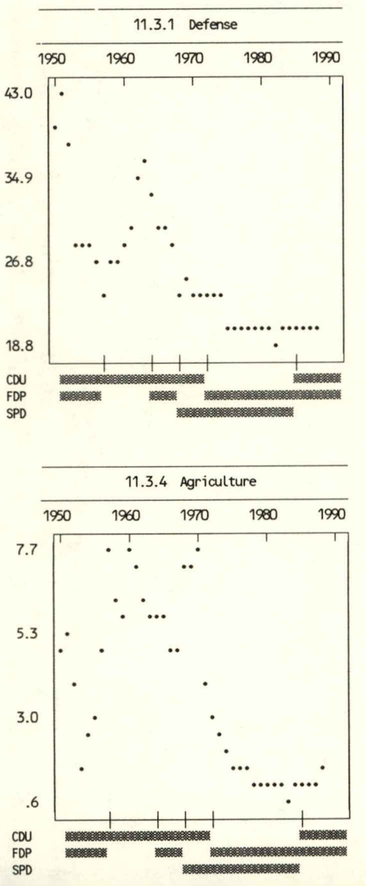

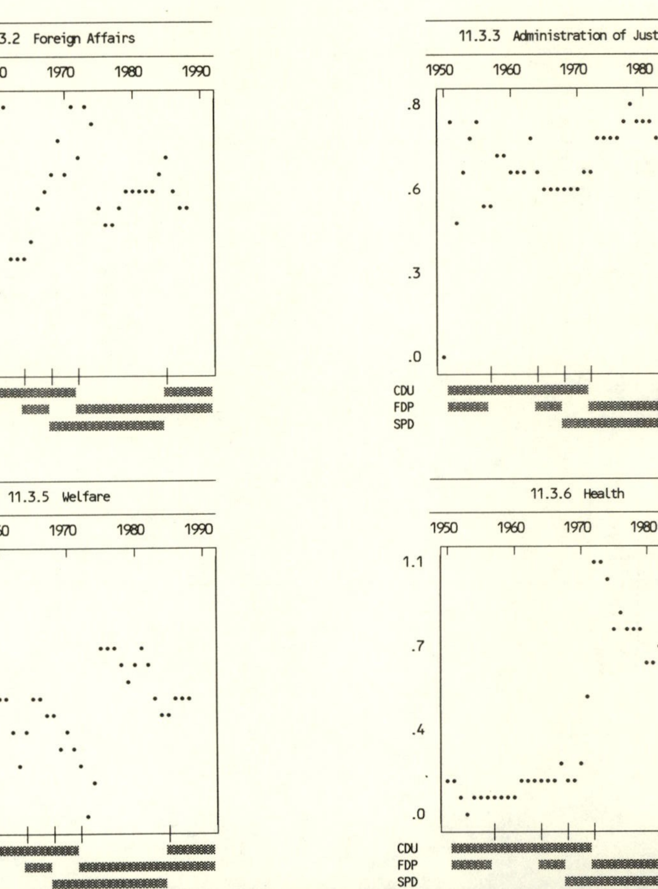

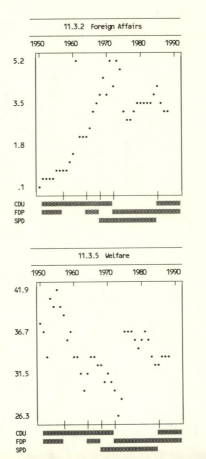

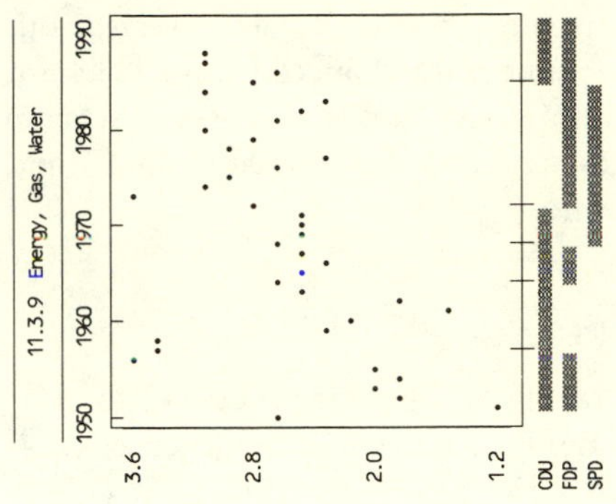
11.3.9 Energy, Gas, Water
3.6
2.8
2.0
1.2
1950
1960
1970
1980
1990
CDU
FDP
SPD

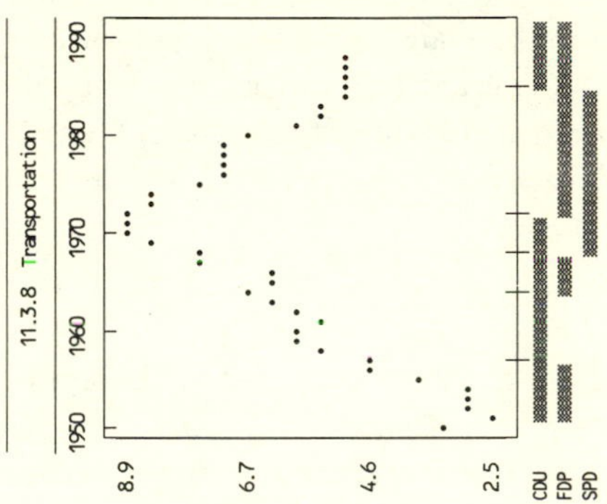
11.3.8 Transportation
8.9
6.7
4.6
2.5
1950
1960
1970
1980
1990
CDU
FDP
SPD

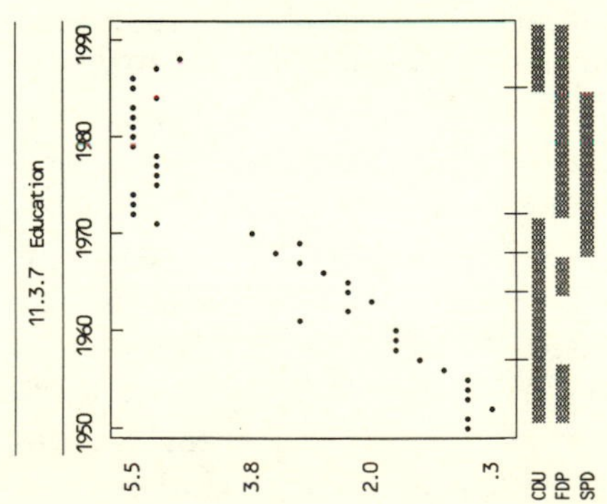
11.3.7 Education
5.5
3.8
2.0
.3
1950
1960
1970
1980
1990
CDU
FDP
SPD

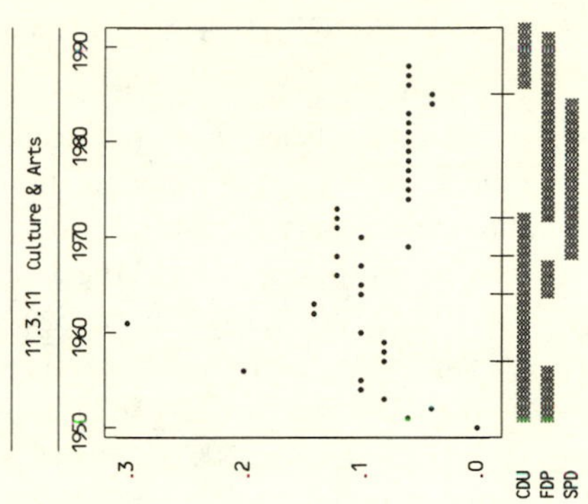
11.3.11 Culture & Arts
.3
.2
.1
.0
1950
1960
1970
1980
1990
CDU
FDP
SPD

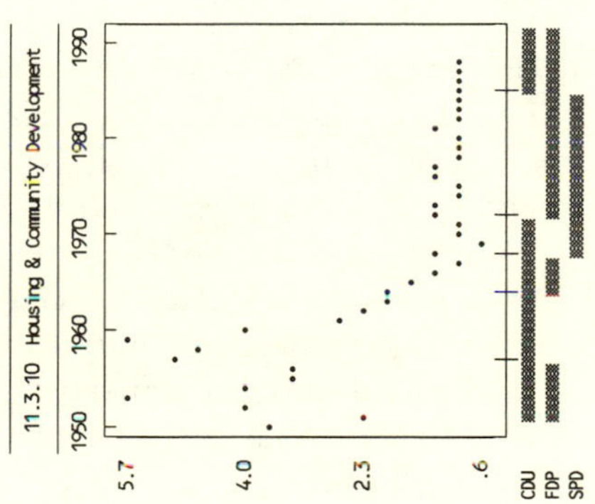
11.3.10 Housing & Community Development
5.7
4.0
2.3
.6
1950
1960
1970
1980
1990
CDU
FDP
SPD

ratchet effect, that is, the overall postwar trends are never totally reversed. But nevertheless, the return of the CDU to power under the chancellorship of Helmut Kohl had also a step effect, notable in several policy domains. These effects are more striking when we examine the linkages between party program leanings and the subsequent general pattern of public policy.

PARTY PROGRAM-TO-POLICY CONGRUENCE

Our ultimate concern is with the translation of programmatic concerns into commensurate policies by the political parties. But the assertion of congruence is sustained only if party emphases statistically predict policy priorities. How well *do* the German party programs forecast policy? In this section we address this question by examining in detail the best-fitting of the three models in our research design. The statistical results are displayed in Table 11.1.

The overall pattern of the results of the German analyses is strikingly like that of the Austrian case. As in Austria, there are no equations where the simple agenda model stands alone; there are a few in the mandate category, but the majority of policy indicators, including the general left-right index, are best predicted by the ideology model, distinguished by inclusion of the term for alternation between CDU- and SPD-led governments. Even the patterns of contradiction are somewhat comparable to those found in Austria.

Best-Fitting Models

The dominant positive message of Table 11.1—already anticipated by the simple time-series plots presented in Figure 11.3—is the importance of party alternation. In examining these coefficients, under the "Ideology" column, however, one must bear two things in mind. First, Germany has an unusual history. Second, Christian parties, such as the CDU, are not to be confused with "conservative" parties elsewhere. There is a strong tradition for Christian parties to follow a path that might appear to true conservatives to be "governmental paternalism." The CDU has never advocated dismantling the welfare state; rather, it has supported its management in conformity with a mix of collective social obligations within a solid, mixed-capitalist economy. Thus it is not unreasonable that the CDU was sympathetic to welfare policy.

For all of its apparent potency, we must view the party alternation variable with some caution. It may convey a confusing message in Germany. The CDU took over after the founding of the Federal Republic in 1949. The tasks confronting the party required a national effort—a suspension to some extent of "normal politics." The German people had to be housed. The elementary infrastructure of the country had to be restored. In addition, the Berlin blockade of 1948–1949, just before the inauguration of the first government of the Federal Republic, neutralized much of the opposition to German rearmament, making it clear that Ger-

Table 11.1
Best-Fitting Models Between Party Program Emphases and Policy Priorities: West Germany, 1948 – 1987*

Mandate Models

Policy Priority (Program Emphasis)	Constant a	Chr. Democrat (Out) (+) Agenda or (–) Mandate	Chr. Democrat (x Gov) Mandate	Soc. Democrat (Out) (+) Agenda or (–) Mandate	Soc. Democrat (x Gov) Mandate	Free Democrat (Out) (+) Agenda or (–) Mandate	Free Democrat (x Gov) Mandate	Adj R^2	Added by Mandate
Foreign Affairs (Foreign Policy)	.29					.24		.79	.02
Education (Education)	2.17	.47	$\underline{-.74}$					.48	.36

$$[\quad E_i = a + bP_i^A + b(P_i^A \times G) + \ldots bP_i^n + b(P_i^n \times G) \quad]$$

Ideology Models

Policy Priority (Program Emphasis)	Constant a	Ideology Chr. Dem. Gov = 1	Chr. Democrat (Out) (+) Agenda or (–) Mandate	Chr. Democrat (x Gov) Mandate	Soc. Democrat (Out) (+) Agenda or (–) Mandate	Soc. Democrat (x Gov) Mandate	Free Democrat (Out) (+) Agenda or (–) Mandate	Free Democrat (x Gov) Mandate	Adj R^2	Added by Mandate	Added by Ideology
Left-Right (Left-Right	1.69	–2.45	$-.04^{n}$	.08		$\underline{-.14}$	-1.86^{n}	1.86	.90	.90	.10
Health (Soc.Just.&Soc.Ser.)	5.46	–5.10	$-.38^{n}$	.41	$-.03^{n}$	.02			.94	.87	.07
Transportation (Tech.& Infrastr.)	7.66	–6.51			.32	$\underline{-.42}$	.85	$\underline{-1.00}$	.72	.17	.16
Agriculture (Agriculture)	–.36	1.64			.40		.33		.63	.15	.03
Welfare (Soc.Just.&Soc.Ser.)	–71.6	101.5	8.52	$\underline{-9.00}$	.83	$\underline{-.36}$	$-.90^{n}$	.51	.63	.46	.11
Defense (Foreign Policy)	74.2	–46.8	-2.12^{n}	2.19	$.35^{n}$	–.93		–.66	.60	.41	.05
Hous. & Com. Dev't (Tech. & Infrastr.)	1.16	6.37			$-.41^{n}$	.36			.59	.23	.18
Culture & Arts (Arts, Sport, etc.)	.17	–.08				$\underline{-.02}$	.04	$\underline{-.05}$	.34	.29	.11

$$[\quad E_i = a + bP_A + bP_i^A + b(P_i^A \times G) + \ldots bP_i^n + b(P_i^n \times G) \quad]$$

* Indicating only those b's (unstandardized regression coefficients) that attained .05 significance. Coefficients in the opposite direction from theoretical expectation are underlined. Coefficients for negative mandates are indicated by ^{n}. In Germany, there were no policy domains best explained by the agenda model alone.

many would have to carry a goodly share of the cost of the cold war. This set in place certain policy patterns that were extrapartisan. With economic recovery, the universal economies of scale that accompany routinization of national and alliance defense (after the cold war shock of the Berlin crisis in the early 1960s), and the adjustments made possible by SPD-led *Ostpolitik*, Germany's policy priorities could not be viewed as having attained an approximation of "normality" until, one could argue, the mid-1970s.

It may be reasonable to view the dummy variable for chancellor's party (CDU = 1, 1949–1968 and post-1982; SPD = 0, 1969–1982) as less an indication of standing differences between parties—the use to which the comparable term is put in the other country chapters—and more a surrogate for the development of Germany's peculiar postwar policy agenda, that is, the oddity of its history.

Thus, there are some counterintuitive coefficients for the indicator of Christian Democratic leadership of the German governments. Left-right conforms clearly to an image of the CDU as right of center, with a coefficient of –2.45. However, the other coefficients do not at all paint a picture of a conservative CDU. The odd case of welfare has been considered in the previous section. It is reasonable that a right-of-center party would de-emphasize health priority (–5.10) and that it would support housing and community development (6.37) or agriculture (1.64). But the negative coefficient for defense (–46.8) is, at first sight, bewildering.

The peculiar historical factors reflected in the CDU dummy variable are clearer if we first look back to Figure 11.3.1, as an example. It plots the share of outlays for defense. The early years under CDU leadership (1950–1969) saw an erratic pattern, generally falling after the Berlin Blockade (which had occurred just before our time series begins), and then rising again with the Berlin crisis of the early 1960s, followed by another decline during the Erhard and Kiesinger years later in that decade. The SPD under Brandt and Schmidt slowed but sustained a decline in defense priority, which finally leveled out and actually reversed a bit under Kohl's CDU government.

One would be hard-pressed to say specifically what the difference between parties was, based on this erratic line. But it is clear that the steady decline in defense priority was maintained by the SPD, whereas the CDU has a very mixed record. Nevertheless, the *b* for the CDU (i.e., dummy variable of 1 for CDU chancellor) term, reported in Table 11.1, is strongly negative (–46.8), suggesting that the SPD is generally a better friend of the military than is the CDU—a misleading suggestion. It results from the CDU's being at extreme ends of a downward trend, with a high value in the beginning and a low value at the end.

The defense coefficients for the party programs are reminiscent of the Australian findings, in that the apparent contradictions may not be real. The general programmatic emphasis on international concerns is *positively* related to defense priorities for the right-of-center party and *negatively* for the party of the Left (and the liberals) when accounting for governmental incumbency. That is, the incumbency effect for the CDU program's congruence with foreign policy priority is 2.19, whereas the paired out-of-office effect is –2.12. The opposite is true of the SPD, with an opposition *b* of +.35 and an incumbency coefficient of –.93. Again, it is the conservative stress on "peace through strength" and the leftist party concern for "peace through disarmament" that probably lies beneath these sharply distinguished findings. It is interesting that this phenomenon occurs in a country where defense and foreign affairs policy priorities are *inversely* correlated over time. The difference here, of course, is that foreign affairs policy is dominated by the FDP.

Were we writing an entire chapter on the determinants of defense spending in the Federal Republic, with governing party as one of many independent variables, we could perform a variety of forms of statistical microsurgery on this pattern in order to describe more precisely the impact of party alternation. But as our major task here, as elsewhere in the book, is to map in very broad terms the impact of party on the policy agenda and the fulfillment of the mandate, we see no need for such detailed study of a single policy in a single country. Rather, we have indulged in this modest side trip entirely to suggest caution in the interpretation of the statistical measure we are using for the effects of alternation between the CDU and the SPD.

Although we may be capturing with that term (CDU × Gov) some artifactual elements in the German experience, we are nevertheless persuaded that it is necessary to include it, especially since we wish to retain maximum comparability of our analyses across chapters. And even though the peculiarities of time and party alternation in several countries—France, Austria, and Germany so far—suggest caution, it is still true that there are political reasons for switches in government and the demarcation between one political era and another. They will often reflect changing majority demands and expectations. Our basic position is that this is a political reality we have to live with in the statistical investigation, rather than an irritating distraction to be eliminated or ignored. (See the methodological discussion in Appendix B.)

Rather than viewing the peculiarity of German party alternation as an aberration or a bothersome statistic analyzed for the sake of cross-national consistency, therefore, we use it as a means to clarify the role of party programs. If indeed there are extraparty elements that constrained policy choice, the party alternation (ideology) term may flush out that influence, sharpening the variance in policy that might more appropriately be expected to flow from specific programmatic differences.

Let us return to the other specifics of Table 11.1: Although the simple agenda model was improved in all cases by either mandate or ideology elements, there is still considerable evidence of parties' being able to see their programmatic emphases translated into policy, irrespective of the advantage of incumbency. The poor record of the SPD in fulfilling a mandate when in government is somewhat balanced by its having significant, positive agenda coefficients (transportation, agriculture, welfare, and defense) when in opposition.

As anticipated, the FDP exerts a role well in excess of its electoral or parliamentary numbers. The one instance of clear policy hegemony in Germany is foreign affairs, which is completely overshadowed by the FDP programs, explaining 79 percent of the variance ($b = .24$). In addition to foreign affairs, the FDP programs work as a significant mandate in the general left-right domain (1.86), in welfare (.51), and possibly in defense (–.66). To these must also be added the fact that the major parties, in government, have apparently taken the FDP seriously enough to cue *negative* mandates in regard to left-right (–1.86) and welfare (–.90). Thus the small number of liberals, although certainly not dominating the setting of the full range of policy priorities, are a clear and effective force across a set of issues.

Other instances of the negative mandate suggest that there is more potency to the election programs than is conveyed by the simple translation of programs by governing parties. SPD governments, although not implementing the general left-right tendencies of their own programs, have rejected those of the CDU at a statistically significant level (–.04). A similar fate has befallen the SPD programs at the hands of the CDU in health (–.03) and housing (–.41).

The case of health policy is almost a textbook example of how the statistics should work. First, its .94 is the largest R^2 in the German findings. Second, it is a tidy fit to theory. The simple difference between CDU and SPD occupancy of the chancellorship is 5.10 percent for health, with the rightist party being less sympathetic. Third, when we take account of the CDU's or the SPD's having been out of office, their programs are negatively reflected in health policy priorities (–.38 and –.03, respectively). Finally, the major parties use their time in office not only to implement standing ideological differences but also to enact that which was emphasized in the most recent election program (.41 for the CDU; .02 for the SPD). The minor coalition partner is not of consequence. That is about all one needs to know to be fully prescient as to the share of central government funds devoted to health policy.

The left-right situation is one of the sharpest in the German findings (with the previously noted exception of the SPD). In discussing the background of the parties, we called attention to the moderating elements in their history. Certainly the general left-right trends (Figure 11.1) do not convey a picture of extremism. The German SPD is slightly to the right of the American Democrats and even further right of British Labour. Likewise, the CDU has shown its moderate acceptance of much that constitutes the core of the modern welfare state.

The biggest message is, perhaps, that conveyed by the left-right equation. It suggests that there is indeed a dominant strain of ideology that permeates the role of the German parties in the policy process. The R^2 of .90 is the highest in any of the ten countries for the capacity of the left-right program indicator to forecast the general direction of policy priorities. The dummy variable indicates that CDU-led governments had a strong rightist effect on policy ($b = -2.45$). That is by far the largest element in the equation. But most of the programs matter too, in particular the CDU's and FDP's. The CDU suffers a negative mandate (–.04) as a result of SPD-led governments. CDU occupancy of the chancellery boosts the program *b* to a significant .08. All but one of the *b*s for left-right are statistically significant. Moreover, if the equation is at least a partial image of the bargaining process, it is clear that the FDP is the biggest player, both as winner and as loser (accounting for those rare occasions when the FDP has not been in government).

The factor analysis by which the left-right policy indicator was constructed yields a score that has a mean of 0 and a standard deviation of 1. Thus the –1.86 negative mandate and the +1.86 incumbency *b*s for the FDP are very impressive (roughly two-thirds as important as changing governments between CDU and SPD). The FDP's policy priorities have survived the push and shove of coalition government quite successfully, being by far the most effective elements in the equation that explains 90 percent of the variance in left-right policy priority. The overall picture for specific policies—as contrasted to general left-right leanings—still provides no ringing endorsement for the clarity of the mandate in Germany, but there are certainly no grounds for rejection.

The interparty differences in spending priorities, indicated in the "Ideology" column, are sometimes striking, if not always in the direction one would expect, based on common assumptions about the biases of each of the two major German parties. We have already addressed the apparent oddity of the –46.8 coefficient for defense under the CDU compared to the SPD. And there is the striking gain for welfare under the CDU. Of course, in addition to being elements of a particular history, these may also be part of that which distinguishes an archetypically *Christian* party in Europe from its *conservative* counterparts.

It would be difficult after these deviations to claim that the message conveyed by the indicator of interparty differences, which we have sometimes referred to as standing "ideology," is clear and unequivocal. Nonetheless, one can conclude from Table 11.1—supplemented by careful inspection of the plots in Figure 11.3—that party alternation in Germany is important and that party labels provide the voter with a useful tool for predicting the policy consequence of who is and who is not in charge.

The effects of underlying ideology are pervasive enough to account for some of the patchy programmatic effects, even in government. Somewhat more of the SPD's government programs have a significant relationship with policy, but many of the signs are still negative, indicating that the opposite of what the party said it wanted actually gets done. In the case of the CDU, many of the coefficients are nonsignificant. The FDP maintains a preeminent position on defense when in government and on foreign policy irrespective of government membership.

For Table 11.1 as a whole, however, what comes through is the effect of party alternation, which in consistency and power seems to overwhelm the programmatic emphases. If—and it is a potent *if*—we can treat this as a genuine effect of party rather than a reflector of the odd sequence of postwar German politics, then it argues strongly that left-right divisions structure German and Austrian politics to a much greater extent than they do those of other countries examined so far in this book. The moral is that electors in Germany and Austria should bestow their mandate, not so much on what the two major parties say in their current program, as on the basis of past record and ideology. But they had better follow the current pronouncements of the FDP.

Nonconformists and Contradictions

Unlike the Austrian case, there were two instances of failure to reach R^2 of .25—administration of justice and public utilities (energy, water, and so on). Across the countries analyzed to this point, there is no apparent pattern to the few policies that fail to conform to the hypothesized models we employ. Neither types of political systems nor substantive policies are demonstrating any commonality, a point to which we shall return in Chapter 14. In any event, nine of eleven policy areas do conform in Germany, and the German models that pass the threshold average 66 percent congruence—a very strong showing, assuming that the instances of contradiction are not too distracting.

As noted above, there is a pattern to the contradictions that resembles the Austrian case in that they are heavily concentrated in the Social Democratic column. Table 11.1 shows that the SPD programs do not predict either of the two policies best-fitted by the mandate model alone. But more disconcerting is the fact that four of the seven significant coefficients for the SPD in the long list of policies best-fitted by the ideology model are clearly contradictory (left-right, –.14; transportation, –.42; welfare, –.36; and culture and arts, –.02). This SPD pattern overwhelms any other findings in Table 11.1 that are contradictory to theoretical expectations. (Defense, again, is a potentially counterintuitive case, which we will discuss below.)

The SPD occupied the chancellery from 1966 to 1982, first under Willy Brandt, in a grand coalition with the CDU, 1966–1969, and later under Helmut Schmidt, a coalition with the FDP. A price seems to have been paid by the SPD in each instance. The shift from CDU-led to SPD-led governments had clear policy consequences, but these were not generally in the direction one might have expected, based upon trends in the SPD programs. To the extent that a mandate has operated in Germany, it has not done so through the SPD program.

The CDU has three positive mandate coefficients and two contradictions, –.74 in education and –9.00 in welfare, and the minority FDP has three positive and two contradictions, transportation, –1.00, and culture and arts, –.05. Neither of these seems to us to constitute the base for a generalization. Although the CDU, like the SPD, does not garner an impressive string of *b*s when in government, it still has only two really contradictory coefficients—education and welfare.

Row-wise, the contradictions are relatively scattered, but they do seem to detract markedly in the cases of transportation (SPD and FDP), welfare (CDU and

SPD), and culture (SPD and FDP). From the standpoint of policies, however, as contrasted to parties, two of these three cases—with culture the exception—are overwhelmingly responsive to alternation in office, that is, the ideology term. Moreover, as we have argued both in the theoretical discussion in Chapter 3 and in several country contexts, the conformity of a governing party to long-standing policy orientations can be as much a fulfillment of a mandate as is translation of the specifics of programmatic emphases. But that fact cannot, of course, be used as a case for the veracity of the programs, at least not in the face of evidence to the contrary, such as we have here.

The CDU *b* in welfare is an even more egregious deviation from expectation than is the SPD –.36. The CDU is simply and clearly contradictory in this policy. Although there is evidence of an ironic agenda effect, with the CDU and SPD programs being reflected in policy when they are *out* of government (b = 8.52 and .83, respectively), neither this nor the contradictory in-government terms match the striking impact of CDU occupancy of the chancellor's office, which, due to peculiar historical developments, has a very strong net *positive* effect. These results together lead to the conclusion that welfare is simply an unusual case.[2]

In sum, we would argue that the mandate is weak, if not absent, in the case of the SPD. And contradictory results further detract from the fulfillment of the mandate in two policy areas, cultural affairs and welfare. These deviations and contradictions, however, should not obscure the strongly positive messages of these analyses.

CONCLUSION

The two major German parties, the CDU/CSU and the SPD, are distinctive, predictable, and relatively consistent in their broad policy commitments. Each has remained relatively true to its respective left or right heritage, as far as the content of election programs is concerned. This argues convincingly against the claim that they are catch-all parties. But the history of German parties cannot be written without giving major attention to the liberal FDP. Insofar as the liberals have stayed true to a heritage, it is not evident in the left or right leaning of their programs. In that regard, the FDP has been blatantly and effectively opportunistic.

Although at first glance one might conclude that the CDU (in league with its Bavarian counterpart, the CSU) has, through occupying the chancellery for all but twelve years of the Federal Republic's first four decades, exercised general hegemony over policy evolution and distribution, our analyses show clearly that the two major alternations in power have made a big difference. The SPD's coming to power in 1969 shifted policy priorities in a manner that was not wholly redressed by the CDU's return in 1982.

The FDP has enjoyed privilege well beyond its popular base. Although sometimes barely topping the minimum 5 percent vote threshold required for representation in the Bundestag, the liberals have nonetheless retained a firm grip on their favored policy areas—foreign policy and defense. The picture of seeming instability or opportunism in the FDP's left-right trend is belied by its dogged ability to see its programmatic emphasis on foreign policy translated into spending on foreign affairs, irrespective of whether the party was in government (which, of course, it was for all but seven years out of the thirty-eight covered by most of our analysis here). And in the closely allied field of defense policy, the FDP exercises preeminent, though not exclusive, sway, in this case, with advantage from the mandate—that is, through occupancy of government posts. The same is true, more subtly, in the strong linkage of FDP left-right program stands to left-right policy.

Perhaps setting the German case most apart from the countries analyzed so far is the vitality of this link between general left-right ideological leanings in the party programs and subsequent general left-right policy priorities. German policy is uncommonly driven by broad ideological differences between the parties. It is the most elaborate of our models—incorporating party alternation as well as indicators for all three parties in and out of government—that best conveys the left-right program-to-policy process . Not only are the left-right programmatic emphases of parties positively reflected in policy when each party gets into government (except for the SPD), but the programs of those in opposition are often reflected negatively in policy priorities. Both rejection and acceptance are measurable parts of the mandate at the broad level of left-right differences. Of course, it is the left-right differences that tell the most interesting story.

The general finding is that Germany's policy priorities are uncommonly guided by ideological considerations, relative to the lesser influence of specific party programmatic emphases. The two big shifts in power, from a CDU-dominated government to the SPD and back, have made a lasting and predictable mark on the policy priorities of the Federal Republic. This is verified both by visual inspection of time trends and by intricate analyses where alternation in power is cast against the influence of current electoral programs.

The odd pattern of coalition in Germany works in interesting ways. The FDP, unlike most other minor parties in the "two and one-half" party systems, has been a major actor in government. It has taken those opportunities in government to focus its influence. In most areas, our analyses suggest, this brokering party takes modest advantage. But in its most salient domains—foreign affairs and defense—it holds the lead. To what extent is this a forecast of patterns in other countries where coalitions are the rule? We should gain more insight as we proceed through the final two country chapters in our analyses—the Netherlands and Belgium.

NOTES

1. The German case is interesting in that the current analyses can be compared to a previous study for which programs were especially coded to match the policy categories used by the Federal Statistics Office (Hofferbert and Klingemann 1990). The advantage from

such specialized coding is that the tailor-made categories cover a majority of programmatic content. The disadvantage is loss of cross-national comparability. In fact, programmatic categories for coding matched to expenditure records did not yield any stronger or clearer results than are obtained in the procedures used in this chapter. Thus there was little internal advantage to be gained in employing a unique German coding system, and there is great disadvantage in losing the grounds for generalization from one set of country findings to another.

2. The equation for welfare looks bizarre, nearly to the point of unbelievability. The dummy variable indicating a CDU chancellor gets a *b* over 100, with a constant of –71.6. In order to unravel this, one must compare the statistical results in Table 11.1 (and Appendix Table A11.3) with the graphic presentation in Figure 11.3.5. In the latter, it is clear that welfare priorities rose early on, quite steeply, under the CDU, then, still under the CDU—dropped precipitously (apparently as a nearly one-to-one exchange for defense spending after the 1960s Berlin crisis), with minimum interruption through the first half of the SPD period (i.e., the Brandt years). The first Schmidt budget, reflected in outlays completed in 1975, restored welfare to a priority higher than its historical average, with the next dip to occur with the first Kohl (CDU) budget.

This concatenation could be statistically accommodated, if we were vitally interested in the particular equation, by a variety of transformations, including multiple polynomials. Such, however, is—we note again—beyond our principal interests. There is a straightforward reason, portrayed in Figure 11.3.5, for the strange welfare constant of –71.6 and the *b* of 101.5 in Table 11.1. Once the actual effect of the dummy variable is entered into the equation, the trend line shifts from moderately negative to steeply positive and, in effect, cuts dramatically below the 0 point, to a negative –71.6. The effect of the CDU chancellor term then is to add 101.6 to the intercept, thereby returning it to a more believable 29.9. Thus, the point from which the impact of party programs on welfare priority begins, once the effect of the party alternation is accommodated, is 29.9 percent.

This does nothing to redeem the poor performance of the party programs—with the exception of the FDP's—in welfare, but at least it transforms seemingly wild statistical figures to a comprehensible reality.

12

The Netherlands

INSTITUTIONAL AND POLITICAL CONTEXT

What European country has had a dozen different parties in parliament since World War II? In what country has a Christian Democratic party been in every postwar government? Where have there been repeated crises, with extended periods of haggling between potential coalition parties, essentially leaving the country without a proper government for weeks and, sometimes, months on end? What country seems to have prospered economically and to have preserved its place within the Western alliance in spite of widespread domestic opposition? Italy, right? Yes, but also the Netherlands. The comparison is apt, but probably odious for some people in both countries.

The Dutch cabinet always has at least two but usually four parties represented, and five are not unknown. Of the two houses in parliament, the lower is by far the more important. Since 1946, the lower house—the Tweede Kamer—has never had fewer than seven parties holding seats, and it once reached fourteen. The Dutch system of proportional representation, whereby votes are cast for party lists rather than for individual candidates, allows a party to gain seats with a very small number of votes. The result is that the percentage of votes is reflected more accurately in the Dutch parliament than in all but one other modern European legislature, that of Denmark.

Interestingly, it has often been the case—more in earlier years than recently—that Dutch cabinet coalitions would be formed of more parties than necessary or of a combination in excess of what is necessary for a parliamentary majority. There are complex reasons for this, that are not so clear as in the other similar case, that of Austria. But such factors are not centrally relevant to our concern here. For all the seeming fractionalization within the Dutch parliaments and governments, there are essentially three parties that have endured. It is to these three that we will give our attention here.

The Labor Party (PvdA—Partij van de Arbeid) is essentially a social democratic party, favoring a solid welfare state, progressive taxation, and substantial redistribution of wealth. The PvdA has been a fervent advocate of peaceful internationalism, skeptical on increases in defense spending, and opposed to such NATO policies as cruise missiles. It has been (largely symbolically) critical of the Netherlands' (largely symbolic) monarchy. The Labor Party averages around 30 percent of the vote in parliamentary elections. The party, which we will most commonly refer to by as PvdA, has alternated in the governing coalitions, serving for twenty-two of the forty-five years covered by our analysis.

The center in the Netherlands is represented by the Christian Democratic Appeal (CDA—Christen Democratisch Appel). The CDA is a modern merger of previously quite separate Roman Catholic and Protestant *confessional* parties. The centrist, mildly welfare-state-oriented Catholic People's Party (Katholieke Volkspartij—KVP), joined forces in the 1970s with the Calvinist, bourgeois Anti-Revolutionary Party (ARP) and another Protestant group, the Christian Historical Union (CHU). In spite of somewhat differing views on the role of the state in the modern economy, the uniting groups sought to sustain a confessional force in an increasingly secular polity. The result has been a party with a decidedly Christian democratic outlook—not unlike that of the CDU in Germany. By that we mean a party oriented toward upholding Christian values in politics, along with economic stability and growth, but still essentially in support of at least the basics of the welfare state. "Right-of-center" is sometimes used in reference to the CDA, but rarely "conservative." The CDA customarily receives a bit over 30 percent of the vote. Either the earlier KVP or the successor CDA has been in every postwar Dutch cabinet. In our analyses, we incorporate the KVP until 1977 and then the CDA as its successor, and we refer to the pair by the recent initials CDA.

A more typically, but not entirely, conservative path is taken by the Dutch liberals, the People's Party for Freedom and Democracy (VVD—Volkspartij voor Vrijheid en Democratie). Founded in 1948 out of the prewar Liberal State and Liberal Democratic parties, the *liberal* label is earned in good part because of the VVD's secularism. It draws support from middle-class white-collar workers and upper-class businesspeople (Banks 1992, 546). The liberals have averaged around 13 percent of the vote and have served in government a little less than half of the time between the war and the mid-1980s.

The apparent class cleavage in Dutch politics is between the VVD and the more socialist PvdA. They have alternated but have not served together in the government since the 1950s. The CDA has been the constant party, building coalitions from either the left, with the PvdA, or from the right, with the VVD, and incorporating other bits and pieces as convenient. Several other parties entered and left the public arena with some regularity, but none had the size or the endurance to be a lasting element in the policy process during the period we are investigating.

The Netherlands has produced a good number of political scientists who have placed their own national experience in a comparative context (Daalder 1966 and 1987; Lijphart 1968, 1977, and 1984; Andeweg 1982; Keman 1988). Throughout their writings there is extensive discussion of the relative rigidity of social cleavages, both interreligious and interclass, in Dutch society, with attention to how these cleavages manifest themselves in political life. The concept of *pillarization* has evolved, suggesting that the social structure is—or has been—a series of parallel but separate religious and class hierarchies, with little real grass-roots integration. These *pillars* are described as capped by stable elites, such as religious figures, business leaders, and labor union officials.

One thesis offers the concept of *consociationalism,* whereby policy is made quietly and political life ordered by these elites from the various pillars. This variation on elite theory does not see the process as necessarily selfish but rather as a way of preserving national peace and progress by diverting and diluting overt conflicts between the various pillars (Daalder 1966 and 1987). Whether this ever existed as a distinct mode of policymaking and whether it still exists are vigorously disputed within the scholarly community (Lijphart 1977 and 1988; Peters, Doughtie, and McCulloch 1977). Particular attention has been paid to the increasing secularization of society (accompanied naturally by declining legitimacy of a bargaining process loaded in favor of the ecclesiastics) and the increasing openness of competitive policymaking.

It is not our intent to engage in or to seek to resolve these essentially domestic disputes. However, we ought to consider the manner in which the factors they involve might affect the functioning and accountability of parties in the Dutch policy process. We have already suggested that coalition governments are likely to result in a cloudy mandate, at best. Who has won when, after an election, a few professional politicians from four or five parties get together in closed rooms and haggle over cabinet portfolios and, presumably, policy? What does it mean for the relevance of party programs when, as in Italy or the Netherlands, one can be sure that the major party in the cabinet will be the same one that has been there for forty years, no matter how the other parties fare?

Our analyses in other coalition systems have not borne out the pessimistic expectation that coalitions will essentially filter out or homogenize party programs before they can be reflected in policy. But if the common view is true that in the Netherlands, for a goodly portion of the period we are studying, policies were made by a group of ecclesiastics, businessmen, and union leaders committed to keeping the lid on any serious conflict, what is the point to party programs at all? And even if the bishops and other capstones of the Dutch society fall from their respective pillars, it still leaves in place multiparty, potentially immobilized coalitions, whose role may be more open and real than heretofore, but nonetheless are impotent to translate into policy the competing concerns contained in the programs offered to the electorate by the separate parties. After the 1972 election, it took 163 days before a government could even be *formed,* let alone get down to the business of somehow honoring the wishes of the electorate. An even longer interregnum occurred in 1977.

Party program-to-policy linkages may be further weakened by the somewhat ambivalent stance that Dutch cabinets have toward the parties. Although, constitutionally, in the Netherlands ministers are part of the Queen's government and bear responsibilities that go beyond party, it is clear that they are answerable to parliament, which in practice can dismiss them. There is no separation of powers, as in the United States, but neither are the powers fused as in Britain. Ministers in the Netherlands cannot be members of parliament. Both MPs and ministers can introduce legislation, but most—if not all—initiatives come from the government. Hence the cabinet is clearly the most powerful institution in the Dutch system.

The relations between parliament and government have, to some extent, changed over time. Until the 1970s, ministers and supporting parties remained rather independent from each other. On the one hand, parties tended to seek to influence governmental decisions through the usual legislation techniques. On the other hand, government and the ministers tended to take a position above politics. Being in the Queen's government led ministers to feel that because they were close to the throne, they were less partisan (Andeweg 1982, 50). Another reason for this attitude may have been that the majority of ministers were selected on grounds of expertise rather than political skill.

Since the mid-1970s, however, the bonds between cabinet and supporting parties have become tighter, with less freedom for either actor to go its own way. This development, some have argued, has sustained a paradoxical process where there is strong competition at the party level and in the election, but cooperation in the cabinet. Since we are applying a common set of models to all countries, we will not be digging deeply into such things as changes before and after the 1970s. But the descriptive material is such as to sustain a pessimistic stance toward the likelihood of clear party program-to-policy accountability in the Netherlands. However, if evidence of accountability is uncovered by our analyses, it will warrant a conclusion that the Netherlands is not so uniquely burdened after all.

PROGRAM AND POLICY TRENDS

Dutch Data

We have already noted the manner in which in our data series the Catholic People's Party (KVP) was treated as the predecessor to the Christian Democratic Appeal (CDA). That is, for the years 1946 through 1977, the figures we give as belonging to the CDA were those of the KVP. The KVP had been by far the biggest of the religious parties in the cabinet, serving continuously until the reorganization that resulted in the CDA. In turn, the CDA has been in all successive governments. This results in a single time series that is generally in accord with Dutch historical reality. By way of reminder, then, the three parties included are the Labor Party (PvdA), the Christian Democrats (CDA), and the liberals (VVD). All competed for the entire period, and all were potential partners in the various coalitions formed along the way.

Policy data represent, as in the Swedish case, outlays by ministries rather than outlays for specific functional categories. This modification probably results in some loss of variance in policy indicators, with consequent reduction in the value of the coefficients in our statistical models. But the overall consistency of categories was much more reliable for ministries than for functional expenditure categories. We incorporated eight ministries into our analyses. The same caution discussed at greater length with respect to the Swedish data apply here (see Chapter 9). There is always the possibility of some modest or hidden functional reallocations across ministries for purely political reasons. Data were available for the period 1951 through 1986, which means that spending figures are led to match to party program entries from 1949 through 1984. The expenditure shares for the Ministries of Justice and of the Interior were summed to make the index of public order policy. The Justice Ministry is concerned with courts, public prosecution, and prisons. The Ministry of the Interior is concerned with police and internal-order programs. Merged, they come quite close to that which has been labeled *administration of justice* in most of the other countries.

In the normal experimentation to fit party program material to policy domains, we encountered no unusual conditions. We found that an aggregation of four categories produced cleaner results for defense policy. Thus to create the index we label "foreign +," for each of the three parties we added the percentages for military +, peace, internationalism +, and European Community +. The decision to add these was guided by a factor analysis of all three parties, which indicated that the four items constituted a strong, single dimension. The pairings between specific program emphases and policy domains, therefore, are as follows:

Party Program	*Policy Area (Ministry)*
Foreign Policy +	Defense
Foreign Special Relations +	Foreign Affairs
Agriculture	Agriculture
Social Justice	Welfare
Technology and Infrastructure	Housing
Technology and Infrastructure	Transport & Waterworks
Education	Education
Law and Order	Public Order*

*Sum of percentages of outlays for Ministries of Justice and of the Interior.

One additional feature of the data will be clear from the statistical analyses but can benefit from special notice. The Christian Democratic Appeal (CDA) and its predecessor have participated in every postwar government. Therefore, any coefficient for CDA automatically is equal to CDA × Gov. There is no interactive term involved in this instance. The CDA is always in government.

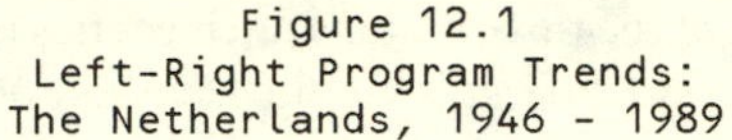
Figure 12.1
Left-Right Program Trends:
The Netherlands, 1946 - 1989

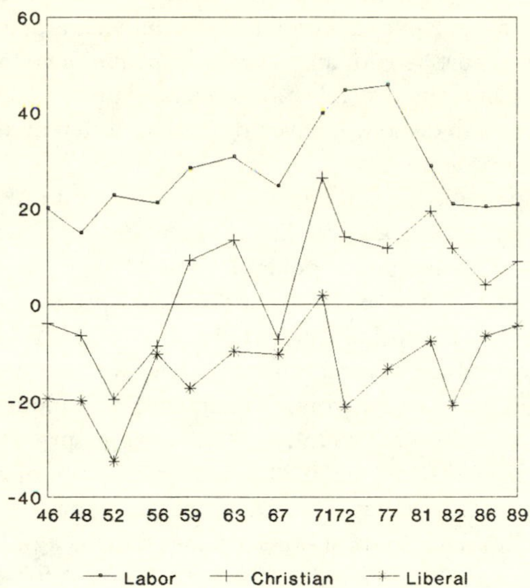

The left-right program indicator was constructed exactly as in all of the other countries. And the left-right policy priority factor was also built as in all the other countries, save Austria. A strong single factor emerges, with the following loadings at the left end: housing = .86; education = .83; welfare = .37. Loaded at the right end are: public order = –.56 and defense = –.90.

Left-Right Trends

The trends for the Labor, Christian, and liberal parties are plotted in Figure 12.1. This is a classic case of stable partisan differentiation. It is as tidy a spread for a multiparty system as we have yet seen. In all other countries with at least three parties there has been substantial leapfrogging by at least two of the contestants. Here, however, although the CDA sometimes moves into space formerly or subsequently occupied by one of the other two, it never crosses over. The VVD does occupy nearly the same space as the CDA for a few years, but they never pass each other. PvdA never crosses the space of the VVD, and it never shares a common space with the CDA. It is not difficult at all, from the evidence of Figure 12.1, to understand how the CDA has stayed in government, alternately building coalitions with the PvdA and with the VVD. It is also understandable why, for the past few decades, the PvdA and VVD have not been together or able to unite to throw out the seemingly entrenched CDA.

The clear separation of the three major Dutch parties is not due to inflexibility. There are substantial period differences in the left-right positions of each of them. What is more, there is a modest, but noticeable, common leftward movement of all three. But each has its own clear domain. As Keman has argued from other evidence, there is no support here for any claim that the major contending parties in the Netherlands are indistinguishable or are catch-all parties (Keman 1988). Voters who are motivated to do so will have no problem differentiating these parties on the basis of their programs.

If we now compare the lines in Figure 12.1 to the trend in Figure 12.2, it appears that there may indeed be some linkage between the two general left-right scales of party programs and public policy. It is hard to spot commensurate shifts by individual parties, but the overall leftward tilt of the programs (12.1) comports with the rather steeper leftward movement of policy (12.2). This correspondence is rather more obvious than in most other countries we have so far studied.

The policy trend itself is eminently familiar, with only modest variation from the pattern seen across the other countries. After the high priority on defense and infrastructural policies during the 1950s, there is a steady movement leftward. The leftward trend does moderate earlier and more gradually in the Netherlands than is common elsewhere. In most other settings there is a rather sharp flattening or even rightward shift in the 1970s. The Netherlands' leftward slope began to curve gradually in the 1960s but actually continued modestly leftward until the end of the period included here. There is no question, however, about the moderation over the latter half of the time series.

Although it seems that the general programmatic leanings of the major parties and that of policy priority, on the broad left-right scales, were more or less in accord, it is difficult to spot any general policy consequences of particular reconstitutions of governments. Of course, the CDA is invariant. Nevertheless, looking at the lines that indicate when the PvdA and VVD exchanged places, it is difficult to spot any corollary in the general policy curve. It remains to be seen if a connection is any clearer in specific policy areas.

Specific Policy Trends

The plots in Figure 12.3 indicate the percentages of funds allocated to the various ministries. As in about half of the other countries, foreign affairs and defense (12.3.1 and 12.3.2) follow inverse trends, with the heavy element of development assistance in the former displacing some of the decline in the latter. Defense does follow the standard pattern of early response to the cold war, relatively regular decline, and then some flattening of decline from the 1970s on. Education (12.3.4) and housing (12.3.7) follow the now-familiar curve, rising early and then declining later. Welfare is a bit erratic but also shows a strong rise from the early 1960s into the 1980s, where it then dips steeply (12.3.3).

Figure 12.2
Left-Right Expenditure Priority Factor Scores:
The Netherlands, 1949 - 1986

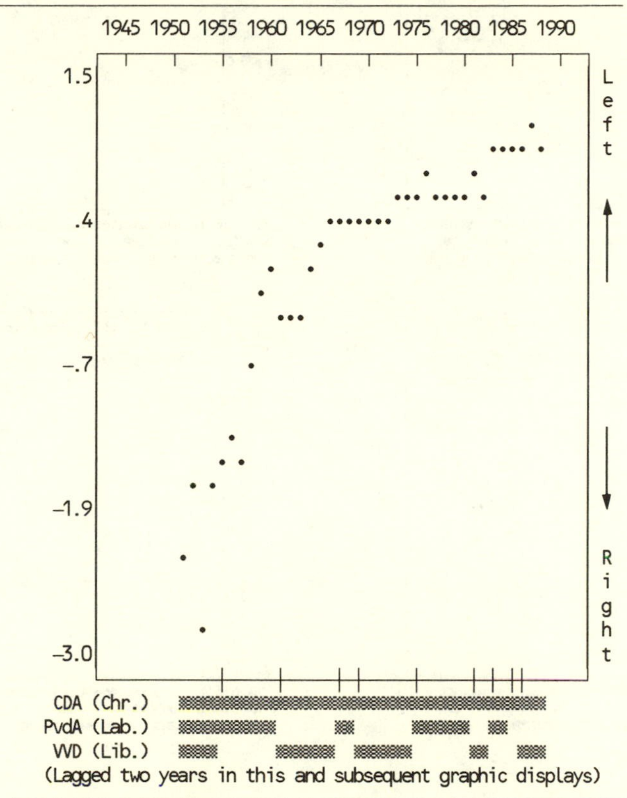

Structure of Policy Factor Score

Policy Area	Factor Loading
Housing	.86
Education	.83
Welfare	.37
Public Order	–.56
Defense	–.90

Figure 12.3
Trends in Expenditure Priorities: The Netherlands, 1951 – 1986

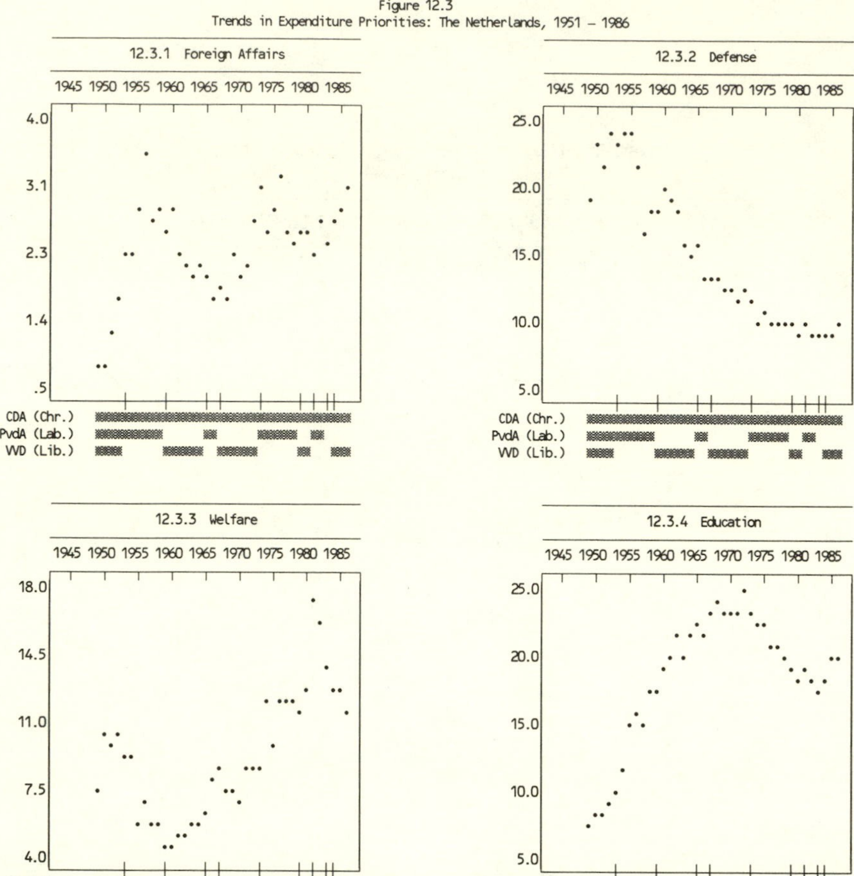

Transportation and waterworks cannot be ignored, especially in a country where 30 percent of the land is below sea level and kept more or less dry by an elaborate, publicly maintained waterworks system (12.3.8). The curve does reflect, much as do public utilities and transportation, elsewhere, an early postwar capital investment that became more efficient with completion of modernization projects.

Agriculture (12.3.6) is typical, with perhaps a somewhat steeper rise than in most countries, before the steep decline set in. But public order (12.3.5), which in most countries is the one apparently conservative policy that enjoyed steady growth was spared that privilege in the Netherlands.

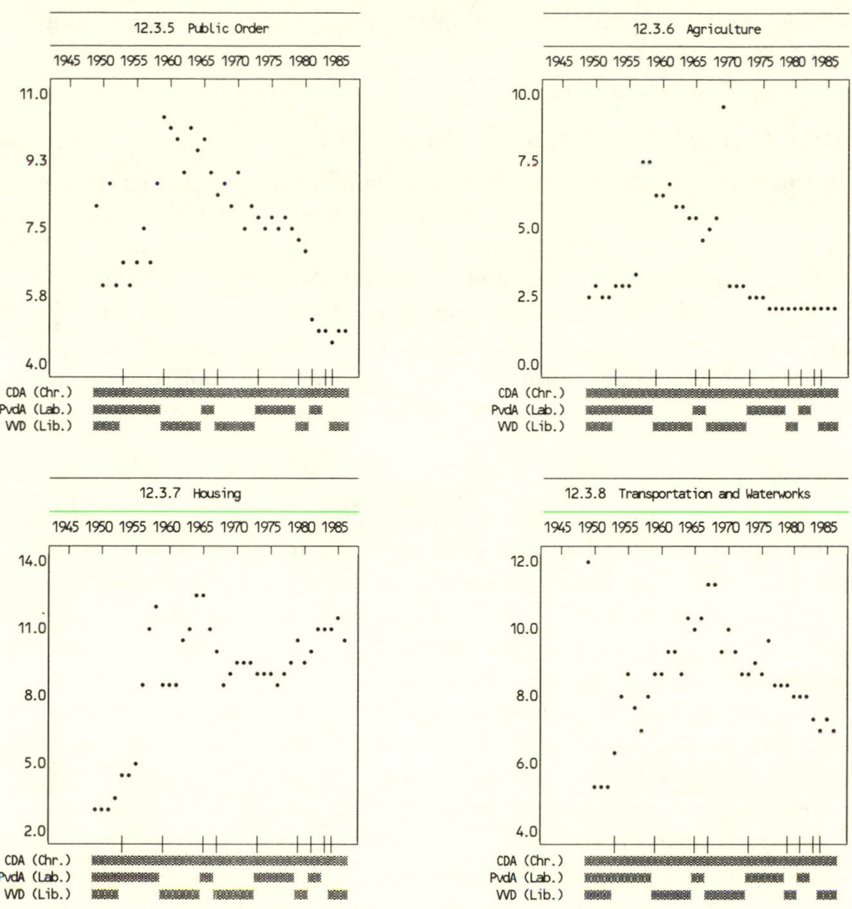

The fact that one party has served continuously in government, and that the other two have alternated rather regularly, makes spotting policy consequences of government reorganization difficult. Were not more-sophisticated and more-accurate statistical procedures available and about to be reported, we might be tempted to speculate about the frequency with which there does seem to be an inflection in the curves at the end of the long service of the PvdA on a succession of Dutch cabinets. The sharp alternation between PvdA and the liberals, against the backdrop of CDA continuity, may constitute for the Netherlands a competitive situation comparable to that found in other countries, even though the latter had more comprehensive party turnover in government. Confirmation of that impression, however, requires more-complex procedures than merely scanning the plots.

PARTY PROGRAM-TO-POLICY CONGRUENCE

The Dutch analyses yield the interesting and convenient result that one model fits best across all but two of the policy areas; those two are not explained by any of the three models. This is the complex ideology equation, which was also the dominant process model for Austria and Germany. Of the seven fields (including left-right) modeled in Table 12.1, the average R^2 is .54, or slightly higher than that of Britain. The mandate and ideology terms do well in all seven areas; however, their effect is as much to restructure the equation in order to emphasize the significance of alternation of coalition partners as it is to boost the R^2.

Best-Fitting Models

It is useful to call attention to what is *not* prominent in the findings. There is very little evidence of a general agenda effect, whereby a particular party significantly relates to a policy field, irrespective of that party's holding office, or receives deferential acknowledgment of its programmatic concerns, specifically when out of office. The pure agenda model did not, alone, fit best any policy domain in the Netherlands.

Furthermore, scanning down the columns for the PvdA and the VVD out of office, one sees no pattern of positive signs, indicating an agenda effect, in interaction with the programs of the other parties. Only two such instances appear above the .05 level: welfare for the PvdA (.50) and housing for the VVD (.98).

What is clear and is backed up by the pattern of cases that did not quite reach .05 significance levels (see also Appendix Table A12.3) is the consistent mandate impact of the CDA, as well as more than a few cases of negative mandate against the PvdA and VVD, when accounting for their times out of power. The negative mandate occurs when the effect of a party's having been out of power yields an inverse congruence between its programmatic emphases and the enacted policies. It is the opposite of the agenda effect, whereby the term that accommodates a party's having been *out* of office nevertheless yields a positive coefficient. Given that the CDA is always in power, it incurs neither the risk of a negative mandate nor the benefit of an agenda effect. Actually, whether the negative mandate indications under PvdA and VVD are a result of each other's antipathy in office or of the brokerage by the CDA cannot be determined by our analysis.

Since the dominant feature of the Dutch policies is their common fit to the ideology model, it is reasonable to give extended attention to the feature that distinguishes that model from the rest. The model includes the dummy variable for Labor (PvdA) participation in government, as well as the multiplicative terms for in-government programs for all three parties (CDA being always uniform in

Table 12.1
Best-Fitting Models Between Party Program Emphases and Policy Priorities:
The Netherlands, 1949–1988 *

	Ideology Models											
Policy Priority (Program Emphasis)	Constant a	Ideology Labor Gov = 1	Labor (Out)(x Gov): (+) Agenda (–) or Mandate	Labor (Out)(x Gov): Mandate	Liberal (Out)(x Gov): (+) Agenda (–) or Mandate	Liberal (Out)(x Gov): Mandate	Mandate Chr.Dem.App'l (In Gov)	Adj R^2	Added by Mandate	Added by Ideology
Left–Right (Left–Right)	1.77	–3.10	$-.03^{n}$	.08			.02	.73	.00	.21
Housing (Tech. & Infrastr.)	7.92	–6.75		.82	.98	<u>–1.30</u>	.65	.74	.08	.10
Defense (Foreign +)	20.5	1.15			-2.16^{n}		.90	.62	**	**
Education (Education)	20.9	10.2		<u>–2.74</u>				.56	.30	.06
Foreign Affairs (Spec. For. Rel's)	2.41	.50		–.76		–.14		.47	.20	.06
Agriculture (Agriculture)	–2.70	5.65	$-.85^{n}$	<u>–2.14</u>	1.45	.49	1.99	.41	.10	.25
Welfare (Social Justice)	4.03	–3.77	.50	.71	$-.43^{n}$	.56		.26	.05	.08

[$E_i = a + bP_A + bP_i^A + b(P^A i \times G) + \ldots bP_i^n + b(P_i^n \times G)$]

* Indicating only those b's (unstandardized regression coefficients) that attained .05 statistical significance. Coefficients in the opposite direction from theoretical expectation are <u>underlined</u>. Coefficients for negative mandate are indicated by ^{n}. There were no cases of either the agenda or the mandate model fitting best in The Netherlands.

** Adjusted coefficient nearly identical for agenda, mandate, and ideology models.

that regard) and out-of-government terms for the PvdA and the liberals (VVD). But it is the dummy variable for PvdA/VVD alternation that concerns us most here.

There is no doubt about the basic programmatic and ideological leanings of these two parties. As Figure 12.1 makes crystal clear, neither has ever entered the turf that has at some time been occupied by the other. It is almost as though the CDA devotes itself to the separation of the two wings. Yet a careful reading down the "Ideology" column in Table 12.1 reveals some serious anomalies. A negative sign is found where a positive would be expected from Labor's participation in government for left-right, housing, and welfare. An unexpected positive sign is found for agriculture and, it could be argued, defense. Clear conformity to the customary expectations from a Labor party are seen in the cases of education and foreign affairs only. Thus, although the ideology model fits best in terms of overall statistical power, five of the seven budgetary categories are misfits.

A bit of reflection on these findings, placed against the backdrop of the left-right trends for the three parties (Figure 12.1), may bring into focus a good example for the ideal type of competition featured in Downs's simplest, single-dimensional, power-driven, vote-maximization theory. The CDA plays a delicate game of holding the center, moving tactically near but never beyond either of the opponents. The result is never a majority of votes for the CDA but rather a clear grasp on the median voter and the presumption of initiative in forming a government.

That the CDA strategy is not wholly free of policy content, however, is verified by the subsequent record that the CDA gained the clearest set of policy results. The column under "Mandate Chr. Dem. App'l" in Table 12.1 supports that claim, with four out of seven significant, positive coefficients. A glance at Appendix Table A12.3 shows that the balance of the coefficients, although not statistically significant, are likewise all positive for the CDA.

More often than not, the VVD sees its policy objectives reflected in legislation that matches its programmatic emphases, when accounting for incumbency, with the one exception of housing (–1.30). The PvdA has a less impressive record of program fulfillment. But neither party attains sufficient success in converting programmatic emphases into policy priority to at all neutralize the strikingly contrary findings from the alternation term.

The reversals of their seeming ideological commitments when either the liberal VVD or the socialist PvdA are in office seem to illustrate near-classic cases of opportunistic parties, sacrificing policy for portfolios. They maintain purity in their ideological pronouncements while participating in governments that most often produce contrary policies. The backdrop shows the CDA shepherding the process, determining payoff matrices, foiling the programmatic aspirations of the real combatants, and tidily bringing its own policy concerns from program to legislation.

Nonconformists and Contradictions

Two policy domains failed to attain R^2 .25: public order and transportation and waterworks. In the case of public order, as we remarked above, we combined the indicators for the Ministries of the Interior (police, and so on) and of Justice (courts, prosecution, and so on). Separate analyses did not improve the explanation. Attention might also be drawn to the very curvilinear pattern of public-order policy priorities (Figure 12.3.5). In most, but not all, other countries we saw a steep rise in priority for administration of justice and such related functions. In fact, all three major Dutch parties increased their attention to law and order in their programs. The simple trends (correlation with year) are all positive: CDA = .74; VVD = .32; PvdA = .22. However, the trend for public order-expenditure is negative, –.41. Dutch parties talk a lot about law and order, but they seem not to do all that much once in office.

Growth of central government concern for public order has been nearly universal and is, in most countries, reflected in shifting fiscal resources. The CDA programmatic emphasis on law and order did relate significantly to policy priority at the simple correlation level with an *r* of .45. In fact, at the level of simple correlations, public order was among the higher correlations. But that may be saying nothing more than that if one ignores the interplay between parties in and out of government, bivariate relations are oversimplifications. As before, our goal is to check the fit of the theory, not to explain policy variance. Thus, we can conclude here that the general theory does not fit public-order policy.

Waterworks and transportation may be so basic in the Netherlands, after centuries of the effort to push away the sea, that they are simply taken for granted. In the first half of the postwar period, a substantial share of outlays was devoted to this policy area, probably in major capital improvements, followed by a decline in priority (Figure 12.3.8). But that curve generally describes the postwar experience with infrastructure in most countries. We shall not go beyond such musings. As with public order, we have no further interest in this policy domain, except to note its exceptionalism.

Aside from these two nonconformities, there are only a few obvious contradictions in the coefficients listed in Table 12.1: two for Labor (PvdA) × government (agriculture = –2.14; education = –2.74) and one for the Liberals (VVD) × government (housing = –1.30). These seem to be genuine contradictions—where the policy priority goes in the opposite direction of the governing party's program. There may be a pattern here, visible only when viewed across several countries, where the frequency of misfits or contradictions for both agriculture and education is greater than that in other policy domains. We will give this further attention in Chapter 14.

Two seeming contradictions are probably not contradictory. These are the negative coefficients for the PvdA and the Liberals, in government, on foreign affairs

(–.76 and –.14, respectively). We have noted that foreign affairs–policy priority in the Netherlands is negatively correlated with defense, the former representing an alternative to peace through strength, and consisting in large measure of development assistance to Third World nations (mostly to former Dutch colonies). But the independent variable in the foreign affairs policy equations is the composite foreign + indicator, composed mostly of positive references to the military, NATO, and other aspects of the Western alliance. Thus, inverse coefficients here are not surprising and, in fact, are quite plausible.

CONCLUSION

Do these findings support or contradict a claim that party democracy works in the Netherlands? This is not a book about the Netherlands. It is about democracy in general. There are many other facets of that country's political life that would have to be taken into account and weighed both empirically and normatively before even a tentative answer could be given to the question. We can, however, address one critical nexus of the chain of elements that constitute a working democracy, namely, the congruence between the preelection statements of competing parties and what is done by the government that subsequently takes office.

There is little argument that votes matter in the Netherlands, if mattering means getting a substantial portion of the distribution of interests in the society represented through occupancy of parliamentary seats. But if a parliament only "parls" and does not get reflected in policy what was supported by the electorate, the chain has a weak link. If those who are ostensibly answerable to parliament in fact bargain away the terms upon which they sought office, then the chain is further weakened.

There is a vigorous left-right battle fought in the Netherlands, and it has been fought clearly for at least the whole postwar period. The Labor party (PvdA) and the liberals (VVD) have selected weapons appropriate for that battle. But while those two parties fight on the open plain, the Christians have occupied the city. The Christians are not deaf to the left-right struggle. Their own programs are the best single predictor of left-right policy from corresponding programmatic emphases ($r = .49$). But they seem to attain their victories through the misadventure and/or power hunger of their coalition allies.

This CDA impact seems to take place openly, as a way of effectuating through legislation the signals raised in its election programs. There is no evidence of a cabal, except that somewhere along the line whichever of the two other parties is the coalition partner of the moment has to give up, tacitly or overtly, many of its major programmatic and ideological concerns. Of course, as long as enough voters prefer that confessional (Calvinist *or* Catholic) interests override those of class, the CDA will sustain its brokerage role. But who is to say that, just because voters choose not to align along the dictates of class-based left-right disputes, the result is any the less *democratic?* It is frustrating perhaps for the Left (PvdA) and for the

Right (VVD) that neither can attract sufficient voters to play on its field. But such has been their lot.

In that most unlikely of circumstances where the electoral rules were changed and a single-member, plurality system were introduced, the CDA would probably be the big loser. Perhaps then the VVD and the PvdA would be more prone and/or competent to honor their election programs through action. But that is not the direction of twentieth-century political reform—quite the opposite, if the preference for proportional representation of the new Central and Eastern European democracies is any guide.

Much has been made of political transformations in the Netherlands during the 1970s. And these may indeed in some domain be important. In the face of declining fortunes, probably because of the general secularization of the population, the Calvinists and the Catholics buried the hatchet in order to sustain a lasting presence of a confessional party on the Dutch cabinet. The bringing together of Protestant and Catholic political forces is more the norm than the exception in those European countries where both are potent forces. Certainly, as the cases of both the Dutch CDA and the German CDU illustrate, the result is not a conventional conservative movement but one that dulls the edges of the welfare state without doing it lasting damage.

13

Belgium

INSTITUTIONAL AND POLITICAL CONTEXT

Belgium is a telling example of the political cleavages scattered by history throughout Western Europe. Wedged between the Netherlands, Germany, and France, the country straddles the linguistic boundary between the Germanic and Romance languages. In Flanders, the most populous and prosperous northern part, Flemish (Dutch) is spoken; in Wallonia, the smaller and poorer southern half, French is spoken. The expanding Belgian and European Community capital, Brussels, is physically located in Flanders, but most residents speak French, a fact that has prevented any tidy settlement of linguistic differences by division of the country into autonomous regions.

The first political cleavage to develop in modern Belgium was neither ethnic nor linguistic but rather religious. This may seem at first glance odd for a country that is overwhelmingly Catholic. But in the mid-nineteenth century, an opposition developed between traditional Catholics and secularizing liberals, primarily over the place of church schools within the education system. This division engendered a Catholic and a Liberal Party. The schools question itself was not finally settled until a compromise was reached in 1958.

In the meantime, another sociopolitical cleavage had been institutionalized at the party level by the emergence of a Labor (later Socialist) Party in 1885, which was explicitly oriented toward extending social welfare and industrial democracy. This coincided with some of the interests of social Catholicism, a movement that took its start from the papal encyclicals on the rights of workers, in the late nineteenth century. The movement became the dominant tendency within the Catholic Party (which, significantly, changed its name to the Social Christian Party in the early twentieth century). Both Socialists and Social Christians thus became associated with popular workers' movements and trade unions, though the Christians also tried to mobilize farmers and the bourgeoisie under their political banner.

In the traditional three-party system that dominated Belgian politics until the 1960s, there was thus a basis for cooperation between any pair of parties. Socialists and Liberals could agree on strengthening secular as opposed to religious education. Socialists and Social Christians could combine to advance welfare and social services. Social Christians could combine with Liberals to defend the traditional social order and political institutions against Socialist incursions. In fact, coalition governments of all three types existed, although there has always been more of a tendency for Liberals and Socialists, whether jointly or apart, to combine with the Christians rather than separately with each other. This is reflected in the fact that, over the postwar period, through the 1980s, the Social Christians were out of office only once, in the mid-1950s, for just under four years. Coalition governments tend to be based on the Christians' participation and on their providing the prime minister.

Belgium has a classic parliamentary system, in which the government depends on attracting a majority of votes cast on motions of confidence. Only one government since World War II was based on a single-party parliamentary majority. In 1950, the Christians won 108 out of 212 seats, forming Belgium's sole postwar noncoalition government, which lasted until the election of 1954. That, in turn, was shortly followed by the only coalition that excluded the Christians—the rare instance of Socialist-Liberal cooperation. Up to the 1960s the coalitions were made up of two or three parties—nearly always the Christians and one or the other of the two major alternatives. Since the 1960s, the coalitions have been larger, incorporating various small parties.

The prime cause for this broadening in order to include lesser parties as coalition partners was the political prominence of linguistic-ethnic cleavages after the settlement of the issue of religious schools in 1958. These tensions had always been there, of course, but they had been diverted, partly by the schools question, as the Flemings were more traditional and Catholic than the Walloons, and partly by the collaboration of more extreme Flemish nationalists with the Germans during the war. For the first part of the postwar period, the Social Christians, therefore, gained politically as the more *Flemish* party. Starting in the early 1960s, this position was challenged by the rise of the People's Union (Volksunie—VU), which focused Flemish demands for regional autonomy and for restrictions on the Brussels "cancer" eating into the Flemish heartland.

Proportional representation allowed the VU, along with the Walloon and Brussels *defense* parties (the Walloon Party—Rassemblement Wallon, RW; and the Francophone Democratic Front—Front Démocratique des Bruxellois Francophones, FDF) to gain parliamentary representation quickly. This put pressure on the established parties to respond to their separate ethnic constituencies. Over a ten-year period, all three formally split into Flemish, Walloon, and Brussels wings. They continued, however, to share some facilities (such as research institutes), to subscribe to substantially common electoral programs, and to enter and leave governments together. They now described themselves as party *families* rather than *parties.*

In the years before the splits, the Social Christians held between 45 and 50 percent of the seats in parliament. Their share, summing the Flemish and Walloon fractions, dropped to a range of 29 to 39 percent after the breakup. The other two families sustained about the same level of parliamentary representation as in the period before the schisms: the Liberals ranging from 10 to 25 percent; the Socialists from 25 to 40 percent. Clearly, the previously dominant Social Christian Party was a big loser in the difficult years after 1968–1970. But no party was able to recover sufficiently from the linguistic breach to act again as a really unified political force.

Paralleling the party developments, a series of constitutional reforms legalized the existence of separate cultural communities, with power over economic, cultural, and social affairs. These communities were recognized in Flanders and Wallonia and covered the separate linguistic groups in Brussels. Jurisdiction was to include delivery of a range of services through regional, linguistically based governments. A full territorial division of powers, however, was bedeviled by the question of Brussels. It has 10 percent of the national population, but does not fit with either of the other two regions. Recognition of Brussels as a third region would tilt the national balance in favor of French speakers, a condition unacceptable to the Flemish national majority.

As a result of this ever-present stumbling block to negotiations, the need to get a two-thirds parliamentary majority for constitutional amendments, and the growing fragmentation of the party systems, both elections and government reformations between elections became more frequent in the late 1960s and the 1970s. The policy agenda was dominated by the need to get and keep not two but three or four ideological families together for long enough to pass an agreed-upon constitutional amendment. Other considerations, including fulfillment of other policy aspirations, tended to go by the board.

The political situation was exacerbated by—and perhaps contributed to—economic stagnation and strong regional imbalances in unemployment and prosperity. Comparative survey research across several countries showed that pessimism toward their political system has increased most rapidly among the Belgians (Inglehart 1990). It is hard to avoid the impression that Belgian government in the latter two thirds of the postwar period has been more an exercise in crisis management than a considered implementation of substantive policy programs.

This is not to say that water doesn't flow or schools don't operate, that soldiers are unpaid or pension checks unsent. Normal governmental jobs get done by a professional bureaucracy. But professional bureaucracies are under no political or moral obligation to adapt to the wishes of the electorate or to the promises for change presented to the voters by competing political parties. Nor does the context of crisis mean that changes cannot be made in policy priorities. Rather it suggests that there may be less likelihood of clear linkage between party programs and policy priorities than we have found in more "normal" countries.

Crises mean there are bigger issues than those of the most recent election. Between 1945 and 1988, Belgium had thirty-four different governments. Unstable coalitions, dependent on diverse and cantankerous splinter parties that are organized for purposes of constitutional change, may require sacrifice or postponement of current concerns in favor of efforts to resolve the definition of the regime itself. That task may leave little time, talent, or energy to attend to the mundane policy preferences of the moment (Dewachter 1987).

In each chapter since taking leave of the Westminster systems (Britain, Australia, Canada) we have opened with a pessimistic assessment of the likely fate of party program-to-policy linkages, first in presidential and then in various types of coalition systems. These were not set up as straw men. Yet in each case, with variations on the theme, we have found our pessimism largely unfounded. Such is not to be the case with Belgium.

PROGRAM AND POLICY TRENDS

Belgian Data

The analyses here are confined to the programs of the three major party families. They are the more or less continuous entities, although some tactical decisions were required for organization of the data, necessitated by the divisions of the parties in the 1960s and 1970s into linguistic groups. After the splits, the separate branches did issue separate election programs. Once the divorces were complete, and the original party ceased issuing a program under its specific banner, we used the two main branches (Flemish and Wallonian sections) and computed the mean scores for program themes. Thus, we include in our analyses the following:

Christian:
- 1946–1971:
  - Christian People's Party (Christelijke Volksparij/Parti social chrétien)
- 1974–1981 (Mean of):
  - Flemish—Christian People's Party
  - Walloon—Social Christian Party

Liberal:
- 1946–1971:
  - Liberal Party (Liberale Partij/Parti libéral, in 1961 renamed Party of Liberty and Progress)
- 1974–1981 (Mean of):
  - Flemish Liberal Party (Partij voor Vrijheid en Vooruitgang)
  - Francophone Liberal Party (Parti de la liberté et du progrés, in 1976 renamed Parti des réformes et de la liberté, and in 1979 renamed Parti des réformateur libéral)

Socialist:
1946–1977:
Socialist Party (Belgische Socialistische Partij/Parti socialiste belge)
1978–1981 (Mean of):
Flemish Socialist Party (Belgische Socialistische Partij, in 1980 renamed Socialistische partij)
Francophone Socialist Party (Parti socialiste)

Although the other regional parties that served as minor members of some post-1973 cabinets are included and coded in the Manifestoes Research Group data set, we did not include them in the present analyses. Their programs tend to be highly concentrated on matters of prime concern to specific regions, with many of the issues important for the larger parties, and of most relevance to the policies we examine here, getting no attention from these smaller parties. They have no time-series continuity at all and thus would be very difficult to accommodate statistically. Further, the three major families have held most of the seats in Parliament and have always provided the prime minister.

Policy indicators for Belgium are quite well documented in the *Statistical Yearbook* (published in Flemish and French). Modest variations in categories did require some aggregation, but it was nevertheless possible to use eleven categories, which together account for an average of 90 percent of Belgian central governmental outlays.

Special note should be taken of two categories: public enterprises and regional subsidies. Belgium has a fairly large public-enterprise sector and an elaborate system of subsidies to selected private undertakings, which have been, to some extent, protectorates of the Socialists. Efforts to reduce the size of the public sector, and the subsidies necessary to keep the various firms afloat, have been at the center of policy dispute, when policymakers have not been wholly distracted by constitutional issues. A comparable category has not been included among the policy domains analyzed in the other countries. We found that party program emphases on productivity provided the best fit for public enterprise policy priority.

Regional assistance has climbed significantly since 1968. Settling the structure of regional governments will, no doubt, lead to even greater increases in this category. Essentially, regional assistance takes the form of block allocations to enable the regional governments to take up human services that had heretofore been the core of the centrally administered, very large Belgian welfare state. After some experimentation with alternative programmatic emphases, we found that the most interesting statistical results were obtained by pairing emphases on national effort *and* social harmony with the policy priority for regional assistance.

As in some other settings, the most interesting results for foreign affairs and defense policy were obtained by pairing them with an aggregated foreign policy

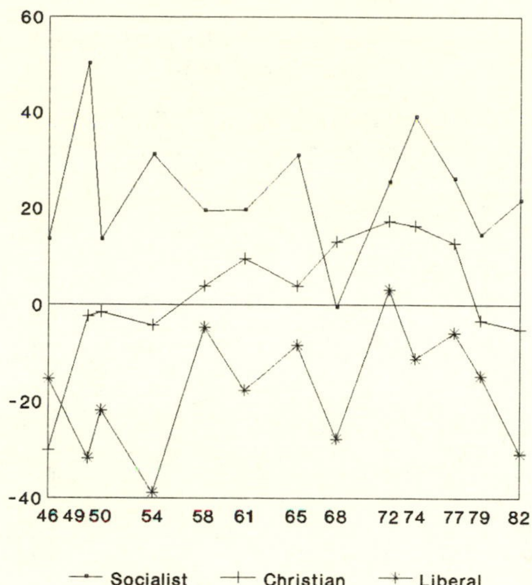

measure from the party programs. That combination and the other pairings of program emphases to policy domains are as indicated below:

Party Program	*Policy Area*
Social Services +	Pensions
Social Services +	Family Assistance
National Effort/Social Harmony	Regional Aid
Education	Education
Social Justice	Health
Law & Order	Administration of Justice
Productivity	Public Enterprises
Technology & Infrastructure	Transport & Communication
Agriculture	Agriculture
Foreign Policy*	Foreign Affairs
Foreign Policy*	Defense

*Sum of Special Foreign Relations +, Military +, Peace, Internationalism +.

The left-right program indicator is the same as in all the other countries (Figure 13.1). The policy factor for left-right, detailed in the note to Figure 13.2, is particularly interesting for what it says about the place of regionalism on the Belgian agenda. The policy factor has on the left end pensions (for all retired work-

Figure 13.2
Left–Right Expenditure Priority Factor Scores:
Belgium, 1945 - 1983

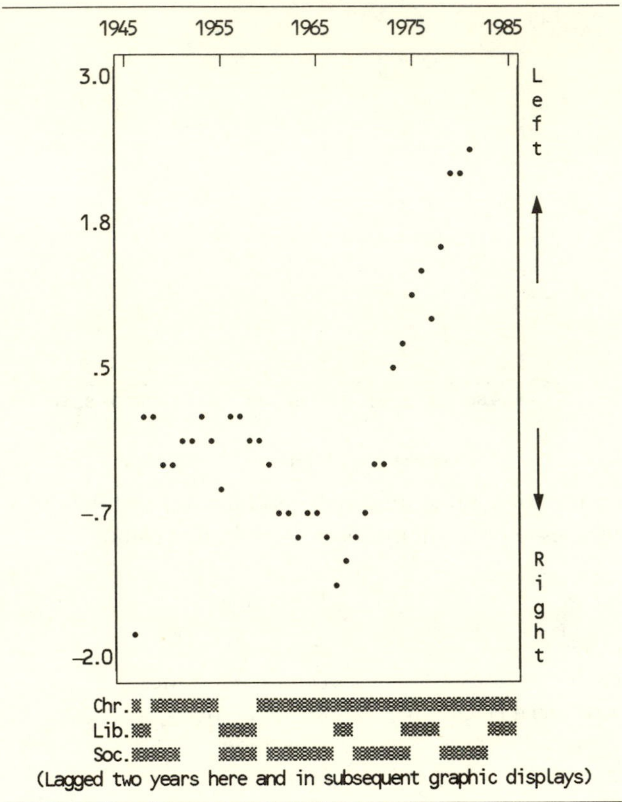

(Lagged two years here and in subsequent graphic displays)

Structure of Policy Priority Factor

Policy Area	Factor Loading
Pensions	.93
Regional Aid	.89
Defense	–.60
Agriculture	–.69
Adm. of Justice	–.74

ers, both governmental and private sector), with a factor loading of .93; and regional aid, at .89. It is clear that supporting decentralization in Belgium and responding to the demands for regional control of public resources, are very much a *leftist* position, whereas preservation of the traditional role of the central government is a goal of the *right.* On the right side of the factor score are defense (–.60), agriculture (–.69), and, interestingly, administration of justice (–.74). Administration of justice, in other countries, has been an oddity, that is, it is a preferred domain of conservatives that has resisted the otherwise leftist policy trend over the postwar period. But that is not so in Belgium, where support for courts and police has fairly steadily dropped, probably also as a part of the general drive to remove power from Brussels in order to enhance the scope of regional governments.

Left-Right Trends

The time trends for the three Belgian parties (or party families) are presented in Figure 13.1. The general spread looks remarkably like that in the Netherlands, but quite a bit less tidy. The three parties occupy generally distinct domains, most of the time staying well separated from one another in a substantively consistent manner. The Socialists are clearly on the left; the Liberals, supporting free-enterprise as well as anticlerical positions, anchor the right. These two never leapfrog, although on occasion—especially during the time of party reorganization—they do each move into space occupied at another time by their most fervent opponent. As in the Netherlands, the Christians and the Liberals show generally leftward trends, *r* with year being respectively .61 and .32, with no trend evident either visually or statistically for the Socialists.

Also, as in the Netherlands, the opposition is between Socialists on the left and Liberals on the right, with Christians coming in between. Although comparable to their Dutch counterpart, the Belgian Liberals contrast with the centrist location of their cognate parties in Britain, Germany, and Scandinavia. There are two distinct tendencies within the general family of liberal parties. One is supportive of a broad range of social services, many "new left" issues such as the environment, and diversified political participation. The other is individualistic, cautious of governmental power, and fiscally orthodox. What they all share, of no small consequence in the European context, is a commitment to civil liberties and secularism.

The central position of the Christians in the picture explains why it is more natural for them to form coalitions with either the Liberals or the Socialists, and why it is far less common—but not unknown—for the latter two to serve together. It is when dimensions of conflict arise other than left-right, such as anticlericalism or ethnic concerns, that there may be grounds of agreement between Liberals and Socialists.

The conflicts of the late 1960s are abundantly clear from Figure 13.1, with 1968 in Belgium being the only instance among our ten countries in which a Socialist party obtained a negative score on the left-right scale. The Socialists are outflanked to the left by the Christians, and the Liberals stake a solid claim well off to the right.

The Belgian Christians, for all their visibility in the center, have not been as adept as their Dutch counterparts in keeping the left and right at bay. They leapfrogged the Liberals to the right, early on, and the Socialists to the left, after 1968. The one time they obtained a majority in parliament, 1950, was after making a substantial leftward leap programmatically. The party may have never subsequently been wholly at ease in coalition, sharing cabinet places with others, while brokering the policy process, as have the Dutch Christians. If there ever was a firm basis for expecting a majority, after the glory days in the 1950s, it certainly ceased to be realistic after the linguistic and regional split. In the turbulent situation of Belgian politics, the Christians have been unable to secure sufficient loyalty from a large enough confessionally inclined electorate to ensure lasting coalition dominance.

The Dutch Christians were able to surmount the Catholic-Protestant difference to present a united front of confessional partisanship, attracting those voters not comfortable with the more class-based left-right split that was being fought out between Liberals and Socialists. Over the past generation in Belgium, the regional-linguistic gap has proven far harder to bridge than has the Calvinist-Catholic cleavage to the north. One should not, however, ignore the fact that the premiership has been held by a Christian Party member most of the time since the war. And that party has been a major force, if not dominant, in every government since 1958. As we shall later see, however, the degree of policy success from brokerage apparently enjoyed by the Dutch Christians has not been achieved by their Belgian cousins.

The left-right policy trend has a twist to it that makes it unlike that of any of the other countries in our set (Figure 13.2). Belgium has not stinted on defense, relative to other small European countries, and it is, after all, the seat of both the European Community and of NATO. But the left-right curve is nearly the reverse of most other countries, with a leap to the left in the early years, followed by a downward slope, reversed sharply after 1968. The latter upswing is unequivocally due to the joint influence of pension expenditures in an aging population and the major shifting and infusion of funds into regional assistance.

This uncommon bifurcation of the trend either conceals or completely overwhelms any obvious variations associated with shifting composition of governments. However, as we have found before, visual inspection of trend lines is not nearly so precise as is statistical analysis, to which we shall turn shortly. Before that, however, we need to examine the trends for specific policy domains, in order to see if there are shifts in priority that are excessively smoothed by the general left-right measure plotted in Figure 13.2.

Specific Policy Trends

The plots in Figure 13.3 show clearly that 1968 was a watershed year. After 1968, policy priority for regional assistance and income support (pensions, family aid) grew rapidly, whereas agriculture, health, administration of justice, and education dipped sharply. Education looks much as it does elsewhere, and almost certainly reflects changing demographics.

Foreign affairs (Figure 13.3.3) has a special Belgian twist in that it is overwhelmed by aid to Zaire during the years when that country was ceasing to be the Belgian Congo. The curves for defense and for transportation are not noticeably unusual, compared to other countries. But there does appear to be a sufficiently sharp break in 1968 in enough policy domains to have reverberated through the entire structure of policymaking and execution.

The questions for us, and for the links in the chain of democratic theory with which we are concerned, are the following: To what extent are these uncommon shifts consonant with the programs presented by the parties to the electorate? Was this a process that, while different in content from that of other countries, was, nevertheless, comparable in form? A party system functioning as a positive component of the democratic process can present dramatic changes to the electorate, as long as the course of that policy is forecast in the programs presented to the voters.

The visual presentations take no account of party programs and give at best a crude picture of the policy correlates of changes in government. For these purposes, we need to proceed to the statistical analyses.

PARTY PROGRAM-TO-POLICY CONGRUENCE

The most important message of Table 13.1, which presents the best-fitting models for Belgium, is the one not seen. Four policy indicators—left-right, pensions, transportation and communication, and agriculture—fail to reach R^2 .25 by any of the three models. This is the largest proportion of nonconformists we have had across the ten countries. And of the eight equations that do reach or surpass 25 percent of the variance, the mean R^2 is only .49, which is second lowest, just ahead of Australia.

Of the eight policy areas passing the threshold, there is less concentration in the "Ideology" column than has been the case with most of the other coalition systems. Still, half the cases do gain substantially by inclusion of the ideology term, measuring, in this case, the presence of the Socialists in or out of government. Two areas of policy priority—defense and subsidies for enterprises—are

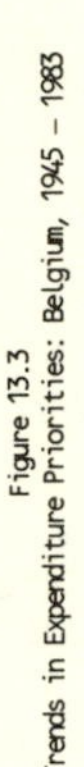

Figure 13.3
Trends in Expenditure Priorities: Belgium, 1945 – 1983

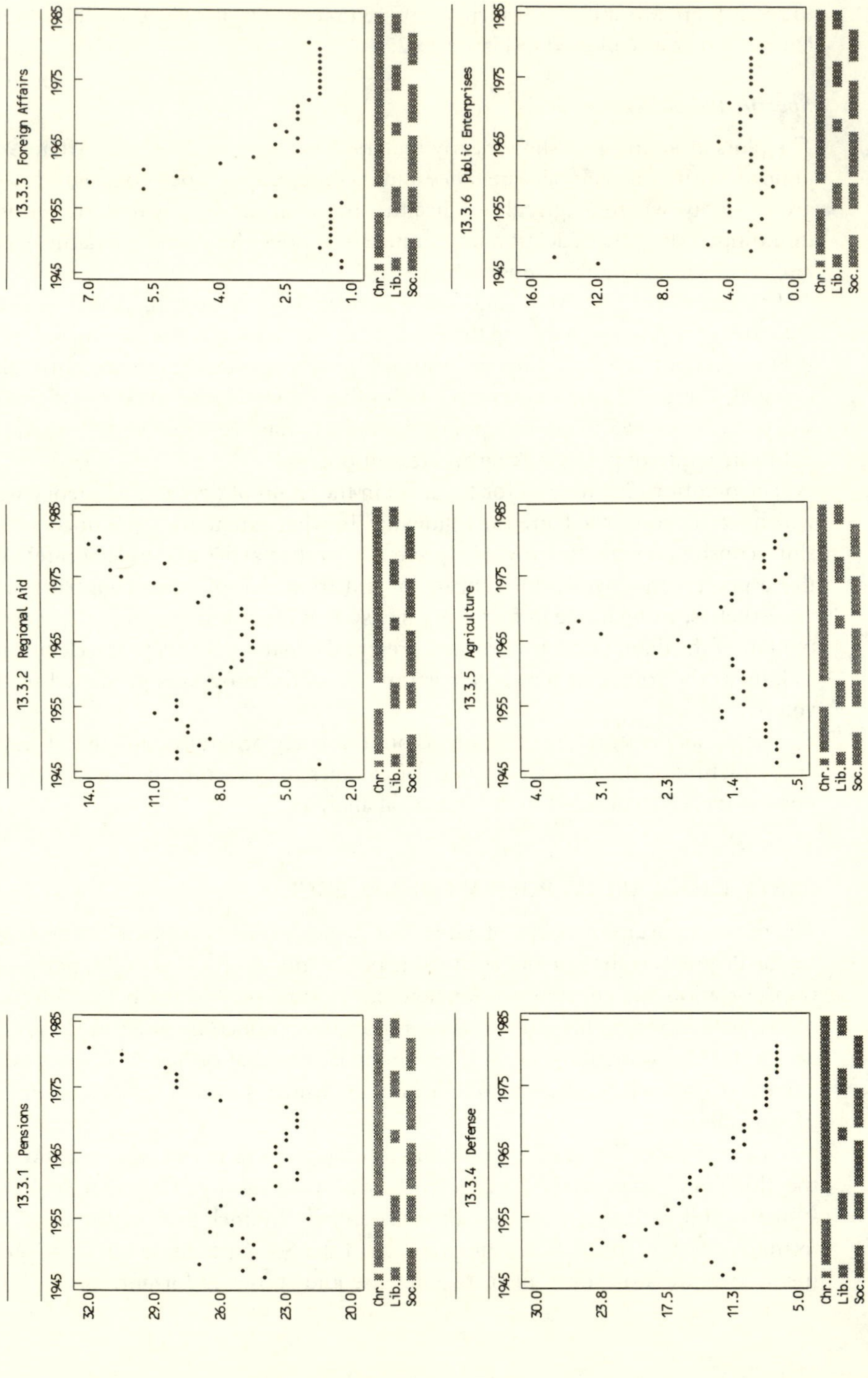

13.3.1 Pensions
13.3.2 Regional Aid
13.3.3 Foreign Affairs
13.3.4 Defense
13.3.5 Agriculture
13.3.6 Public Enterprises
1945
1955
1965
1975
1985
Chr.
Lib.
Soc.

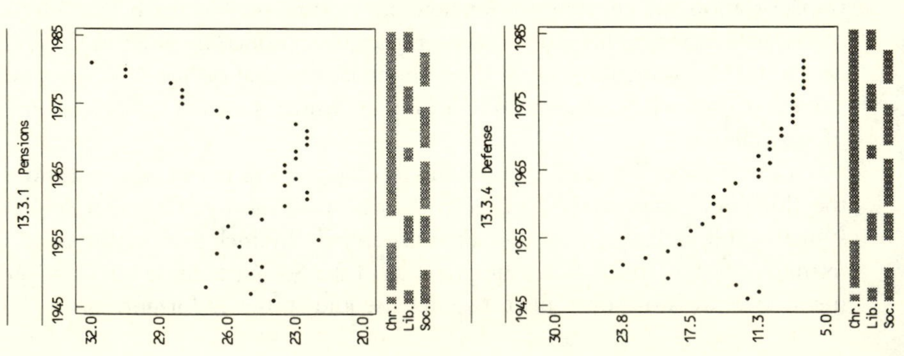

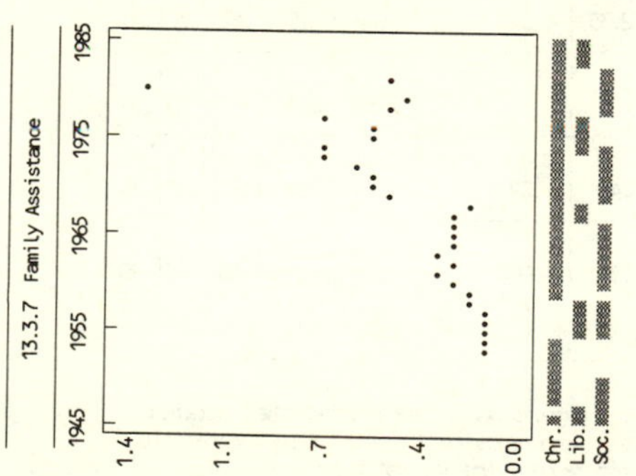
13.3.7 Family Assistance
1945
1955
1965
1975
1985
1.4
1.1
.7
.4
0.0
Chr.
Lib.
Soc.

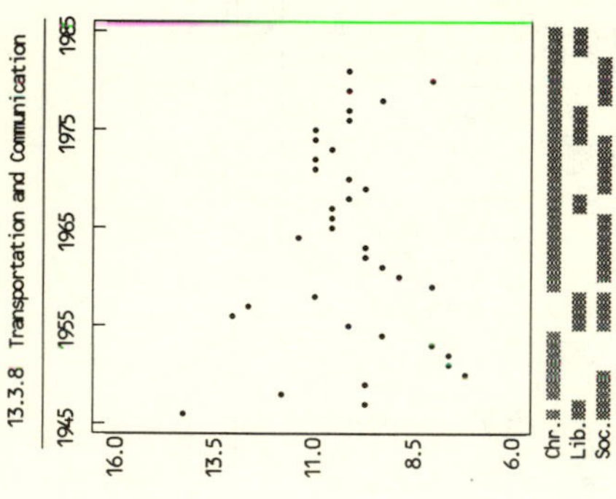
13.3.8 Transportation and Communication
1945
1955
1965
1975
1985
16.0
13.5
11.0
8.5
6.0
Chr.
Lib.
Soc.

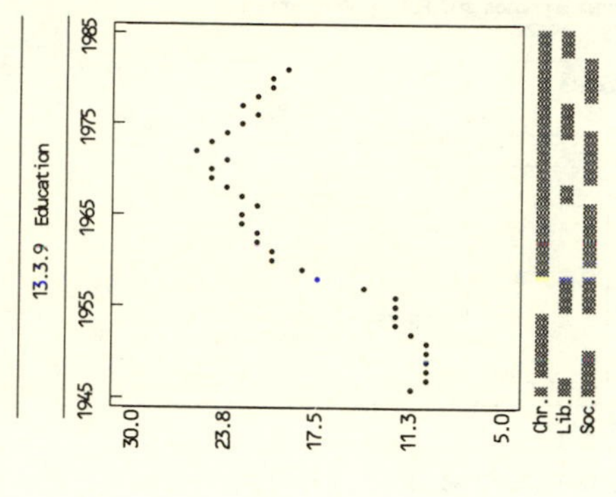
13.3.9 Education
1945
1955
1965
1975
1985
30.0
23.8
17.5
11.3
5.0
Chr.
Lib.
Soc.

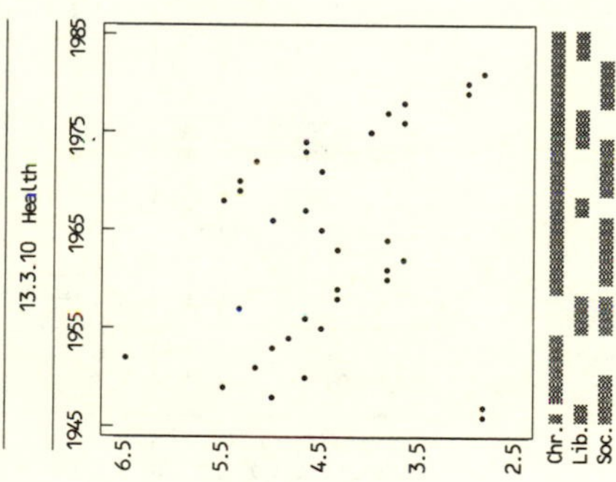
13.3.10 Health
1945
1955
1965
1975
1985
6.5
5.5
4.5
3.5
2.5
Chr.
Lib.
Soc.

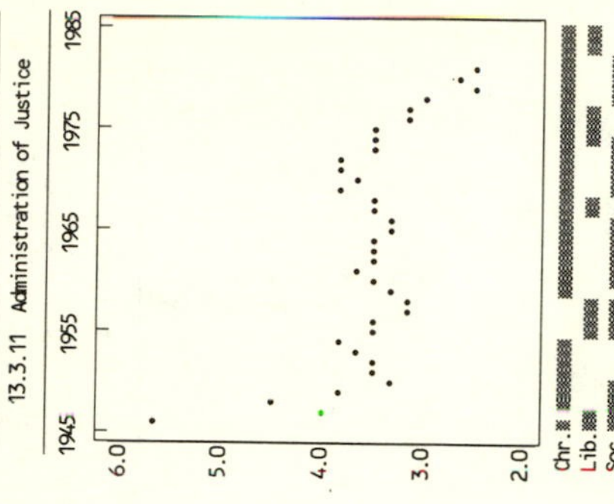
13.3.11 Administration of Justice
1945
1955
1965
1975
1985
6.0
5.0
4.0
3.0
2.0
Chr.
Lib.
Soc.

Table 13.1
Best-Fitting Models Between Party Program Emphases and Policy Priorities: Belgium, 1948 – 1987*

Agenda Models

Policy Priority (Program)	a	Christian	Liberal	Socialist	Adj R^2
Defense (Foreign Policy)	2.53	.70		.87	.58
Enterprise (Productivity)	2.71			2.35	.37

$$[\quad E_i = a + bP_i^A + \ldots bP_i^n \quad]$$

Mandate Models

Policy Priority (Program Emphasis)	Constant a	Christian (+) Agenda (Out)	Christian (–) Mandate	Christian Mandate (x Gov)	Liberal (+) Agenda (Out)	Liberal (–) Mandate	Liberal Mandate (x Gov)	Socialist (+) Agenda (Out)	Socialist (–) Mandate	Socialist Mandate (x Gov)	Adj R^2	Added by Mandate
Admin. of Justice (Law & Order)	3.03	.18		–.10							.50	.12
Health (Social Justice)	4.18							.16		–.11	.33	.04

$$[\quad E_i = a + bP_i^A + b(P_i^A \times G) + \ldots bP_i^n + b(P_i^n \times G) \quad]$$

Ideology Models

Policy Priority (Program Emphasis)	Constant a	Ideology Socialist Gov = 1	Christian (+)(–) Agenda Mandate (Out)	Christian Mandate (x Gov)	Liberal (+)(–) Agenda Mandate (Out)	Liberal Mandate (x Gov)	Socialist (+)(–) Agenda Mandate (Out)	Socialist Mandate (x Gov)	Adj R^2	Added by Mandate	Added by Ideology
Education (Education)	11.2	8.20	$-1.01^{\underline{n}}$	2.35	$-1.30^{\underline{n}}$		.42	–.54	.63	.30	.23
Foreign Affairs (Foreign Policy)	5.73	9.86					$2.65^{\underline{n}}$	–2.96	.62	.03	.59
Regional Subsidies (Social Harmony)	7.23	4.28	$-.63^{\underline{n}}$	.49	.29			–3.40	.50	.12	.25
Family Assistance (Social Services)	.57	.85	$-.09^{\underline{n}}$	.35	$-.09^{\underline{n}}$	.10		–.13	.40	.05	.20

$$[\quad E_i = a + bP_A + bP_i^A + b(P_i^A \times G) + \ldots bP_i^n + b(P_i^n \times G) \quad]$$

* Indicating only those b's (unstandardized regression coefficients) that attained .05 statistical significance. Coefficients in the opposite direction from theoretical expectation are underlined. Coefficients for mandate are indicated by $\underline{n}$.

reflective of certain party programs, regardless of time in office. Moreover, although it appears that priority for administration of justice and priority for health are subject to the program mandate, irrespective of differences that can be attributed to alternation of the Socialists in and out of government, both in fact feature contradictory coefficients, a general concern to which we turn a bit later.

Best-Fitting Models

Any programmatic concern with welfare-state services is going to be confounded by the post-1968 flow of resources from previously national human-services outlays into block allocations for comparable purposes under the expanding rubric of regional subsidies. As the party most supportive of decentralization, the Socialists have, in effect, seen their concerns with such domains as health, education, and family assistance become manifest through decentralization by means of regional subsidies, which they also support. But if that is the case, why then is there an apparent contradiction between the Socialist program and regional subsidies (–3.40)?

The –3.40 for the linkage between emphases on national interest/social harmony in the program and the share of central outlays given over for regional subsidies may be a case equivalent to the one linking emphases on peace issues to defense priority, where it is probably theoretically consistent and plausible for different parties to get different signs on the coefficient. The coding instructions for this area of program emphasis call for assigning a sentence in a party program to *national interest/social harmony* if it expresses an "appeal for national effort and solidarity; need for nation to see itself as united; appeal for public spiritedness; decrying anti-social attitudes in a time of crisis; support for public interest; national interest; bipartisanship."

The Socialists have been the champions of increased autonomy for the linguistic regions, especially Flanders, where there is a high concentration of industrial workers. The Christians, for whom the *b* is a positive .49 between social harmony and regional aid, have been rather more defensive of the center. It is an argument with some appeal that both the Socialist and the Christian coefficients reflect mandate fulfillment. When the Socialists emphasize national effort and social harmony, they are seeking to preserve the Belgian polity by meeting the demands of the regional claimants. When the Christians seek to preserve the polity, they do so by resisting the same claims.

We believe that a similar reversal of customary signs is also warranted in the domain of foreign affairs, matched to the set of programmatic themes we have added to make an index of foreign policy. That index is heavily weighted toward a promilitary, strong-defense posture. Even if Belgian foreign affairs expenditure priorities had not spiked around the time of Congolese independence, the slope would still have been upward, in contrast to that of defense, which was downward. Thus Belgium is one of those countries where defense and foreign policy expenditure priorities have been, in a sense, substitutes for each other, and investment in foreign affairs may be taken to be a conscious departure from peace through strength. So a decrease in the Socialist program's concerns for promilitary foreign policy should logically be associated with subsequent increases in foreign affairs–spending priority.[1]

Assuming that the logic in these two cases—regional subsidies and foreign affairs—is not too contorted, it still leaves three significant, contradictory negative *b*s for the Socialists, as contrasted to only two for clear conformity to the mandate. We do offer the excuse that much that is advocated by the socialists through their emphasis on social justice and social services may in fact be attained by regional subsidies, which we have sought to predict by looking at Socialist emphases on social harmony. But it still leaves the utility of the program (at least as we have coded it) open to serious challenge.

We shall shortly give more-detailed attention to the most striking nonconforming and contradictory cases. It is worth noting here, however, that there is only one apparent theoretical contradiction for the Christians or for the Liberals. However, the Liberals have only one instance where, in government, they attain a significant reflection of their program in policy priority—family assistance (.10). The contradictions are clearly concentrated in the Socialist column. Those plus an unusually large number of unexplained policy domains raise serious challenges to the role of parties in the Belgian policy process—challenges to which we must return after reviewing those cases that do conform to theory.

The Belgian case is seductively complex, tempting the analyst to dig ever deeper into the morass of complexity in that small country's political life. However, one should not let the prospect of complexity cloud that which may be clear. Relative clarity marks the congruence of several important policy domains to alternations in government. The Socialists have participated in government about twice as long as the Liberals, and overlap between the two is uncommon. Thus the alternation term—"Socialist Gov," under the "Ideology" column in Table 13.1—comes close to measuring the standing differences between Christian/Socialist governments (positive signs) and Christian/Liberal governments (implicit negative signs). Education (8.20), foreign affairs (9.86), regional subsidies (4.28), and family assistance (.85) have all been in unequivocally better favor when the Socialists were in government. The message of the election program content may be muddled to begin with or get garbled in translation to policy, but that does not detract from these few but vital areas of government activity where the standing party differences seem to provide a clear cue to the voter as to the direction of policy.

Besides reading these ideology coefficients as exclusively a fulfillment of Socialists objectives, one could—with slightly less accuracy, to be sure—read these figures as domains that suffer relative loss under Belgium's Liberals, with their stress on the free market, tight controls on government spending, and preservation of national unity.

To these theoretically consistent findings must be added those instances of significant negative mandate. Even though there were very few years when the Christian party was out of government, they were sufficient to yield three instances of negative mandate, whereby, compared to the effect of being in government, their presence in opposition led to policy priorities counter to their programmatic emphases: education (–1.01), regional subsidies (–.63), and family assistance (–.09). The Liberals, owing to their being in opposition, suffer reverses for their stands in education (–1.30) and family assistance (–.09). In addition, because the customary direction of the signs in foreign affairs policy must be reversed, the positive 2.65 for the Socialists' opposition effect also suggests a negative mandate in that volatile policy area.

There are two policies with reasonably strong agenda congruence—whereby a party's program predicts policy priority, exclusive of other parties, even accounting for being out of government. The Socialists maintain dominance over the share of expenditures used to support public enterprises (2.35). This category includes subsidies to industries, state-owned and otherwise, along with some economic management and planning expenses. It is clearly a domain of classic socialist concern. When the Socialists emphasize productivity, it is a signal that this class of expenditures will be favored, regardless of how often the Socialists have been in government.

A multiparty agenda effect also operates in defense policy for both the Christians and the Socialists. Two devastating invasions in this century plus the centrality of NATO in Belgian affairs have probably been major factors in bringing about a defense policy that is, in effect, nonpartisan. The Liberals, although not producing a statistically significant *b*, also relate positively to defense policy in the agenda model (see Appendix Table A13.1).

These two policies indicate an agenda as contrasted to a mandate role of the party programs. The same is true, in a more complex manner, for those few other positive coefficients obtained by parties' "out" of government term, indicated under the mandate and ideology models: administration of justice for the Christians (.18), along with health (.16) and education (.42) for the Socialists (.16).

The appearance of agenda effects for the Socialists, paired with contradictions in office, may also be a sign of Christian Party maneuvering, not unlike that seen in the Netherlands. Further evidence of Christian control is seen in the remarkable consistency of that party's coefficients in three of the four policies fitted best by the ideology equation. In education (2.35), regional subsidies (.49), and family assistance (.35), the Christians get negative *b*s for those few years when they were out of office, and positive *b*s for the many when they were in. No other instances in Belgium match this performance for program mandates.

The strength of the party alternation term in the expected direction stands in sharp contrast to the situation in the Netherlands (Chapter 12). Recall that we surmised that the Dutch Socialists and, to a lesser extent, Liberals were essentially manipulated by the Center-hogging Christians into sacrificing party policy objectives (both long-term ideology and current programmatic foci) in order to get into government. This classic behavior in conformity with Downs's theory is not as apparent in Belgium. The overall linkage of parties to policies is, to be sure, weak in Belgium, but where it is present, it confirms the general policy relevance of long-standing ideology for the Socialists and the Liberals.

Nonconformists and Contradictions

As noted above, a full third of the policy domains (including left-right) failed to have 25 percent or more of their variance forecast by any of the three models. And once one has accounted for the nonconformists, there are at least four important contradictions—three for the Socialists and one for the Christians.

The one Christian contradiction is for administration of justice (–.10). We noted above in this domain of policy Belgium is unlike the other countries, in that administration of justice declined over time and it loaded heavily on the right side of the left-right policy factor score. On its face, this would seem to be the expected association—law and order being usually associated with rightist or conservative causes. However, aside from Belgium, that has not proved to be the case—a matter to which we shall return in the general discussion in Chapter 14. Christian parties, such as Belgium's, although not conservative in the usual sense of the British Tories or the American Republicans, can nonetheless usually be expected to be concerned more than the Left or the Liberals with matters of law and order. In the Dutch case, however, the fact is that the CDA most often gave no attention to matters of law and order in its programs, and when it did, those matters simply do not show up in later policy. Beyond noting that, we are not moved to speculate.

The contradiction of the socialists in health is merely one of several, including, among the ideology models, education (–.54) and family assistance (–.13). This, along with the apparent contradictions in foreign affairs and regional subsidies (discussed above), suggests a pattern of nonfulfillment of programmatic emphases. Like their Dutch counterpart, it appears that the Belgian Socialists pay a price in policy aspirations foregone in order to serve in governments.

CONCLUSION

The decisions of well-informed Belgian voters will not be helped as much by party history or current programs as are those of their counterparts in other democracies. In many policy domains neither long-standing ideological differences nor the most recent programs provide useful signals as to the direction of policy. Socialist and Liberal programs are hardly worth reading as predictors of policy, with a few important exceptions. The Christians' programs provide some better guidance, with several exceptions, but the record is hardly patterned enough to be a very useful guide.

What does matter, however, in several policy domains is the standing ideological differences between these two parties. In the domain that is all-important to Belgium over the last generation—subsidies to the ethno-linguistic regions—Socialist or Liberal participation in government makes a major difference in expenditure share. The same is true of a few other areas of varying fiscal importance. It applies to education, which before being displaced by ethno-linguistic conflict was the most contentious area of public policy in Belgium, and at an average of 19 percent continues to be the largest area of central government spending, even counting the increase in regional assistance.

For the Socialists and Liberals, therefore, it is the standing ideological differences that provide the voter with the best clue to subsequent government priorities. These cannot be measured accurately for the Christians, since they have not been out of government enough to provide a good contrast. However, theirs is the program that is most useful as a signal of upcoming government action, providing significant positive guidance to policy priorities in three areas. Both the Christian and the Liberal programs, however, are more useful in indicating what will not be a favored policy priority if either party is excluded from government (a rare circumstance, to be sure, for the Christians). In spite of the relative strength of the party alternation term, however, general ideological positions, as measured by left-right programmatic trends, are of no value in anticipating general policy directions.

In all, it is a weak record. Belgian politicians, at least for the generation after the mid-1960s, have been too engaged in defining the *political* community to worry much about the government (Easton 1953). The frustration the Belgians reveal in survey research (Inglehart 1990) has here its policy counterpart. Elections, or at least the issues talked about at election time by the parties, do not seem to matter. A relatively small crowd has circulated through the corridors of responsibility—we are hesitant to say "corridors of *power*." They trade office in a seemingly random search for solutions to bedeviling constitutional problems, driven by historic antagonisms that neither time nor prosperity has been able to assuage. And one of the victims may well be party democracy.

NOTES

1. The trend—that is, correlation with time—in the Socialist foreign policy emphases is indeed –.39, whereas the foreign affairs expenditure share, minus the peak years between 1959 and 1963, is .40. And the simple *r* between the two is –.26.

14

Parties, Policies, and Democracy

INTRODUCTION: AGENDAS AND MANDATES

This book is about the role of political parties in the policy processes of modern democracies. We have studied the parties and policies of ten democracies over four decades. We have applied a common mode of analysis to several policies in each country, using similar measures and the same statistical procedures. Our quest has been to find common patterns across the parties and policies of the ten countries. On average, about 50 percent of policy variance has been accounted for—an uncommonly high figure in the social sciences. However, that should be read as testimony to the success of the theory, not as evidence of how much we understand about this or that policy in this or that country. In nearly all of the policy/country situations, a bit more statistical exploration could have produced unique explanations with higher R^2s and richer descriptions. But our aim has *not* been to explain why a particular policy or country is as it is. We have indeed examined particular policies, parties, and countries, but always with the goal of discovering general patterns. This chapter assesses the success of that search.

Our general outline is common in cross-national research and true to many comparative studies—a theoretical and methodological introduction, followed by a series of country studies, concluded with a summary chapter (Almond and Verba 1963; Budge, Robertson and Hearl 1987; Laver and Budge 1993; Verba, Nie, and Kim 1978). The common goal is to conclude with a set of cross-system, cross-time observations, based on various dynamics discovered within the country studies. That usually means that the actual number of cases upon which the theoretical speculations are based is between five and a dozen or so. Our circumstance is no different. We are now looking for very general patterns of comparability across countries in an effort to stimulate theoretical speculation. We certainly would not view any of that speculation as firmly anchored in solid evidence but as merely suggested by what seem to be similarities and differences across the ten countries we have studied.

In modern democratic theory political parties are seen as the primary institutional means for mediating between society and government. Parties are supposed to play a comprehensive role—before, during, and after elections. In contrast to interest groups, parties span a broad range of human concerns. They identify, select, define, and focus those concerns toward modes of action that can be addressed by voters and government. Competing parties present transpolicy programs in the context of the contest for office. They structure the voter's choice. Once in office, parties are the major organizing institutions that form, operate, and control the policymaking process. The concern of this book is with this mediating and integrating role of parties as bridges between society and government.

The formal election programs are the clearest available statement of policy intentions expressed by the leadership of competing parties. Our task has been to test variations on a theory of the policy impact of parties, as indicated by the signaling capacity of election programs.

Party programs can anticipate policy in two ways: through the *agenda* and through the *mandate*. The effective policy agenda and its evolution may be tracked in the programs of the set of parties in a country. The validity of the parties' presentation of the agenda is measured by the extent to which policy follows a path similar to that of the party programs. That is, parties are effective articulators of a policy agenda to the extent that the profiles of policies *enacted* by governments reflect the profiles of programs that parties have presented to the electorate. Collectively and over time, the parties that compete in a country present a changing set of programmatic concerns, which provide evidence of the shifting boundaries of policy discourse. If these also correspond with the boundaries of changing government action, then we can claim that the parties have portrayed the effective agenda from which the policy process has proceeded. Policymaking has been structured by the process of competition through which the agenda has been publicly forged.

Confirmation of the agenda thesis is not contingent upon parties' holding office but rather upon their holding a legitimate and effective place in the public forum. A more restrictive and more democratic form of linkage of parties to policy is the *mandate*, whereby policies enacted by governments reflect more clearly the programmatic emphases of the winners than they do those of the losers of the immediate past election.

Neither societies nor their problems are stagnant. The world turns and so does the policy agenda. Furthermore, politicians are not superhuman. The concerns and prescriptions of even the most recent election may not endure throughout a government's tenure in office. Definitions of problems may prove inaccurate, just as remedies may prove ineffective. Politicians as policymakers are mortal, and mortality should not be confused with mendacity. There are more and better explanations for variation in the program-to-policy fit than saying that politicians are liars. For many reasons perfectly compatible with the rules of the democratic game, decisionmakers may choose to accommodate the claims of their opponents. That is, there are democratic reasons why a party in office might enact policies compatible with the programmatic emphases of parties not in office.

One reason why winners accommodate losers is, of course, that winners and losers are not always clearly distinguishable. In systems of separated powers, when the executive and the legislative branches are occupied by different parties, there are no clear winners. Likewise in fluid coalition systems—the most common among modern democracies—more than one party is in government; furthermore, the composition of government can be changed by formal parliamentary action without an election.

Another reason for winners to accommodate losers is that losers speak for real people with real problems. Even a small party, with a very particular set of policy concerns, may—by focusing on these specific concerns all the time—come up with the most efficient and logical solution. The very attractiveness of the solution is the incentive for the winning party to take it up. Losing an election ought not to be fatal or even significantly damaging to the losers, at least not on a steady basis. If it is, their willingness to continue playing the democratic game is apt to wane. Interests of losers of elections need not be thereby deemed illegitimate. In fact, most public issues are not and need not be conceived to be somehow mutually exclusive. It is reasonable to expect public policy to reflect the terms of a complex process of bargaining. Analysis of the program-to-policy congruence, therefore, needs to take account of that bargaining process. That is, measures must accommodate the possibility of simultaneous agenda and mandate effects. Our research design has allowed for that simultaneity.

Likewise, our research has allowed for a version of the mandate that is evident in policy priority differences associated with the simple alternation of parties in government. The analysis of program trends has shown that each of the major parties occupies a distinctive ideological space and rarely exchanges places in that space with opponents. This ideological location may (but need not necessarily be) independent of specific variations in programmatic emphases from election to election. Our most elaborate—and ultimately most powerful—statistical model was designed to capture this alternation effect as well as the policy reflection of programs of incumbents and opposition.

Each of three variations on the theory was incorporated into a slightly different statistical model of program-to-policy congruence. The results of the research can be addressed under several headings:

- Patterns of nonconformity and contradiction
- The implications of programmatic and policy trends
- A reexamination of party politics in the policy process

NONCONFORMISTS AND CONTRADICTIONS

General Patterns

The general spread and level of congruence of policy priorities by party programs and alternation in office is rather impressive, with R^2s averaging above 50 percent.

That figure reflects the deflation caused by nonconforming policies, that is, policies that did not attain R^2 of .25, approximately 12 percent of the cases. However, if the seemingly successful R^2s are replete with contradictory coefficients, then the claim of explanatory success is rather hollow. In fact, only about 5 percent of the coefficients in all of the best-fitting models are contradictory to theoretical expectation.

The nonconformists and contradictions are summarized by policy area in Table 14.1. Note should be made of what is not illustrated in the table, namely cross-national and cross-party patterns. Three countries had no nonconforming policies: France, Sweden, and Austria. And, as noted in Chapter 13, Belgium had four, as well as a rather high number of contradictions. No other country had more than two nonconforming policies. An examination of the parties that accounted for the contradictory *b*s revealed no partisan pattern. That is, on a broad cross-national basis, conservative, liberal, and socialist parties did not appear strikingly more likely than the others to produce policies contradictory to their programmatic emphases, although there was a concentration of socialist contradictions in certain countries, a pattern to which we give our attention later in this chapter.

Some caution is in order regarding the distributions displayed in Table 14.1, since not all of the policies were represented in every country's data. Furthermore, occasionally a country had more than one policy domain under what is here included as a single entry, for example, social security *and* welfare or public utilities *and* transportation. At most, one should draw very broad conclusions from the apparent patterns of nonconformity and contradiction illustrated in Table 14.1.

The first entry is revealing. In seven of the ten countries the linkage between left-right programmatic trends and left-right policy trends either failed to reach .25 or it was affected by significant contradictions, not readily seen as statistical artifacts. The countries where left-right conformed cleanly were Canada, Sweden, and the Netherlands. This offers no apparent pattern to the broad ideological structuring across parties, countries, and policy domains.

The democratic policy process cannot be understood as a straightforward general confrontation of left versus right, with policy rewards going, across a wide partisan range, to the victors. There is certainly a complex, enduring structure from the party programs to policy. But it is at a substantively specific level rather than at the general level of left-right ideological confrontation. Even if, as we learned from Gilbert and Sullivan, "Every boy and every gal that's born into this world alive, is either a little liber-al or else a little conserva-tive," modern democracies have failed to accommodate their policy processes to that fact.

Specific Policy Domains

It must be kept in mind that the entries ("#") in Table 14.1 relate to individual equations, not to countries. Thus, although there are 6 contradictions listed for social services/welfare and for education in the second column, these are from 128 coefficients for those two areas in the best-fitting models in the ten countries.

Table 14.1
Nonconformist Policies and Contradictory Regression Coefficients

Policy	Nonconformists[1]	Contradictions[2]
Left-Right	###	####
	Human Services Entitlements	
Soc.Sec./Welfare	##	######
Education		######
Health	##	##
	Economy and Infrastructure	
Public Works[3]	####	####
Agriculture	##	##
Housing	#	#
	Quality of Life	
Adm. of Justice	##	###
Culture/Arts/Environ.	#	##
	External Policy	
Foreign Affairs		##
Defense		#

\# Each #-symbol refers to a single country/policy coefficient.

1 No model reached R^2 .25 (approx. 12% of cases).

2 One or more b's statistically significant in direction opposite to theoretical expectation (approx. 5% of coefficients).

3 Public Works = Transportation, public utilities, communication, waterworks, energy.

Table 14.1 does show a modest concentration of contradictions in the realm of human services entitlements. Recall that when the nonconformity of social security and health was observed in Britain, we offered the tentative hypothesis that entitlements may be beyond the reach of partisan impact. We would not, however, see the frequency of contradiction as confirmation of that expectation. By far the majority of cases of human services policies—where most of the entitlements are concentrated—were well accounted for by the partisan variables in the various models. (As with most other policies, these were most often the ideology models, including the term for party alternation.) As the trends in our left-right policy scores clearly indicate, human services–policy priorities have been on the rise, relative to other categories, at least until the 1970s. That might suggest a process somewhat out of control. Most of the time in most of the countries, however, that trend was indeed congruent with the changing agendas of the parties. Therefore, perhaps we can say that there is a hint here that there is somewhat less room for partisan control—less *Spielraum*—than in other policy domains.

Outside the human services realm, two other policy areas are deserving of commentary: public works and administration of justice. Public works, including transportation and other infrastructural facilities, are capital-intensive. Trends in priority for these policies are nearly all curvilinear, rising and then falling. The time trends reveal a high priority in the immediate postwar years, followed by a significant drop. One can reasonably assume that the investment was a combination of repairs to war-damaged facilities and a response to several years of unmet demand during the depression and war. Highways, railroads, electric lines, and so on are expensive to build and relatively cheap to maintain. Although preferred by conservatives over more immediately redistributive public services, public works are often partially self-financing, once in place, and tend not to be the stuff of intense partisan dispute. The Dutch do not argue much about the dikes. They just fix them. Thus, we see the frequency with which there is no satisfactory explanation of public works–policy priority by party programs and partisan alternation in government.

An occasional eyebrow may be raised by our classification in Table 14.1 of administration of justice under "Quality of Life." We did this in part because there is no other convenient category. Furthermore, there is little that more dramatically reduces quality of life than a disintegration of public order. But the classification is also designed to draw attention to the interesting pattern of this domain of policy. Administration of justice, as represented in the expenditure figures in our analyses, includes spending on national courts, prisons, police, prosecution, and related legal services.

The concern here is with party programs in national elections and national policy priorities. In many of the countries, the various functions of the justice system are concentrated in subnational jurisdictions. We do not (nor is it theoretically relevant that we should) capture the largest part of such inputs into society. We capture those that are subject to national decision processes and that are thus subject to influence from national election programs and changes in party composition of national governments. Our suspicion is that at the national level, the marginal growth is not in the traditional realms of courts, police, and prisons.

In most of the country analyses, we have treated justice policy as an anomaly, in that it is the one apparently right-wing policy priority that has most steadily and uniformly risen. Justice policy, however, may not be all that right-wing, at least on the margins where the expanded priority has taken place. Our statistical results may be the consequence of unavoidable but misleading aggregation. Administration of justice is not only cops and courts. It is also consumer-protection programs, legal aid to the poor, and the rising tide of litigation by "ordinary people" in the name of social justice. On the one hand, the rising priority for justice policy may be a sad commentary on the increased necessity for the state to replace deteriorating traditional structures of social control. But it may also be an indicator of an ever-more-egalitarian legal system. In such a case, party program emphases on law and order could reasonably be expected to relate poorly to such egalitarian services within the legal system.

Without detailed data collection and analysis, well beyond the central purposes of this study, we cannot resolve these questions regarding specific policy domains. It is sufficient for present purposes to raise a cautionary flag.

PROGRAM AND POLICY TRENDS

In spite of the spotty record of relationship between left-right programmatic trends and comparable trends in overall policy, the nearly universal centrality of that dimension makes it interesting and important for understanding the politics and policies of modern democracies.

Left-Right Programmatic Trends

There is no uniform programmatic movement of most parties either to the right or to the left across the ten countries. But it is worthwhile to review here the trends for the ten different party systems, as illustrated as Figure X.1 in each of the country chapters.

What can be seen in these trends? First, in each of the countries, the parties generally keep their distance—or at least the leading left and right parties do so. There is no evidence of power-hungry clustering around the median at the risk of loss of ideological identity. Leapfrogging is indeed rare between the left and right parties, occurring once in Austria and once in Australia and never in the other eight countries.[1] No one seeks security at the fringe, but all move generally back and forth across fairly wide but distinct bands. Parties in the center show great flexibility in the quest for coalition potential but never permanently move so far into their opponents' turf as seriously to risk the loyalty of ideologically committed followers.

In the discussion of Downs's theory of competition in Chapter 2, we offered the proposition that there might be less variance in parties in multiparty systems than in a two- or three-party setting. The multiparty rigidity would be due to the combatants' having reconciled to permanent minority status and thus the need not to build but rather to hold their market share. Sartori (1976) took that further and suggested that in multiparty, polarized situations, the parties steadily move to the extremes—a hypothesis for which we find no support.

The Right has generally shown more flexibility or, the other way around, less rigid commitment to principle than the Left. Table 14.2 documents this assertion. The standard deviations of left-right scores show a clear differentiation between Left, Center, and Right—with the general variance rising respectively from a mean of 10.4 for the socialists, 13.2 for the center, to 15.1 for the right. That same array holds more or less well for the individual countries.

This patterning of flexibility suggests that the Left has been more dogged in pursuit of, if not a utopia—as in the early days of European socialism—at least a definition of society substantially different from what it was for the first half of the century. Because of the essential orientation toward preserving that which is, as opposed either to pursuing a utopian goal or to rolling back the clock, the Right has more room for maneuver—more *Spielraum*—than the Left.

The graphic presentation of trends in the country chapters showed that the leftist parties tend to tilt a bit rightward over time. Rather than being evidence of abandonment of socialists' goals, however, this tilt may well mark their recognition of general success in building the welfare state. Certainly the trends in policy, which will be reviewed below, would lend credence to that assessment.

There is no evidence of either rigidity or clustering to the extremes or to the center. To the extent that there has been any reduction in differentiation, that is, a general convergence, it happened in all countries at about the same time—during the 1960s and early 1970s—when Western democracies were commonly confronted with perhaps their greatest recent internal challenge to institutional legitimacy. Far from shattering the party systems, with parties' searching out unique bases in secure ideological homes that ensure places in government but preclude majority victory, the parties moved more or less together, a bit to the left (enough to pull some of the teeth of the radicals). If we stretch the reach of the data, to be sure, it appears that in the postradical period—the 1970s through 1980s—all major competitors moved into and stayed within a rather narrower band of competition than in the years prior to the late 1960s. The challenges of that period did not eliminate interparty distance. They did not induce opportunistic leapfrogging. But they seem rather to have diluted any urge to seek sustenance at the fringes.

These ten cases provide no evidence that lack of hope for gaining a majority encourages parties to metastasize ideologically. Stable but small parties in multiparty systems are programmatically flexible, yet they still hover about as near to one another as do those in less-diffuse party systems.[2]

Table 14.2
Left-Right Programmatic Flexibility:
Variation (Standard Deviation) by Party*

	Socialist/ Soc. Dem.	Liberal/ Center	Conservative/ Christian
	S 14.41	S 24.59	As 20.51
	As 13.91	D 15.60	GB 19.15
	NL 13.42	As 14.84	S 18.34
	F 12.24	B 11.44	D 17.90
	B 11.78	F 11.38	Al 17.88
	CDN 10.19	GB 10.92	USA 14.03
	GB 10.10	NL 8.47	B 12.34
	D 8.09	CDN 8.31	NL 12.25
	USA 5.20		F 9.58
	Al 4.17		CDN 8.55
Mean	10.35	13.19	15.08

* Standard Deviation of Left-Right Program Orientation

Al = Australia; As = Austria; B = Belgium; CDN = Canada; D = Germany; F = France; GB = Britain; NL = Netherlands; S = Sweden; USA = United States

Sartori argued that the greater the number of enduring parties, the greater the tendency of parties to take up extreme positions—the process of *center-fleeing* (Sartori 1976; Powell 1987). There is in these trends neither a cross-national nor a secular pattern of center-fleeing as a function of relative party system diversity. Even in the most seemingly atomized system—Belgium—none of the combatants consistently hovers near the extremes. Party elites who prepare the election programs, if they have even a remote prospect of participating in government, must anticipate not only the impact of their policy formulations on the election but also their own potential credibility as policymakers. And our data may be reflecting the fact that none of the parties we include for these ten countries is prepared consistently to dismiss that chance to play a policymaking role and thus to resort to center-fleeing.

This hint at a containing function is reinforced by the fact that the parties of most countries seem to have converged around the time period in recent history when the societies themselves were most cleft by serious internal contradictions and ideological stridency. The only exception, as has been discussed at some length in Chapter 13, is Belgium, where the party system essentially disintegrated for a time during the troublesome 1960s and early 1970s.

More striking than the contrasts between systems of differing numbers of parties are the longitudinal similarities across countries irrespective of number of parties. None of the major parties has taken a completely rigid position. Flexibility is the rule. But flexibility is not so great that it erodes the relative identity of the combatants. Parties seem attentive to their birthrights, as we suggested in Chapter 1, as long as the issue content of that heritage maintains contemporary relevance. Tactical movements together and apart are evident from election to election. But major trends are likewise obvious—not trends that respond to the peculiarities of election laws or nation-specific oddities but trends across parties and across countries that respond to broad cultural changes.

Left-Right Policy Trends

Even more striking than the similarity of general trends in party programs are the trends in policy, as clearly displayed in Figure 14.1. Nine of the ten countries show a steady movement of policy leftward until sometime in the 1970s, after which point the leftward movement ceases, or at least slows dramatically. Immediately after World War II, most Western democracies demobilized their armed forces. That process, however, was short-lived. First the Berlin Blockade (1948–1949) and then the Communist invasion of South Korea (1950) brought about a thoroughgoing reorientation of policy. National defense was not completely restored to its wartime footing, but it was restored to such an extent that dreams of a massive peace dividend were effectively postponed. NATO was clearly led by the rising priority in the United States for defense, at around two-thirds of national expenditures. But the United States brought along even the most reluctant of

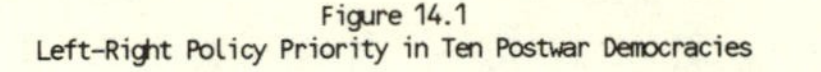

Figure 14.1
Left-Right Policy Priority in Ten Postwar Democracies

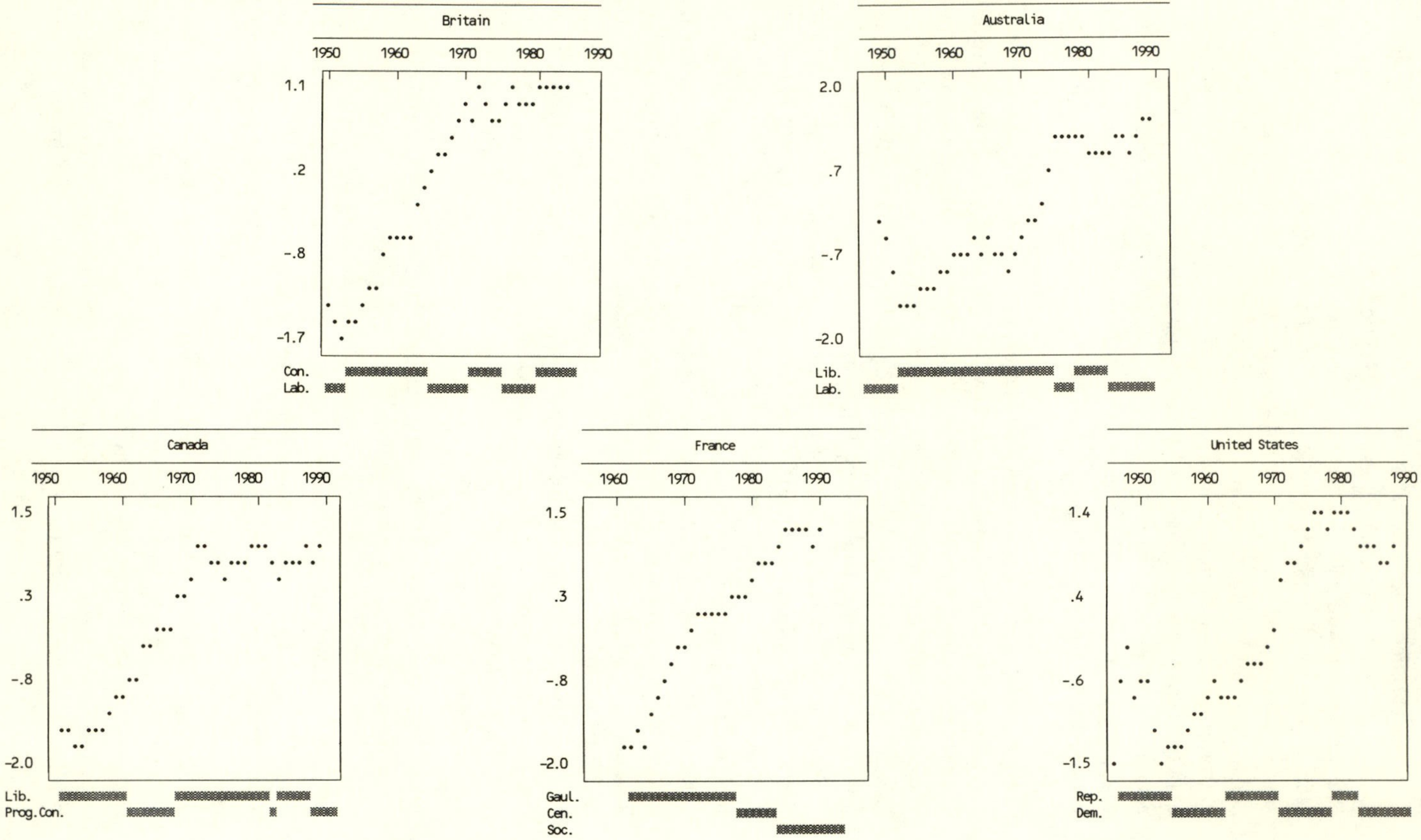

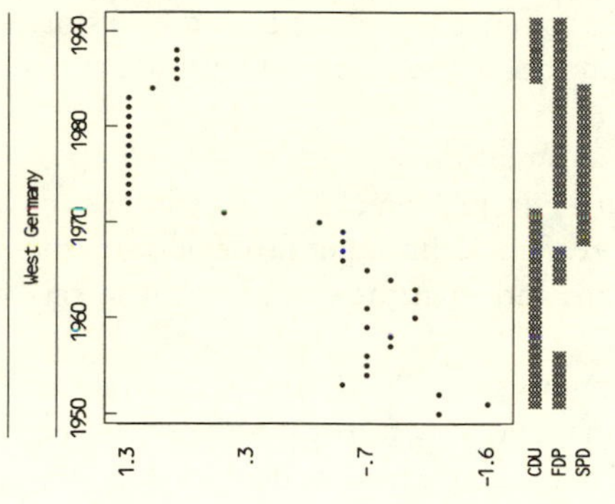
West Germany
1950
1960
1970
1980
1990
1.3
.3
-.7
-1.6
CDU
FDP
SPD

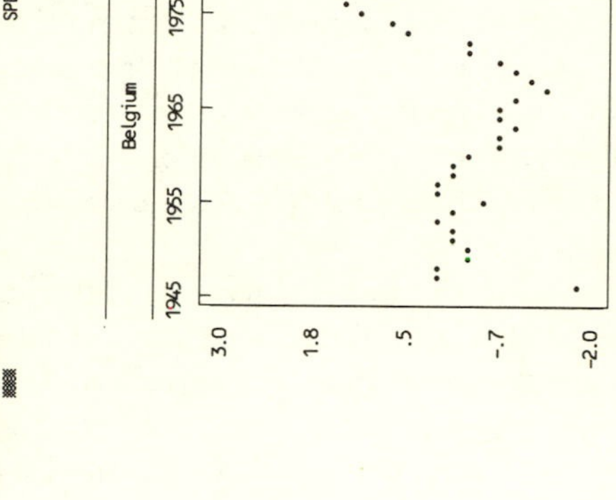
Belgium
1945
1955
1965
1975
1985
3.0
1.8
.5
-.7
-2.0
Chr.
Lib.
Soc.

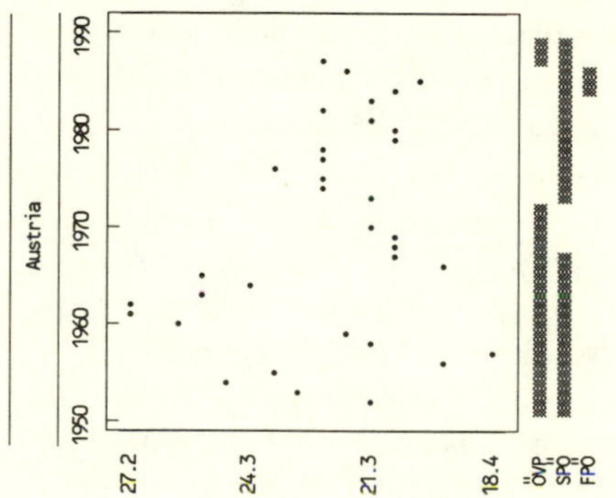
Austria
1950
1960
1970
1980
1990
27.2
24.3
21.3
18.4
ÖVP
SPÖ
FPÖ

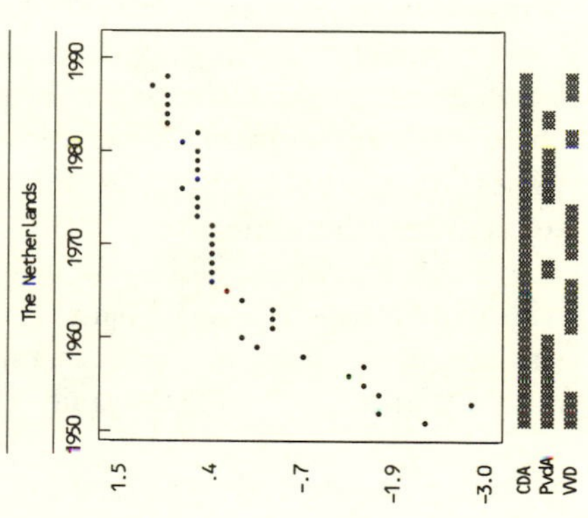
The Netherlands
1950
1960
1970
1980
1990
1.5
.4
-.7
-1.9
-3.0
CDA
PvdA
VVD

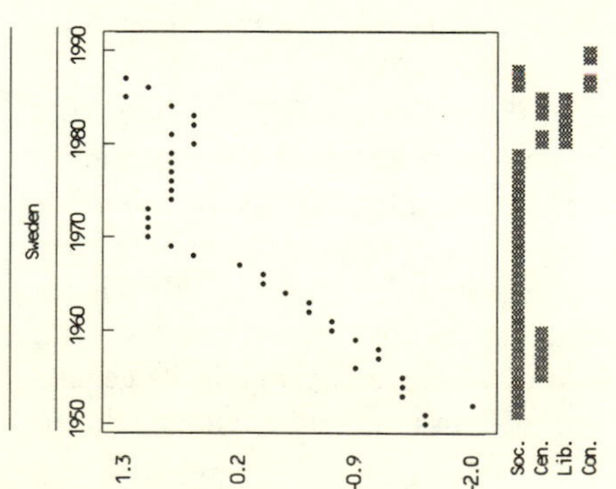
Sweden
1950
1960
1970
1980
1990
1.3
0.2
-0.9
-2.0
Soc.
Cen.
Lib.
Con.

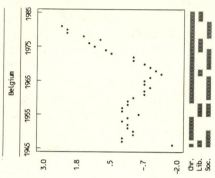

European partners. Countries sorely pressed to repair war damage and to restore their economies were nonetheless to commit the largest share of their budgets to national defense.

Although the image in popular discourse is that this pattern continued up to the fall of communism in Central and Eastern Europe, in fact it reached its apogee in the early 1950s, with defense's share thereafter declining in favor of domestic projects—first infrastructural modernization and then the commitment to services and redistribution of the welfare state.

From the early 1950s on, two policy domains generally declined: defense and agriculture. Others rose first and later declined, notably transportation, housing, and other infrastructural areas. Human services generally moved upward in their share of the budget, with the most dramatic rise being in health policy. Social security rose with the aging of the population. Education rose and then dropped modestly, probably as a function of the changing age composition of the population. And we have already noted the steady rise in priority for administration of justice.

To capture this movement across countries, we designed a scoring strategy that sought to use country-specific statistical categories to produce scores that would be generally comparable in relative form if not in absolute magnitudes. The extent of cross-national similarity of trends is confirmed by the correlations reported in Table 14.3. These are the pairwise correlations between countries over time in their left-right policy scores.

One country stands out as odd—Austria. As we noted in Chapter 10, Austria, because of its occupied status, had no military expenses until 1955. In effect, by being occupied, Austria "escaped" the early cold war. The subsequent buildup never matched that of any of the Warsaw Pact or NATO countries. But the defense trend, unlike that trend in the other democracies, was upward—from nothing to about 7 percent of outlays. Given that defense has anchored the right of the left-right score in the other countries, this Austrian peculiarity colors the entire policy trend there. Whereas the trend for the other nine countries (i.e., correlation coefficient of left-right score with year) ranges from a low of .72 to a high of .96, Austria's trend is negative, –.63. That means that although every other country moved strongly to the left, Austria, reflecting its belated if modest defense buildup, moved to the right, but less steadily than the opposite trend in the other countries.

Exceptions, even though vital as anchors for theoretical confidence, should not dominate one's vision, at least not when the pattern from which the exception is taken is so striking as that revealed in Table 14.3. The simple fact is that there has been a cross-nationally common program of policy reformulation over the postwar years. As important as the direction—leftward until rather recently—is the commonality. The national averages in correlation with other countries range from Belgium's .59 to France's .88. That is to say, France is closer in its general policy trend to those of the other nine countries than is any other country in the

Table 14.3
Correlations over Time Between Left-Right Policy Scores in Ten Countries

	GB	As	CND	F	USA	S	Al	D	NL	B
Britain		.72	.94	.94	.85	.91	-.77	.85	.92	.52
Australia			.71	.84	.91	.55	-.42	.85	.70	.87
Canada				.92	.88	.93	-.72	.88	.83	.44
France					.94	.85	-.71	.94	.89	.69
USA						.78	-.58	.97	.82	.71
Sweden							-.80	.76	.83	.24
Austria								-.57	-.78	-.25
Germany									.81	.70
Netherlands										.53
Mean r	.84	.77	.82	.88	.86	.77	-.63	.85	.80	.59
Trend	.89	.92	.85	.96	.93	.72	-.63	.92	.86	.82

* Standard Deviation of Left-Right Program Orientation

set. Aside from Belgium (and Austria), however, the countries are quite closely clustered, with the minimum mean being .77. The weakest pair is Belgium and Sweden (again, omitting Austria) at .24, whereas the United States and Germany have virtually identical left-right policy trends, with an *r* of .97.

That there is a leveling or at least a reduction in the leftward slope nearly everywhere denotes the completion (if not the success) of the welfare-state program advocated by the Left so vigorously throughout the years. And perhaps it is the very inflexibility—or determination—of the Left (Table 14.2) that accounts for this success. The impact of party alternation coupled with the complex interplay of party programs seems to have had the effect of ratcheting policy leftward, with it moving when leftist parties were in power and/or when their programmatic commitments were so inclined. The generally negative coefficients for the dummy variable denoting rightist parties in power, and the reflection of their programmatic commitments, indicate not so much reversal as hesitation in the trend leftward.

The hesitation beginning in the mid-1970s, so clearly illustrated in Figure 14.1, however, has been lasting and generally nonpartisan. To be sure, the Right has been in office more than the Left since that time. But even leftist governments, as exemplified by François Mitterrand's dramatic turn toward austerity after only eighteen months in office, have had to acknowledge that the drive toward entitlements and away from defense and infrastructure was not to be permanent. At the time of this writing, it was too early to forecast the direction of post–cold war policy. Stasis is not the norm. Democratic policy processes are too dynamic for a long level line. Some would predict that the emergence of quality-of-life issues will restructure public discourse along a new dimension, other than left-right. Alternatively, it can also be argued that those issues will themselves become the core of a newly constituted left-right contest, without a shift of dimensions of competition (see Inglehart 1990; Fuchs and Klingemann 1993).

POLITICS AND THE POLICY PROCESS

The writings of some leading commentators on contemporary policymaking could lead to the conclusion that democracy is doomed either to the Scylla of chaos or to the Charybdis of elitism. Those fates are incompatible with the premises of democratic theory. Our analysis casts doubt on both pessimistic diagnoses and offers support for the idea that party democracy works by and large as it is supposed to. In particular the analysis affirms the positive role of parties as essential instruments of democratic government.

Chaos is widely believed to follow from the multitude of veto groups, the omnipresence of logrolling, and the dynamics of voting cycles, whereby rational individual (or distinct group) self-interest tends to produce collective irrationality. Seen from what we earlier called an "ant's eye view," the day-to-day democratic process indeed appears disorderly, if not actually unseemly. Candidates for office chastise one another's chastity or lack thereof. They give circuitous and equivocal responses to clear questions. They sponsor campaign advertisements that divert rather than focus public attention. In office, they grapple endlessly with what seem to be the same old questions—more justice for less money, peace but pride, growth without pain, and the never-ending conflict between liberty and equality. Budgets are late. Politicians dip into the till. Unholy alliances yield holier-than-thou denials of deviation. Promises to hold the line on taxes fall before the claims of competing interest groups. From close-up, it is an unpretty sight.

Yet underlying the fray there is order. Note that we are not arguing for the *wisdom* of modern democracies. Rather we are arguing for their being *democratic.* The contestants for office collectively say in public what they intend to do. And then they usually do what they said they would do. Yet they do not wholly exclude or close the door on those who at the moment are out of electoral favor. None of the resolutions is permanent. Yet they get the democratic job done for their time.

Left parties take leftist stands. Right parties take rightist stands. And center parties wander about in the middle. All keep somewhat to their own turf, yet they sustain sufficient flexibility to accommodate to the evolution of voters' aspirations and the needs of new times. In the process, the parties each bundle issues into a finite package. These bundles of issues are voted upon in ways that evade cycles and instability, which are just not evident from the orderly way in which policy priorities evolve over time.

Between elections, elements of the opposition that are not dramatically incompatible may be accommodated. Members of coalitions bargain and exchange. This is facilitated through what we have called *saliency theory,* where parties rarely commit themselves in direct opposition to the bundles of aspirations expressed by their opponents. Instead, each party tries to construct its own unique bundle, leaving quietly open the possibility of selective borrowing from the other players. Our analyses affirm the extent to which this happens.

None of the major parties ever strays for long or widely from the common policy agenda. Yet none is obliged by the overpowering short-term lust for office to abandon wholly its historic identity. Thus even the relatively small third parties in several countries seem able to exercise major influence over special policies featured in their election programs.

The result has been the pursuit of a policy agenda that is remarkably similar across the set of modern democracies put under our lens. That similarity is the antithesis of chaos. Yet is it the result of manipulation by a hidden set of elites? With the full array of evidence behind us, we are suspicious of an explanation of such orderliness based on dominance by capitalist or bureaucratic elites. Shifting from defense, where the military-industrial complex makes its money, to welfare, where the better-off pay out more than they get back, hardly comports with an interpretation of the policy process as driven by power brokers beyond the reach of the electorate, unless one is now prepared to argue that a bureaucratic elite has replaced the military-industrial plutocrats of yore. Furthermore, if there are such elites, subtly adjusting governmental outlays to serve their desires in some nonobvious fashion, they have to be coordinating them on a massive international scale, which seems unlikely.

The final criticism, of course, is that elites of privilege and power let the appearance of democracy run on while they manipulate the agenda in such a way as to avoid zones of policy that might impinge on their core interests. We have shown, however, that the policies enacted largely reflect the broad and changing agenda advocated by sets of combatants in openly fought election campaigns. Neither elitist manipulation nor chaos will accommodate the evidence we have presented. The evidence covers a broad span of time, over many countries, across a wide spectrum of policies, with a multitude of competing parties. And it sustains a pluralist theory of democracy.

The main conclusion we reach is that party programs generally function according to the requirements of democratic theory—or at least those key requirements that we have been able to examine here. Which party is in office and what it has advocated are both very useful in trying to understand why policies look as they do. Parties have changed their relative concerns over the years. Those changes have been broadly reflected in policy priorities. In spite of common changes, the major partisan combatants have maintained clear and consistent programmatic differences from one another. And those programmatic differences have often mattered for subsequent policy. Parties in office are generally held accountable by their policies for what could have been expected from the information available to the voters at election time.

The organization of the country chapters in this book reflects our a priori expectations of the relative levels of accountability across countries. We had expected the Westminster systems (Britain, Australia, and Canada) to be the most accountable. We thought these would be followed, with reduced accountability, by the systems with separated powers (France and the United States). Still further down the list in terms of the power of the program-to-policy congruence would be the minority coalition arrangements in Sweden and the stable coalitions of Austria and Germany. Last and least accountable would be fluid, multiparty coalitions, represented here by the Netherlands and Belgium.

Figure 14.2 presents a reasonably comprehensive summary of the cross-national performance of our overall theory. The bars indicate the number of statistically significant (<.05) *b*s recorded for each country in the set of best-fitting models—either agenda, agenda plus mandate, or agenda plus mandate plus ideology. The actual total number of coefficients indicated by the bars must be viewed with caution, as it is affected by three sources of variation: (1) the number of policy areas included (indicated by the bracketed figures following the country name), (2) the number of parties in each country's analyses, and (3) the overall power of the models analyzed. As a corrective for some of the extraneous variation, we also indicate beneath the bars the percentage of statistically significant coefficients fitting in each column. The countries are arrayed from top down according to the relative percentage strength of the agenda over the sum of other models.

A Brief Review

A short review of what determines where a particular coefficient fits and what it means will be helpful at this point. The *agenda* model measures the accommodation of the policy process to the various concerns of the parties, without their having to be in government. There are two ways a coefficient may come to be listed in the "Agenda" column. It may represent the program-to-party congruence in a particular policy in a country when that policy is best accommodated by the various party programs, irrespective of incumbency. That is, a policy is predicted at better than R^2 .25, but the prediction is not improved by accounting for any of the parties' being in or out of government. The other source of coefficients in the "Agenda" column reflects the cumulative nature of the three models. An entry in that column can come from a positive *b* for a party if its program predicts policy shares even for the term in the *mandate* and *ideology* equations that accounts for that party's time out of office relative to its time in office. (Given that our selections here are from best-fitting models, no policy/party linkage has more than one opportunity to show up in Figure 14.2.)

Either source of agenda coefficients indicates, as we read the evidence, that for a party's program to anticipate policy priority, it is not necessary for the party to be in government. Theoretically we view this as the party's having participated in

Figure 14.2
Distribution of Statistically Significant Coefficients from Best-Fitting Models

	Agenda	Mandate: Negative	Mandate: Positive	Ideology	Mean Adj. R^{2}*
Sweden [8]** %	73.7	21.1	5.2		.58
France [10] %	67.6	20.6	11.8		.80
Britain [8] %	60.0	5.0	20.0	15.0	.49
Canada [11] %	35.9	20.5	20.5	23.1	.57
Belgium [8] %	30.4	26.1	26.1	17.4	.49
Germany [10] %	29.4	20.6	26.5	23.5	.66
Netherlands [7] %	18.2	27.3	22.7	31.8	.54
USA [12] %	16.1	29.1	38.7	16.1	.52
Austria [12] %	12.9	32.1	25.0	25.0	.65
Australia [7] %	9.0	36.4	36.4	18.2	.40
Column %	37.0	23.7	21.8	17.5	Mean of Mean R^2s .52

* Average of those equations included in the tables of best-fitting models (excluding those not reaching R^2 .25).

** Bracketed figure indicates number of policy domains for which one of the three models attained R^2 = or > .25.

█ = One statistically significant b.

▒ = Weak signal of policy priorities.

[ ] Box in Agenda column encloses countries in which 60 percent of the coefficients fit agenda model.

Box in Mandate - Ideology columns encloses countries in which 60 percent of the coefficients fit mandate - ideology model.

a process of discourse that pointed the direction of governmental action, even though that party may have been occasionally or even consistently out of office.

A negative mandate entry, as in Figure 14.2, represents the reverse of the second agenda coefficient discussed above. That is, it reflects the fact that a party receives a negative coefficient for the statistical term accounting for the party's having been out of office. This inverse congruence comports fairly well with classical conceptions of interparty competition, whereby winners actively reject the agenda of the losers. The negative mandate works to drive policy in the direction opposite to a particular party's programmatic emphases when account is taken of that party's having been out of office, compared to what happens as a function of its having been in.

The negative mandate, contrary to a possible first impression, is quite consistent with saliency theory. According to that theory, competition is structured not by parties taking diametrically opposed positions, for or against, particular policies, but by their stressing those things that they most desire and by their ignoring those things they either oppose or in which they are not interested. That still leaves room for maneuver by incumbent parties that wish to follow the message of the election. They may give priority to those issues they themselves stressed, or they may reduce the priority given to those stressed by their opponents. Party A's program ignores infrastructure. Party B's program stresses it. Party A wins and then reduces the priority for infrastructure. We would label that a case of the *negative mandate.* The voter is given important guidance by the program: Vote against the party whose program you disapprove of most. We see this as no less consistent with democratic theory or the saliency argument than is the *positive mandate.*

A statistically significant coefficient for the positive mandate says that being in office has enhanced the congruence between program emphases of a party and subsequent policy priorities. Again, the voter is given important guidance by the program. Vote for the party whose program you approve of. If the programs of the contesting parties fitted a traditional conception of interparty competition, the voter could endow a negative and a positive mandate simultaneously. The parties would be overtly *pro* or *con* on the issues important to the voter. A vote for one would be clearly a vote against the other. The saliency theory, however, modifies the old adage: If a party can't say something good about an issue area, it doesn't say anything at all. This circumstance may present the voter with a less vehement message than that conveyed by a sharp *pro* versus *con* fight, but the message is not, as a consequence, any less clear. The signaling capacity of the combination of affirmative programmatic emphases and selective silence provides the means for a quite clear mandate.

Finally, the *ideology* coefficients tallied in the fourth column in Figure 14.2 tell us how common it is that the simple change from one major party to another adds to the efficiency of party programs alone as predictors of policy priority. This element of the process, which we have measured by the alternation of a major party in and out of government, reflects standing interparty difference not captured by variation in specific programmatic emphases of the party's election programs. As we have seen, in some policies in particular countries, this index of ideological consistency may be more powerful as a signal of policy than are the more specific concerns expressed in contemporary election programs. As such, it is a form of mandate. It says that the voter may expect the standing policy differences between Party A and the others to persist if A is voted in and to diminish if A is voted out. To the extent that ideology operates to the exclusion of congruence between current programs and policies in the near term, of course, it detracts from the mandate role of *programs* but not from the mandate role of *elections.*

Two Special Cases

The distributions for Belgium and the Netherlands in Figure 14.2 are indicated by bars with lighter shading than those of the other countries, which is supposed to suggest that neither party programs nor alternation in office of major parties does a very good job of signaling Belgian or Dutch policy priorities. In Belgium, four of twelve policies failed even to reach R^2 .25. That in itself argues that there is at best an intermittent and weak electoral mandate in the Belgian policy process.

Only two of nine policy domains were nonconformists in the Netherlands, but other factors, not obvious in Figure 14.2, suggest that Dutch voters have at best a minimal opportunity to endow their governments with a clear electoral mandate. That it might be otherwise is suggested by the fact that the ideology model is best-fitting for a higher proportion of policies in the Netherlands than in any of the other nine countries. But that is misleading on two grounds. First, the Christian Democratic Appeal (CDA) is always in government (as is its counterpart in Belgium most of the time), so there is constrained alternation. We have measured such alternation as the presence of Labor (PvdA) in government, which nearly always means the exclusion of the Liberals. The term representing Labor-Liberal alternation into and out of CDA-dominated coalitions indeed predicts policy strongly. But it is nearly always *opposite* to the direction traditionally associated with each of those parties, suggesting that each has made a series of Faustian bargains. When Labor (PvdA) has been in, policy has moved to the right. When the (right-wing) Liberals have been in, policy has moved to the left. Thus the competition that exists—which is far from total, given the Christian Democrats' dominance—offers the voters at best a chance for a perverse mandate.

Although not conforming well to any of our models, the Belgian and Dutch findings do not at all deviate from our general theoretical expectations. We predicted there would be a low level of party accountability in these countries. They have, relative to the set analyzed here, the most nearly fragmented party systems. There are more participating parties. There has been more volatility in the set of consequential parties. And the process of forming and maintaining governments has, because of the fluidity of their party systems, been much more tedious and fractious than in the other eight countries. Thus, however unfortunate for the quality of Dutch or Belgian democracy, these cases fit with our overall theory-based expectations.

Beyond these two cases, however, our expectations about the institutional conditions enhancing and inhibiting party accountability were largely unfulfilled. Interestingly, beyond the Dutch and Belgian cases, the lack of fulfillment of our expectations was due more to our having found evidence of effective mandates where not expected than to our not having found such evidence where it was expected. That is, the mandate seems to work across a wider range of institutional circumstances than traditional reasoning would lead one to expect.

The Unremarkable Westminster Systems

Constitutional theory led us to expect that the Westminster systems would be the most likely sites for the mandate and ideology models. Britain, Canada, and Australia are, by and large, majoritarian. Party discipline is well developed and applied. Yet the mandate occurs no more frequently in the Westminster systems than it does elsewhere. The Westminster countries are most distinguished by their diversity. One feature of the findings for the Westminster systems is abundantly clear and contrary to our initial hypothesis: Parties there are *not,* by virtue of the presumed advantages of single-party parliamentary institutions, more accountable for seeing their pronouncements through to policy. The mean adjusted R^2 for the set (.47) is a bit below the mean for the ten countries (.52), and Britain's R^2 is rather substantially down the list. The range of explanation is encouraging for the general theory, but not for the usefulness of the specific hypothesis regarding the Westminster systems. The uncommon extent of spread across the three models in the Westminster systems, however, discourages us from much more speculation.

It may be concluded with certainty that the three categories, Westminster (Britain, Canada, Australia), presidential (France, United States), and coalition (the rest), do not show the kind of respective decline in program-to-policy congruence that we assumed when ordering the country chapters in this book. Neither in terms of R^2 nor in type of process model are the Westminster systems more accountable than the coalitions in terms of policy response to electoral promise. This is an important and challenging message for constitutional theory and design.

Figure 14.2 shows one dimension that does *not* array the countries' party and policy systems. What is not evident is what *does* array them. Clearly what does not array them coherently is the organization by constitutional arrangement commonly expected to enhance or inhibit party accountability.

The Agenda Countries

As suggested by the two boxes in Figure 14.2 indicated by dashed lines, the ten countries divided rather neatly into two sets: Three in which over 60 percent of the coefficients fit under the *agenda,* and seven in which 60 percent of the coefficients fit under one or more of the variations on the *mandate* (including *ideology* in that set). In Sweden, France, and Britain, although the parties indeed are clearly and consistently distinguishable in their programmatic emphases, governments are maximally accommodating to the programs of a broad set of parties rather than to just those holding posts in government at a particular time.

In the Swedish case, this accommodation is, in all likelihood, due to the small size and social homogeneity of the country, as well as to the tradition of using nonpartisan policy instruments, such as the expert commission. Swedish partisan differences, for all their apparent drama, do not seem to run deep. Deep divisions would hardly be expected in a country with virtually no minorities, one religion, and a generally wealthy populace.

France obtains from its constitution and leadership what Sweden gets from its culture. That France should be such an accommodating system, however, will strike some as strange. Few affluent modern democracies have a more volatile political history. The present constitution was written in the wake of a virtual coup d'état. However, what we may also be seeing is the capacity of the strong presidency, instituted by the Fifth Republic's constitution, to lead the policy process. President de Gaulle argued for a system *above* party. His political style was to be aloof from the general grubbiness of partisan combat, yet what he and his followers have built is not so much a system *above* parties as *across* them. More than in any other country we have analyzed, what French parties emphasize and the manner in which their emphases change, collectively, presages the contours of policy. The range of partisan concern is broad, thanks in particular to the historic role of the French Communists, but it is nonetheless accommodated by policy. Who wins has proven to be less important than the collective concerns of the partisan combatants in French policy formation.

France's history of political instability under former constitutions contrasts sharply with the post-1958 years. Transfers from one party to the other in government have been smooth. Even the periods of cohabitation, with different parties controlling the National Assembly and the presidency, have led to no inconveniences of lasting note. The Gaullists and the Center have on occasion produced a common election program, as have the Socialists and the Communists. The constitution might have allowed French presidents, at least for a time, to ignore the parties, or the power conferred could have been used to pursue exclusively the priorities of the president's party. However, successive presidents—Gaullist, Center, and Socialist—have used the concentrated power of the office to reach across the parties, to accommodate their respective agendas, and thus apparently to retain and build the legitimacy of the system. That legitimacy, as French history illustrates, is an essential precondition to democracy (Lipset 1959). That it does not make for a clear operation of the mandate—a more refined and focused aspect of democratic policymaking—is, of course, a point to note.

It is indeed surprising that in Britain the agenda should so clearly predominate over variations on the mandate. It suggests a transpartisanship in British policymaking that is hardly suggested by the common reading of constitutional theory. Single-member districts yield clear parliamentary majorities, alternating between two distinct parties. Each party has the instruments for strong discipline over MPs. The Cabinet is a powerful policymaking body. The instruments seem to be in place to yield clear winners and to endow those winners with the power to implement their electoral promises and to ignore or contravene the concerns of the losers.

But it often does not happen that way. To be sure, in a noticeable number of policy areas, the positive mandate and ideology effects are evident, as seen in Figure 14.2. The few cases where the ideology term is important do set Britain a bit apart from the other two agenda-dominant countries (Sweden and France). But little we know of the formal structure and workings of British politics would lead us to expect governments to be so apparently solicitous of out-parties, including the perennially out Liberals. Certainly the message of common criticism would not lead one to expect more accommodation of out-parties in Britain than in the United States, given the U.S. electorate's penchant for electing a president of one party and a Congress of the other. Yet these expectations are contradicted by the evidence as we have analyzed here.

The British reality appears to be an exception to legal theory. As we noted in Chapter 4, the real world of society and politics often contrasts with governmental and legal theory. And, indeed, such is the case in Britain. As we have noted, Britain has a three-party, not a two-party, system, even if one ignores the various regional parties, such as the Scottish or Welsh Nationalists. Rarely does one party receive a majority of votes. Thus the consistently clear majorities of seats in Parliament are based actually on a mere plurality of votes. The claim on a mandate is thus weaker than legal theory might suggest.

Given that parliamentary majorities are structured by institutional means rather than by social realities, it seems that British governments are more prone to taking over obviously popular ideas from the opposition and the Liberals than to adhering steadfastly to their own partisan schedules. Formal investment of power does not automatically translate into political security. As a consequence, all parties, not just the government one, get some of their program adopted through moral or intellectual persuasiveness or through the ruling party's fears of adverse electoral repercussions. Institutional arrangements have created an illusion of potency that politicians know full well better than to flout.

Let us turn to the common Anglo-American comparison, where the election of the American president for a fixed term, independent of the legislative branch, contrasts with a parliamentary system, where the prime minister is the leader of the majority party. The U.S. phenomenon does not seem to have diluted the congruence between party promise and policy performance, relative to a variety of parliamentary systems, and most notably to the presumed classic case of accountability—Britain.

There is one aspect of agenda congruence that is patterned and requires special attention. This is the large number of countries in which smaller leftist or liberal parties' programs have very strong predictive power on foreign and defense policy.

The Canadian NDP, the British Liberals, the French Communists, the Swedish Communists, and the German FDP all have quite high party program regression coefficients in the best-fitting equations for defense and/or foreign affairs policy. These parties have some strong influence in other areas. For example, the French Communists are deferred to in at least four policies. The British Liberals see their programmatic emphases reflected in environmental-protection policy. But it is defense and foreign affairs that stand out as being subject to strong minor-party influence across several countries. In the West German case, elsewhere we attributed this to the "blackmail potential" whereby the FDP has most of the time been in a position to make or break the governing coalition (Hofferbert and Klingemann 1990). The multinational pattern raises doubts about that nationally unique explanation. With the exception of a brief three-year period in the 1980s for the French Communists, none of the other parties of concern here (Canadian NDP, French or Swedish Communists, British Liberals) has ever even been in a postwar government. Yet their programs show up nearly as well in external policy as does that of the German FDP.

We suggested that winners may accommodate the programmatic emphases of parties out of government in those domains of special concern to the out-parties. A small party may focus its attention on a very narrow set of policy concerns, gaining justified respect for producing efficient and logical solutions. If the Canadian NDP or the British Liberals or the Swedish Communists ever have the political good fortune to emulate the German FDP in gaining cabinet membership, it will not be surprising if their first portfolio is the Foreign Ministry.

Given the specific domains where this minor party pattern most often seems to occur—defense and foreign affairs—there is added reason for an open door to outsiders' ideas. These are the policy domains that have the least clarity in terms of domestic interests. The conscience-to-pocketbook ratio may be larger here than in most other domains. Likewise, the political payoff of program fulfillment—or the costs of nonfulfillment—may be relatively lower for the incumbents.

The Mandate Countries

The strength of the *agenda* effect means that the policy-relevant aggregation process is performed frequently in a transparty fashion. At least one test of party performance—aggregation of interests in such a way as to enter them effectively into the policy process—seems to be passed.

But for democratic theory, more is required. Elections have to matter. Signals provided before an election by competing parties have to be discernibly different. And those signals have to be reliable guides to probable policy choices by winners, as contrasted to losers. In short, there needs to be evidence of a *mandate* operating between the parties and the policy process.

In at least five or, with some generosity, seven, of the ten countries, the various forms of the mandate (negative, positive, and ideology) seem to hold consequential sway in the policy process.[3] Occupancy of office frequently has a strong effect on the ability of parties to implement policies stressed in their programs and/or policies characteristic of their standing differences from their opponents. Interestingly, the incidence of the negative mandate is about equal to that of the positive.

We have repeatedly stressed that the three models are cumulative—each a part of a common theory—and not distinct from one another. According to saliency theory, the implementation of a positive mandate in some policy areas by a government need not be to the exclusion of another party's concerns. In addition, all along we have insisted that standing interparty differences (the measurement of which we have treated as an indicator of *ideology*) can be an important basis for a party mandate. Voters have available both the current program and the standing record.

The ideology model, furthermore, need not add much variance to be quite instructive. In many cases, as seen in the far right column of the summary table in each chapter, it is often the case that the ideology term boosts the R^2 by only a few percentage points over the mandate model. But the regression coefficients (*b*s) for the ideology term are most commonly far larger than any other component of the model. This is because the emphases of each party's program usually sustain a constant interparty difference. Thus, if that is of policy consequence, it is picked up by the ideology term, leaving for the pure *program effect* modest temporal variations around the generally constant differences between the parties. What is important about the ideology term is not that it is insensitive to variations in programmatic emphasis, but rather that it provides a shorthand reference for those and any other unmeasured differences in policy patterns associated with party alternation. The ideology model shows, in effect, how efficient it would be for the voter seeking to confer a mandate to do so exclusively on the basis of established interparty differences.

As noted by the larger of the boxes within Figure 14.2, with some indulgence toward the Netherlands and Belgium, seven of the ten countries are characterized by the predominance of variations on the mandate. There is a peculiarity of four of these that deserves our attention—the institutionalization of traditional cleavages.

Traditional Versus Modern Cleavages

In Germany, Austria, Belgium, and the Netherlands, the dominant partisan cleavage continues to be more "traditional" than "modern." That is, in all four countries the avowedly *Christian* party has maintained a preeminent role right up to the present. The opposition liberals and socialists, whatever their other differences, share a commitment to secularism, if not avowed anticlericalism. In Germany and the Netherlands the supporters of Christian parties have by now successfully bridged historical Catholic-Protestant antagonisms while keeping their confessional identity.

In Catholic Austria, the regionally based clerical-anticlerical cleavage may have historically been a lesser challenge, but the People's Party has nevertheless served as a broad umbrella under which all who are concerned with traditional values of family and Church could be comfortably covered. It provides an arena of defense against the spread of "moral decay" from Vienna westward. Of course, in Belgium the dominant cleavage is not exclusively or even predominantly between Christian and secular parties, although that is very much in evidence, but it is rather another traditional demarcation—linguistic-regional differences. But we wish here to focus particularly on the interparty differences between Christian parties and their opponents.

Again we stress for the non-European reader a point that is better known to the European: Christian parties are not always to be equated with conservative parties. That they may both score within the rightist range on our left-right scale is simply due to the scale's having summed both traditional family values and social harmony, central in the Christian party repertoire, and the equally rightist commitments of conservative parties to the market economy, orthodox fiscal policy, and skepticism about the welfare state. As long as the policies do not threaten their traditional commitments, the Christian parties have generally been quite accommodating to the core of the welfare state.

It is, as we have noted in the German, Austrian, Dutch, and Belgian chapters, the leftist parties in competition with the Christians who have the most difficulty translating their particular programmatic concerns into policy priorities. When pitted directly against conventional conservatives, the leftists have fared relatively better (e.g., the Canadian New Democrats or the French Communists, even when not in government). The bulk of contradictory coefficients are concentrated in the socialist columns for Germany, Austria, Belgium, and the Netherlands. This is probably due to the relative flexibility of the Christian parties in dealing with those issues at the heart of the socialist agenda. Aside from sectarian-secular issues, the Christians can be quite nimble, creating a moving target for the socialists.

Perhaps ironically, the continuation of a premodern cleavage, deftly maneuvered by the defenders of Christian values into the context of a contemporary industrial democracy, seems to create the very conditions that make for fulfillment of theoretically key attributes of a modern democracy. The forecasts of policy differences' flowing from standing distinctions between the parties, coupled with differential program foci, are more accurate, generally, in the countries whose central dimension of competition is also the most traditional. Lipset and Rokkan

(1967) saw class conflict, resulting from industrialization and urbanization, displacing or at least crosscutting territorial, religious, and linguistic cleavages (see also the discussion in Chapter 1). Our analysis suggests that for a country to function according to certain central precepts of modern democratic theory, it is not always necessary to have abandoned the battle lines of "pre"-modern politics.

None of the three agenda-dominant countries has a significant Christian party. They all have viable conservative parties and equally viable parties to the left of center, if not well out on the left wing. And in two of the three most accommodating countries—Sweden and France—there are even some policies that have been adapted to the concerns of the domestic Communists.

It appears that class conflict is more readily fitted to the politics of accommodation than are religious-secular differences. Yet modernization theory, such as put forth by Lipset and Rokkan (1967), asserts that class cleavages will displace or at least take precedence over traditional identities. We would argue, however, that class conflict is easier to bargain over in the policy process than are more fundamental cultural values. If one steps outside the immediate concern of this book and looks at the emergence of bloody ethno-religious strife in the industrialized post-Communist world, the seeming indelibility of traditional cleavages is starkly evident. In the more genteel context of the established democracies, those cleavages are managed in the relatively civilized parliamentary contest over policy. But the divisions are still sharp and visible. Why is this?

Governments cannot grant an ethnic group half of its language. It cannot parcel out the accoutrements of religious identity. Those distinctions exist not only at the level of specific "interest" but also at the level of identity. Wages, hours, working conditions, housing allotments, teachers' salaries, all can be negotiated and bargained for in fractions. The essential values of the "modern" cleavage are continuous variables, subject to fine-tuned logrolling. Here we speculate that the modern issues of industrial society lend themselves to different patterns of management and resolution than did the cleavages of premodern times. It means, ironically, that the latter may be better fitted to our theory of party democracy than are the former.

In Chapter 1, Figure 1.2, we presented a diagrammatic model of the policy process, whereby a flow of functions performed by various sets of actors expressed their interests more or less through particular stages. Our speculation is that the demands articulated out of the (here oversimplified) conflict between labor and business, and the variations on that central theme of industrial society, lend themselves to compromise by bargaining and may be dealt with before the sharpening of issues at the party program–formulation stage—the stage at which political parties theoretically become the central actors. In contrast, traditional cleavages often do not get "resolved" until the final vote in parliament, if then.

Labor and management, the guardians of the class struggle, resolve most of their differences in a day-to-day, cumulative manner beyond the walls and halls of government, as such, in a more or less stable framework. It is usually the definition or amendment of that framework that gets passed over to the public-policy process. And even there, the historical identity of clearly left and clearly right parties can survive a lot of compromise and cumulative change—in a way that the identity of Christian parties cannot.

In 1967 Reinhard Bendix wrote a stimulating essay, "Tradition and Modernity Reconsidered," in which he sought to emphasize the staying power of preindustrial social cleavages and their ability to be accommodated and adapted to quite modern institutional settings (Bendix 1967). We can think of no more dramatic illustration of that thesis than that among the sharpest, most policy-relevant grounds for competition in contemporary policymaking would be those between parties' speaking for cleavages rooted in the eighteenth century (see Table 1.1 and Lipset and Rokkan 1967, 47).

CONCLUSION

Our aim has been to examine general patterns of the role of parties in the policy process of modern democracies. We have stressed that we are not interested in explaining why particular policies are as they are. Nor have we been interested in the peculiarities of specific countries or parties, except insofar as they might provide clues to more general features of the democratic policy process. The aim of this chapter has been to draw together such generalizations as our research will support. As the discussion has necessarily been somewhat broad and technically focused so far, a summary of these general observations is in order.

By means of a cross-time, cross-country, comparable index of left-right party program content, we have confirmed the presence of certain patterns. Generally, there are few secular trends over the postwar years in the left-right movement of parties, although the socialist and social democratic parties have some tendency to move toward the center. In general, the socialist and social democratic parties have less temporal variance in the broad direction of their election programs than do the center parties; and the center parties have less than do the parties to the right.

Most consequential parties maintain their distance from one another. "Left" parties tend to be more steady in their leftist commitment than "right" parties are to their rightist commitments. Rarely do they cross over one another's issue domains. But there is no evidence of party rigidity or flights to extreme positions, not even in multiparty systems, where such behavior has been predicted by some scholars.

It is easy to discover a similar cross-nationally comparable left-right dimension of postwar policy variance, even based upon nation-specific indicators. Following the peak in defense commitments in the early 1950s, nearly all countries' policy priorities moved steadily leftward, well into the 1970s, after which they either leveled or even moved a bit rightward.

The congruence of party programs and policy priorities along the left-right dimensions, however, is notable for its infrequency. The policy processes of modern democracies, in spite of the centrality of the left-right dimension in both party rhetoric and policy production, are not reliably captured by that dimension. Policy responds to party concerns, but it is at substantively specific levels rather than at the general level of left-right ideological confrontation.

Contrary to the popular belief that the cold war steadily drove up the priority of national defense policy, the clear pattern has been for defense commitments to decline and welfare priority to rise from the early 1950s well into the 1970s. That the trend flattened after the 1970s may be due to many complex processes, but no small part is that the core of the welfare state had largely become established policy.

Education priority rose and then leveled or fell, no doubt largely in response to the movement of the postwar baby boom through the public school systems of the countries studied. Similar curvilinear patterns, with early rise and later fall in priority, were also the norm in infrastructure policies, where initial capitalization was required to compensate for delayed investment during the depression and war years.

Certain parties seem to have advantages in certain substantive areas. In particular, defense- and foreign affairs–policy priorities stand out as being especially attuned to the concerns articulated in minor (usually liberal) parties' programs.

Although here and there we find evidence that entitlements in the human services have low program-to-policy congruence, there are also several cases where such congruence is substantial. One cannot say, therefore, that the growth of entitlements has uniformly reduced the flexibility of parties or their capacity to articulate and enact policy changes.

Party involvement in the democratic policy process is a reasonably civil business. The parties provide a flexible means for articulating issues in the public arena. The range of parties capable of articulating issues and seeing that articulation reflected in authoritative decisions is quite wide. Few parties capable of significant electoral support fail to see some policy reflection of some of their issue concerns. Thus, winning a place in government is not an all or nothing affair.

At the same time that a good deal of transparty accommodation takes place, there are nonetheless sufficient substantive differences between the parties, publicized in their formal programs, to present the electorates with choices rather than echoes. And those choices, when reflected in the parties' gaining positions in government, are meaningful in terms of alternative policy patterns following the election. In spite of many strong grounds for skepticism, we find a remarkably high congruence between the themes stressed in party election programs and the subsequent policies enacted by the parties that get into government. This reflection is about equally divided between rejection of out-party preferences and enactment of preferences of governing parties.

Over and above the predictive capacity of party election programs, the voters have available an additional piece of useful information, namely the standing policy differences among major parties. These differences, while generally reflected in current programmatic emphases, have a predictive capacity beyond that of the immediate election documents. Ideology matters, and it is only under the most inconvenient circumstances that there are no policy reflections of such longtime standing interparty differences.

In sum, there is evidence of considerable policy accountability of parties in modern democracies. However, the variation from country to country in levels and forms of accountability (agenda, mandate, ideology) does not conform to the expectations deduced from institutional and constitutional arrangements for party vitality in the policy process. Some countries have forms of Roman Law, some the Common Law. Some are federations and some are centralized. Some have parliaments and prime ministers; some have separated powers and presidents. But these differences do not relate to variation in level or form of party accountability.

Number of parties and structure of coalitions is a one-tailed influence, with the extreme (Netherlands and Belgium) being distinguished by the predicted lesser potency of parties. A multiparty system with loose coalitions appears to be a sufficient, but not necessary, condition for low accountability.

The extent to which policy priority accommodates the preferences of parties in and out of government or, in contrast, the extent to which policymakers adopt the preferences of parties in government or reject preferences of those out of government is not a function of obvious institutional or constitutional features. Rather, the conditions for accountability are there in nearly all modern democracies. Governing officials can rightly be held accountable for fulfilling their mandates. Institutional barriers are no excuse for failure.

Interparty bargaining is important in all ten countries, as indicated by the frequency with which policies reflect *agenda* influences. Institutions that guarantee a place at the table for multiple parties—that set up barriers to the "tyranny of the majority"—are not sham gestures toward collaboration. But those same constitutional barriers, so often cited as the key to governmental immobility, nonetheless allow party democracy usually to function. The role enshrined by history in party systems finds its way into the reality of policymaking. The concerns expressed by the parties in the election become, for the most part, the concerns embodied in policy after the election. The rational, information-maximizing voter would have little difficulty in attaching accountability to the actions of policymakers in at least nine of the ten countries studied here. And the vitality of opposition provides a guarantee that the voter's information costs will be, at most, marginal.

We stand by our formulation of the theory of party functions that we set out in Chapter 1: Modern politics is party politics. Political parties are the major actors in the system that connects the citizenry and the governmental process. Parties sort through citizens' demands, most of which have been articulated by interest groups and the mass media. The parties turn the demands into political issues by working out policy alternatives in light of the general principles for which the respective parties stand. In this way political parties aggregate demands into loosely coherent policy packages—a process that gives voters a choice in elections. Political parties form governments and act as opposition in legislatures. They may occupy the upper echelons of the bureaucracy. Thus, they are crucial to political decisionmaking and implementation. From this perspective, political parties must choose policies. They have to rule, and they have to take responsibility for their decisions. They are the major actors in representative democratic systems when it comes to solving societal problems. We have no reason to retract that statement.

Our research has not examined all the links in the chain of the democratic process. But we have singled out a few that have long been claimed by many critics to be fatally weak. Having analyzed the congruence between party election programs and policy priorities across ten countries over four decades, we find that those links in the democratic chain are far stronger than heretofore believed.

NOTES

1. The Canadian Liberals and Progressive Conservatives leapfrog regularly, but it is reasonable to argue that it is not a case of Left versus Right crossing over. Rather, the Canadian "Liberals," unlike the Australian "Liberals," really do seem to be "liberals," if we compare the location and behavior of the Canadian Liberals to the German FDP, the British Liberals, or the Austrian FPÖ. The key Canadian difference is that the Liberals there are unique in often heading the government, something never done by their counterparts elsewhere. There is never any leapfrogging between Canada's leftist party, the New Democrats, and either of the two major parties. However, the Liberal/Progressive Conservative competition does look a bit like a relatively clear (and very unusual) example of the kind of behavior predicted by Downs's model in its pure form.

2. One nation-specific note is warranted. Tweedledum/Tweedledee can be put to rest for the United States. The Democrats are, on average, to the left of several European social democratic parties. The Republicans average to the right of their closest counterparts in Canada, Germany, the Netherlands, and the United Kingdom.

3. We have given ample attention to the lack of clear fit of the Netherlands and Belgium to either an agenda or a mandate explanation. But there are elements, noted in the concluding sections of Chapters 12 and 13, which still are worth attention under those categories—in particular, the mandate congruence of the CDA programs in the Netherlands and the ideology effects of Socialist/Liberal alternation in Belgian governments. Thus, we retain them in Figure 14.2, but with the caution implied by the bars with lighter shading.

Appendix A: Party Program–Coding Procedures and Categories

CODING PROCEDURES

Strategy

The comparative party program data are the product of deliberation and experimentation over many years by a group of scholars from several countries.[1] Although the basic outlines were fixed at the beginning of the project, the details are the product of a lengthy process of international communication and cooperation leading to the resolution of technical problems that could not be identified ahead of time but had to be resolved as they occurred. Whereas this is true of most collaborative research projects, it was particularly the case with this project because of the need to achieve a very high degree of comparability in data collection and analysis over very different and contrasting countries. The only basic point fixed at the outset was that a specific form of content analysis would be used to transform the party program texts into numerical records. That decision stemmed from previous research experience with election programs (Robertson 1976; Budge and Farlie 1977).

Content analysis has a long history in the social sciences, and our use is not particularly novel. The only thing requiring comment is our definition of the *counting unit*—that is, the symbols used to constitute an observation. Particularly since the development of computer-aided content analysis, there has been a tendency to define specific words or precise phrases as the symbols to be searched for and counted in written material. Thus we might have looked for the number of occurrences of the word "socialism" as an indicator of left-wing economic policy, or the frequency of mention of the phrase "public order" to indicate traditional conservative concerns with social tension. There are two reasons for not doing so. The first is that a cross-national study cannot rely on the identity of meaning of such simple lexical units, regardless of quality of translation. Even between British and American English, the word "socialism" differs intensely in connotation, and the French idea of "ordre publique" has greatly different undertones from the common law conception of "public order."

Equally important, single words or predetermined phrases could not capture what was wanted from the party programs, which was to measure the relative stress on certain ideas, policies, issues, and concerns. It is these, however expressed, that we needed to capture. Consequently, we adopted a natural unit, the sentence, as the counting unit. This involved not an automatic count, but a coding procedure. Each sentence was examined, and the coder then had to decide which of the long list of fifty-four concept categories, if any, it expresses. This approach involves more risk of error than counting specified words, but it allows for a much richer description of the content. Sentences that do not fit into one of the categories are treated as uncodable.

The coding scheme is given in detail below. It was developed from an earlier scheme designed for the analysis of British party manifestoes and later applied to U.S. platforms (Robertson 1976; Budge and Farlie 1977). Lengthy meetings of the experts who were to study the individual countries sought on this basis to create a list of categories that expressed (1) as closely as possible the most important issues and concerns in comparative politics that were common to at least several countries and (2) did so in a way that had an internationally comparative meaning. Inside these relatively broad categories, special subcategories could be used to catch more precise shades of meaning peculiar to a particular political system. The scope of the coding frame had to be very wide to cover issues adequately in so many countries, and hence many never were used fully in one country or another. Even where categories attract zero scores they reflect a political reality. It is a fact that, let us say, anticlericalism is never an issue in British politics but can be important in countries as different as Belgium and Israel, thus distinguishing the three from one another.

The fifty-four categories were grouped into seven "domains," that is, common sets of categories covering broad areas of political discourse. These domains, the content of which are shown below, are deliberately a priori theoretical groupings of common issues. They contain varying numbers of primary categories. The number of such categories, however, is not a measure of their relative importance but rather of the inherent complexity of the area of policy conflict they cover.

It can be argued that both the fifty-four initial categories and the seven domains are often too detailed and should have been collapsed somewhat. The reader will note that, occasionally in the analyses, we indeed do collapse some categories to gain more precision of measurement. However, it is always possible to collapse detailed categories. But excessively aggregated categories, without that detail, cannot be separated. The primary responsibility at the outset of the project was to produce—with enormous labor—a general purpose data set, as rich and refined as possible, and with as precisely comparable a meaning for each variable in all countries and parties as could be attained.

Tactics

The tasks of coordination of coding have fallen into two successive stages: (1) the pre-1980 data, coordination of which was generally provided out of the University of Essex, and (2) the post-1980 data, which continues to be coordinated through the Research Unit on Institutions and Social Change of the Science Center–Berlin. Maintenance and updating is now guided by a detailed handbook (Volkens 1992) and direct coordination between Berlin and cooperating scholars in various countries.

Coordination of a multinational team is never easy or inexpensive. However, from the outset the project's procedures achieved an uncommon level of standardization. As explained above, the many election manifestoes, party platforms, and so on were coded into a standard coding frame in as uniform a way as possible. The coding frame was itself elaborated at face-to-face "bargaining sessions" between the various national specialists early in the project. From the very beginning, therefore, everyone was clear about what the various themes and categories were intended to cover. The inevitable difficulties and problems associated with individual coding decisions were fully discussed by the national specialists at regular intervals, and we are satisfied that the greatest possible standardization was achieved.

In several early cases, the documents, although collected by a national researcher, were sent to the University of Essex for coding and analysis. One of the editors of the original volume published by the project (Hearl) personally supervised these operations, employing a team of four assistants who referred all doubtful decisions to him. Over time, of course, these assistants became steadily more expert at the coding task. In the majority of cases, checks of one kind or another were performed, usually by the national researcher, on the accuracy and consistency of the coding. Details of these checks are in the individual chapters of Budge, Robertson, and Hearl (1987).

The mutually agreed-upon coding rules allowed for individual national circumstances by permitting the use of subcategories. In other words, each national researcher had full freedom to break down any of the standard categories in such a way as to be able to capture concerns particular to each country's context, subject only to the condition that this be done in such a way as to permit the reaggregation of these subcategories back to the standard ones for the purposes of comparative analysis. Some country contributors made extensive use of this facility, and others used it either only to a limited extent or not at all.

The standard categories were grouped into the seven themes or domains listed with each set below. The full coding frame, consisting of the standard categories, grouped by domain, is also given. It should be noted that the specifications are intended to be descriptive and illustrative of the types of issue covered by each category rather than exhaustive definitions.

CODING CATEGORIES FOR PARTY ELECTION PROGRAMS

Domain 1: External Relations

Foreign Special Relationships: Positive
Favorable mention of other countries where these are either specially dependent on or are specially involved with the relevant country. For example, former colonies; in the West German case, East Germany; in the Swedish case, the rest of Scandinavia; the need for cooperation with and aid to such countries; their importance to the economy and defense programs of the relevant country.

Foreign Special Relationships: Negative
Same as preceding, but negative.

Decolonization
Favorable mentions of decolonization, need for relevant country to leave colonies; greater self-government, and independence; need to train natives for this; need to give special aid to make up for colonial past. This also includes negative references to Soviet Imperialism in Eastern Europe, especially in the United States.

Military: Positive
Need for strong military presence overseas, for rearmament and self-defense, need to keep to military treaty obligations, need to secure adequate manpower in military.

Military: Negative
Same as preceding, but negative.

Peace
Declaration of belief in Peace and peaceful means of solving crises; need for international disarmament and desirability of relevant country joining in negotiations with hostile countries.

Internationalism: Positive
Support for UN, need for international cooperation, need for aid to developing countries, need for world planning of resources, need for international courts, support for any international aim or world state.

Internationalism: Negative
Same as preceding, but negative.

European Community: Positive
Favorable mentions of European Community in general; desirability of relevant country joining (or remaining a Member); desirability of expanding it and/or of

increasing its competences; favorable mentions of Direct Election; pro–European Unity in general.

European Community (and Europe): Negative
Same as preceding, but negative.

Domain 2: Freedom and Democracy

Freedom and Domestic Human Rights
Favorable mentions of importance of personal freedom, civil rights; freedom of choice in education; freedom from bureaucratic control, freedom of speech; freedom from coercion in industrial and political sphere; individualism.

Democracy
Favorable mention of democracy as method or goal in national and other organizations; support for worker participation, for involvement of all citizens in decisionmaking, as well as generalized support for symbols of democracy.

Constitutionalism: Positive
Support for specified aspects of a formal constitution, use of constitutionalism as an argument for policy as well as generalized approval for "constitutional" way of doing things.

Constitutionalism: Negative
Same as preceding, but negative.

Domain 3: Government

Decentralization: Positive
Support for devolution, regional administration of politics or economy, support for keeping up local and regional customs and symbols, deference to local expertise in planning, etc.

Decentralization: Negative
Same as preceding, but negative.

Government Efficiency
Need for efficiency in government (e.g., merit system in civil service), economy in government, cutting down civil service; improving governmental procedures; general appeal to make process of government and administration cheaper and more effective.

Government Corruption
Need to eliminate corruption in government, and associated abuse, e.g., regulation of campaign expenses; need to check pandering to selfish interests.

Government Effectiveness and Authority
This includes references to government stability, especially in Italy.

Domain 4: Economy

Enterprise
Favorable mention of private property rights; personal enterprise and initiative; need for the economy of unhampered individual enterprise; favorable mention of free enterprise capitalism; superiority of individual enterprise over state, and over state buying or management systems.

Incentives
Need for financial and other incentives and for opportunities for the young, etc.; encouragement to small businesses and one-man shops; need for wage and tax policies designed to induce enterprise; Home Ownership.

Regulation of Capitalism
Need for regulations designed to make private enterprise work better; actions against monopolies and trusts and in defense of consumer and small businessmen; anti-profiteering.

Economic Planning
Favorable mention of central planning of consultative or indicative nature; need for this and for government department to create national plan; need to plan imports and exports.

Corporatism (Applicable to the Netherlands and Canada only)
Favorable mentions of the need for the involvement of employers and Trade Union organizations in overall economic planning and direction through the medium of "tripartite" bodies such as the SER in the Netherlands.

Protectionism: Positive
Favorable mention of extension or maintenance of tariffs, to protect internal markets; or other domestic economic protectionism.

Protectionism: Negative
Same as preceding, but negative.

Economic Goals
General statements of intent to pursue any economic goals that are policy nonspecific.

Keynesian Demand Management
Adjusting government expenditure to prevailing levels of employment and inflation.

Productivity
Need to encourage or facilitate greater production, need to take measures to aid this, appeal for greater production, and importance of productivity to the economy; increase foreign trade; special aid to specific sectors of the economy; growth; active manpower policy; aid to agriculture, tourism, and industry.

Technology and Infrastructure
Importance of modernizing industrial administration, importance of science and technological developments in industry; need for training and government sponsored research; need for overhaul of capital equipment, and methods of communication and transport (including Merchant Marine); development of Nuclear Energy.

Controlled Economy
General need for direct government control of economy; control over prices, wages, rents, etc. This covers *neither* Nationalization *nor* Indicative planning.

Nationalization
Government ownership and control, partial or complete, including government ownership of land.

Economic Orthodoxy and Efficiency
Need for traditional economic orthodoxy, e.g., balanced budget, retrenchment in crisis, low taxation, thrift and savings; support for traditional economic institutions such as the Stock Market and banking system; support for strong currency internationally.

Domain 5: Welfare and Quality of Life

Environmental Protection
Preservation of countryside, forests, etc.; general preservation of natural resources against selfish interests; proper use of national parks; soil banks, etc.

Art, Sport, Leisure, and Media
Favorable mention of leisure activities, need to spend money on museums, art galleries, etc.; need to encourage worthwhile leisure activities, and to provide cultural and leisure facilities; to encourage development of the media, etc.

Social Justice
Need for fair treatment of all men; for special protection for exploited; fair treatment in tax system; need for equality of opportunity; need for fair distribution of resources and removal of class barriers; end of discrimination.

Social Services Expansion: Positive
Favorable mention of need to maintain or expand any basic service or welfare scheme; support for free basic social services such as public health, or housing (excludes education).

Social Services Expansion: Negative
Same as preceding, but negative.

Education: Pro-Expansion
The need to expand and/or improve education provision at all levels (exclusive of technical training, fitted under Technology and Infrastructure, above).

Education: Anti-Expansion
Same as preceding, but negative.

Domain 6: Fabric of Society

Defense of National Way of Life: Positive
Favorable mentions of importance of defense against subversion, necessary suspension of some freedoms in order to defend this; support of national ideas, traditions, and institutions.

Defense of National Way of Life: Negative
Same as preceding, but negative.

Traditional Morality: Positive
Favorable mention of, e.g., prohibition, censorship, suppression of immorality and unseemly behavior; maintenance and stability of family.

Traditional Morality: Negative
Same as preceding, but negative.

Law and Order
Enforcement of all laws; actions against organized crime; putting down urban violence; support and resources for police; tougher attitudes in courts, etc.

National Effort/Social Harmony
Appeal for national effort and solidarity; need for nation to see itself as united; appeal for public-spiritedness; decrying anti-social attitudes in a time of crisis; support for public interest; national interest; bipartisanship.

Communalism, Pluralism, Pillarization: Positive
Preservation of autonomy of religious, ethnic, linguistic heritages within the country. Preservation and/or expansion of schools with a specific religious orientation.

Communalism, Pluralism, Pillarization: Negative
Same as preceding, but negative.

Domain 7: Social Groups

Labor Groups: Positive
Favorable references to Labor, working class, unemployed, poor; support for Labor Unions, free collective bargaining, good treatment of manual and other employees.

Labor Groups: Negative
Same as preceding, but negative.

Agriculture and Farmers
Support for agriculture, farmers; any policy aimed specifically at benefiting these.

Other Economic Groups
Favorable references to any Economically defined group not covered above (Labor; Agriculture). For example, employers, self-employed, middle-class, and professional groups in general.

Underprivileged Minority Groups
Favorable references to underprivileged minorities who are defined neither in economic nor in demographic terms, e.g., the handicapped, homosexuals, etc.

Noneconomic Demographic Groups
Favorable mentions of, or need for, assistance to Women, Old People, Young People, linguistic groups and national minorities; special interest groups of all kinds.

NOTES

1. Adapted from Budge, Robertson, and Hearl (1987), Appendix B, pp. 456–467. The titles of the actual party program documents for the years up to the early 1980s are contained in Budge, Robertson, and Hearl (1987, Appendix A). For those, plus updates through the early 1990s, see Volkens (1992).

Appendix B: Special Methodological Considerations

The order of our concerns here puts us in an unusual methodological position.[1] The election programs are a formalization by collective elites of their policy intentions. Thus the documents are clues to future events—events guided by the intentions which the documents reflect. We are interested in *signaling* or *congruence,* not in *causation.* That is, we are more concerned to trace out the forecasts from a set of independent variables than we are to account fully for the variance in a set of dependent variables. This reverses the common scientific focus on the dependent variable. However, we find talk of dependent and independent variables itself out of place, given that the political process is a system, by which we mean at a minimum that it is a complex of moving parts, all of which affect and are affected by one another. No one element is a primordial cause of any other in such a continuous process.

All versions of regression analysis are statistical devices designed to help us find out how much variation in one or more independent conditions are associated with another condition we consider as the dependent condition. In our case, the independent conditions are the party program emphases, and the dependent conditions are expenditure shares. The very language of dependence and independence, however, suggests causation. But there are other reasons for wanting to know how well one set of conditions forecasts another. Moreover, that knowledge can be useful even without assuming that a deliberate change in the measured independent variables would of itself produce a predictable change in the dependent variables.

To understand why people stop at an intersection with a stop-light system, it is enough to know whether the light is red or green. The color of the light is the independent variable. The stopping or going is the dependent variable. But does the red light *cause* the cars to stop? Or is it the registration of the red on the retina of the drivers? Or was it the city ordinance passed by the city council that caused the drivers to stop? Or was it the drivers' manual that all drivers study? Or was the *cause* the foot that pushed the pedal that activated the disk pad that pushed against the disk that … ? Causation is a tricky concept—a fact that is sometimes forgotten by statistical aficionados who gain undue confidence in their techniques at the expense of the logic of the things they are trying to observe in the real world.

We can risk one more metaphor. Riders know that a nervous or unhappy horse lays back its ears, which can be a prelude to misbehavior. The rider's behavior can be appropriately modified upon observing laid-back ears. And that change in rider's behavior need not always include full knowledge of the source of the horse's unhappiness. But the appropriate behavioral modification is most assuredly not to push the horse's ears forward. Likewise, if someone sneaked into party headquarters and changed the original copy of the text of a party program, it is unlikely such an act would have much policy consequence.

For one who is indeed interested in primal causes, the amendment of which is sure to yield predictable changes in the value of dependent variables (the source of unhappiness and the means for its elimination), there are several features of the statistical association that give hints of things not yet included in the equation. And if one wishes to intervene for some desired end, it is necessary to identify malleable elements of the system that are susceptible to deliberate manipulation and promise to have predictable, independent effects.

But causal language sometimes confuses more than it helps understanding. Such has been the history of the (essentially epistemologically nonsensical) debate over whether politics or economics is more important as a determinant of policy. A test of mandate theory does not require a demonstration of causation between party program emphases and policy products. It need only demonstrate that the pronouncements of the parties are available and project what the parties later do. That is, first, we want to see how much the set of programs has forecast the contours of policy over time, and, second, we want to see to what extent the *choice* posed by the competing programs forecast differences in policy, depending on who got into government.

In any regression analyses, there are confounding considerations that can disguise "true causation." And when the observations are successive over time, these are especially tricky to spot. However, a series of statistical tools is available to help the search for causation by checking for the presence of such confounding factors. Although our purpose here is not such a search for causation, the manner in which we have organized and analyzed the data needs discussion, and consideration needs to be given to our logic in those instances where we have not employed some of the diagnostic and data "cleansing" techniques often employed in time-series analysis. In particular, we need to discuss: (1) exogenous, socioeconomic influences on policy priorities; and, (2) several time-series analytic techniques, including our exclusion of prior policy values from the equations ("endogenous dependent variables"), de-trending, autocorrelation, and tests of significance.

EXOGENOUS SOCIOECONOMIC INFLUENCES ON POLICY

It could be argued, in classic terms of "which is more important—society or politics?" that parties write their programs and enjoy their mandates because of certain objective conditions or problems of the time and place. The framework we present in Chapter 1 recognizes this explicitly. Mandate theory most assuredly does not rest on a demonstration that party programmatic emphases are independent of the economic or demographic context. The programs of governing parties may anticipate changes in education-spending priorities, as has been found to be strikingly the case in the United States (Budge and Hofferbert 1990). But it might also be demonstrated that spending shares for education are statistically very strongly related to the proportion of the population between the ages of five and twenty, a society-to-policy linkage that hardly requires complex explanation. Moreover, the linkage between emphases on social justice in the party programs and subsequent priorities for health policy may be shown to be "spurious" when one controls statistically for the aging of the population.

Far from accepting such potential evidence of antecedent or primal factors as diminishing the impact of the party mandate, however, we would see it as an indication of parties' responsiveness to the society around them and of their relative ability and commitment to follow through on that agenda. In fact, the variation in the tightness of this fit might well be used, in future research, as a rather good measure of political responsiveness. The tighter the fit of "exogenous" circumstances to the party agenda, the more responsive the party to its social calling. Likewise, the more snug the fit of the agenda to policy products, the more accountable the party to its mandate. It is in this very sense that parties may be considered *mediating* institutions. To "control" for the effect of socioeconomic circumstances on the party agenda, while trying to assess the latter's "nonspurious" impact on later policy, would be to use statistical gadgetry to argue that party programs are most appropriately written in a vacuum.

This is clearly not the case. Without considering general societal influences further, we focus on the crucial political linkage that is necessary to test for party program reflections on the policy agenda, and if it is absent, we need no longer concern ourselves with it. That is, the connection between some programmatic emphases and some of the policy product is the central linkage. If we find some prima facie important connections, then future research on broader systemic processes will be well advised to take account of our findings.

ENDOGENOUS VARIABLES

The question may also be raised of why we do not include in our analyses a lagged endogenous variable, that is, the cumulative effect of past spending shares on current percentages. Technically, this means that in order to explain the percentage of spending for a particular policy area in a certain year we would have included the same policy's share in the previous year. That is, each year's spending percentage—our "dependent variable"—would be an "independent variable" the next year. This is designed to control for the incremental nature of changes in a time series. Again, if one were interested in a specific causal linkage, in some strict sense, a case might be made for such controls. Certainly the current level of spending on a particular public function is a major element in planning the coming year's allocation. An analogy might be made to testing the impact of an experimental medicine. The effects of a medicine cannot be adequately assessed without controlling for the before-and-after magnitude of, and trend in, the condition it is designed to treat. Although the human body is a system, the theory of medicine is eminently bivariate and causal. Politics is a system and policies are designed to be medicinal. In those instances, trials should likewise account for the magnitude and trend of prior conditions.

But our concerns here are, again, not causal in the medicinal sense. Rather, they are with the signaling capacity of our independent variables, not unlike some physiological symptom that may itself be an early-warning signal. The elimination or amendment of such a signal will have in itself no curative impact on the onset of the disease for which it serves as a precursor. The mandate is essentially a mechanism by which voters have available a set of alternative signals that may be harbingers of alternative future actions. Testing the clarity of that signaling would be confused by incorporation of past policy indicators or multiple lagged program variables. (See King et al. 1993, for a more technical consideration of this point.)

DE-TRENDING

Time-series analysis always confronts the question of whether to de-trend and also how to deal with potential autocorrelation. We do not follow a "standard" set of procedures, for both substantive and technical reasons. De-trending is designed to remove the effect of common time trends. Thus, if emphases of party programs and expenditure priorities on, for example, environmental matters are both rising, de-trending removes that joint upward slope, leaving the variance to be accounted for to be that which is time independent. We do not do this to the data.

The logic is akin to that which we pursued above in discussing the hypothesized linkage between antecedent socioeconomic conditions, party program emphases, and expenditures. The difference here is that a time trend is taken to incorporate a host of unmeasured prior causal conditions that could be jointly affecting both programmatic emphases and spending priorities. De-trending would remove any "contamination" such as responsiveness of parties to their social contexts, although with a time trend, unlike a specified causal model (for example, incorporating demographic composition as a causal factor that determines education's shares of party election programs and of expenditures), contextual circumstances are merely taken as subsumed in the trends. We find useful an analogy to physical training. The more one trains, the faster one can run. There is a high time-series correlation between training and speed. Control for time, however, and the relationship disappears, suggesting no "true" relationship between training and speed.

De-trending is appropriate only when (1) one has no idea what is responsible for the longitudinal relationship or (2) when there is a specific known but unmeasured and theoretically irrelevant time-associated variable affecting the dependent variable. Neither of these conditions applies to our analyses. Thus, we conduct our analyses with various models using simple, lagged annual data on party programmatic emphases regressed on percentages of public expenditures for the various functions.

AUTOCORRELATION

Tests for autocorrelation confront a related but different set of considerations. "Autocorrelation" means that the deviation of adjacent observations (in our cases, time periods one year apart) from values predicted by a model are somehow themselves related. Thus, when a least-squares line (that is, a straight line) is estimated through a curvilinear time trend, the residuals of each year are less different from the year before and from the year after than would be the case if there were no such curvilinear time trend, that is, if the residuals were randomly distributed. As with mutual trends between independent and dependent variables, autocorrelation suggests the presence of unmeasured influences in the process being modeled, influences that distort the results of the equation and that suggest other "causes."

Again, the presence of antecedent or additional influences is not at all theoretically bothersome in assessing the congruence of election programs and subsequent policy. It is a stimulant to curiosity and a challenge to more-elaborate inquiry. But it does not detract from the predictive power of the party statements, although it may reduce the numeric magnitude of statistical coefficients, again an element of conservatism in our approach.

The manner in which we organize the data, in our effort to reflect the real political world, actually guarantees a bit of autocorrelation, in that the value of adjacent independent variables—the party program indicators—are identical in many cases. Taking the British case, for example, there have been twelve elections over the period we analyze, meaning that programmatic emphases can take on a maximum of twelve different values, although there are thirty-six yearly observations. Thus, to the extent that, for example, emphases on agriculture predict agricultural spending shares—which themselves are not without some serial consistency—the residuals for 1959 through 1964 are bound to be related, since the values of the independent variables for those years are identical. It happens that 1964 was the first election after 1959 in Britain. Autocorrelation is not a fault of the method of analysis, simply a description of the real world. We must accept that our regression results will be a bit affected by these factors, but not in a manner that detracts from our use of them.

TESTS OF SIGNIFICANCE

The final technical consideration we should address is our use of tests of significance. The level of a significance test indicates the likelihood that a particular relationship will occur by chance in an infinity of random samples. We analyze data for every party program and every year's expenditure in the postwar period up through the last election for which we have data. It is a record of every case, not a sample of anything. When one has a universe of cases, tests of significance merely summarize the relative goodness of fit in a particular relationship. A test of significance on a universe of cases tells us about how much we can expect the future to look more or less like the past, if we assume that the general structure of relationships between things in the future will look something like the way they did in the past. On the basis of only three of four decades of human experience, that is a pretty heroic assumption—but it is the weakest we can make if any time-series analyses are to be taken as saying something enduring.

We use a .05 cutoff and simply indicate by parentheses around coefficients (in the full tables in the following appendix) those relationships that do not attain that level. This is our way of noting that which we accept as worth thinking about and that which it is probably a waste of time to discuss. The decimal value of a standard error would be more precise. But since we are reporting the results of dozens of equations, a presentation of so many additional statistics would be visual overkill, not to mention that it would convey a sense of precision to which we lay no claim.

These various methodological and technical conventions have all been chosen or rejected as most appropriate to the basic theoretical orientation. The decisions we have taken reflect our concern with party competition expressed as issue saliency, rather than as interparty confrontation over a common set of issues centrally relevant to all contestants. Saliency denotes a tendency of each competing party to select from the universe of issue positions those elements that are most coherent with its standing self-definition, coupled with criteria of the moment, such as electoral advantage, leadership preference, or fluid objective conditions.

The logic and mechanics of organizing the party program data according to duration of government are spelled out in detail in Chapter 3, as is the substantive justification for selecting a two-year lead for the policy indicators. Decisions about not "controlling" for social or economic conditions, de-trending, removing autocorrelation, and inserting autoregressive endogenous variables (i.e., expenditure $T_{-1} \dots T_{-n}$) all reflect our view of the party program as an aid to the process by which (1) the electorate opts for parties out of a set in which the saliency of issues of each is different from the others, and (2) the extent to which differential salience in the election program is later reflected in differential action priorities, as measured by allocation of monetary resources to various policy domains.

NOTES

1. The basic theme of this appendix is also considered in an exchange between some of the present authors (plus Michael D. McDonald), on the one hand, and Gary King and Michael Laver, on the other. That exchange revolved around the technical procedures used in Budge and Hofferbert (1990). The exchange is in King et al. (1993).

Appendix Tables

Table A5.1
Agenda: Australia, 1950 - 1988

Expenditure Area (Program Emphasis)	a	b Lib	+	b Lab	Adj. R^2
Left - Right (Left-Right)	.29	(.04)	-	(.01)	.00
Defense (Foreign Policy)	39.8	.98	+	(.29)	.31
Foreign Affairs (Foreign Policy)	2.23	-(.01)	-	(.03)	.20
Admin. of Justice (Law & Order)	1.31	(.23)	+	(.23)	.12
Agriculture (Agriculture)	3.11	-(.04)	+	.04	.23
Welfare (Social Justice)	2.02	-(.22)	+	.47	.34
Housing (Tech. & Infrastr.)	.71	-(.25)	+	(.52)	.00
Education (Education)	1.83	(.03)	+	(.09)	.09
Transportation (Tech. & Infrastr.)	2.74	(.00)	-	(.03)	.00

Note: Appendix tables are keyed to chapters, e.g., Tables A5.1, A5.2, and A5.3 supplement Chapter 5.

Table A5.2
Mandate: Australia, 1950 - 1988

Expenditure Area (Prog.) Emphasis	a	b Lib (out)	+	b (Lib x Gov)	+	b Lab (out)	+	b (Lab x Gov)	Adj R^2
Left - Right (Left-Right)	.60	-.73	+	.74	-	.03	-	.56	.13
Defense (Foreign Policy)	45.7	-1.14	+	1 .65	+	(.58)	+	(26)	.49
Foreign Affairs (Foreign Policy)	1.96	(.08)	-	(.05)	-	.07	+	(.34)	.37
Admin. of Justice (Law & Order)	1.34	.02	+	1 .01	-	1.45	+	1 .89	.32
Agriculture (Agriculture)	3.37	-(.25)	+	(.18)	-	.03	-	(.16)	.29
Welfare (Social Justice)	2.26	-(.22)	-	(.66)	+	.32	+	(.18)	.37
Housing (Tech. & Infrastr.)	.59	.09	-	.10	-	(.17)	+	.11	.41
Education (Education)	1.61	-(.09)	+	(.18)	+	(.01)	+	.36	.30
Transportation (Tech. & Infrastr.)	2.77	(.07)	-	(.07)	-	(.03)	-	(.05)	.00

Table A5.3
Ideology: Australia, 1950 - 1988

Expenditure Area (Prog.) Emphasis	a	b Lib Ch (0/1)	+ b Lib (out)	+ b (Lib x Gov)	+ b Lab (out)	+ b (Lab x Gov)	Adj. R^2
Left - Right (Left-Right)	[Unstable due to multicollinearity between Lib government 0/1 & program variables]						.31
Defense (Foreign Policy)	47.0	- (2.02)	- (1.33)	+ (1.85)	- (.58)	- (.23)	.48
Foreign Affairs (Foreign Policy)	2.00	- (.04)	+ (.07)	- (.04)	- .07	+ (.34)	.35
Admin. of Justice (Law & Order)	1.72	- (.48)	- (.05)	+ 1.41	- 1.31	+ 1.68	.33
Agriculture (Agriculture)	3.37	(.00)	- (.25)	+ (.18)	+ .03	- (.16)	.24
Welfare (Social Justice)	4.95	- 3.05	- 1.02	+ (.39)	+ .40	- (.21)	.52
Housing (Tech. & Infrastr.)	1.12	.68	+ (.04)	- (.04)	+ (.01)	+ (.01)	.52
Education (Education)	.82	(.95)	+ (.08)	+ (.01)	+ (.00)	+ .42	.32
Transportation (Tech. & Infrastr.)	3.72	- 1.19	- (.02)	+ (.04)	- .01	- .22	.17

Table A6.1
Agenda: Canada, 1950 – 1988

Expenditure Area (Program Emphasis)	a	b PgC*		b Lib		b NDP	Adj R^2
Left – Right (Left–Right)	2.57	.08	+	(.03)	–	(.08)	.62
Defense (Spec. For. Rel's)	7.59	4.52	+	1.44	+	8.12	.64
Foreign Affairs (Spec. For. Rel's)	1.76	.68	–	(.01)	–	.42	.32
Admin. of Justice (Law & Order)	1.88	–(.26)	–	.28		**	.33
Agriculture (Agriculture)	3.67	.03	+	(.03)	–	.23	.16
Welfare (Social Services)	5.04	–.36	+	(.02)	+	(.00)	.10
Health (Social Services)	7.30	–.77	+	(.01)	+	.19	.59
Social Security (Social Services)	13.3	–.41	–	(.01)	+	(.07)	.16
Education (Social Services)	3.24	–.37	–	(.01)	+	.14	.40
Transportation (Tech. & Infrastr.)	4.66	(.06)	–	.07	–	(.06)	.22
Housing (Tech. & Infrastr.)	.28	–.05	+	.06	+	(.04)	.67
Culture and Arts (Art, Sport, etc.)	.75	.02	+	.05	–	.14	.12

* PgC = Progressive Conservative Party
** No law and order emphases by the New Democratic Party (NDP)

Table A6.2
Mandate: Canada, 1950 – 1988

Expenditure Area (Program Emphasis)	a	b PgC (out) +	b (PgC x Gov) +	b Lib + (out) +	b (Lib x Gov) +	b NDP	Adj R^2
Left – Right (Left-Right)	2.47	(.02)	+ (.01)	+ .07	+ (.02)	– .08	.60
Defense (Spec. For. Rel's)	8.01	6.20	– 9.75	+ 1.73	– (.23)	+ 3.26	.69
Foreign Affairs (Spec. For. Rel's)	1.76	.69	– (.14)	– (.02)	+ (.04)	– (.44)	.29
Admin. of Justice (Law & Order)	1.86	–(.64)	+ (.71)	+ (.11)	– (.04)	*	.44
Agriculture (Agriculture)	2.05	.20	– .21	+ .27	– .26	+ .03	.57
Welfare (Social Services)	5.49	–. 51	+ .74	– .40	+ .46	+ (.01)	.16
Health (Social Services)	7.18	–.92	+ .72	– .29	+ .31	+ .23	.71
Social Security (Social Services)	13.2	–.54	+ .65	– (.27)	+ (.27)	+ .11	.25
Education (Social Services)	3.20	–.45	+ .41	– .18	+ .18	+ .16	.49
Transportation (Tech. & Infrastr.)	4.97	–(.50)	+ .27	– .28	+ .24	– (.62)	.41
Housing (Tech. & Infrastr.)	.13	–.04	– .02	+ .14	– .08	– .02	.71
Culture and Arts (Art, Sport, etc.)	.75	.13	– (.10)	+ (.03)	– (.11)	– .20	.19

* No law and order emphases by the New Democratic Party (NDP)

Table A6.3
Ideology: Canada, 1950 – 1988

Expenditure Area (Program Emphasis)	a	b PgCPM (0/1) +	b PgC (out)	b (PgC + x Gov) +	b Lib (out)	b (Lib + x Gov) +	b NDP	Adj R^2
Left – Right (Left-Right)	2.75	–.60	+ (.03)	+ (.07)	+ .12	– (.04)	– .08	.68
Defense (Spec. For. Rel's)	6.67	7.21	+ 6.88	– 14.34	+ (.95)	+ (.79)	+ 2.63	.72
Foreign Affairs (Spec. For. Rel's)	1.74	(.13)	+ .70	– (.22)	– .03	+ (.59)	– (.45)	.27
Admin. of Justice (Law & Order)	1.99	–.48	– (.62)	+ (.84)	+ .26	– (.27)	*	.59
Agriculture (Agriculture)	2.17	–(.48)	+ .19	– .20	+ .33	– .33	+ (.02)	.57
Welfare (Social Services)	5.83	–12.7	– .60	+ 1.15	+ (.52)	– (.49)	+ (.58)	.35
Health (Social Services)	7.40	–8.19	– .98	+ .98	+ (.31)	– (.31)	+ .26	.79
Social Security (Social Services)	13.4	– 10.4	– .62	+ .98	+ (.49)	– (.52)	+ .15	.40
Education (Social Services)	3.39	–6.87	– .50	+ .63	+ .32	– .34	+ .18	.64
Transportation (Tech. & Infrastr.)	5.12	–2.20	– .59	+ .36	– .15	– .20	– .89	.46
Housing (Tech. & Infrastr.)	–.56	2.70	– .03	– .13	– .19	+ .24	+ .07	.79
Culture and Arts (Art, Sport, etc.)	.76	–(.13)	+ .12	– (.08)	+ (.09)	+ (.04)	– .20	.18

* No law and order emphases by the New Democratic Party (NDP)

Table A7.1
Agenda: France, 1958 – 1988

Expenditure Area (Program Emphasis)	a	b Gaul	b Soc	b Cen	b Comm	Adj R^2
Left-Right (Left-Right)	3.40	– .06	– .02	– .04	– .10	.85
Defense (International)	18.8	3.17	+ 1.09	– (2.35)	+ 1.04	.57
Foreign Affairs (International)	3.48	1.44	+ 1.42	– .57	+ .38	.84
Admin. of Justice (Public Order)	4.70	– .21	+ .21	+ .36	– (.03)	.68
Agriculture (Agriculture)	3.08	– .35	+ .26	+ (.01)	+ .33	.47
Welfare (Social Justice)	–20.1	3.12	– 1.30	+ 1.95	+ .99	.65
Housing (Tech. & Infrastr.)	.31	.44	+ 2.06	– .62	+ 1.18	.67
Education (Social Justice)	–26.4	4.60	– .62	+ 2.80	+ .15	.88
Culture (Art, Sport, etc)	4.62	.72	+ .25	+ (04)	– 1.35	.83
Tran. & Commun. (Tech. & Infrastr.)	3.19	–(.02)	– (.16)	+ .16	+ .58	.22

Table A7.2
Mandate: France, 1958 – 1988

Expenditure. Area (Program Emphasis)	a	b Gaul (out)	b (Gaul x Prs)	b Soc (out)	b (Soc x Prs)	b Cen (out)	b (Cen x Prs)	b Comm (out)	Adj R2
Left-Right (Left-Right)	3.6	– .06	+ (.00)	– .03	– .04	– .09	+ .66	– .09	.92
Defense (International)	20.9	4.46	+ (.31)	+ (.23)	– 5.93	– 2.85	+ (.00)	+ 1.72	.82
Foreign Affairs (International)	5.7	3.84	– 1.43	+ (.22)	– 1.75	– 2.11	[Zeroed out]		.89
Admin. of Justice (Public Order)		[Multicollinearity]							
Agriculture (Agriculture)	3.6	(1.95)	– (2.23)	+ .22	– (6.12)	– (.01)	–(2.25)	+ (.17)	.43
Welfare (Social Justice)	–19.6	12.3	– 9.13	– .63	– 9.63	+ 1.88	– 5.50	+ .17	.91
Housing (Tech. & Infrastr.)	9.5	.49	+ (.55)	+ 3.62	+ 3.24	– .86	+ (.11)	+ 3.82	.79
Education (Social Justice)	–21.1	(5.51)	– (1.46)	– .60	– 1.81	+ 2.33	– .75	+ .25	.88
Culture (Art, Sport, etc)	–4.4	(.17)	+ (.98)	+ .56	+ (.01)	+ (.18)	+ 1.12	+ 1.70	.91
Tran. & Commun. (Tech. & Infrastr.)	11.2	(.14)	+ (.05)	– 1.51	– 2.44	+ .39	– (.03)	– 1.56	.81

Table A7.3
Ideology: France, 1958 – 1988

a	b Gaul Prs (0/1) +	b Gaul (out) +	b (Gaul x Prs)+	b Soc (out) +	b (Soc x Prs) +	b Cen (out) +	b (Cen x Prs) +	b Comm	Adj R^2

[All models failed to run due to multicollinearity with Gaul Prs]

Table A8.1
Agenda: United States, 1948 - 1990

Expenditure Area (Program Emphasis)	a	b Rep	+	b Dem	Adj. R^2
Left-Right (Left-Right)	-.29	-(.01)	-	-(.01)	.00
Defense (Spec. For. Rel's)	36.2	-3.45	+	5.91	.40
Foreign Affairs (Spec. For. Rel's)	2.78	-.26	+	.37	.19
Admin. of Justice (Law & Order)	.41	(.01)	+	.05	.80
Agriculture (Agriculture)	1.27	.11	+	(.13)	.28
Social Security (Social Justice)	17.6	-4.03	+	1.13	.44
Welfare (Social Justice)	11.2	-1.47	+	(.43)	.14
Health & Medicare (Social Justice)	6.53	-1.83	+	(.41)	.15
Education (Education)	-.44	.14	+	.94	.52
Transportation (Tech. & Infrastr.)	2.91	.12	-	(.03)	.10
Energy (Tech. & Infrastr.)	.94	.12	-	.11	.39
Commerce & Housing (Tech. & Infrastr.)	1.66	(.01)	-	(.07)	.03
Comm. & Reg'al Dev't (Tech. & Infrastr.)	.90	.19	-	.13	.46
Environ. Protect. (Environ. Protect.)	1.76	.12	-	.07	.26

Table A8.2
Mandate: United States, 1948 - 1990

Expenditure Area (Program Emphasis)	a	b Rep	+ b (Rep x Pr)	+ b Dem	+ b (Dem x Pr)	Adj R^2
Left-Right (Left-Right)	.23	-(.02)	- (.01)	+ (.02)	- (.02)	.00
Defense (Spec. For. Rel's)	46.9	-8.70	+ 6.54	+ (.85)	+ 8.00	.48
Foreign Affairs (Spec. For. Rel's)	3.59	-.57	+ (.41)	- (.07)	+ .60	.21
Admin. of Justice (Law & Order)	.40	-(.00)	+ .09	- (.03)	+ .08	.84
Agriculture (Agriculture)	1.33	(.32)	- (.22)	+ .12	- (.16)	.26
Social Security (Social Justice)	19.9	-6.35	+ 4.12	- (.16)	+ (.16)	.55
Welfare (Social Justice)	13.1	-2.64	+ 1.61	- (.11)	- 1.52	.29
Health & Medicare (Social Justice)	8.43	-3.00	+(1.60)	- (.19)	- (1.55)	.24
Education (Education)	.20	-(.02)	+ .48	+ .61	+ .52	.87
Transportation (Tech. & Infrastr.)	2.42	(.09)	+ (.16)	- .09	+ .23	.32
Energy (Tech. & Infrastr.)	.84	.21	- .11	- .09	- (.02)	.55
Commerce & Housing (Tech. & Infrastr.)	1.58	-(.06)	+ (.13)	- .11	+ (.08)	.01
Comm. & Reg'al Dev't (Tech. & Infrastr.)	.66	.17	+ (.08)	- .16	+ .11	.54
Environ. Protect. (Environ. Protect.)	1.69	-(.01)	+ .16	- .09	+ .15	.34

Table A8.3
Ideology: United States,1948 - 1990

Expenditure Area (Program Emphasis)	a	b Rep Pr (0/1)	+ b Rep	+ b (Rep x Pr)	+ b Dem	+ b (Dem x Pr)	Adj R^2
Left-Right (Left-Right)	-6.9	7.57)	- (.01)	+ (.00)-	(.03)	+ (.39)	.11
Defense (Spec. For. Rel's)	48.5	-(9.86)	- 9.04	+ 6.74 +	(3.46)	+(5.39)	.47
Foreign Affairs (Spec. For. Rel's)	4.09	-(3.14)	- .68	+ .47 +	(.76)	- (.23)	.43
Admin. of Justice (Law & Order)	.38	(.03)	+ (.00)	- (.02)+	.08	+ .07	.84
Agriculture (Agriculture)	1.43	-(.18)	+ (.33)	- (.22)+	(.12)	- (.19)	.24
Social Security (Social Justice)	20.1	-(.24)	- 6.42	+ 4.19 -	(.15)	+ (.05)	.54
Welfare (Social Justice)	12.3	(1.01)	- 2.31	+(1.28)-	(.16)	-(1.10)	.28
Health & Medicare (Social Justice)	11.5	-(4.11)	- 4.32	+ 2.95 +	(.10)	- 3.27	.27
Education (Education)	.51	-2.18	- .09	+ .49 +	.99	- (.01)	.92
Transportation (Tech. & Infrastr.)	.55	2.60	+ .09	+ (.10)-	.14	+ .60	.64
Energy (Tech. & Infrastr.)	1.22	-.52	+ .21	- .10 -	.08	- (.08)	.58
Commerce & Housing (Tech. & Infrastr.)	1.44	(.20)	- (.06)	+ (.12)-	.11	+ .11	.00
Comm. & Reg'al Dev't (Tech. & Infrastr.)	.09	.79	+ .17	+ (.06)-	.17	+ .22	.58
Environ. Protect. (Environ. Protect.)	1.85	-.46	- (.01)	+ .19 -	.06	+ (.09)	.40

Table A9.1
Agenda: Sweden, 1948 - 1990

Expenditure Area (Program Emphasis)	a	b SDP	+ b Lib	+ b Cen	+ b Con	+ b Com	Adj. R^2
Left-Right (Left-Right)	.14	-(.10)	+ .02	+ (.00)	+ .03	+ (.02)	.71
Defense (Peace)	17.3	-1.34	+ .75	- (.33)	+ (.57)	+ .33	.58
Foreign Affairs (Peace)	1.60	.19	- (.14)	+ (.22)	+ (.10)	+ .07	.54
Admin. of Justice (Law & Order)	2.00	(.01)	- .21	+ .60	+ .16	+ (.03)	.68
Agriculture (Agriculture)	3.64	(.03)	+ .98	- (.04)	- (.02)	- 1.80	.57
Soc.Sec. & Soc.Serv's (Social Services)	31.0	-(.04)	+ .09	+ .14	- (.05)	- .11	.38
Education & Culture (Education)	16.2	-(.14)	- (.13)	+ (.17)	- .23	+ (.04)	.09
Transp.& Communica's (Tech. & Infrastr.)	6.25	(.19)	- (.37)	+ .61	+ (.44)	+ (.10)	.25

Table A9.2
Mandate: Sweden, 1948 - 1987

Expenditure Area (Program Emphasis)	a	b SDP	+ b (SDPxGv)	+ b Lib	+ b (LibxGv)	+ b Cen	+ b (CenxGv)	+ b Con	+ b (ConxGv)	+ b Com	Adj R^2
Left-Right (Left-Right)	.32	-(.07)	+ (.06)	+ .02	+ (.04)	+ (.00)	+ (.01)	+ .02	+ (.01)	+ (.02)	.68
Defense (Peace)	17.1	-(.01)	- (.92)	+ 1.12	-(12.9)	- (.95)	+(2.30)	+ (.50)	-(1.44)	+ (.16)	.55
Foreign Affairs (Peace)	1.62	-(.09)	(.30)	- .20	+ 2.72	+ (.21)	+ (.38)	+ (.10)	+ (.31)	+ (.04)	.52
Admin. of Justice (Law & Order)	2.09	-(.06)	+ (.06)	- .23	+ .95	+ .57	- (.33)	+ .18	+ (.12)	+ (.01)	.64
Agriculture (Agriculture)	3.90	(.11)	+ (.00)	+ 1.20	+ (.00)	- (.08)	- .10	- (.03)	+ (.55)	- (.66)	.69
Soc.Sec. & Soc.Serv's (Social Services)	31.7	-.45	+ .38	+ .07	+ .29	+ .18	+ (.00)	+ (.03)	+ (.00)	- .15	.59
Education & Culture (Education)	16.2	(.67)	- .90	-+ (.25)	- (.09)	+ .22	- .47	- .37	+ (.09)	- (.17)	.56
Transp.& Communica's (Tech. & Infrastr.)	7.04	-(6.14)	+(6.76)	- (.58)	+(12.4)	+ (.38)	- (.09)	+ (.29)	+ (.00)	+ (.02)	.27

Table A9.3
Ideology: Sweden, 1950 - 1987

Expenditure Area (Program Emphasis)	a	b SDP PM (Dum)	+ b SDP	+ b (SDP•Gv)	+ b Lib	+ b (LibxGv)	b Cen	+ b (CenxGv)	+ b Con	+ b (ConxGv)	+ b Com	Adj R^2
Left-Right (Left-Right)	-.41	(.73)	- (.00)	- (.01)	+ .02	+ (.03)	+ (.00)	+ (.01)	+ .03	+ (.01)	+ (.02)	.67
Defense (Peace)	2.45	(14.6)	+ (.64)	-(1.57)	+(1.12)	+ (.00)	- (.95)	+(2.30)	+ (.50)	-(1.44)	+ (.16)	.54
Foreign Affairs (Peace)	4.70	-(3.08)	- (.22)	+ (.43)	- (.20)	+ (.00)	+ (.21)	- (.38)	+ (.10)	+ (.33)	- (.04)	.50
Admin. of Justice (Law & Order)	1.58	(.51)	+ (.11)	- (.12)	- .23	+ (.25)	+ .57	- (.33)	+ .18	+ (.12)	+ (.01)	.63
Agriculture (Agriculture)	4.09	-(.18)	+ (.12)	+ (.00)	+ 1.21	+ (.00)	- (.09)	- .10	- (.03)	+ (.45)	- (.60)	.68
Soc.Sec. & Soc.Serv's (Social Services)	28.9	(2.79)	- (.17)	+ (.10)	+ .07	+ (.17)	+ .18	+ (.00)	+ (.03)	+ (.00)	- .15	.57
Education & Culture (Education)	8.77	(7.47)	+(3.25)	-(3.47)	+ (.25)	+ (.00)	+ .22	- .47	- .36	+ (.09)	- .17	.55
Transp.& Communica's (Tech. & Infrastr.)	4.95	(2.10)	+ (.39)	+ (.24)	- (.58)	+ (.00)	+ (.38)	- (.09)	+ .29	+ (.00)	+ (.02)	.25

Table A10.1
Agenda: Austria, 1951 - 1988

Expenditure Area (Program Emphasis)	a	b ÖVP	+	b SPÖ	+	b FPÖ	Adj. R^2
Left-Right (Left-Right)	22.4	-(.02)	-	(.05)	-	.07	.20
Defense (Internationalism)	5.44	(.09)	-	.42	-	(.06)	.10
Foreign Affairs (Peace + Int'ism)	.35	(.01)	+	.01	+	(.00)	.12
Admin. of Justice (Law & Order)	5.84	-(.18)	-	.30	-	.19	.38
Agriculture (Agriculture)	1.73	(.05)	+	(.05)	-	(.05)	.00
Social Security (Social Justice)	14.2	-(.17)	-	-(.19)	-	.59	.27
Family Ass't (Social Justice)	8.09	-.29	+	.35	+	(.12)	.31
Education (Education)	9.49	(.00)	-	.09	-	(.06)	.21
Public Utilities (Tech. & Infrastr.)	.14	-(.05)	+	.05	+	.06	.26
Culture and Arts (Art, Sport, etc.)	.09	.03	-	(.02)	+	.06	.24

Table A10.2
Mandate: Austria, 1951 - 1988

Expenditure Area (Program Emphasis)	a	b ÖVP (out)	+	b (ÖVP x Gov)	+	b SPÖ (out)	+	b (SPÖ x Gov)	+	b FPÖ (out)	+	b (FPÖ x Gov)	Adj R^2
Left-Right (Left-Right)	20.5	(.00)	+	(.05)	+	(.18)	-	(.04)	-	.10	+	.27	.35
Defense (Internationalism)	6.70	-(.14)	+	(.21)	-	.58	+	(.09)	-	(.14)	-	1.02	.17
Foreign Affairs (Peace + Int'ism)	.41	(.00)	+	(.01)	+	.02	-	.02	+	(.00)	+	(.02)	.60
Admin. of Justice (Law & Order)	5.25	-.80	+	2.53	-	(.21)	-	(.10)	+	(.08)	+	(.05)	.76
Agriculture (Agriculture)	2.12	-(.06)	+	.16	-	(.02)	+	(.04)	-	(.03)	-	(.11)	.32
Social Security (Social Justice)	11.8	.67	-	.63	-	(.05)	-	(.08)	-	.76	-	(.41)	.36
Family Ass't (Social Justice)	12.4	-1.06	+	(.36)	+	.19	-	.28	+	.32	+	(.02)	.72
Education (Education)	9.61	(.07)	+	(.11)	-	.17	-	.25	+	(.12)	+	(.21)	.59
Public Utilities (Tech. & Infrastr.)	.47	-.02	+	(.02)	+	(.02)	+	.05	+	(.00)	+	.39	.96
Culture and Arts (Art, Sport, etc.)	.17	(.01)	+	.02	+	(.00)	-	.07	+	.05	-	(.01)	.82

Table A10.3
Ideology: Austria, 1951 - 1988

Expenditure Area (Program Emphasis)	a	b ÖVP Ch (0/1)		b ÖVP (out)		b (ÖVP x Gov)		b SPÖ (out)		b (SPÖ x Gov)		b FPÖ (out)		b (FPÖ x Gov)	Adj R^2
Left-Right (Left-Right)	21.2	-11.7	-	(.01)	+	.07	+	.92	-	.82	-	.13	+	.28	.42
Defense (Internationalism)	4.72	3.62	-	(.16)	+	(.18)	-	.98	+	.95	-	(.11)	-	(.40)	.38
Foreign Affairs (Peace + Int'ism)	.42	-(.04)	+	(.00)	+	.02	+	(.00)	+	(.01)	-	.03	+	(.01)	.60
Admin. of Justice (Law & Order)	2.06	4.28	+	1.53	-	(.42)	-	.36	+	.84	-	.35	-	.27	.88
Agriculture (Agriculture)	.95	1.85	+	(.03)	+	(.01)	-	(.10)	+	.25	-	(.05)	+	(.04)	.51
Social Security (Social Justice)	21.6	-11.8	-	(.74)	+	(.93)	+	(.07)	-	.65	-	.77	-	(.21)	.46
Family Ass't (Social Justice)	3.06	11.2	+	(.28)	-	1.12	+	(.09)	+	(.27)	+	.33	-	(.17)	.81
Education (Education)	9.56	(.05)	+	(.07)	+	(.12)	-	.17	-	(.23)	+	(.11)	+	(.20)	.58
Public Utilities (Tech. & Infrastr.)	.79	-(.03)	+	(.03)	+	(.03)	+	(.01)	+	(.04)	+	(.00)	+	.33	.95
Culture and Arts (Art, Sport, etc.)	.08	.30	+	(.01)	-	(.01)	-	.02	+	(.00)	+	.02	-	(.01)	.89

Table A11.1
Agenda: West Germany, 1950 - 1988

Expenditure Area (Program Emphasis)	a	b CDU	+	b SPD	+	b FDP	Adj. R^2
Left - Right (Left-Right)	.42	(.00)	+	-(.03)	+	-(.09)	.00
Defense (Foreign Policy)	30.0	(.07)	-	(.11)	-	.49	.19
Foreign Affairs (Foreign Policy)	.07	-(.01)	+	(.02)	+	.23	.77
Admin. of Justice (Law & Order)	.60	(.03)	-	(.01)	+	(.04)	.14
Agriculture (Agriculture)	-.05	.24	+	.37	+	.41	.48
Welfare (Soc. Just. & Serv's)	31.5	(.19)	+	(.30)	-	.69	.17
Health (Soc. Just. & Serv's)	-.06	(.00)	+	(.04)	+	(.03)	.07
Education (Education)	2.17	(.19)	+	(.10)	+	(.05)	.12
Transportation (Tech. & Infrastr.)	2.88	.18	+	.26	-	.12	.55
Energy, Water, Gas (Tech. & Infrastr.)	2.52	(.03)	+	(.01)	-	.04	.03
Housing & Comm.Dev't (Tech. & Infrastr.)	4.86	-(.07)	-	.24	-	(.01)	.36
Culture and Arts (Art, Sport, etc.)	.11	(.00)	-	.01	-	.03	.05

Table A11.2
Mandate: West Germany, 1950 - 1988

Expenditure Area (Program Emphasis)	a	b CDU (out)	b (CDU x Gov)	b SPD (out)	b (SPD x Gov)	b FDP (out)	b (FDP x Gov)	Adj R^2
Left - Right (Left-Right)	.09	-.02	+ .16	- .04	- (.08)	- (.59)	+ .58	.80
Defense (Foreign Policy)	27.5	-(.13)	+ .01	+ (.30)	- (.35)	+ (.19)	- .52	.55
Foreign Affairs (Foreign Policy)	.29	-(.10)	- (.01)	- (.01)	+ (.04)	+ .24	- (.02)	.79
Admin. of Justice (Law & Order)	.61	.05	- .05	- (.07)	+ (.06)	+ (.02)	+ (.00)	.17
Agriculture (Agriculture)	.23	.22	- (.38)	+ .50	- (.17)	+ .40	- (.05)	.60
Welfare (Soc. Just. & Serv's)	32.9	(.50)	- .87	+ .62	- .71	- .97	+ (.38)	.35
Health (Soc. Just. & Serv's)	.21	(.03)	+ (.00)	- .02	+ .04	+ (.00)	- (.01)	.87
Education (Education)	2.17	.47	- .74	- (.03)	- (.02)	+ (.11)	+ (.05)	.48
Transportation (Tech. & Infrastr.)	3.67	(.19)	- (.04)	+ .16	+ (.01)	+ (.08)	- (.20)	.56
Energy, Water, Gas (Tech. & Infrastr.)	2.46	-(.04)	+ (.11)	+ (.03)	+ (.09)	- .33	+ .24	.09
Housing & Comm.Dev't (Tech. & Infrastr.)	5.07	-(.02)	+ (.00)	- .25	- (.07)	+ (.22)	+ (.27)	.41
Culture and Arts (Art, Sport, etc.)	.09	(.00)	+ (.00)	+ (.00)	- (.01)	+ .03	- .03	.23

Table A11.3
Ideology: West Germany, 1950 - 1988

Expenditure Area (Program Emphasis)	a	b CDU Ch (0/1)	b CDU (out)	b (CDU x Gov)	b SPD (out)	b (SPD x Gov)	b FDP (out)	b (FDP x Gov)	Adj R^2
Left - Right (Left-Right)	1.69	-2.45	- .04	+ .08	- (.01)	- .14	- 1.86	+ 1.86	.90
Defense (Foreign Policy)	74.2	-46.8	- 2.12	+ 2.19	+ .35	- .93	- (.03)	- .66	.60
Foreign Affairs (Foreign Policy)	-1.6	1.94	+ (.07)	- (.10)	- (.01)	+ (.06)	+ .25	- (.01)	.79
Admin. of Justice (Law & Order)	.43	(.19)	+ (.14)	- (.14)	- (.08)	+ (.04)	+ (.17)	+ (.00)	.16
Agriculture (Agriculture)	-.36	1.64	+ (.14)	- (.02)	+ .40	- (.10)	+ .33	+ (.04)	.63
Welfare (Soc. Just. & Serv's)	-71.6	101.5	+ 8.52	- 9.00	+ .83	- .36	- .90	+ .51	.63
Health (Soc. Just. & Serv's)	5.46	-5.10	- .38	+ .41	- .03	+ .02	+ (.00)	- (.02)	.94
Education (Education)	4.03	-(1.93)	- (.11)	+ (.27)	- (.01)	+ (.00)	+ (.10)	+ (.00)	.48
Transportation (Tech. & Infrastr.)	7.66	-6.51	+ (.15)	+ (.18)	+ .32	- .44	+ .85	- 1.02	.72
Energy, Water, Gas (Tech. & Infrastr.)	1.82	(1.05)	- (.04)	+ (.08)	+ (.00)	+ .17	- .45	+ .37	.11
Housing & Comm.Dev't (Tech. & Infrastr.)	1.16	6.37	+ (.02)	- (.22)	- .41	+ .36	- (.53)	+ (.54)	.59
Culture and Arts (Art, Sport, etc.)	.17	-.08	- (.01)	+ (.01)	+ (.00)	- .02	+ .04	- .05	.34

Table A12.1
Agenda: The Netherlands, 1949 - 1988

Expenditure Area (Program Emphasis)	a	b PvdA	+ b VVD	+ b CDA*	Adj R^2
Left-Right (Left-Right)	-.35	(.02)	+ .03	+ .03	.52
Defense (Foreign +)	21.9	-(.17)	- 2.19	+ 1.06	.62
Foreign Affairs (Spec. For. Rel's)	2.66	-(.28)	- (.03)	- (.14)	.21
Public Order (Social Harmony)	1.13	(.41)	+ (.08)	+ .57	.17
Agriculture (Agriculture)	2.46	(.06)	+ .55	- .14	.06
Welfare (Social Justice)	4.61	.42	- (.05)	+ (.25)	.13
Housing (Tech. & Infrastr.)	3.46	.58	+ .48	+ (.30)	.56
Education (Education)	18.0	-.85	- (.45)	+ 1.39	.20
Trans. & Waterw'ks (Tech. & Infrastr.)	7.58	.24	+ (.17)	- (.16)	.02

* Christian Democratic Appeal (CDA) is always in government. Therefore, the "CDA" term throughout is equivalent to "CDAxGov."

Table A12.2
Mandate: The Netherlands, 1949 - 1988

Expenditure Area (Program Emphasis)	a	b PvdA (out)	+ b (PvdA x Gov)	+ b VVD (out)	+ b (VVD x Gov)	+ b CDA*	Adj R^2
Left-Right (Left-Right)	-.25	(.02)	- (.01)	+ (.01)	+ (.02)	+ .04	.51
Defense (Foreign +)	20.8	-(.29)	+ (.35)	- 2.20	+ (.34)	+ .98	.63
Foreign Affairs (Spec. For. Rel's)	2.62	-(.44)	- (.35)	+ (.05)	- .17	+ (.28)	.41
Public Order (Social Harmony)	6.14	(.40)	+ (.05)	- (.10)	+ (.36)	+ .47	.14
Agriculture (Agriculture)	2.13	-(.08)	- .77	+ (.42)	+ .06	+ (.83)	.16
Welfare (Social Justice)	4.85	.47	+ .33	+ (.42)	+ .42	- (.01)	.18
Housing (Tech. & Infrastr.)	2.52	.65	- (.11)	+ .80	- (.70)	+ .79	.64
Education (Education)	21.0	-.47	- 1.27	+ (.61)	- 1.43	+ .87	.50
Trans. & Waterw'ks (Tech. & Infrastr.)	7.50	.25	- (.23)	+ (.11)	- (.33)	+ (.18)	.00

* See note to Table A12.1

Table A12.3
Ideology: The Netherlands, 1949 - 1988

Expenditure Area (Program Emphasis)	a	b PvdA Gov (0/1) +	b PvdA (out) +	b (PvdA x Gov) +	b VVD (out) +	b (VVD x Gov) +	b CDA*	Adj R^2
Left-Right (Left-Right)	1.77	-3.10	- .03	+ .08	+ (.03)	+ (.02)	+ .02	.73
Defense (Foreign +)	20.5	1.15	- (.23)	+ (.26)	- 2.16	+ (.35)	+ .90	.62
Foreign Affairs (Spec. For. Rel's)	2.41	.50	- (.25)	- .76	+ (.06)	- .14	+ (.25)	.47
Public Order (Social Harmony)	6.37	-(.29)	+ (.30)	+ (.20)	- (.07)	+ (.20)	+ .47	.11
Agriculture (Agriculture)	-2.7	5.65	- .85	- 2.14	+ 1.45	+ .49	+ 1.99	.41
Welfare (Social Justice)	4.03	-3.77	+ .50	+ .71	- .43	+ .56	+ (.09)	.26
Housing (Tech. & Infrastr.)	7.92	-6.75	+ (.07)	+ .82	+ .98	- 1.30	+ .65	.74
Education (Education)	20.9	10.2	- (.28)	- 2.74	- (.46)	- (.15)	+ (.55)	.56
Trans. & Waterw'ks (Tech. & Infrastr.)	11.1	-4.48	- (.13)	+ (.38)	+ (.24)	- (.72)	+ (.08)	.09

* See note to Table A12.1

Table A13.1
Agenda: Belgium, 1946 - 1983

Expenditure Area (Program Emphases)	a	b Chr +	b Lib +	b Soc	Adj R^2
Left-Right (Left-Right)	.00	(.00)	+ (.02)	+ (.01)	.00
Pensions (Social Services)	28.7	-.67	+ (.05)	+ (.00)	.17
Regional Aid (Social Harmony)	10.1	-.19	+ -(.17)	+ (.40)	.13
Family Aid (Social Services)	1.00	-.06	- (.02)	- (.04)	.15
Education (Education)	16.6	(.61)	- (.53)	+ .22	.10
Health (Social Justice)	4.82	-(.04)	- .17	+ .06	.29
Enterprise (Productivity)	2.71	-(.03)	- (.02)	+ 2.35	.37
Transp. & Commun. (Tech. & Infrastr.)	9.81	(.04)	+ (.06)	- (03)	.00
Admin. of Justice (Law & Order)	3.07	.12	+ (.03)	+ (.05)	.38
Foreign Affairs (Foreign Policy)	2.53	-(.01)	+ (.00)	- (.01)	.00
Defense (Foreign Policy)	5.12	.70	+ (.27)	+ .87	.58
Agriculture (Agriculture)	1.77	-(.11)	- (.03)	+ (.03)	.00

Table A13.2
Mandate: Belgium, 1946 - 1983

Expenditure Area (Program Emphases)	a	b Chr (out)+	b (Chr x Gov)+	b Lib (out)+	b (Lib x Gov)+	b Soc (out)+	b (Soc x Gov)	Adj R^2
Left-Right (Left-Right)	.51	.08 -	.09 +	(.04)-	(.03)-	(00) +	(.05)	.06
Pensions (Social Services)	29.2	- .72 -	(.11)-	(.08)-	(.18)+	(.28)-	(28)	.17
Regional Aid (Social Harmony)	10.4	- .48 +	.38 +	(.04)-	(.33)-	(.43)-	(.81)	.25
Family Aid (Social Services)	1.05	- .10 +	(.04)-	(.62)+	(.05)-	(.04)+	(.01)	.20
Education (Education)	16.9	-1.07 +	1.94 -	.89 +	(.37)+	(.03)+	(.53)	.40
Health (Social Justice)	4.81	-(.11)+	(.01)-	(.11)-	(.05)+	.16 -	.11	.33
Enterprise (Productivity)	2.45	-(.25)+	(.34)-	(.54)+	(.45)+	2.67	[*]	.35
Transp. & Commun. (Tech. & Infrastr.)	9.65	(.20)-	(.16)+	(.06)+	(.10)-	(.15)+	(.15)	.00
Admin. of Justice (Law & Order)	3.03	.18 -	.10 +	(.05)-	(.03)+	(.10)-	(.15)	.50
Foreign Affairs (Foreign Policy)	2.14	-(.31)+	(.25)-	(.05)+	(.03)+	.39 -	(.23)	.03
Defense (Foreign Policy)	5.03	(.67)-	(.02)+	(.31)-	(.14)+	1.10 -	(.18)	.55
Agriculture (Agriculture)	1.98	-(.10)-	(.13)-	(.76)+	(.05)+	(.10)-	.02	.00

[*] Zeroed out due to collinearity with preceding term

Table A13.3
Ideology: Belgium, 1946 - 1983

Expenditure Area (Program Emphases)	a	b SocGov (0/1) +	b Chr (out)+	b (Chr x Gov)+	b Lib (out)+	b (Lib x Gov)+	b Soc (out)+	b (Soc x Gov)	Adj R^2
Left-Right (Left-Right)	-.26	1.03 +	.82 -	.10 +	(.04)-	(.02)+	(.03)-	(.03)	.07
Pensions (Social Services)	29.5	-(.29) -	.71 -	(.12)-	(.09)+	(.17)+	(.24)-	(.24)	.14
Regional Aid (Social Harmony)	7.23	4.28 -	.63 +	.49 +	.29 +	(.40)+	(.67)-	3.4	.50
Family Aid (Social Services)	.57	.85 -	.09 +	.35 -	.09 +	.10 +	(.03)-	.13	.40
Education (Education)	11.2	8.20 -	1.01 +	2.35 -	1.30 +	(.58)+	.42 -	.54	.63
Health (Social Justice)	4.49	(.37) -	(.12)+	(.02)-	(.12)-	(.05)+	(.21)-	(.16)	.31
Enterprise (Productivity)	2.70	-(.28) -	(.24)+	(.31)-	(.55)+	(.43)+	2.74	[*]	.33
Transp. & Commun. (Tech. & Infrastr.)	8.10	2.44 +	(.27)-	(.20)+	(.02)+	(.01)+	.18 -	.34	.12
Admin. of Justice (Law & Order)	3.24	-(.28) -	(.20)-	.11 +	(.03)-	(.04)+	(.03)+	(.03)	.50
Foreign Affairs (Foreign Policy)	5.73	9.86 +	(.20)-	(.38)-	(.11)-	(.04)+	2.65 -	2.96	.62
Defense (Foreign Policy)	5.67	-(.79) +	(.63)+	(.03)+	(.32)-	(.13)+	(.92)+	(.04)	.53
Agriculture (Agriculture)	2.67	-.95 -	(.05)-	.21 -	(.06)+	(.01)+	(.04)+	.14	.05

[*] Zeroed out due to collinearity with preceding term

Bibliography

In addition to full citations for all items noted in the text, this bibliography also includes items of general interest in order to provide readers more detail on particular political systems and processes.

Abramovitz, Alan I. 1980. "The United States: Political Culture Under Stress." In *The Civic Culture Revisited,* ed. Gabriel A. Almond and Sidney Verba. Boston: Little, Brown.

Agger, Robert E., Daniel Goldrich, and Bert Swanson. 1964. *Rulers and the Ruled: Political Power and Impotence in American Communities.* New York: John Wiley.

Alber, Jens. 1986. "Germany." In *Growth to Limits: The West European Welfare States Since World War II,* vol. 2, ed. Peter Flora. Berlin: de Gruyter.

Almond, Gabriel, and Sidney Verba. 1963. *The Civic Culture.* Princeton: Princeton University Press.

Amenta, Edwin, and Theda Skocpol. 1989. "Taking Exception: Explaining the Distinctiveness of American Public Policies in the Last Century." In *The Comparative History of Public Policy,* ed. Francis G. Castles. New York: Oxford University Press.

Anderson, James E. 1974. *Public Policy-Making.* New York: Praeger.

Andeweg, Rudi B. 1982. *Dutch Voters Adrift: On Explanations of Electoral Change,* 1963–1977. Leiden: published by the author.

APSA (American Political Science Association). 1950. *Toward a More Responsible Two-Party System.* New York: Rinehart.

Arrow, Kenneth J. 1951. *Social Choice and Individual Values.* New York: John Wiley.

______. 1984. *Individual Choice Under Certainty and Uncertainty, Collected Papers of Kenneth J. Arrow,* vol. 3. Cambridge, Mass.: The Belknap Press of Harvard University Press.

Bachrach, Peter, and Morton S. Baratz. 1962. "Two Faces of Power." *American Political Science Review* 56:947–953.

______. 1963. "Decisions and Non-Decisions: An Analytic Framework." *American Political Science Review* 57:632–642.

Banfield, Edward. 1961. *Political Influence.* New York: Free Press of Glencoe.

Banks, Arthur S. 1992. *Political Handbook of the World.* Binghamton, N.Y.: CSA Publications.

Barry, Brian. 1970. *Sociologists, Economists and Democracy.* London: Macmillan Company.

Bendix, Reinhard. 1967. "Tradition and Modernity Reconsidered." *Comparative Studies of Society and History* 9:292–346.

Berelson, Bernard R., Paul F. Lazarsfeld, and William N. McPhee. 1954. *Voting: A Study of Opinion Formation in a Presidential Campaign.* Chicago: University of Chicago Press.

Berglund, Sten, and Ulf Lindstrom. 1978. *The Scandinavian Party System(s).* Lund: Studentlitteratur.

Bloomberg, Warner, Jr., and Morris Sunshine. 1963. *Suburban Power Structures in Public Education.* Syracuse: Syracuse University Press.

Bonjean, Charles, and David M. Olson. 1964. "Community Leadership: Directions of Research." *Administrative Science Quarterly* 4:278–300.

Budge, Ian, and Dennis Farlie. 1977. *Voting and Party Competition: A Theoretical Critique and Synthesis Applied to Surveys From Ten Democracies.* New York: John Wiley.

______. 1982. *Voting and Party Competition: A Spatial Synthesis and a Critique of Existing Approaches Applied to Surveys from Ten Democracies.* New York: John Wiley.

______. 1983. *Explaining and Predicting Elections: Issue Effects and Party Strategies in Twenty-Three Democracies.* London: George Allen and Unwin.

Budge, Ian, and Hans Keman. 1990. *Parties and Democracy: Coalition Formation and Government Functioning in Twenty States.* Oxford: Oxford University Press.

Budge, Ian, and Richard I. Hofferbert. 1990. "Mandates and Policy Outputs: U.S. Party Platforms and Federal Expenditures." *American Political Science Review* 84:111–131.

Budge, Ian, David Robertson, and Derek Hearl (eds.). 1987. *Ideology, Strategy, and Party Change: Spatial Analysis of Post-War Election Programs in Nineteen Democracies.* London: Cambridge University Press.

Burns, James MacGregor. 1963. *The Deadlock of Democracy.* Englewood Cliffs, N.J.: Prentice-Hall.

Butler, David E. 1984. "Reflections on the Electoral Debate in Britain." In *Choosing an Electoral System,* ed. Arend Lijphart and Bernard Grofman. New York: Praeger.

Cairns, Alan C. 1968. "The Electoral System and the Party System in Canada." *Canadian Journal of Political Science* 1: 55–80.

Cameron, David R. 1978. "The Expansion of the Political Economy: A Comparative Analysis." *American Political Science Review* 72:1243–1261.

Campbell, Angus, Phillip Converse, Warren E. Miller, and Donald E. Stokes. 1960. *The American Voter.* New York: John Wiley & Sons.

Castles, Francis G. 1982. "The Impact of Parties on Public Expenditures." In *The Impact of Parties,* ed. Francis G. Castles. London: Sage.

______. 1988. *Australian Public Policy and Economic Vulnerability.* Sidney: Allen & Urwin.

Clark, Peter B. 1960. "Civic Leadership: The Symbols of Legitimacy." Paper delivered at the 1960 Annual Meeting of the American Political Science Association, New York, September 1960.

Clarke, Harold, Jane Jensen, Lawrence LeDuc, and Jon Pammett. 1979. *Political Choice in Canada.* Toronto: McGraw-Hill Ryerson.

______. 1984. *Absent Mandate: The Politics of Discontent in Canada.* Agincourt, Ont.: Gage Publishing.

Clarke, Harold, and Andrew Skalaban. 1992. "France." In *Electoral Change, Responses to Evolving Social and Attitudinal Structures in Western Countries,* ed. Mark Franklin et al. Cambridge: Cambridge University Press.

Conradt, David P. 1980. "Changing German Political Culture." In *The Civic Culture Revisited,* ed. Gabriel A. Almond and Sidney Verba. Boston: Little, Brown.

Converse, Philip, and Roy Pierce. 1986. *Political Representation in France.* Cambridge: Harvard University Press.

Crewe, Ivor, and Bo Saarlvik. 1980. "Party Strategies and Issue Attitudes." In *Comparative Party Politics,* ed. Z. Layton-Henry. London: Macmillan.

Cutright, Phillips. 1965. "Political Structure, Economic Development, and National Social Security Programs." *American Journal of Sociology* 30:537–550.

Dahl, Robert A. 1958. "A Critique of the Ruling Elite Model." *American Political Science Review* 52:463–469.

______. 1961. *Who Governs.* New Haven: Yale University Press.

______. 1967. *Pluralist Democracy in the United States.* Chicago: Rand McNally.

Daalder, Hans. 1966. "The Netherlands: Opposition in a Segmented Society." In *Political Oppositions in Western Democracies,* ed. Robert A. Dahl. New Haven: Yale University Press.

______. 1987. "The Dutch Party System: From Segmentation to Polarization—And Then?" In *Party Systems in Denmark, Austria, Switzerland, the Netherlands, and Belgium,* ed. Hans Daalder. New York: St. Martin's Press.

Dalton, Russell J. 1989. *Politics in West Germany.* Glenview, Ill.: Scott, Foresman.

Dalton, Russell J, and Martin P. Wattenberg. 1992. "The Not So Simple Act of Voting." In *Political Science: The State of the Discipline,* 2nd ed., ed. Ada Finifter. Washington, D.C.: American Political Science Association.

Davis, O. A., A. H. Dempster, and A. Wildavsky. 1966. "A Theory of the Budgetary Process." *American Political Science Review* 60:529–547.

Dawson, Richard E., and James A. Robinson. 1963. "Inter-Party Competition, Economic Variables, and Welfare Policies in the American States." *Journal of Politics* 25:265–289.

Dewachter, Wilfried. 1987. "Changes in a Particratie: The Belgian Party System from 1944 to 1986." In *Party Systems in Denmark, Austria, Switzerland, The Netherlands, and Belgium,* ed. Hans Daalder. New York: St. Martin's Press.

Downs, Anthony. 1957. *An Economic Theory of Democracy.* New York: Harper.

Dreijmanis, J. 1982. "Austria: The 'Black'-'Red' Coalitions." In *Government Coalitions in Western Democracies,* ed. Eric C. Browne and J. Dreijmanis. New York: Longman.

Dunleavy, Patrick. 1989. "The United Kingdom." In *The Comparative History of Public Policy,* ed. Francis G. Castles. Oxford: Oxford University Press.

Dye, Thomas R. 1966. *Politics, Economics, and the Public.* Chicago: Rand McNally.

Easton, David. 1953. *The Political System. An Inquiry into the State of Political Science.* Chicago: University of Chicago Press.

Engelmann, Frederick C. 1988. "The Austrian Party System: Continuity and Change." In *Parties and Party Systems in Liberal Democracies,* ed. Steven B. Wolinetz. London: Routledge.

Flora, Peter (ed.). 1986. *Growth to Limits: The Western European Welfare States Since World War II,* 2 vols. Berlin, New York: de Gruyter.

Flora, Peter, and Arnold J. Heidenheimer (eds.). 1980. *The Development of the Welfare State in Europe and North America.* New Brunswick, N.J.: Transaction Books.

Flora, Peter, et al. 1983. *State, Economy, and Society in Western Europe 1815–1975,* Vol. 1: *The Growth of Mass Democracies and Welfare States.* Frankfurt: Campus Verlag.

Franklin, Mark. 1992. "Britain." In *Electoral Change, Responses to Evolving Social and Attitudinal Structures in Western Countries,* ed. Mark N. Franklin et al. Cambridge: Cambridge University Press.

Fried, Robert C. 1971. "Communism, Urban Budgets, and the Two Italies: A Case Study in Comparative Urban Government." *Journal of Politics* 33:1008–1051.

Frognier, Andre. 1975. "Parties and Cleavages in the Belgian Parliament." *Legislative Studies Quarterly* 3:109–131.

Fuchs, Dieter. 1993. "A Metatheory of the Democratic Process." Manuscript, Science Center—Berlin.

Fuchs, Dieter, and Hans-Dieter Klingemann. 1990. "The Left-Right Scheme." In *Continuities in Political Action: A Longitudinal Study of Political Orientations in Three Western Democracies,* ed. M. Kent Jennings and Jan van Deth. Berlin: de Gruyter.

______. 1993. "Citizens and the State: A Changing Relationship?" In *Citizens and the State,* ed. Hans-Dieter Klingemann and Dieter Fuchs. Oxford: Oxford University Press.

Fukuyama, Francis. 1989. "The End of History?" *National Interest,* Summer 1989.

______. 1992. *The End of History and the Last Man.* New York: Free Press.

Gerlich, Peter. 1987. "Consociationalism to Competition: The Austrian Party System Since 1945." In *Party Systems in Denmark, Austria, Switzerland, The Netherlands, and Belgium,* ed. Hans Daalder. New York: St. Martin's Press.

Ginsberg, Benjamin. 1976. "Elections and Public Policy." *American Political Science Review* 70:41–50.

Goetschy, Janine. 1987. "The Neo-Corporatist Issue in France." In *Political Stability and Neo-Corporatism: Corporatist Integration and Societal Cleavages in Western Europe,* ed. Ilja Scholten. London: Sage.

Greenstone, J. David, and Paul Peterson. 1968. "Reformers, Machines, and the War on Poverty." In *City Politics and Public Policy,* ed. James Q. Wilson. New York: John Wiley.

Greenwood, G. 1978. *Australia: A Social and Political History.* Sydney: Angus & Robertson.

Grumm, John. 1971. "The Effects of Legislative Structure on Legislative Performance." In *State and Urban Politics,* ed. Richard I. Hofferbert and Ira Sharkansky. Boston: Little, Brown.

Haerpfer, Christian. 1985. "Electoral Volatility and Partisan Change in the Austrian Party System." In *Electoral Volatility in Western Democracies,* ed. Ivor Crewe and David Denver. London: Croom Helm.

Herson, Lawrence. 1961. "In the Footsteps of Community Power." *American Political Science Review* 55:817–831.

Hicks, Alexander M., and Duane H. Swank. 1992. "Politics, Institutions, and Welfare Spending in Industrialized Democracies, 1960–1982." *American Political Science Review* 86:658–674.

Hofferbert, Richard I. 1966. "The Relation Between Public Policy and Some Structural and Environmental Variables in the American States." *American Political Science Review* 60:73–82.

______. 1972. "State and Community Policy Studies: A Review of Comparative Input-Output Analyses." In *Political Science Annual,* vol. 3, ed. James A. Robinson. Indianapolis: Bobbs-Merrill.

______. 1974. *The Study of Public Policy.* Indianapolis: Bobbs-Merrill.

Hofferbert, Richard I., and Hans-Dieter Klingemann. 1990. "The Policy Impact of Party Programs and Government Declaration in the Federal Republic of Germany." *European Journal of Political Research* 18:277–304.

Hofferbert, Richard I., and Ian Budge. 1992. "The Party Mandate and the Westminster Model: Election Programmes and Government Spending in Britain, 1948–85." *British Journal of Political Science* 22:151–182.

Hollingshead, August. 1949. *Elmtown's Youth.* New York: John Wiley.

Holmberg, Sorem. 1989. "Political Representation in Sweden." *Scandinavian Political Studies* 12:1–36.

Hunter, Floyd. 1953. *Community Power Structure.* Chapel Hill: University of North Carolina Press.

Inglehart, Ronald. 1977. *The Silent Revolution: Changing Values and Political Styles Among Western Publics.* Princeton: Princeton University Press.

———. 1990. *Culture Shift in Advanced Industrial Society.* Princeton: Princeton University Press.

(IMF) International Monetary Fund. Annual. *Government Finance Statistics Yearbook.* Washington, D.C.: IMF.

Irvine, William P. 1987. "Canada 1945–1980: Party Platforms and Campaign Strategies. In *Ideology, Strategy and Party Change: Spatial Analyses of Post-War Election Programmes in Nineteen Democracies,* ed. Ian Budge, David Robertson, and Derek Hearl. Cambridge: Cambridge University Press.

Jaensch, D. 1983. *The Australian Party System.* Sydney: Allen & Urwin.

Jennings, M. Kent. 1963. "Public Administrators and Community Decision-Making." *Administrative Science Quarterly* 7:18–43.

Jones, Charles O. 1970. *An Introduction to the Study of Public Policy.* Belmont, Calif.: Wadsworth.

Kaase, Max. 1984. "Personalized Proportional Representations: The 'Model' of the West German Electoral System." In *Choosing an Electoral System,* ed. Arend Lijphart and Bernard Grofman. New York: Praeger.

Katz, Richard S. 1987. "Party Government and Its Alternatives." In *The Future of Party Government,* Vol. 2: *Party Governments—European and American Experiences,* Rudolf Wildenmann, gen. ed.; ed. Richard S. Katz. Berlin, New York: de Gruyter.

Kaufman, Herbert, and Victor Jones. 1954. "The Mystery of Power." *Public Administration Review* 14:205–212.

Kavanagh, Dennis. 1980. "Political Culture in Great Britain: The Decline of Civic Culture." In *The Civic Culture Revisited,* ed. Gabriel A. Almond and Sidney Verba. Boston: Little, Brown.

Keman, Hans E. 1988. *The Development Toward Surplus Welfare.* Amsterdam: CT Press.

Key, V. O., Jr. 1966. *The Responsible Electorate.* New York: Vintage.

King, Anthony. 1973. "Ideas, Institutions, and the Policies of Government." *British Journal of Political Science* 3:291–314.

King, Gary, Michael Laver, Richard I. Hofferbert, Ian Budge, and Michael D. McDonald. 1993. "On Party Platforms and Government Spending." *American Political Science Review* 87:774–780.

Kingdon, John W. 1984. *Agendas, Alternatives, and Public Policies.* Boston, Toronto: Little, Brown.

Klingemann, Hans-Dieter. 1986. "Der vorsichtig abwägende Waehler. Einstellungen zu den politischen Parteien und Wahlabsicht. Eine Analyse anlässlich der Bundestagswahl 1983." In *Wahlen und politischer Prozess: Analysen aus Anlass der Bundestagswahl 1983,* ed. Max Kaase and Hans-Dieter Klingemann. Opladen: Westdeutscher Verlag.

Klingemann, Hans-Dieter, and Martin P. Wattenberg. 1992. "Decaying Versus Developing Party Systems: A Comparison of Party Images in the United States and West Germany." *British Journal of Political Science* 22:131–149.

Laver, Michael, and Ian Budge. eds. 1993. *Party Policy and Coalition Government in Western Europe.* London: Macmillan.

Lehmbruch, Gerhardt, and Philippe Schmitter, eds. 1982. *Patterns of Corporatist Policy-Making.* Beverly Hills, Calif.: Sage.

Lijphart, Arend. 1968. *The Politics of Accommodation: Pluralism and Democracy in the Netherlands.* Berkeley: University of California Press.

______. 1977. *Democracy in Plural Societies.* New Haven: Yale University Press.

______. 1984. *Democracies.* New Haven: Yale University Press.

______. 1988. "From the Politics of Accommodation to Adversarial Politics in The Netherlands: A Reassessment." *West European Politics* 12:139–153.

Lindblom, Charles E. 1959. "The Science of Muddling Through." *Public Administration Review* 19:79–88.

Lineberry, Robert L., and Edmund P. Fowler. 1967. "Reformism and Public Policies in American Cities." *American Political Science Review* 61:701–716.

Lipset, Seymour Martin. 1959. "Some Social Requisites of Democracy: Economic Development and Political Legitimacy." *American Political Science Review* 53:69–105.

Lipset, Seymour Martin, and Stein Rokkan. 1967. "Cleavage Structure, Party Systems and Voter Alignments: An Introduction." In *Party Systems and Voter Alignments,* ed. Seymour Martin Lipset and Stein Rokkan. New York: Free Press.

Lorwin, V. 1966. "Belgium: Religion, Class and Language in National Politics." In *Political Oppositions in Western Democracies,* ed. Robert A. Dahl. New Haven: Yale University Press.

Luebbert, G. M. 1986. *A Theory of Government Formation in Multiparty Democracies.* Stanford, Calif.: Stanford University Press.

Luther, K. 1987. "The Transformation of the Freedom Party of Austria from Old Nazi to Liberal Party." In *Liberal Parties in Western Europe,* ed. Emil Kirchner. Cambridge: Cambidge University Press.

Lynd, Robert, and Lynd, Helen. 1929. *Middletown.* New York: Harcourt, Brace.

______. 1937. *Middletown in Transition.* New York: Harcourt, Brace.

March, James G., and Johann P. Olson. 1984. "The New Institutionalism: Organizational Factors in Political Life." *American Political Science Review* 78:734–749.

Marin, Bernd. 1987. "From Consociationalism to Technocorporatism: The Austrian Case as a Model-Generator?" In *Political Stability and Neo-Corporatism,* ed. Ilja Scholten. London: Sage.

Martin, Roscoe C., et al. 1961. *Decisions in Syracuse.* Bloomington: Indiana University Press.

Merelman, Richard M. 1968. "On the Neo-Elitist Critique of Community Power." *American Political Science Review* 62:451–460.

Michels, Roberto. 1915. *Political Parties: A Sociological Study of the Oligarchical Tendencies of Modern Democracies,* trans. Eden and Cedar Paul. London: Jarrolo and Sons.

Miller, Arthur, and Brad Lockerbie. 1992. "United States of America." In *Electoral Change: Responses to Evolving Social and Attitudinal Structures in Western Countries,* ed. Mark Franklin et al. Cambridge: Cambridge University Press.

Miller, Delbert C. 1959. "Industry and Community Power Structure: A Comparative Study of an American and an English City." *American Sociological Review* 24:804–814.

Mills, C. Wright. 1956. *The Power Elite.* New York: Oxford University Press.

Moore, Barrington, Jr. 1966. *Social Origins of Dictatorship and Democracy: Lord and Peasant in the Making of the Modern World.* Boston: Beacon Press.

Mosca, Gaetano. 1939. *The Ruling Class,* trans. Hannah D. Kahn. New York: Macmillan.

Mughan, Anthony. 1992. "Belgium." In *Electoral Change: Responses to Evolving Social and Attitudinal Structures in Western Countries,* ed. Mark N. Franklin et al. Cambridge: Cambridge University Press.

OMB (Office of Management and Budget). Annual. *Historical Tables: Budget of the United States Government.* Washington, D.C.: U.S. Government Printing Office.

Olson, Mancur J.R. 1983. *The Rise and Decline of Nations: Economic Growth, Stagflation, and Social Rigidities.* New Haven: Yale University Press.

Olson, Sven. 1986. "Sweden." In *Growth to Limits: The West European Welfare States Since World War II,* vol. 1, ed. Peter Flora. Berlin: de Gruyter.

Ordeshook, Peter C. 1986. *Game Theory and Political Theory.* Cambridge: Cambridge University Press.

Oskarson, Maria. 1992. "Sweden." In *Electoral Change: Responses to Evolving Social and Attitudinal Structures in Western Countries,* ed. Mark Franklin et al. Cambridge: Cambridge University Press.

Pappi, Franz Urban, and Peter Mnich. 1992. "Germany (BRD)." In *Electoral Change: Responses to Evolving Social and Attitudinal Structures in Western Countries,* ed. Mark N. Franklin et al. Cambridge: Cambridge University Press.

Parry, R. 1986. "United Kingdom." In *Growth to Limits: The West European Welfare States Since World War II,* ed. Peter Flora. Berlin: De Gruyter.

Peters, B. G., J. C. Doughtie, and M. K. McCulloch. 1977. "Types of Democratic Systems and Types of Public Policy: An Empirical Examination." *Comparative Politics* 9:237–255.

Pétry, François. 1987. "France 1958–81: The Strategy of Joint Government Platforms." In *Ideology, Strategy and Party Change: Spatial Analyses of Post-War Election Programmes in Nineteen Democracies,* ed. Ian Budge, David Robertson, and Derek Hearl. Cambridge: Cambridge University Press.

———. 1988. "The Policy Impact of Canadian Party Programs: Public Expenditure Growth and Contagion from the Left." *Canadian Public Policy/Analyse de Politique* 14:376–389.

Polsby, Nelson W. 1963. *Community Power and Political Theory.* New Haven: Yale University Press.

Pomper, Gerald. 1968. *Elections in America.* New York: Dodd Mead.

Powell, G. Bingham. 1970. *Social Fragmentation and Political Hostility: An Austrian Case Study.* Stanford, Calif.: Stanford University Press.

———. 1987. "The Competitive Consequences of Polarized Pluralism." In *The Logic of Multi-Party Systems,* ed. M. J. Holler. Dordrecht: Martinus Nijhoff.

———. 1990. "Holding Governments Accountable: How Constitutional Arrangements and Party Systems Affect Clarity of Responsibility for Policy in Contemporary Democracies." Paper delivered to the annual meeting of the American Political Science Association. San Francisco, Calif., August 1990.

Pridham, Geoffrey. 1977. *Christian Democracy in Western Germany.* London: Croom Helm.

Rallings, Colin. 1987. "The Influence of Election Programmes: Britain and Canada 1945–79." In *Ideology, Strategy, and Party Change: Spatial Analysis of Post-War Election Pro-*

grams in Nineteen Democracies, ed. Ian Budge, David Robertson, and Derek Hearl. London: Cambridge University Press.

Riker, William. 1962. *The Theory of Political Coalitions.* New Haven: Yale University Press.

Robertson, David. 1976. *A Theory of Party Competition.* London and New York: Wiley.

Rossi, Peter. 1947. "Community Decision-Making." *Administrative Science Quarterly* 1:415–443.

Rose, Richard. 1989. *Politics in England,* 5th ed. Glenview, Ill.: Scott, Foresman.

Saarlvik, Bo, and Ivor Crewe. 1983. *Decade of Dealignment.* New York: Cambridge University Press.

Sabatier, Paul A. 1991. "Toward Better Theories of the Policy Process." *PS: Political Science and Politics* 24 (June):144–156.

Sabatier, Paul A., and Jenkins-Smith, Hank C. 1993. *Policy Change and Learning: An Advocacy Coalition Approach.* Boulder, Colo.: Westview Press.

Sartori, Giovanni. 1976. *Parties and Party Systems.* Cambridge: Cambridge University Press.

Schattschneider, E. E. 1935. *Politics, Pressures, and the Tariff.* Englewood Cliffs, N.J.: Prentice-Hall.

______. 1960. *The Semi-Sovereign People.* New York: Holt, Rinehart and Winston.

Schmidt, Manfred G. 1989. "Learning from Catastrophes: West Germany's Public Policy." In *The Comparative History of Public Policy,* ed. Francis G. Castles. New York: Oxford University Press.

Scholten, Ilja. 1987. "Corporatism and the Neo-Liberal Backlash in The Netherlands." In *Political Stability and Neo-Corporatism,* ed. Ilja Scholten. London: Sage.

Schultze, Robert O. 1961. "The Bifurcation of Power in a Satellite City." In *Community Political Systems,* ed. Morris Janowitz. Glencoe, Ill.: Free Press.

Sharkansky, Ira. 1971. "Economic Development, Regionalism and State Political Systems." In *State and Urban Politics,* ed. Richard I. Hofferbert and Ira Sharkansky. Boston: Little, Brown.

Sharkansky, Ira, and Richard I. Hofferbert. 1969. "Dimensions of State Politics, Economics, and Public Policy." *American Political Science Review* 63:867–880.

Smith, David E. 1985. "Party Government, Representation and National Integration in Canada." In *Party Government and Regional Representation in Canada.* Vol. 36 in the Research Studies conducted for the Royal Commission on the Economic Union and Development Prospects for Canada, ed. P. Aucoin. Toronto: University of Toronto Press.

Statistisches Bundesamt. Annual. *Rechnungsergebnisse der staatlichen Haushalte.* Wiesbaden: Federal Statistical Office.

Steiner, K. 1972. *Politics in Austria.* Boston: Little, Brown.

______ (ed.). 1982. *Tradition and Innovation in Contemporary Austria.* Palo Alto, Calif.: SPOSS.

Strom, Kaare. 1984. "Minority Governments in Parliamentary Democracies: The Rationality of Nonwinning Cabinet Solutions." *Comparative Political Studies* 17:199–277.

Thorburn, Hugh. 1985. *Party Politics in Canada,* 5th ed. Scarborough: Prentice Hall.

Tufte, Edward. 1978. *Political Control of the Economy.* Princeton: Princeton University Press.

van den Brande, A. 1987. "Neo-Corporatism and Functional Integral Power in Belgium." In *Political Stability and Neo-Corporatism*, ed. Ilja Scholten. London: Sage.

van der Eijk, Cees, and Kees Niemller. 1992. "Netherlands." In *Electoral Change, Responses to Evolving Social and Attitudinal Structures in Western Countries*, ed. Mark N. Franklin et al. Cambridge: Cambridge University Press.

von Beyme, Klaus, and Manfred Schmidt (ed.). 1985. *Policy and Politics in the Federal Republic of Germany.* Aldershot: Gower.

Verba, Sidney, Norman Nie, and J. O. Kim. 1978. *Participation and Political Equality.* New York: Cambridge University Press.

Volkens, Andrea. 1992. *Comparative Manifestos Project: Dataset CMP92.* Berlin: Science Center Berlin, Research Unit on Institutions and Social Change.

Volkens, Andrea, and Derek Hearl. 1990. *Content Analysis of Party Programmes in Comparative Perspective: Handbook and Coding Instructions.* Berlin: Science Center Berlin, Research Unit on Institutions and Social Change.

Walker, Jack L. 1969. "The Diffusion of Innovation Among the American States." *American Political Science Review* 63:880–899.

Warner, W. Lloyd, and Paul S. Lunt. 1941. *The Social Life of a Modern Community.* New Haven: Yale University Press.

Wattenberg, Martin P. 1990. *The Decline of American Political Parties 1952–1988*, 3rd ed. Cambridge, Mass., London: Harvard University Press

Wildavsky, Aaron. 1964. *Leadership in a Small Town.* Ottawa: Bedminster Press.

______. 1984. *The Politics of the Budgetary Process*, 4th ed. Boston, Toronto: Little, Brown.

______. 1988. *The New Politics of the Budgetary Process.* Glenview, Ill.: Scott, Foresman.

Williams, Oliver P., and Charles R. Adrian. 1963. *Four Cities.* Philadelphia: University of Pennsylvania Press.

Wilson, Frank L. 1988. "The French Party System in the 1980s." In *Parties and Party Systems in Liberal Democracies*, ed. Steven B. Wolinetz. London: Routledge.

Wolinetz, Steven B. 1988. "The Netherlands: Continuity and Change in a Fragmented Party System." In *Parties and Party Systems in Liberal Democracies*, ed. Steven B. Wolinetz. London: Routledge.

Wright, Gerald C., Robert S. Erikson, and John P. McIver. 1988. "Public Opinion and Policy Liberalism in the American States." *American Journal of Political Science* 31:980–1001.

Wright, Jack F.H. 1980. *Mirror of the Nation's Mind: Australia's Electoral Experiments.* Sydney: Hale and Iremonger.

______. 1984. "An Electoral Basis for Responsible Government: The Australian Experience." In *Choosing an Electoral System*, ed. Arend Lijphart and Bernard Grofman. New York: Praeger.

About the Book and Authors

In democracies, contemporary politics *is* party politics, and parties serve to organize the political process even as they ensure democratic representation of minority and majority policy preferences. How do they do this? In great part, as this ambitious survey shows, parties translate policy preferences into policy priorities by articulating and enacting clearly defined party platforms. There is, this international author team demonstrates, a strong connection between what parties say they will do in an election campaign and what they actually do when elected. In sum, we are shown that political parties deserve more credit than they often receive.

This book addresses questions central to the operation of modern democracies and can be used to inform institutional development in emerging democracies. It is at once an ambitious summary of original research and a model text for students of comparative politics. First the theory and method are introduced. Then, ten key countries are covered in parallel detail, with the discussions proceeding from general consideration of institutional and political context and program and party trends to more specific examinations of the congruence between party programs and policy outcomes. The data for all countries and parties span the post–World War II period up to the late 1980s. The analyses employ agenda, mandate, and ideology models and expenditure analyses across key policy arenas.

Because of its commitment to comparative rather than merely descriptive analysis, *Parties, Policies, and Democracy* offers convincing answers to basic questions about the functioning of democratic political systems. Rigorous comparative analysis of forty years' experience across ten countries demonstrates that political parties in contemporary democracies work better than critics have claimed. This is important news for emerging democracies just now establishing institutions and policies that bear watching over the *next* forty-year period.

Hans-Dieter Klingemann is professor of political science at the Free University of Berlin and director of the Research Unit on Institutions and Social Change in the Science Center–Berlin (Wissenschaftszentrum–Berlin für Sozialforschung). **Richard I. Hofferbert** is professor of political science at the State University of New York at Binghamton and recurring visiting research professor at the Science Center–Berlin. **Ian Budge** is professor of government at the University of Essex, Colchester.

Index